Cases in Collective Bargaining and Industrial Relations

A Decisional Approach

Sterling H. Schoen
Professor of Management

Raymond L. Hilgert
*Professor of Management
and Industrial Relations*

*Both of the School of Business Administration
Washington University
St. Louis, Missouri*

1989 Sixth Edition

IRWIN

Homewood, IL 60430
Boston, MA 02116

© RICHARD D. IRWIN, INC., 1969, 1974, 1978, 1982, 1986, and 1989

Sponsoring editor: William R. Bayer
Project editor: Suzanne Ivester
Production manager: Stephen K. Emry
Cover Design: Studio M
Compositor: Better Graphics, Inc.
Typeface: 10/12 Century Schoolbook
Printer: R. R. Donelley & Sons

LIBRARY OF CONGRESS
Library of Congress Cataloging-in-Publication Data

Schoen, Sterling Harry, 1918–
    Cases in collective bargaining and industrial relations : a
decisional approach / Sterling H. Schoen, Raymond L. Hilgert.—6th
ed.

        p.   cm.
    Includes bibliographies and indexes.
    ISBN 0-256-06990-5 (pbk.)
    1. Collective labor agreements—United States—Cases.
I. Hilgert, Raymond L.   II. Title.
KF3408.A4S3 1989
344.73′0189—dc 19
[347.304189]   88–21824
                                                          CIP

Printed in the United States of America
1 2 3 4 5 6 7 8 9 0 D O 5 4 3 2 1 0 9 8

Preface

This sixth edition provides a convenient but extensive set of cases in a variety of union-management problem situations. The book is probably most appropriate as a supplementary text in basic or survey courses in collective bargaining, labor economics, and industrial relations. The cases vary in length, complexity, and numbers of issues. Therefore, the collection of cases is of sufficient magnitude and depth that the book would be suitable for advanced courses or case courses in the field of collective bargaining and labor relations.

A major objective is to provide a means by which students can apply principles, concepts, and legal considerations that they have learned to realistic decision situations and confrontations between labor and management. We have used the cases in seminars and classes and have found them to be challenging and fascinating learning instruments.

The cases are representative of the types of problems that continue to confront management and labor unions. Cases such as these test analytical ability in dealing with challenging human relations and union-management situations in a way useful even for students who do not have a management or labor relations career in mind.

In an effort to reflect the impact of recent trends, we have collected representative cases dealing with problems that focus upon current issues both in the private and public sectors. Some 30 percent of the cases in the sixth edition are new to this collection. The cases we have retained from previous editions provide continuity and balance, and these cases are "timeless" in the evaluation of union-management relations.

Part One of the book presents a collection of National Labor Relations Board cases as restructured from published reports of the NLRB and court decisions. Our intent has been to describe each situation from the perspective of impartial writers reporting the facts and issues of the case. The case format has been developed as follows: the background information of the case is first presented, including relevant legal issues; the position of the union(s) or person(s) is stated; and the position of the management or company is stated. An introductory discussion and important and substantive sections of the Labor Management Relations Act (as amended) are included at the outset of Part One to enable students to become familiar with the provisions of the Act that are applicable throughout the cases.

We believe that the legal obligations and responsibilities of unions and management under the Labor Management Relations Act continue to be among the most dynamic and important areas of collective bargaining today. Case studies such as those in the first section enable the student to appreciate the nature of this Act, its application in numerous union-management situations, and the duties and legal obligations of management and union representatives to carry out their bargaining responsibilities in good faith.

Part Two consists of cases adapted from grievance-arbitration decisions. We are grateful to the Bureau of National Affairs, Inc., (Stanley E. Degler, vice president and executive editor) for permission to adapt certain published cases from *Labor Arbitration Reports*. Here, too, the approach has been to restructure these actual arbitration cases in a convenient format. The highlights and issues of each case are provided through relevant background information, including the contractual clauses, rules, practices, and the like, which are pertinent. Principal arguments of the union and management sides are then presented. Cases in this part demonstrate complexities and controversial areas that continue to manifest themselves in the ongoing relationships between management and union personnel. We also have included a brief introductory discussion of the major considerations involved in grievance-arbitration procedures from which these cases emanate.

For both the NLRB and labor arbitration cases—which have not been selected with any intent of presenting "good" or "bad" or "right" or "wrong" union-management practices—the student should ask, "What are the problems or principal issues?" "What is at stake between the parties?" "What is justice or equity in the situation?" "What does the law require?" "What does the contract say on the issue(s)?" "How have previous NLRB decisions or previous labor arbitration decisions handled similar circumstances?" These types of questions, and the more specific questions we have developed at the conclusion of each case, urge students toward a deep analysis of issues. Decisions of the NLRB, the courts, and labor arbitrators for these cases are included in an instructor's manual. It has been the authors' experience that most students want to compare their decisions and approaches with those of authorities in the field.

Index and classification tables are included in each section of the book prior to the cases. These tables briefly cite the major issues of each case; for the NLRB cases, legal provisions are indicated. Selected bibliographies are also provided for more detailed reading in areas that either directly or indirectly are involved in the cases and materials in both sections of the book.

Although we cannot recognize everyone who has had a part in developing this book, we wish to acknowledge the following professors who reviewed the text and instructor's manual and who offered numerous helpful suggestions and insights: Geraldine Ellerbrock of California Polytechnic State University at San Luis Obispo; Brian Heshizer of Cleveland State University; Stanley Huff of Denison University; Chalmer Labig of Oklahoma State University; and Mitchell Novit of Indiana University. We are particularly grateful to Karl Sauber of the St. Louis office of the National Labor Relations Board, whose assistance in developing several cases for Part One was invaluable. The cooperation of Charles Riley of the St. Louis office of the Federal Mediation and Conciliation Service in providing us with FMCS materials is similarly acknowledged.

Sterling H. Schoen
Raymond L. Hilgert

Contents

PART TWO
Case Problems in Union-Management Relations: Cases from Grievance Arbitration   217

Legal Aspects of Collective Bargaining

National Labor Relations Board Cases

INTRODUCTION TO THE LABOR MANAGEMENT RELATIONS ACT (LMRA)

SELECTED BIBLIOGRAPHY

PARTIAL TEXT OF THE LABOR MANAGEMENT RELATIONS ACT

INDEX TO CASES FOR PART ONE

THE CASES

Introduction to
The Labor Management
Relations Act (LMRA)

This introductory section will briefly introduce the principal provisions of the Labor Management Relations Act (LMRA) of 1947 as amended. A partial text of this Act follows this introductory section. For even more analytical understanding of the provisions of the Act and its applications, a selected bibliography for reading is included at the end of this introductory section. It also is recommended that the student of collective bargaining and industrial relations contact a regional or national office of the National Labor Relations Board (NLRB) to obtain various NLRB publications that explain detailed principles and procedures involved in administration of the law. For example, a publication included in the bibliography entitled, *A Guide to Basic Law and Procedures under the National Labor Relations Act,* is prepared by the Office of the General Counsel of the NLRB; this booklet is very helpful for understanding many of the day-to-day activities of the Board and some of its most recent thinking. Parts of this publication have been excerpted and included in this introductory section.

The LMRA of 1947, also known as the Taft-Hartley Act in recognition of the principal congressional authors of the law, is the principal labor legislation governing the "rules of the game" of collective bargaining for the private sector of the U.S. economic system.[1] The LMRA of 1947 constituted a major amendment and revision of the National Labor Relations (Wagner) Act of 1935. The Act since has been amended a number of times (1951, 1958, 1959, 1969, 1973, 1974, and

---

[1] The Railway Labor Act of 1926 (as amended) governs collective bargaining in the rail and airline industries. Although the Railway Labor Act is not widely applicable and some of its provisions are considerably different from those in LMRA, its premises and procedures were drawn upon by the framers of the National Labor Relations (Wagner) Act of 1935, upon which the Act of 1947 subsequently was based. The student is encouraged to study the provisions of the Railway Labor Act, as well as a history of labor laws in the railroad industries, which led to the passage of the Railway Labor Act of 1926.

1980); the 1974 amendments primarily focused upon health care institutions. As it stands today, the Act is the fundamental legislative basis for the majority of union-management relationships in the United States.[2] The LMRA is an extremely complex document in and of itself. Of even greater complexity, however, is the body of administrative laws and decisions that has evolved over the years of its existence in hundreds of thousands of union-management cases. The Act is constantly being tested, evaluated, and reevaluated by the NLRB, the courts, and by the Congress of the United States in the light of changing times, new confrontations, and new decisions. It is not the purpose of this section to completely interpret the Act nor to present it in its entirety. Rather, selected parts of the Act will be discussed to underscore the major elements of the Act governing the collective bargaining process. An understanding of these parts of the Act should provide sufficient insights on which analysis of various aspects of specific union-management cases may be based.

EXCERPTS AND COMMENTS ON THE TEXT OF THE LABOR MANAGEMENT RELATIONS ACT, 1947, AS AMENDED

Section 1. The Statement of Findings and Policy

The LMRA begins with a statement to the effect that industrial strife interferes with the normal flow of commerce. The purpose of the Act is to promote the full flow of commerce by prescribing and protect-

---

[2] One of the major developments in contemporary labor relations has been at the federal government employee level. Executive Order 10988, originally signed by President Kennedy in 1962, was replaced by Executive Order 11491, issued by President Nixon in 1970. (Executive Orders 11616 and 11636 issued by President Nixon in 1971, and Executive Order 11838, issued by President Ford in 1975, amended Executive Order 11491.) These orders provided federal employees with union representation and collective bargaining rights. Subsequently, in 1978, Title VII of the Civil Service Reform Act replaced these Executive Orders and consolidated into law provisions for civilian federal government employees to govern collective bargaining in the federal sector. Title VII of the Civil Service Reform Act (Public Law 95–454) closely parallels the LMRA in many fundamental areas, with many of its provisions similar to various provisions in LMRA governing union-management relations in the private sector. Of course, federal government employees do not have the right to strike nor to have a "union shop," and a number of key areas remain outside the scope of bargaining in the federal sector. For example, most wages and certain working conditions are set by Congress, and a number of areas of employee concern are handled under federal and civil service regulations. Further, this Act created a new administrative agency, the Federal Labor Relations Authority (FLRA), whose functions are similar to those of the National Labor Relations Board (NLRB). Numerous cases decided in the federal sector have drawn heavily for precedent and policy from decisions of the NLRB in the private sector. Included in the bibliography

ing rights of employers and employees and by providing orderly and peaceful procedures for preventing interference by either with the legitimate rights of the other.

This statement of public policy also points out that the labor law of the land is designed to regulate both unions and employers in the public interest. The Act encourages employees to exercise their right to organize labor unions and to bargain collectively with their employers as a means of balancing bargaining power. At the same time, the Act encourages union and employer practices that are fundamental to the friendly adjustment of industrial disputes, with the objective of eliminating some union and employer practices that impair the public interest by contributing to industrial unrest and strikes.

The NLRB, which is the federal agency administering the Act, has consistently interpreted this section to mean that the public policy of the United States is to promote and encourage the principle of unionism.

Section 2. Definitions

This section of the Act defines various terms used in the statement of the Act, and also outlines the coverage of the Act. By its terms, the Act does not apply to employees in a business or industry where a labor dispute would not affect interstate commerce. In addition, the Act specifically states that it does not apply to the following:

Agricultural laborers, as defined by the Fair Labor Standards Act (Wage-Hour Law).

Domestic servants.

Any individual employed by one's parent or spouse.

Government employees, including those of government corporations or the Federal Reserve Bank, or any political subdivision such as a state or a school district.[3]

---

at the end of this introductory section are a number of sources to consult for public sector bargaining law, cases, and decisions.

The U.S. Postal Service was brought under partial coverage of the LMRA through enactment of the Postal Reorganization Act of 1970 (Public Law 91–375). This law granted the NLRB jurisdiction over the U.S. Postal Service for various aspects of bargaining unit determination, unfair labor practices, and related matters. The authors have included one case from the postal sector in this part of the text.

[3] A number of states have laws—which vary widely in scope and coverage—to provide collective bargaining rights and procedures for state and local government employees, including teachers and employees of government operated health care facilities. In 1984, Illinois became the most recent state to enact a comprehensive labor relations law for its public employees.   *(continued on next page)*

Independent contractors who depend upon profits, rather than commissions or wages, for their income.

Employees and employers who are subject to provisions of the Railway Labor Act.

Supervisors are excluded from the definition of employees covered by the Act. Whether or not a person is a supervisor is determined by authority rather than by title. The authority required to exclude an employee from coverage of the Act as a supervisor is defined in Section 2(11) of the Act.

All employees properly classified as "managerial," not just those in positions susceptible to conflicts of interest in labor relations, are excluded from the protection of the Act. This was the thrust of a decision of the Supreme Court in 1974.

The 1974 amendments to LMRA (Public Law 93–360) brought all private health-care institutions, whether or not operated for a profit, under the coverage of the Act. Section 2(14) defines a private health care institution as, "any hospital, convalescent hospital, health maintenance organization, health clinic, nursing home, extended care facility, or other institution devoted to the care of sick, infirm, or aged person."

An *employer* is defined in the law as including "any person acting as an agent of employer, directly or indirectly." A *person* is defined to include "one or more individuals, labor organizations, partnerships, associations, legal representatives, trustees, trustees in bankruptcy, or receivers."

The term *labor organization* means any organization, agency, or employee representation committee or plan in which employees participate and that exists for the purpose, in whole or in part, of dealing with employers concerning grievances, labor disputes, wages, rate of pay, hours of employment, or conditions of work.

Section 2(12) defines the meaning of the term *professional employee,* for which specific organizational rights are guaranteed in a later section.

The following sources are recommended for a review of legislation governing collective bargaining for state, local, and municipal government employees: Marvin J. Levine, *Labor Relations in the Public Sector: Readings and Cases,* 2d ed. (Columbus, Ohio: Grid, 1985); and Michael T. Leibig and Wendy L. Kahn, *Public Sector Organizing and the Law (Washington, D.C.:* The Bureau of National Affairs, Inc., 1987).

Sections 3, 4, 5, 6. The National Labor Relations Board

Section 3 creates the NLRB as an independent agency to administer the Act. The NLRB consists of five members appointed by the President of the United States.

Section 3 also authorizes the appointment of a General Counsel of the Board, who is given supervisory authority over the Board attorneys and officers and employees in the regional offices of the Board.

Sections 4 and 5 outline certain compensation, procedural, and administrative authorities granted to the NLRB by the Congress.

However, the key section is Section 6, which gives the Board authority to establish rules and regulations necessary to carry out provisions of the LMRA. *In effect, this section empowers the NLRB to administer and interpret the labor law in whatever manner it deems appropriate to the situations encountered.*

In order to do this, the Board has developed various standards—for the most part, dollar sales or volume standards—by which it determines whether or not a business enterprise is deemed to be interstate commerce and thus covered under the provisions of the Act.[4]

---

[4] For example, the NLRB has used a standard of $500,000 total annual volume of business to determine whether a *retail enterprise* should be considered interstate. For *nonretail businesses* the Board uses two tests: *(a)* direct sales to consumers in other states or indirect sales through others, called outflow, of at least $50,000 a year; or *(b)* direct purchases of goods from suppliers from other states or indirect purchases through others, called inflow, of at least $50,000 a year.

Among the NLRB jurisdictional standards in effect since July 1, 1976, are the following:

Office buildings: Total annual revenue of $100,000, of which $25,000 or more is derived from organizations that meet any of the standards except the indirect outflow and indirect inflow standards established for nonretail enterprises.

Public utilities: At least $250,000 total annual volume of business, or $50,000 direct or indirect outflow or inflow.

Newspapers: At least $200,000 total annual volume of business.

Radio, telegraph, television, and telephone enterprises: At least $100,000 total annual volume of business.

Hotels, motels, and residential apartment houses: At least $500,000 total annual volume of business.

Transit systems: At least $250,000 total annual volume of business.

Taxicab companies: At least $500,000 total annual volume of business.

(continued on next page)

The Board has developed detailed rules, policies, and procedures by which it determines appropriate collective bargaining units, holds representational elections, investigates labor disputes, and other such matters. *The NLRB by its policies and rulings in effect can and does reshape the Act, subject only to review of the federal courts.* The Appendix to this introductory section will provide an overview of the general operations of the NLRB and the magnitude of those operations.

Privately operated health care institutions: At least $250,000 total annual volume of business for hospitals; at least $100,000 for nursing homes, visiting nurses' associations, and related facilities; and at least $250,000 for all other types of private health care institutions defined in the 1974 amendments to the Act.

Associations: These are regarded as a single employer in that the annual business of all association members is totaled to determine whether any of the standards apply.

Enterprises in the territories and the District of Columbia: The jurisdictional standards apply in the territories; all businesses in the District of Columbia come under NLRB jurisdiction.

National defense: Jurisdiction is asserted over all enterprises affecting commerce when their operations have a substantial impact on national defense, whether or not the enterprises satisfy any other standard.

Private universities and colleges: At least $1 million gross annual revenue from all sources (excluding contributions not available for operating expenses because of limitations imposed by the grantor).

Symphony orchestras: At least $1 million gross annual revenue from all sources (excluding contributions not available for operating expenses because of limitations imposed by the grantor).

Ordinarily if an enterprise does the total annual volume of business listed in the standard, it will necessarily be engaged in activities that "affect" commerce. The Board must find, however, based on evidence, that the enterprise does in fact affect commerce.

The Board has established the policy that if an employer whose operations affect commerce refuses to supply the Board with information concerning total annual business, and so on, the Board may dispense with this requirement and exercise jurisdiction.

Section 14(c) (1) authorizes the Board, in its discretion, to decline to exercise jurisdiction over any class or category of employers where a labor dispute involving such employers is not sufficiently substantial to warrant the exercise of jurisdiction, provided that it cannot refuse to exercise jurisdiction over any labor dispute over which it would have asserted jurisdiction under the standards it had in effect on August 1, 1959.

Finally, the NLRB has adopted other standards and policies that it uses in determining its jurisdiction, depending upon various types of businesses and unique conditions involved. For example, in 1976 the NLRB changed its policy of exempting nonprofit, noncommercial, and charitable institutions from coverage of LMRA. The Board asserted that it would use the same general revenue standards for these types of institutions to determine whether an employer's operations "substantially affect interstate commerce" and thus should be subject to provisions of the Act.

Section 7. Rights of Employees

This section is perhaps one of the most significant in the Act. It guarantees employees the right to self-organization; to form, join, or assist labor organizations; to bargain collectively through representatives of their own choosing; and to engage in (or refrain from) certain other concerted activities for the purpose of collective bargaining or other mutual aid or protection.

Examples of employee rights protected by Section 7 are:

Forming or attempting to form a union among the employees of a company.

Joining a union.

Assigning a union to organize the employees of any company.

Going out on strike for the purpose of attempting to obtain improved wages, hours, or other conditions of employment.

Refraining from joining a union in the absence of a valid union shop agreement.

UNFAIR LABOR PRACTICES: EMPLOYERS

The unfair labor practices of employers are listed in Section 8(a) of the Act; those of labor organizations in Section 8(b). Section 8(e) lists an unfair labor practice that can be committed only by an employer and a labor organization acting together.

Section 8(a) (1). Employers are forbidden from engaging in practices that would interfere with, restrain, or coerce employees in the exercise of rights guaranteed by Section 7.

Section 8(a) (1) constitutes a broad statement against interference by the employer; employers violate this section whenever they commit any unfair labor practices. Thus, a violation of Section 8(a) (2), (3), (4), or (5) also results in a violation of Section 8(a) (1).

Various acts of an employer may independently violate Section 8(a) (1). Examples of such violations are:

Threatening employees with loss of jobs or benefits if they should join or vote for a union.

Threatening to close down the plant if a union should be organized in it.

Questioning employees about their union activities or membership in such circumstances as will tend to restrain or coerce the employees.

Spying on union gatherings, or pretending to spy.

Granting wage increases deliberately timed to discourage employees from forming or joining a union.

Threatening to terminate credit at the company store or to force employees to move out of company housing if the union wins bargaining rights for the employees.

Circulating antiunion petitions among employees.

Section 8(a) (2). Employers may not dominate or interfere with the formation or administration of any labor organization or contribute financial or other support to it.

In this regard, the Board distinguishes between "domination" of a labor organization and conduct that amounts to little more than illegal "interference." When a union is found to be "dominated" by an employer, the Board will normally order the organization completely disestablished as a representative of employees. But if the organization is found only to have been supported by employer assistance amounting to less than domination, the Board usually orders the employer to stop such support and to withhold recognition from the organization until it has been certified by the Board as a bona fide representative of employees.

In recent years, there has been a growth in various types of labor-management cooperative efforts such as quality circles, quality-of-worklife programs, employee involvement groups, labor-management participation teams, and the like. In general, these types of efforts do not of themselves violate Section 8(a) (2), unless one becomes of such a nature that it leads to a circumvention of the negotiated labor agreement or some other interference with union or employee rights.

An employer violates Section 8(a) (2) by engaging in activities such as:

Assisting employees in organizing a union or an employee representation plan by providing financial support, legal counsel, or active encouragement.

Conducting a straw vote to determine whether employees favor an inside union, as opposed to one affiliated with one of the national unions.

Signing a union security contract with an inside union to forestall an organizing drive by an outside union.

Exerting pressure on employees to join a particular union.

Permitting a union to solicit dues checkoff authorizations from new employees as they go through the hiring process.

Permitting officers of one union to leave their machines to solicit union members while denying officers of a competing union these same privileges.

Section 8(a) (3).   This section prohibits discrimination in hiring or tenure of employment or any term or condition of employment that tends to encourage or discourage membership in any labor organization. This provision, together with Section 8(b) (2), prohibits the closed shop, in which only persons who already hold membership in a labor organization may be hired. It also prohibits discriminatory hiring-hall arrangements by which only persons who have "permits" from a union may be hired. However, a proviso of this section permits an employer and labor union to agree to a union shop, where employees may be required to join a union after 30 days of employment.

Section 8(a) (3) provides that an employee may be discharged for failing to pay the required union initiation fees and dues uniformly required by the exclusive bargaining representative under a lawful union shop contract. The section provides further, however, that no employer can justify any discriminatory action against an employee for nonmembership in a union if the employer has reason to believe that membership in the union was not open to the employee on the same terms and conditions that apply to others, or that the employee was denied membership in the union for some reason other than failure to pay regular dues and initiation fees.

Some examples of types of discrimination in employment prohibited by Section 8(a) (3) include:

Discharging employees because they urged other employees to join a union.

Refusing to reinstate employees when jobs they are qualified for are open because they took part in a union's lawful strike.

Granting of "superseniority" to those hired to replace employees engaged in a lawful strike.

Demoting employees because they circulated a union petition among other employees asking the employer for an increase in pay.

Discontinuing an operation at one plant and discharging the employees involved, followed by opening the same operation at another plant with new employees, because the employees at the first plant joined a union.

Refusing to hire qualified applicants for jobs because they belong to a union. It would also be a violation if the qualified applicants were refused employment because they did not belong to a union, or because they belonged to one union rather than another.

Section 8(a) (4). Employers may not discharge or otherwise discriminate against employees because they have filed charges or given testimony under this Act. Examples of violations of this section are:

Refusing to reinstate employees when jobs they are otherwise qualified for are open because they filed charges with the NLRB claiming their layoffs were based on union activity.

Demoting employees because they testified at an NLRB hearing.

Section 8(a) (5). It is an unfair labor practice for an employer to refuse to bargain collectively with the representatives of the employees. The meaning of "bargaining collectively" is more specifically outlined in Section 8(d) of the Act. Section 8(d) has been interpreted in many ways, and it might be considered as the cornerstone for the basic philosophy of the Act.

Examples of employer violations of this section are as follows:

Refusing to meet with representatives of a certified union because employees have threatened to go on strike.

Insisting that the union withdraw its demand for a union shop before the company would enter negotiations over a contract.

Insisting that members of the negotiating committee of the union be composed of employees of the company.

Refusing to discuss an increase in the price of coffee served in the company cafeteria.

Granting a wage increase without consulting the certified union.

Refusing to supply the union negotiators with information concerning the incentive system.

Subcontracting certain work to another employer without notifying the union that represents the affected employees and without giving the union an opportunity to bargain concerning the change in working conditions of the employees.

Unfair Labor Practices: Labor Organizations

The 1947 and 1959 amendments to the Act made certain activities of labor unions unfair labor practices.

Section 8(b) (1) (A). A labor organization or its agents are forbidden "to restrain or coerce employees in the exercise of the rights guaranteed in section 7." The section also provides that it is not intended to "impair the rights of a labor organization to prescribe its own rules" concerning membership in the labor organization.

Examples of restraint or coercion that violate Section 8(b) (1) (A) when done by a union or its agents include the following:

Mass picketing in such numbers that nonstriking employees are physically barred from entering the plant.

Committing acts of force or violence on the picket line, or in connection with a strike.

Threatening to do bodily injury to nonstriking employees.

Threatening employees that they will lose their jobs unless they support the union's activities.

Stating to employees who oppose the union that those employees will lose their jobs if the union wins a majority in the plant.

Entering into an agreement with an employer that recognizes the union as exclusive bargaining representative when it has not been chosen by a majority of the employees.

Fining or expelling members for crossing a picket line that is unlawful under the Act or which violates a no-strike agreement.

Fining employees for conduct in which they engaged after resigning from the union.

Fining or expelling members for filing unfair labor practice charges with the Board or for participating in an investigation conducted by the Board.

Refusing to process a grievance in retaliation against an employee's criticism of union officers.

Section 8(b) (1) (B).   A labor organization is prohibited from restraining or coercing an employer in the selection of a bargaining representative. The prohibition applies regardless of whether the labor organization is the majority representative of the employees in the bargaining unit. The prohibition extends to coercion applied by a union to a union member who is a representative of the employer in the adjustment of grievances. This section is violated by such conduct as the following:

Insisting on meeting only with a company's owners and refusing to meet with the attorney the company has engaged to represent it in contract negotiations, and threatening to strike to force the company to accept demands.

Striking against several members of an employer association that had bargained with the union as the representative of the employers and secured the signing of individual contracts by the struck employers.

Insisting during contract negotiations that the employer agree to accept working conditions that will be established by a bargaining group to which it does not belong.

Fining or expelling supervisors for the way they apply the bargaining contract while carrying out their supervisory functions.

Section 8(b) (2). This section bars a union from causing or attempting to cause an employer to discriminate against an employee in violation of Section 8(a) (3). It also prohibits the union from attempting to cause an employer to discriminate against an employee whose membership in the union had been denied or terminated, except where this action was taken by the union because the employee failed to "tender" the regular initiation fees and/or periodic dues uniformly required as a condition of acquiring or retaining membership in the union, where a union shop agreement is in effect.

Contracts or informal arrangements with a union under which an employer gives preferential treatment to union members are violations of Section 8(b) (2). It is not unlawful for an employer and a union to enter into an agreement whereby the employer agrees to hire new employees exclusively through the union hiring hall so long as there is neither a provision in the agreement nor a practice in effect that discriminates against nonunion members in favor of union members or otherwise discriminates on the basis of union membership obligations. Both the agreement and the actual operation of the hiring hall must be nondiscriminatory; referrals must be made without reference to union membership or irrelevant or arbitrary considerations such as race.

Examples of violations of Section 8(b) (2) are:

Causing an employer to discharge employees because they circulated a petition urging a change in the union's method of selecting shop stewards.

Causing an employer to discharge employees because they made speeches against a contract proposed by the union.

Making a contract that requires an employer to hire only members of the union or employees "satisfactory" to the union.

Causing an employer to reduce employees' seniority because they engaged in antiunion acts.

Refusing referral or giving preference on the basis of race or union activities in making job referrals to units represented by the union.

Seeking the discharge of an employee under a union security agreement for failure to pay a fine levied by the union.

Section 8(b) (3). This section requires a labor organization to bargain in good faith with an employer about wages, hours, and other conditions of employment if it is the representative of that employer's employees. This section imposes on labor organizations the same duty to bargain in good faith that is imposed on employers by Section 8(a) (5). Both the labor organization and the employer are required to follow the procedure set out in Section 8(d) before terminating or changing an existing contract.

Section 8(b) (3) not only requires that a union representative bargain in good faith with employers but also requires that the union carry out its bargaining duty fairly with respect to the employees it represents. A union, therefore, violates Section 8(b) (3) if it negotiates a contract that conflicts with that duty, or if it refuses to handle grievances under the contract for irrelevant or arbitrary reasons.

Section 8(b) (3) is violated by any of the following:

Insisting on the inclusion of illegal provisions in a contract, such as a closed shop or a discriminatory hiring hall.

Refusing to negotiate on a proposal for a written contract.

Striking against an employer who has bargained, and continues to bargain, on a multiemployer basis to compel it to bargain separately.

Refusing to meet with the attorney designated by the employer as its representative in negotiations.

Terminating an existing contract and striking for a new one without notifying the employer, the Federal Mediation and Conciliation Service (FMCS), and the state mediation service, if any.

Conditioning the execution of an agreement upon inclusion of a nonmandatory provision such as a performance bond.

Refusing to process a grievance because of the race, sex, or union activities of an employee for whom the union is the statutory bargaining representative.

Section 8(b) (4). This section forbids secondary boycotts and certain types of strikes and picketing; it is an extremely complicated section. Secondary boycotts; sympathy strikes or boycotts to force recognition of an uncertified union; a strike to substitute another bargaining representative for one certified by the Board; strikes over so-called union jurisdictional disputes or work assignment disputes; and several other types of unfair acts—all are forbidden under this section.

More specifically, Section 8(b) (4) prohibits a labor organization from engaging in strikes or boycotts or taking other specified actions to accomplish certain purposes or "objects" as they are called in the Act. The actions are listed in clauses (i) and (ii); the objects are described in subparagraphs (A) through (D). A union commits an unfair labor practice if it takes any of the kinds of action listed in clauses (i) and (ii) as a means of accomplishing any of the objects listed in the four subparagraphs.

Clause (i) forbids a union to engage in a strike, or to induce or encourage a strike, work stoppage, or a refusal to perform services by "any individual employed by any person engaged in commerce or in an industry affecting commerce" for one of the objects listed in subparagraphs (A) through (D). Clause (ii) makes it an unfair labor practice for a union to "threaten, coerce, or restrain any person engaged in commerce or in an industry affecting commerce" for any of the proscribed objects.

Section 8(b) (4) (A) prohibits unions from engaging in actions specified in clause (i) or (ii) to compel an employer or self-employed person to join any labor or employer organization; or to force an employer to enter a hot cargo agreement prohibited by Section 8(e).

Section 8(b) (4) (B) contains the Act's secondary boycott provision. A secondary boycott occurs if a union has a dispute with Company A and in furtherance of that dispute causes the employees of Company B to stop handling the products of Company A, or otherwise forces Company B to stop doing business with Company A. The dispute is with Company A, called the primary employer; the union's action is against Company B, called the secondary employer; hence, the term *secondary boycott*. Section 8(b) (4) (B) also prohibits secondary action to compel an employer to recognize or bargain with a union that is not the certified representative of its employees.

Section 8(b) (4) (C) forbids a labor organization from using clause (i) or (ii) conduct to force an employer to recognize or bargain with a labor organization other than the one that is currently certified as the representative of its employees.

Section 8(b) (4) (D) forbids a labor organization from engaging in action described in clauses (i) and (ii) for the purpose of forcing any employer to assign certain work to "employees in a particular labor organization or in a particular trade, craft, or class rather than to employees in another labor organization or in another trade, craft, or class." The Act sets up a special procedure for handling disputes over work assignments under Section 10(k).

A proviso to Section 8(b) (4) makes clear that it is not unlawful for a person to refuse to enter the premises of an employer if the employees of that employer are engaged in a lawful strike ratified or approved by a representative of these employees. Another provision permits informational picketing in various circumstances, so long as such publicity and information picketing do not have the effect of inducing any individual employed by any person other than a primary employer to refuse to pick up, deliver, or transfer goods or not to perform services at the establishment of the employer involved in the dispute.

The following union activities are considered to be unfair labor practices under this section:

Picketing a company after three of its four partners refused to comply with the union's demand that they become members [8(b) (4) (A)].

Insisting that where final court action requires employees to handle goods at premises involved in a labor dispute, the employer must pay triple wages for the day or the entire tour of duty [8(b) (4) (A)].

Picketing the premises of an employer to compel him to cease doing business with another employer who has refused to recognize the union [8(b) (4) (B)].

Threatening an employer by telling him that his business will be picketed if he continues to do business with another employer whom the union has designated as "unfair" [8(b) (4) (B)].

Directing union members not to pick up and deliver products from a plant where the drivers had voted to be represented by a different union, which had received certification from the NLRB [8(b) (4) (C)].

Engaging in a strike to attempt to force the employer to assign to it the job of installing metal doors when the employer had assigned the work to the members of another union [8(b) (4) (D)].

Section 8(b) (5).   A union may not require employees under a union shop agreement to pay an initiation fee which the Board finds excessive or discriminatory. The section states that the Board shall consider in determination of these types of fees the practices and customs of labor organizations in the particular industry and the wages currently paid to employees affected. For example, a local union would probably violate this section by raising its initiation fee from $20 to $500, when other locals of the same union charged from $10 to $100 and the starting rate for the job was $175 per week.

Section 8(b) (6).   This section prohibits what is commonly known as featherbedding. Unions may not force an employer to pay or deliver or to agree to pay or deliver, any money or thing of value for services that are not performed or not to be performed. This section has been narrowly interpreted by the Board and does not include situations in which the work is performed, although it may be "unnecessary."

Section 8(b) (7).   This is a complex provision prohibiting a union that has not been certified as the bargaining agent from picketing or threatening to picket an employer for the purpose of obtaining recognition by that employer or acceptance by his workers as their bargaining representative. Both recognitional and organizational picketing constitute unfair labor practices when: *(a)* the employer has recognized a certified union and a new representation election would be barred under the Act, *(b)* an NLRB election has been conducted during the previous 12 months, or *(c)* a representation petition has not been filed with the Board "within a reasonable period of time not to exceed 30 days from the commencement of such picketing."

However, this section does not prohibit picketing for the purpose of truthfully advising the public (including consumers) that the company does not employ union members, nor have a contract with a union, unless the effect of the picketing is to interfere with deliveries, pickups, and other services required by the picketed employer.

Section 8(e). This complicated provision forbids both labor organizations and employers to enter into agreements commonly known as hot cargo agreements. These are defined as agreements where the employer will not handle, use, sell, transport, or deal in any of the products of another employer as required or forced by the labor organization.

The Act exempts both the construction and garment industries from the conditions of this section. In the construction industry the parties may agree to a clause that restricts the contracting or subcontracting of work to be performed at the construction site. Typically, the union and the employer agree that subcontracted work will go to an employer who has a contract with the union. A union may strike, picket, or engage in any other lawful activity in order to obtain such an agreement with the employer. A labor organization in the garment industry may not only strike, picket, or engage in other lawful activity to obtain such an agreement, but it may also engage in such activities in order to enforce it.

Section 8(f). A union and employer in the construction industry may enter into an agreement whereby employees must join the union not later than 7 days after the date of hire, rather than 30 days, as provided in Section 8(a) (3) for all other employers. The parties may enter into such an agreement without having first established the majority status of the union, as required in Section 9.

FREE SPEECH

Section 8(c). This section of the Act provides that the expression of any views, argument, or opinion shall not constitute or be evidence of an unfair labor practice "if such expression contains no threat of reprisal or force or promise of benefit." Examples of actions this provision does not protect, and that would be ruled as unfair labor practices, are:

> An implied threat by an employer that the organization of a union would result in the loss of certain benefits for employees.

> A threat by an employer to close down a plant to move to another location, in the event of a union's winning an election.

> A statement by a management official to an employee that the employee will lose her job if the union wins a majority in the plant.

THE MEANING OF COLLECTIVE BARGAINING

Section 8(d). This section defines collective bargaining as required from both parties by the Act. This definition imposes a mutual obligation upon the employer and the representative of the employees

> to meet at reasonable times and confer in good faith with respect to wages, hours, and other terms and conditions of employment or the negotiation of an agreement or any question arising thereunder and the execution of a written contract incorporating any agreement reached if requested by either party, but such obligation does not compel either party to agree to a proposal or require the making of a concession.

The duty to bargain thus covers all matters concerning rates of pay, hours of employment, or other conditions of employment. These are called mandatory subjects about which the employer, as well as the employees' representative, must bargain in good faith, although the law does not require "either party to agree to a proposal or require the making of a concession." As determined by the NLRB, mandatory subjects of bargaining include but are not limited to such matters as pensions for present and retired employees, bonuses, group insurance, grievance procedure, safety practices, seniority, procedures for discharge, layoff, recall, or discipline, and the union shop. On nonmandatory subjects, that is, matters that are lawful but not related to "wages, hours, and other conditions of employment," the parties are free to bargain and to agree, but neither party may insist on bargaining on such subjects over the objection of the other party.

Section 8(d) also requires that the parties to a collective agreement follow certain steps in terminating or modifying the agreement. Among these requirements are that the party wishing to terminate or modify a labor contract must notify the other party to the contract in writing about the proposed termination or modification 60 days before the date on which the contract is scheduled to expire. This party also must, within 30 days after the notice to the other party, notify the FMCS of the existence of a dispute if no agreement has been reached by that time, and further notify at the same time any state or territorial mediation or conciliation agency in the state or territory where the dispute occurred.[5]

The NLRB has interpreted this section to mean that employees who go on strike without following the prescribed steps for terminating or modifying the contract lose the protection of the law. They may not appeal to the Board if the employer disciplines or discharges them.

REPRESENTATIVES AND ELECTIONS

Section 9 of the Act is a lengthy section that governs the procedural and legal requirements for the designation of representatives and election of union representatives. It provides for three types of elections among employees:[6]

Representation elections to determine the employees' choice of a collective bargaining agent. These are held upon petition of an individual, employer, employees, or a labor organization. Typically, the NLRB will not hold an election unless the petitioner can show that at least 30 percent of the employees involved have indicated their support for the union, or for an election.

Decertification elections to determine whether or not the employees wish to withdraw the bargaining authority of the union. These are held upon the petition of the employees or a labor organization.

Deauthorization polls to determine whether or not the employees wish to revoke the authority of their union to enter into a union shop contract.

Section 9(a). This section provides that the union representative designated by a majority of employees appropriate for collective bargaining becomes the exclusive representative of the employees in bargaining. When a union majority representative has been chosen, it becomes illegal for an employer to bargain with anyone else.

Sections 9(b) and 9(c). These sections outline in general terms the "rules of the game" for the holding of NLRB elections. Included in 9(b) is the designation that the Board determine what group of employees constitutes an appropriate unit for bargaining. The appropriate

---

[5] Procedures of the FMCS are described in Appendix B to this introductory section.

[6] The Board also conducts "expedited elections" in connection with Section 8(b) (7) (C) and employer last-offer elections in connection with Section 209 of the Act.

bargaining unit may extend to one or more employers, to one or more plants of the same employer, or it may be a subdivision of a plantwide unit such as a unit of skilled craftsmen. It is up to the Board to consider similarities of skills, wages, working conditions; the history of collective bargaining in the company; the wishes of the employees; and any other factors that the Board may consider important in determination of the appropriate unit. In short, employees who possess common employment interests concerning wages, hours, and conditions of employment usually are grouped together in a bargaining unit. However, Section 9(b) specifically limits the Board in its determination of a bargaining unit in several ways. It may not include professional and nonprofessional employees in the same unit, unless a majority of the professional employees votes to be included in the unit. It also prohibits the Board from including plant guards in the same unit with other employees, and from certifying a union of guards if it also includes members who are not guards. The Board also may not use "the extent to which employees have organized" as the controlling factor in deciding the appropriate bargain unit [Section 9(c) (5)].

Section 9(c) (1) authorizes the NLRB to direct an election and certify the results thereof, provided the record shows that a question of representation exists.

An election may be held by agreement between the employer and the individual or labor organization claiming to represent the employees. In such an agreement the parties state the time and place agreed on, the choices to be included on the ballot, and a method to determine who is eligible to vote. They also authorize the NLRB Regional Director to conduct the election.

If the parties are unable to reach an agreement, the Act authorizes the NLRB to order an election after a hearing. The Act also authorizes the Board to delegate to its Regional Directors the determination on matters concerning elections. Under this delegation of authority the Regional Directors can determine the appropriateness of the unit, direct an election, and certify the outcome. Upon the request of an interested party, the Board may review the action of a Regional Director, but such review does not stop the election process unless the Board so orders. The election details are left to the Regional Director. Such matters as who may vote, when the election will be held, and what standards of conduct will be imposed on the parties are decided in accordance with the Board's rules and its decisions.

Section 9(c) (3) prohibits the holding of an election in any collective bargaining unit or subdivision thereof in which a valid election has been held during the preceding 12-month period.

In summary, Section 9 is one of the key sections that constantly confronts both unions and management in collective bargaining relationships, particularly in the formative stages of a labor union in its efforts to gain representational status.

SPECIAL PROVISIONS FOR HEALTH CARE INSTITUTIONS

Representation election procedures are the same for health care facilities as for other establishments.[7] Similarly, as to unfair labor practices, the health care area is covered by the same statutory provisions as those that forbid employer or union discrimination against employees, failure to bargain in good faith, certain unlawful union picketing, and employer domination or support of a labor organization.

But with a goal of minimizing work stoppages at health care institutions and providing continuity of patient care, Congress in 1974 wrote into the Act a new unfair labor practice—*Section 8(g)*. It prohibits a labor organization from striking or picketing a health care institution, or engaging in any other concerted refusal to work, without first giving the employer and FMCS a 10-day notice of such action. The section specifies, "The notice shall state the date and time that such action will commence. The notice, once given, may be extended by the written agreement of both parties."

Additionally, a series of special provisions for the health care industry were added to Section 8(d) of the Act. These health care amendments call for special dispute-settling procedures. A 90-day written notice must be served by employer or union of intent to terminate or modify a collective bargaining contract (30 days more than required by the Act elsewhere). If the dispute continues, the FMCS and similar state agencies must be notified at the 60-day point. If a dispute arises in bargaining for an initial contract, 30 days' notice must be given by the union to the employer, FMCS, and the appropriate

---

[7] In 1975 the NLRB issued its first guidelines for appropriate representational units in private health care institutions. In a series of cases—217 NLRB 131–138—these guidelines limited the number of bargaining units to avoid "proliferation" of units in health care organizations. In 1984, the NLRB ruled that it was no longer going to be held to a "community of interest" standard and would begin using a "disparity of interest" standard in health care bargaining unit determination. (See decision of the NLRB, St. Francis Hospital and IBEW Local 474, 271 NLRB No. 160.) However, in 1988, the NLRB developed and proposed new bargaining unit guidelines for hospitals. Up to eight bargaining units would be considered "appropriate" under the new rules. These are registered nurses; physicians; other professionals; technicians; skilled maintenance employees; office clerical employees; guards; and all other non-professional employees.

agency. In either a contract termination-modification or initial contract dispute, under Section 213 of the Act, the FMCS may, if disagreement continues, invoke a 30-day no-strike, no-lockout period and set up a fact-finding board to make settlement recommendations, while continuing its mediation-conciliation efforts.

All else failing, the 10-day strike or picketing notice must be given as required by Section 8(g).

PREVENTION OF UNFAIR LABOR PRACTICES

Section 10 is very important, in that it outlines the procedural requirements and limitations that are placed upon the Board and interested parties in processing unfair labor practice cases. The LMRA is not a criminal statute. The NLRB's actions are designed to stop unfair labor practices and to restore situations to their "original states"—those that prevailed before the violations occurred—insofar as possible. The orders of the Board serve basically to remedy the situation, not to punish persons who may have violated its provisions. The NLRB is authorized by Section 10(c) not only to issue a cease-and-desist order but "to take such affirmative action, including reinstatement of employees with or without back pay, as will effectuate the policies of this Act."

Sections 10(a), 10(b), 10(c), 10(d). These sections of the Act outline the general procedures by which the NLRB and its regional offices investigate, attempt to prevent, and/or remedy unfair labor practices. Generally, an unfair labor practice charge must be filed with an office of the NLRB within six months of the date of the occurrence of the alleged unfair labor practice. (As of 1980, about 50 regional and other field offices of the NLRB were located in major cities in various sections of the country.) When a charge is received in the office of the Board, an agent will investigate to see whether formal proceedings are warranted.[8] If the regional office of the NLRB is unable to resolve the issue, and the complaint warrants a full hearing, an Administrative Law Judge (ALJ) from the Board's independent Division of Judges may be assigned to conduct a full, formal hearing to take testimony and examine the evidence. If the opinion of the ALJ is that the evidence presented is not sufficient to justify a finding that an unfair labor practice has been committed, the ALJ will issue an order dis-

---

[8] In the event that the regional office refuses to issue a formal complaint, the person(s) who filed the charge may appeal this decision to the General Counsel of the NLRB, who has final authority to determine whether to issue a formal complaint [Section 3(d)].

missing the complaint. However, if the ALJ is of the opinion that an unfair labor practice(s) has occurred, he or she will make an appropriate finding and issue a remedial order. In effect, the findings and orders of the ALJ become recommendations to the NLRB. If there is no appeal of the ALJ's decision, the decision and remedial order (if any) of the ALJ become the decision and the order of the Board. If the case is appealed, the NLRB itself will review the determination made by the ALJ and either reverse, modify, or affirm the decision and order of the ALJ.

A remedial order issued by the NLRB usually will require the person, union, or company involved to cease and desist from the unfair labor practice(s) and to take affirmative action designed to remedy the effects of the unfair labor practice(s). Since the LMRA is not intended to designate criminal penalties, these orders will be designed to restore equity to the situation on the assumption that such equity is necessary to guarantee rights protected under the Act. Examples of affirmative actions required of employers are:

Disestablishing a union dominated by the employer.

Reopening a plant closed in an attempt to thwart the employees' attempts at self-organization.

Offering to hire employees denied employment because of their prounion attitudes or activities.

Offering to reemploy workers who were discharged for union activity; reimburse the employees for all lost wages, including interest; and restore full seniority and all other rights, including promotions, pay increases, pension privileges, and vacation rights that would have been received had the discriminatory discharges not occurred.

Upon request, bargaining collectively with a certain union as the exclusive representative of the employees in a certain described unit and signing a written agreement if an understanding is reached.

Examples of affirmative actions required of unions are:

Notification to the employee and the employer that the union does not object to the reinstatement or employment of certain persons who were discharged or denied employment as a result of certain discriminatory actions by the union.

Ordering the union to refund dues and fees illegally collected, including interest.

Signing an agreement that had been negotiated with the employer.

Sections 10(e) and 10(f).   These sections provide the machinery for the legal enforcement of Board orders and for appeal for relief from Board orders by an employer or union who believes that an order has been issued in error. Normally, the first appeal from an order of the regional office or ALJ will go to the full NLRB itself in Washington, D.C. The NLRB, in order to seek enforcement of its orders, may petition a federal district court or circuit court of appeals for appropriate relief or restraining order. Appeals from a Board or district court order may be made to a federal appeals court, and ultimate appeal can be made to the U.S. Supreme Court. The large majority of cases, however, are not appealed to the federal courts but are decided at Board regional office and/or national NLRB levels.[9]

Section 10(k).   Special procedures for hearing and adjudicating jurisdictional disputes are provided for in this section.

Section 10(l).   This section provides for special priority procedures, including court injunctions, so as to stop quickly certain acts, strikes, and boycotts that may result in "irreparable harm" to the employer. For the most part, these are directed against secondary boycotts and certain types of organizational picketing.

MISCELLANEOUS PROVISIONS

The remainder of the LMRA, although quite extensive in length, is not nearly so important to the duty to bargain collectively as are the provisions discussed to this point. Only brief mention will be made of the more salient miscellaneous provisions covered in the remaining sections that have not been mentioned previously.

Sections 11 and 12—Investigatory Powers and Penalties.   As the title suggests, Sections 11 and 12 outline the legal powers of investigation given the NLRB by the Congress and provide for penalties under the Act.

Sections 13 to 18—Limitations.   Sections 13 through 18 state a series of limitations that the Act is not to be construed as interfering with or diminishing in any way. Section 13 guarantees that the right to strike is still a right not limited by the LMRA. Section 14(a) permits supervisors to be members of a labor organization, but states that

---

[9] Statistically, about 65 percent of the unfair labor practice charges filed with the NLRB are dismissed by the regional offices of the Board or withdrawn by the parties. Of the remainder, over 90 percent usually are settled at the regional office level. Of the cases which are tried by an ALJ, about two thirds are appealed to the full NLRB. Some 25 to 35 percent of Board decisions are appealed to Courts of Appeal; typically the NLRB is sustained in whole or part in about 80 percent of these cases. Only a few cases are reviewed by the Supreme Court, usually some five or fewer annually.

employers are not required to bargain with supervisors as part of labor organizations. Section 14(b) permits so-called right-to-work laws in states where these laws are enacted. Specifically, Section 14(b) allows states to ban union shop contracts if they so choose. In early 1985, Idaho became the 21st state to have a right-to-work law on its statute books. The majority of right-to-work states are located in the southern part of the United States.

Section 19. As amended in legislation passed in 1980, this section provides that any employee who has conscientious objections to joining or financially supporting a labor organization, based on the traditional tenets of a bona fide religion or sect, shall not be required to do so.[10]

However, such an employee may be required to make charitable contributions in an amount equal to union dues and initiation fees, and may be required to pay the costs incurred by the union of any requested grievance-arbitration procedure instituted on his/her behalf.

The language in this section defining conscientious objection is not to be construed in such a way as to discriminate among religions or to favor any religious views.

Sections 201 through 205. These sections create and outline the functions of the FMCS and create a National Labor Relations Panel to advise the President on problems of industrial relations. The National Labor Relations Panel, consisting of representatives of management, labor, and the public, has not been active in recent years.

Sections 206 through 210. The National Emergency Strike provisions, giving the President power to intervene in those types of disputes that he deems to be national emergencies, are outlined in these sections.

Section 301. This section provides that suits for violation of contracts between an employer and a union may be brought in the federal district courts. Unions are made responsible for the acts of their agents; however, money judgments assessed against a labor organization in a district court are enforceable only against the organization as an entity and not against individual members per se.

Section 303. Strikes and boycotts enumerated in Section 8(b) (4) are made illegal, as well as their being made unfair labor practices. Employers may sue to collect damages for injury resulting from such strikes.

---

[10] Section 19 first was added to the Act in the 1974 amendments for health care institutions, but without the grievance-arbitration proviso.

SUMMARY

The remaining provisions of the Act are relatively minor in nature but should be studied by the student of labor relations. Certainly, the complexity of the LMRA will be impressed upon the student by both study and application in case situations. Only by extensive analysis of labor-management cases can the student come to understand and appreciate the intent and effectiveness of the Act and its purpose to govern the duty to bargain collectively.

APPENDIX A

Edited and Updated Excerpts from the Informational Pamphlet, *The NLRB—What It Is, What It Does**

In recent fiscal years, the NLRB has received annually some 40,000 to 45,000 cases of all kinds. About three fourths are unfair labor practice charges. Over the years, charges filed against employers have outnumbered those filed against unions by about 2 to 1. Charges are filed by individual workers, employers, and unions.

What is the structure of the NLRB?   The NLRB has five Board Members and a General Counsel, each appointed by the President with Senate consent. The Board Members are appointed to five-year terms, the term of one Member expiring each year. The statute specifies that the President shall designate one Member to serve as Chairman of the Board. The General Counsel is appointed to a four-year term. Reappointments may be made.

Headquartered in Washington, the NLRB has 33 Regional Offices and 16 smaller field offices throughout the country.

The NLRB's judicial functions are by law separate from its prosecuting functions. The five-member Board acts primarily as a quasi-judicial body in deciding cases upon formal records, generally upon review from Regional Directors' or Administrative Law Judges' decisions. The General Counsel is responsible for the investigation and prosecution of charges of violations of the Act, and he has general supervision of the Regional Offices.

Who enforces Board orders?   The NLRB has no statutory independent power of enforcement of its orders, but it may seek enforcement in the U.S. Courts of Appeals. Similarly, parties aggrieved by its orders may seek judicial review in the courts.

Annually, the U.S. Courts of Appeals hand down some 300 decisions

---

* Published by the NLRB, Washington, D.C.

related to enforcement and/or review of Board orders in unfair labor practice proceedings. Of these, about 80 percent affirm the Board in whole or in part.

How do NLRB procedures work?   Upon the filing of an unfair labor practice charge with an NLRB Regional Office, members of the professional staff of that office investigate circumstances from which the charge arises, in order to determine whether formal proceedings are warranted. Approximately one third of the unfair labor practice allegations are found, after investigation, to require legal disposition. In such a case, the Regional Office works with the parties in an attempt to achieve a voluntary settlement adequate to remedy the alleged violation. A very substantial number of cases are settled at this stage. If a case cannot be settled, then a formal complaint is issued, and the case is heard before an Administrative Law Judge.

NLRB Administrative Law Judges conduct formal hearings and issue decisions, which may be appealed to the five-member Board; if they are not appealed, the Administrative Law Judges' recommended orders become orders of the Board.

The NLRB's traditional emphasis on voluntary disposition of cases at all stages means that only about 5 percent of the unfair labor practice charges originally filed with the Regional Offices are litigated all the way through to a decision of the Board. Yet, despite the small percentage, the Board is still called to decide on the order of 1,200 unfair labor practice cases and 700 representation cases each year.

In representation election cases, the 33 Regional Directors have the authority to process all petitions, rule on contested issues, and direct elections or dismiss the requests, subject to review by the Board on limited grounds. The NLRB, through its Regional Offices, conducts thousands of representation elections a year, in which hundreds of thousands of employees exercise their free choice by secret ballot.

National Labor Relations Board—Statistical Information for Fiscal Year 1986

The following statistics reflect the work of the various NLRB Divisions during the 1986 fiscal year and are based on actions taken during that year and previous years. These data were excerpted and developed from reports provided by the Statistical Services Staff for the office of the General Counsel of the NLRB.

Fiscal year 1986 saw an intake of some 42,136 cases—a number close to that docketed during several previous years, although considerably smaller than the NLRB caseloads during the late 1970s and early 1980s, which were 50,000 or more cases annually. During FY1986 the intake of unfair labor practices (C) cases was 34,433, about the same number as in FY1984 and FY1985. There were 7,703 representation petititons filed in FY1986, a decrease of about 8 percent from both FY1984 and FY1985.

The Board's Regional Offices conducted 3,363 representational (RC and RM) elections during fiscal year 1986. Slightly more than 200,000 employees were eligible to vote in these elections. Unions won 47 percent of these elections, a percentage similar to that during most of the 1980s but considerably lower than the 55 percent or so during most of the 1970s. During FY1986 the Board conducted 857 decertification (RD) elections. Unions were decertified in 75 percent of these elections, about the same percentage as in several previous years.

APPENDIX B—THE FEDERAL MEDIATION AND CONCILIATION SERVICE (FMCS)

Excerpts from the Publication, *Securing Labor-Management Peace Through Mediation**

A strike or lockout is not the only answer when an employer and a union exhaust their bargaining talents and reach a stalemate. *Mediation* is the alternative.

A mediator can help bring reason and a fresh viewpoint to the dilemma, and often points the way to a solution. In fact, 9 out of 10 disputes receiving active mediation assistance are settled peacefully —without a strike. These are pretty good odds that mediation is a course worth trying.

Even when there is no stalemate or imminent deadline—but mounting difficulties clearly signal real trouble ahead—the mediator can be helpful. The mediator's training and skill often can spot difficulties early and help develop a remedy.

Mediation is a free and voluntary process. It can be requested by either party to a dispute, or the mediator may volunteer to help. There is no cost to either side, and mediation is available not only to private industry but also in public employment situations.

The mediator is completely impartial, a confidential advisor who neither takes sides nor forces decisions. The only role that a mediator has is that of a constructive peacemaker who brings objectivity to disputed issues and opens new roads to problem solving and decision making.

Collective bargaining is an indispensable ingredient of a free industrial society. Mediation is a time-tested and productive tool that helps preserve and strengthen our collective bargaining system.

What Is the Federal Mediation and Conciliation Service?   The Federal Mediation and Conciliation Service is an independent agency of the federal government created by Congress with a director appointed by the president. Its primary duty is to promote labor-management peace.

This responsibility is fulfilled by providing mediation assistance in preventing and settling collective bargaining controversies. For this purpose Federal mediators, known as commissioners, are stationed strategically throughout the country.

The Labor Management Relations Act requires that parties to a labor

---

* Published by the FMCS, Washington, D.C.

contract must file a dispute notice if agreement is not reached 30 days in advance of a contract termination or reopening date. The notice must be filed with the FMCS and the appropriate state or local mediation agency.

The notice alerts the service to possible bargaining trouble. If the case falls within the jurisdiction of the service, the regional office then assigns a mediator to check with the employer and union involved to see whether assistance is required.

It is a tribute to the nation's free collective bargaining system that in more than 95 out of 100 cases in which notices are filed, the employers and unions reach agreements on their own without requiring mediation aid. Yet in those cases where third-party assistance is needed it makes good sense to call in the mediator.

Who Are the Mediators?   Mediators are carefully selected and trained. About equal numbers have backgrounds with management and with labor, and many have had some experience with both.

Mediators are picked for the job because of their knowledge and demonstrated skill in collective bargaining. Regardless of background, they are required to maintain strict objectivity as representatives of the public interest.

How Does the Mediator Work?   While methods and circumstances vary, the mediator generally will confer first with one of the parties involved and then with the other to get their versions of the pending difficulties. Then with these problems firmly in mind, the mediator usually will call joint conferences with the employer and union representatives.

Mediators function informally, meeting separately and jointly with the parties to help them find some mutually acceptable solutions.

It is part of the job to listen, review, analyze, suggest, advise, reason, and explore all possible means of reaching an agreement.

The mediator can restart stalled negotiations, improve the bargaining atmosphere, encourage mutual discussions, explore alternative solutions, suggest specific contract clauses that have worked well elsewhere, and provide needed economic data and other information.

The mediator works hard to promote cooperation and understanding between management and labor not only during contract disputes but at other times as well in order to improve day-to-day relations in the workplace.

Through the use of FMCS technical services, unions and employers, with the assistance of the mediator, can improve the labor-management climate. The mediator can give advisory assistance on specific problems and encourage the use of joint labor-management committees. A skilled mediator can provide training and information to improve the knowledge and skill of both parties, can identify trends and developments, can encourage early bargaining to forestall deadline tensions, and will respond to the various needs of labor and management, including government employers and labor organizations, to improve their bargaining relationships.

In addition, the service helps employers and unions in selecting arbitrators to adjudicate labor-management disputes by maintaining a large roster of qualified arbitrators. When an employer and a union need an arbitrator, they need only to notify the service and the service will provide at no charge a listing of qualified arbitrators in their area who are available to hear the dispute. When the parties have agreed on one name from the list, they notify FMCS and the service notifies the arbitrator.

Federal Mediation and Conciliation Service— Statistical Information for Fiscal Year 1985

The following statistics reflect the work of the various FMCS offices as summarized in the Annual Report of the FMCS for fiscal year 1985.

The FMCS maintained some 72 field offices and 8 regional offices throughout the United States. Some 229 mediators were on staff. During FY1985, FMCS received 108,751 formal notices of pending bargaining situations. Of these, 22,736 (20.9 percent) were assigned to mediators. Mediators actively participated and gave mediation assistance in 8,019 cases (35.3 percent of cases assigned) and conducted a total of 23,793 joint conferences with the parties during the year. In the major negotiation cases where FMCS mediators were monitoring or were active in mediating, there were 993 work stoppages (4.4 percent of the FMCS cases assigned).

Selected Bibliography

A Guide to Basic Law and Procedures under the National Labor Relations Act. Washington, D.C.: Office of the General Counsel of the NLRB, U.S. Government Printing Office, 1987.

Allen, Robert E., and Timothy J. Keaveny. *Contemporary Labor Relations.* 2d ed. Reading, Mass.: Addison-Wesley Publishing, 1988.

Baderschneider, Jean A.; Richard N. Block; and John A. Fossum. *The Collective Bargaining Process—Readings and Analysis.* Plano, Tex.: Business Publications, 1983.

Balfour, Alan. *Union-Management Relations in a Changing Economy.* Englewood Cliffs, N.J.: Prentice-Hall, 1987.

Basic Patterns in Union Contracts. 11th ed. (Compiled by editorial staff of BNA, Inc.) Washington, D.C.: Bureau of National Affairs, Inc., 1986.

Begin, James P., and Edwin F. Beal. *The Practice of Collective Bargaining.* 8th ed. Homewood, Ill.: Richard D. Irwin, 1989.

Carrell, Michael R., and Christina Heavrin. *Collective Bargaining and Labor Relations: Cases, Practice, and Law.* 2d. ed. Columbus, Ohio: Merrill Publishing Co., 1987.

Davey, Harold W.; Mario F. Bognanno; and David L. Estenson. *Contemporary Collective Bargaining.* 4th ed. Englewood Cliffs, N.J.: Prentice-Hall, 1982.

Dilts, David A., and Clarence R. Deitsch. *Labor Relations.* New York: Macmillan, 1983.

Estey, Marten. *The Unions.* 3d ed. New York: Harcourt Brace Jovanovich, 1981.

Feldacker, Bruce. *Labor Guide to Labor Law.* 2d ed. Reston, Va. Reston Publishing, 1983.

Fischer, Roger, and William Ury. *Getting to Yes: Negotiating Agreements Without Giving In.* Boston: Houghton Mifflin, 1981.

Fossum, John A. *Labor Relations: Development, Structure, Process.* 4th ed. Homewood, Ill.: BPI/Irwin, 1989.

Gould, William. *A Primer on American Labor Law.* Cambridge, Mass.: MIT Press, 1982.

Gregory, Charles O., and Harold H. Katz. *Labor and the Law*. New York: W. W. Norton, 1979.

Herman, E. Edward; Alfred Kuhn; and Ronald L. Seeber. *Collective Bargaining and Labor Relations*. Englewood Cliffs, N.J. Prentice-Hall, 1987.

Hilgert, Raymond L., and Sterling H. Schoen. *Labor Agreement Negotiations*. Homewood, Ill.: Richard D. Irwin, 1988.

Holley, William H., Jr., and Kenneth M. Jennings. *The Labor Relation Process*. 3d ed. Hinsdale, Ill.: Dryden Press, 1988.

Kochan, Thomas A. and Harry C. Katz. *Collective Bargaining and Industrial Relations*. 2d ed. Homewood, Ill.: Richard D. Irwin, 1988.

Labor Cases. Chicago: Commerce Clearing House.

Labor Relations Reference Manual. Washington, D.C.: Bureau of National Affairs, Inc.

Lewicki, Roy J., and Joseph A. Litterer. *Negotiation*. Homewood, Ill.: Richard D. Irwin, 1985.

Lewicki, Roy J., and Joseph A. Litterer. *Negotiation: Readings, Exercises, and Cases*. Homewood, Ill.: Richard D. Irwin, 1985.

Loughran, Charles S. *Negotiating A Labor Contract*. Washington, D.C.: Bureau of National Affairs, Inc., 1984.

NLRB Decisions. Chicago: Commerce Clearing House.

McGuiness, Kenneth C., and Jeffrey A. Norris. *How to take a Case Before the NLRB*. 5th ed. Washington, D.C.: Bureau of National Affairs, Inc., 1986.

McKelvey, Jean T., ed. *The Changing Law of Fair Representation*. Ithaca: New York State School of Industrial Relations, Cornell University, 1985.

Mills, Daniel Quinn. *Labor-Management Relations*. 3d ed. New York: McGraw-Hill, 1986.

Mills, Daniel Quinn, and Janice McCormick. *Industrial Relations in Transition*. New York: John Wiley & Sons, 1985.

Robinson, James W., and Roger W. Walker. *Introduction to Labor*. 2d ed. Englewood Cliffs, N.J.: Prentice-Hall, 1985.

Rosenbloom, David H., and Jay M. Shafritz. *Essentials of Labor Relations*. Reston, Va.: Reston Publishing, 1985.

Rowan, Richard L., ed. *Readings in Labor Economics and Labor Relations*. 5th ed. Homewood, Ill.: Richard D. Irwin, 1985.

Sandver, Marcus Hart. *Labor Relations: Process and Outcomes*. Boston: Little, Brown, 1987.

Schlossberg, Stephen I., and Judith A. Scott. *Organizing and the Law*. Washington, D.C., Bureau of National Affairs, Inc., 1983.

Simkin, William E., and Nicholas A. Fidlandis. *Mediation and the Dynamics of Collective Bargaining*. 2d ed. Washington, D.C.: Bureau of National Affairs, Inc., 1986.

Sloane, Arthur A., and Fred Witney. *Labor Relations*. 6th ed. Englewood Cliffs, N.J.: Prentice-Hall, 1988.

Taylor, Benjamin J., and Fred Witney. *Labor Relations Law*. 5th ed. Englewood Cliffs, N.J.: Prentice-Hall, 1987.

The Federal Mediation and Conciliation Service. Washington, D.C.: Federal Mediation and Conciliation Service, U.S. Government Printing Office.

Twomey, David. *Labor Law and Legislation*. 7th ed. Cincinnati: South-Western Publishing, 1985.

Zack, Arnold M. *Public Sector Mediation*. Washington, D.C.: Bureau of National Affairs, Inc., 1985.

Partial Text of
The Labor Management
Relations Act, 1947*

**as amended by the Labor-Management Reporting
and Disclosure Act of 1959†, by Public Law 93–360,
1974, and by Public Law 96–593, 1980**

[PUBLIC LAW 101—80TH CONGRESS]
[CHAPTER 120—1ST SESSION]

AN ACT

To amend the National Labor Relations Act, to provide additional facilities for the mediation of labor disputes affecting commerce, to equalize legal responsibilities of labor organizations and employers, and for other purposes.

Be it enacted by the Senate and House of Representatives of the United States of America in Congress assembled.

Short Title and Declaration of Policy

Section 1. (a) This Act may be cited as the "Labor Management Relations Act, 1947."

(b) Industrial strife which interferes with the normal flow of commerce and with the full production of articles and commodities for commerce, can be avoided or substantially minimized if employers, employees, and labor organizations each recognize under law one another's legitimate rights in their relations with each other, and above all recognize under law that neither party has any right in its relations with any other to engage in acts or practices which jeopardize the public health, safety, or interest.

It is the purpose and policy of this Act, in order to promote the full flow of commerce, to prescribe the legitimate rights of both employees and employers in their relations affecting commerce, to provide orderly and peaceful procedures for preventing the interference by either with the legitimate rights of the other, to protect the rights of individual employees in their relations with

---

* Also known as the Taft-Hartley Act.
† Also known as the Landrum-Griffin Act, Public Law 86–257.

labor organizations whose activities affect commerce, to define and proscribe practices on the part of labor and management which affect commerce and are inimical to the general welfare, and to protect the rights of the public in connection with labor disputes affecting commerce.

TITLE I—AMENDMENT OF NATIONAL LABOR RELATIONS ACT

Section 101. The National Labor Relations Act is hereby amended to read as follows:

Findings and Policies

Section 1. The denial by some employers of the right of employees to organize and the refusal by some employers to accept the procedure of collective bargaining lead to strikes and other forms of industrial strife or unrest, which have the intent or the necessary effect of burdening or obstructing commerce by (a) impairing the efficiency, safety, or operation of the instrumentalities of commerce; (b) occurring in the current of commerce; (c) materially affecting, restraining, or controlling the flow of raw materials or manufactured or processed goods from or into the channels of commerce, or the prices of such materials or goods in commerce; or (d) causing diminution of employment and wages in such volume as substantially to impair or disrupt the market for goods flowing from or into the channels of commerce.

The inequality of bargaining power between employees who do not possess full freedom of association or actual liberty of contract, and employers who are organized in the corporate or other forms of ownership association substantially burdens and affects the flow of commerce, and tends to aggravate recurrent business depressions, by depressing wage rates and the purchasing power of wage earners in industry and by preventing the stabilization of competitive wage rates and working conditions within and between industries.

Experience has proved that protection by law of the right of employees to organize and bargain collectively safeguards commerce from injury, impairment, or interruption, and promotes the flow of commerce by removing certain recognized sources of industrial strife and unrest, by encouraging practices fundamental to the friendly adjustment of industrial disputes arising out of differences as to wages, hours, or other working conditions, and by restoring equality of bargaining power between employers and employees.

Experience has further demonstrated that certain practices by some labor organizations, their officers, and members have the intent or the necessary effect of burdening or obstructing commerce by preventing the free flow of goods in such commerce through strikes and other forms of industrial unrest or through concerted activities which impair the interest of the public in the free flow of such commerce. The elimination of such practices is a necessary condition to the assurance of the rights herein guaranteed.

It is hereby declared to be the policy of the United States to eliminate the causes of certain substantial obstructions to the free flow of commerce and to mitigate and eliminate these obstructions when they have occurred by encouraging the practice and procedure of collective bargaining and by protecting the exercise by workers of full freedom of association, self-organization, and designation of representatives of their own choosing, for the purpose of negotiating the terms and conditions of their employment or other mutual aid or protection.

Definitions

Section 2.   When used in this Act—

(1) The term "person" includes one or more individuals, labor organizations, partnerships, associations, corporations, legal representatives, trustees, trustees in bankruptcy, or receivers.

(2) The term "employer" includes any person acting as an agent of an employer, directly or indirectly, but shall not include the United States or any wholly owned Government corporation, or any Federal Reserve Bank, or any State or political subdivision thereof, or any person subject to the Railway Labor Act, as amended from time to time, or any labor organization (other than when acting as an employer), or anyone acting in the capacity of officer or agent of such labor organization.

(3) The term "employee" shall include any employee, and shall not be limited to the employees of a particular employer, unless the Act explicitly states otherwise, and shall include any individual whose work has ceased as a consequence of, or in connection with, any current labor dispute or because of any unfair labor practice, and who has not obtained any other regular and substantially equivalent employment, but shall not include any individual employed as an agricultural laborer, or in the domestic service of any family or person at his home, or any individual employed by his parent or spouse, or any individual having the status of an independent contractor, or any individual employed as a supervisor, or any individual employed by an employer subject to the Railway Labor Act, as amended from time to time, or by any other person who is not an employer as herein defined.

(4) The term "representatives" includes any individual or labor organization.

(5) The term "labor organization" means any organization of any kind, or any agency or employee representation committee or plan, in which employees participate and which exists for the purpose, in whole or in part, of dealing with employers concerning grievances, labor disputes, wages, rates of pay, hours of employment, or conditions of work.

(6) The term "commerce" means trade, traffic, commerce, transportation, or communication among the several States, or between the District of Columbia or any Territory of the United States and any State or Territory, or between any foreign country and any State, Territory, or the District of Columbia, or within the District of Columbia or any Territory, or between points in the same State but through any other State or any Territory or the District of Columbia or any foreign country.

(7) The term "affecting commerce" means in commerce, or burdening or

obstructing commerce or the free flow of commerce, or having led or tending to lead to a labor dispute burdening or obstructing commerce or the free flow of commerce.

(8) The term "unfair labor practice" means any unfair labor practice listed in section 8.

(9) The term "labor dispute" includes any controversy concerning terms, tenure or conditions of employment, or concerning the association or representation of persons in negotiating, fixing, maintaining, changing, or seeking to arrange terms or conditions of employment, regardless of whether the disputants stand in the proximate relation of employer and employee.

(10) The term "National Labor Relations Board" means the National Labor Relations Board provided for in section 3 of this Act.

(11) The term "supervisor" means any individual having authority, in the interest of the employer, to hire, transfer, suspend, lay off, recall, promote, discharge, assign, reward, or discipline other employees, or responsibility to direct them, or to adjust their grievances, or effectively to recommend such action, if in connection with the foregoing the exercise of such authority is not of a merely routine or clerical nature, but requires the use of independent judgment.

(12) The term "professional employee" means

(a) any employee engaged in work (i) predominantly intellectual and varied in character as opposed to routine mental, manual, mechanical, or physical work; (ii) involving the consistent exercise of discretion and judgment in its performance; (iii) of such a character that the output produced or the result accomplished cannot be standardized in relation to a given period of time; (iv) requiring knowledge of an advanced type in a field of science or learning customarily acquired by a prolonged course of specialized intellectual instruction and study in an institution of higher learning or a hospital, as distinguished from a general academic education or from an apprenticeship or from training in the performance of routine mental, manual, or physical process; or

(b) any employee, who (i) has completed the courses of specialized intellectual instruction and study described in clause (iv) of paragraph (a), and (ii) is performing related work under the supervision of a professional person to qualify himself to become a professional employee as defined in paragraph (a).

(13) In determining whether any person is acting as an "agent" of another person so as to make such other person responsible for his acts, the question of whether the specific acts performed were actually authorized or subsequently ratified shall not be controlling.

(14) The term "health care institution" shall include any hospital, convalescent hospital, health maintenance organization, health clinic, nursing home, extended care facility, or other institution devoted to the care of the sick, infirm, or aged person.

National Labor Relations Board

Section 3. (a) The National Labor Relations Board (hereinafter called the "Board") . . . as an agency of the United States, shall consist of five . . . members, appointed by the President by and with the advice and consent of the Senate . . . for terms of five years each, excepting that any individual chosen to fill a vacancy shall be appointed only for the unexpired term of the member whom he shall succeed. The President shall designate one member to serve as Chairman of the Board. Any member of the Board may be removed by the President, upon notice and hearing, for neglect of duty or malfeasance in office, but for no other cause.

(b) The Board is authorized to delegate to any group of three or more members any or all of the powers which it may itself exercise. The Board is also authorized to delegate to its regional directors its powers under section 9 to determine the unit appropriate for the purpose of collective bargaining, to investigate and provide for hearings, and determine whether a question of representation exists, and to direct an election or take a secret ballot under subsection (c) or (e) of section 9 and certify the results thereof, except that upon the filing of a request therefor with the Board by any interested person, the Board may review any action of a regional director delegated to him under this paragraph, but such a review shall not, unless specifically ordered by the Board, operate as a stay of any action taken by the regional director. A vacancy in the Board shall not impair the right of the remaining members to exercise all of the powers of the Board, and three members of the Board shall, at all times, constitute a quorum of the Board, except that two members shall constitute a quorum of any group designated pursuant to the first sentence hereof. The Board shall have an official seal which shall be judicially noticed.

(c) The Board shall at the close of each fiscal year make a report in writing to Congress and to the President stating in detail the cases it has heard, the decisions it has rendered, and an account of all moneys it has disbursed.

(d) There shall be a General Counsel of the Board who shall be appointed by the President, by and with the advice and consent of the Senate, for a term of four years. The General Counsel of the Board shall exercise general supervision over all attorneys employed by the Board (other than trial examiners and legal assistants to Board members) and over the officers and employees in the regional offices. He shall have final authority, on behalf of the Board, in respect of the investigation of charges and issuance of complaints under section 10, and in respect of the prosecution of such complaints before the Board, and shall have such other duties as the Board may prescribe or as may be provided by law. In case of a vacancy in the office of the General Counsel the President is authorized to designate the officer or employee who shall act as General Counsel during such vacancy, but no person or persons so designated shall so act (1) for more than 40 days when the Congress is in session unless a nomination to fill such vacancy shall have been submitted to the Senate, or (2) after the adjournment *sine die* of the session of the Senate in which such nomination was submitted.

* * * * *

[Omitted: Sections 4 and 5—Compensation and offices of the NLRB.]

Section 6. The Board shall have authority from time to time to make, amend, and rescind, in the manner prescribed by the Administrative Procedure Act, such rules and regulations as may be necessary to carry out the provisions of this Act.

Rights of Employees

Section 7. Employees shall have the right to self-organization, to form, join, or assist labor organizations, to bargain collectively through representatives of their own choosing, and to engage in other concerted activities for the purpose of collective bargaining or other mutual aid or protection, and shall also have the right to refrain from any or all of such activities except to the extent that such right may be affected by an agreement requiring membership in a labor organization as a condition of employment as authorized in section 8(a) (3).

Unfair Labor Practices

Section 8. (a) It shall be an unfair labor practice for an employer—

(1) to interfere with, restrain, or coerce employees in the exercise of the rights guaranteed in section 7;

(2) to dominate or interfere with the formation or administration of any labor organization or contribute financial or other support to it: *Provided,* that subject to rules and regulations made and published by the Board pursuant to section 6, an employer shall not be prohibited from permitting employees to confer with him during working hours without loss of time or pay;

(3) by discrimination in regard to hire or tenure of employment or any term or condition of employment to encourage or discourage membership in any labor organization: *Provided,* that nothing in this Act, or in any other statute of the United States, shall preclude an employer from making an agreement with a labor organization (not established, or assisted by any action defined in section 8(a) of this Act as an unfair labor practice) to require as a condition of employment membership therein on or after the 30th day following the beginning of such employment or the effective date of such agreement, whichever is the later, (i) if such labor organization is the representative of the employees as provided in section 9(a), in the appropriate collective bargaining unit covered by such agreement when made, and (ii) unless following an election held as provided in section 9(e) within one year preceding the effective date of such agreement, the Board shall have certified that at least a majority of the employees eligible to vote in such election have voted to rescind the authority of such labor organization to make such an agreement: *Provided further,* that no employer shall justify any discrimination against an employee for nonmembership in a labor organization (A) if he has reasonable grounds for believing that such membership was not available to the employee on the same terms and conditions generally applicable to other members, or (B) if he has

reasonable grounds for believing that membership was denied or terminated for reasons other than the failure of the employee to tender the periodic dues and the initiation fees uniformly required as a condition of acquiring or retaining membership;

(4) to discharge or otherwise discriminate against an employee because he has filed charges or given testimony under this Act;

(5) to refuse to bargain collectively with the representatives of his employees, subject to the provisions of section 9(a).

(b) It shall be an unfair labor practice for a labor organization or its agents—

(1) to restrain or coerce (A) employees in the exercise of the rights guaranteed in section 7: *Provided,* that this paragraph shall not impair the right of a labor organization to prescribe its own rules with respect to the acquisition or retention of membership therein; or (B) an employer in the selection of his representatives for the purposes of collective bargaining or the adjustment of grievances;

(2) to cause or attempt to cause an employer to discriminate against an employee in violation of subsection (a) (3) or to discriminate against an employee with respect to whom membership in such organization has been denied or terminated on some ground other than his failure to tender the periodic dues and the initiation fees uniformly required as a condition of acquiring or retaining membership;

(3) to refuse to bargain collectively with an employer, provided it is the representative of his employees subject to the provisions of section 9(a);

(4) (i) to engage in, or to induce or encourage any individual employed by any person engaged in commerce or in any industry affecting commerce to engage in, a strike or a refusal in the course of his employment to use, manufacture, process, transport, or otherwise handle or work on any goods, articles, materials, or commodities or to perform any services; or (ii) to threaten, coerce, or restrain any person engaged in commerce or in an industry affecting commerce, where in either case an object thereof is:

(A) forcing or requiring any employer or self-employed person to join any labor or employer organization or to enter into any agreement which is prohibited by section 8(e).

(B) forcing or requiring any person to cease using, selling, handling, transporting, or otherwise dealing in the products of any other producer, processor, or manufacturer, or to cease doing business with any other person, or forcing or requiring any other employer to recognize or bargain with a labor organization as the representative of his employees unless such labor organization has been certified as the representative of such employees under the provisions of section 9: *Provided,* that nothing contained in this clause (B) shall be construed to make unlawful, where not otherwise unlawful, any primary strike or primary picketing;

(C) forcing or requiring any employer to recognize or bargain with a particular labor organization as the representative of his employees if another labor organization has been certified as the representative of such employees under the provisions of section 9;

(D) forcing or requiring any employer to assign particular work to employees in a particular labor organization or in a particular trade, craft, or class rather than to employees in another labor organization or in another trade, craft, or class, unless such employer is failing to conform to an order or certification of the Board determining the bargaining representative for employees performing such work:

Provided, that nothing contained in this subsection (b) shall be construed to make unlawful a refusal by any person to enter upon the premises of any employer (other than his own employer), if the employees of such employer are engaged in a strike ratified or approved by a representative of such employees whom such employer is required to recognize under this Act: *Provided further,* that for the purposes of this paragraph (4) only, nothing contained in such paragraph shall be construed to prohibit publicity, other than picketing, for the purpose of truthfully advising the public, including consumers and members of a labor organization, that a product or products are produced by an employer with whom the labor organization has a primary dispute and are distributed by another employer, as long as such publicity does not have an effect of inducing any individual employed by any person other than the primary employer in the course of his employment to refuse to pick up, deliver, or transport any goods, or not to perform any services, at the establishment of the employer engaged in such distribution;

(5) to require of employees covered by an agreement authorized under subsection (a) (3) the payment, as a condition precedent to becoming a member of such organization, of a fee in an amount which the Board finds excessive or discriminatory under all the circumstances. In making such a finding, the Board shall consider, among other relevant factors, the practices and customs of labor organizations in the particular industry, and the wages currently paid to the employees affected;

(6) to cause or attempt to cause an employer to pay or deliver or agree to pay or deliver any money or other thing of value, in the nature of an exaction, for services which are not performed or not to be performed; and

(7) to picket or cause to be picketed, or threaten to picket or cause to be picketed, any employer where an object thereof is forcing or requiring an employer to recognize or bargain with a labor organization as the representative of his employees, or forcing or requiring the employees of an employer to accept or select such labor organization as their collective bargaining representative, unless such labor organization is currently certified as the representative of such employees:

(A) where the employer has lawfully recognized in accordance with this Act any other labor organization and a question concerning representation may not appropriately be raised under section 9(c) of this Act.

(B) where within the preceding 12 months a valid election under section 9(c) of this Act has been conducted, or

(C) where such picketing has been conducted without a petition under section 9(c) being filed within a reasonable period of time not to exceed 30 days from the commencement of such picketing: *Provided,* that when such a petition has been filed the Board shall forthwith, without regard to the provisions of section 9(c) (1) or the absence of a showing of a substantial interest on the part of the labor organization, direct an election in such unit as the Board finds to be appropriate and shall certify the results thereof: *Provided further,* that nothing in this subparagraph (C) shall be construed to prohibit any picketing or other publicity for the purpose of truthfully advising the public (including consumers) that an employer does not employ members of, or have a contract with, a labor organization, unless an effect of such picketing is to induce any individual employed by any other person in the course of his employment, not to pick up, deliver or transport any goods or not to perform any services.

Nothing in this paragraph (7) shall be construed to permit any act which would otherwise be an unfair labor practice under this section 8(b).

(c) The expressing of any views, argument, or opinion, or the dissemination thereof, whether in written, printed, graphic, or visual form, shall not constitute or be evidence of an unfair labor practice under any of the provisions of this Act, if such expression contains no threat of reprisal or force or promise of benefit.

(d) For the purposes of this section, to bargain collectively is the performance of the mutual obligation of the employer and the representative of the employees to meet at reasonable times and confer in good faith with respect to wages, hours, and other terms and conditions of employment, or the negotiation of an agreement, or any question arising thereunder, and the execution of a written contract incorporating any agreement reached if requested by either party, but such obligation does not compel either party to agree to a proposal or require the making of a concession: *Provided,* that where there is in effect a collective bargaining contract covering employees in an industry affecting commerce, the duty to bargain collectively shall also mean that no party to such contract shall terminate or modify such contract, unless the party desiring such termination or modification—

(1) serves a written notice upon the other party to the contract of the proposed termination or modification 60 days prior to the expiration date thereof, or in the event such contract contains no expiration date, 60 days prior to the time it is proposed to make such termination or modification;

(2) offers to meet and confer with the other party for the purpose of negotiating a new contract or a contract containing the proposed modifications;

(3) notifies the Federal Mediation and Conciliation Service within 30 days after such notice of the existence of a dispute, and simultaneously therewith notifies any State or Territorial agency established to mediate and conciliate disputes within the State or Territory where the dispute occurred, provided no agreement has been reached by that time; and

(4) continues in full force and effect, without resorting to strike or lockout, all the terms and conditions of the existing contract for a period of 60 days after such notice is given or until the expiration date of such contract, whichever occurs later.

The duties imposed upon employers, employees, and labor organizations by paragraphs (2), (3), and (4) shall become inapplicable upon an intervening certification of the Board, under which the labor organization or individual, which is a party to the contract, has been superseded as or ceased to be the representative of the employees subject to the provisions of section 9(a), and the duties so imposed shall not be construed as requiring either party to discuss or agree to any modification of the terms and conditions contained in a contract for a fixed period, if such modification is to become effective before such terms and conditions can be reopened under the provisions of the contract. Any employee who engages in a strike within any notice period specified in this subsection, or who engages in any strike within the appropriate period specified in subsection (g) of this section shall lose his status as an employee of the employer engaged in the particular labor dispute, for the purposes of sections 8, 9, and 10 of this Act, as amended, but such loss of status for such employee shall terminate if and when he is reemployed by such employer. Whenever the collective bargaining involves employees of a health care institution, the provisions of this section 8(d) shall be modified as follows:

(A) The notice of section 8(d) (1) shall be 90 days; the notice of section 8(d) (3) shall be 60 days; and the contract period of section 8(d) (4) shall be 90 days;

(B) Where the bargaining is for an initial agreement following certification or recognition, at least 30 days' notice of the existence of a dispute shall be given by the labor organization to the agencies set forth in section 8(d) (3).

(C) After notice is given to the Federal Mediation and Conciliation Service under either clause (A) or (B) of this sentence, the Service shall promptly communicate with the parties and use its best efforts, by mediation and conciliation, to bring them to agreement. The parties shall participate fully and promptly in such meetings as may be undertaken by the Service for the purpose of aiding in a settlement of the dispute.

(e) It shall be an unfair labor practice for any labor organization and any employer to enter into any contract or agreement, express or implied, whereby such employer ceases or refrains or agrees to cease or refrain from handling, using, selling, transporting, or otherwise dealing in any of the products of any other employer, or to cease doing business with any other person, and any contract or agreement entered into heretofore or hereafter containing such an agreement shall be to such extent unenforceable and void: *Provided,* that nothing in this subsection (e) shall apply to an agreement between a labor organization and an employer in the construction industry relating to the contracting or subcontracting of work to be done at the site of the construction, alteration, painting, or repair of a building, structure, or other work: *Provided further,* that for the purposes of this subsection (e) and section 8(b) (4) (B) the terms "any employer," "any person engaged in commerce or in industry affecting commerce," and "any person" when used in relation to the terms "any other producer, processor, or manufacturer," "any other employer," or "any other person" shall not include persons in the relation of a jobber, manufacturer, contractor, or subcontractor working on the goods or premises of the jobber or manufacturer or performing parts of an integrated process of production in the apparel and clothing industry: *Provided further,* that nothing in this Act shall prohibit the enforcement of any agreement which is within the foregoing exception.

(f) It shall not be an unfair labor practice under subsections (a) and (b) of this section for an employer engaged primarily in the building and construction industry to make an agreement covering employees engaged (or who, upon their employment, will be engaged) in the building and construction industry with a labor organization of which building and construction employees are members (not established, maintained, or assisted by any action defined in section 8(a) of this Act as an unfair labor practice) because (1) the majority status of such labor organization has not been established under the provisions of section 9 of this Act prior to the making of such agreement, or (2) such agreement requires as a condition of employment, membership in such labor organization after the seventh day following the beginning of such employment or the effective date of the agreement, whichever is later, or (3) such agreement requires the employer to notify such labor organization of opportunities for employment with such employer, or gives such labor organization an opportunity to refer qualified applicants for such employment, or (4) such agreement specifies minimum training or experience qualifications for employment or provides for priority in opportunities for employment based upon length of service with such employer, in the industry or in the particular geographical area: *Provided,* that nothing in this subsection shall set aside the final proviso to section 8(a) (3) of this Act: *Provided further,* that any agreement which would be invalid, but for clause (1) of this subsection, shall not be a bar to a petition filed pursuant to section 9(c) or 9(e).

(g) A labor organization before engaging in any strike, picketing, or other concerted refusal to work at any health care institution shall, not less than 10 days prior to such action, notify the institution in writing and the Federal Mediation and Conciliation Service of that intention, except that in the case of bargaining for an initial agreement following certification or recognition the notice required by this subsection shall not be given until the expiration of the period specified in clause (B) of the last sentence of section 8(d) of this Act. The notice shall state the date and time that such action will commence. The notice, once given, may be extended by the written agreement of both parties.

Representatives and Elections

Section 9.   (a) Representatives designated or selected for the purposes of collective bargaining by the majority of the employees in a unit appropriate for such purposes, shall be the exclusive representatives of all the employees in such unit for the purposes of collective bargaining in respect to rates of pay, wages, hours of employment, or other conditions of employment: *Provided,* that any individual employee or a group of employees shall have the right at any time to present grievances to their employer and to have such grievances adjusted, without the intervention of the bargaining representative, as long as the adjustment is not inconsistent with the terms of a collective bargaining contract or agreement then in effect: *Provided further,* that the bargaining representative has been given opportunity to be present at such adjustment.

(b) The Board shall decide in each case whether, in order to assure to employees the fullest freedom in exercising the rights guaranteed by this Act, the unit appropriate for the purposes of collective bargaining shall be the employer unit, craft unit, plant unit, or subdivision thereof: *Provided,* that the Board shall not (1) decide that any unit is appropriate for such purposes if such unit includes both professional employees and employees who are not professional employees unless a majority of such professional employees vote for inclusion in such unit; or (2) decide that any craft unit is inappropriate for such purposes on the ground that a different unit has been established by a prior Board determination, unless a majority of the employees in the proposed craft unit vote against separate representation or (3) decide that any unit is appropriate for such purposes, if it includes, together with other employees, any individual employed as a guard to enforce against employees and other persons rules to protect property of the employer or to protect the safety of persons on the employers' premises; but no labor organization shall be certified as the representative of employees in a bargaining unit of guards if such organization admits to membership, or is affiliated directly or indirectly with an organization which admits to membership, employees other than guards.

(c) (1) Wherever a petition shall have been filed, in accordance with such regulations as may be prescribed by the Board—

(A) by an employee or group of employees or any individual or labor organization acting in their behalf alleging that a substantial number of employees (i) wish to be represented for collective bargaining and that their employer declines to recognize their representative as the representative defined in section 9(a), or (ii) assert that the individual or labor organization, which has been certified or is being currently recognized by their employer as the bargaining representative, is no longer a representative as defined in section 9(a); or

(B) by an employer, alleging that one or more individuals or labor organizations have presented to him a claim to be recognized as the representative defined in section 9(a);

the Board shall investigate such petition and if it has reasonable cause to believe that a question of representation affecting commerce exists shall provide for an appropriate hearing upon due notice. Such hearing may be conducted by an officer or employee of the regional office, who shall not make any recommendations with respect thereto. If the Board finds upon the record of such hearing that such a question of representation exists, it shall direct an election by secret ballot and shall certify the results thereof.

(2) In determining whether or not a question of representation affecting commerce exists, the same regulations and rules of decision shall apply irrespective of the identity of the persons filing the petition or the kind of relief sought and in no case shall the Board deny a labor organization a place on the ballot by reason of an order with respect to such labor organization or its predecessor not issued in conformity with section 10(c).

(3) No election shall be directed in any bargaining unit or any subdivision within which, in the preceding 12-month period, a valid election shall have been held. Employees engaged in an economic strike who are not entitled to reinstatement shall be eligible to vote under such regulations as the Board

shall find are consistent with the purposes and provisions of this Act in any election conducted within 12 months after the commencement of the strike. In any election where none of the choices on the ballot receives a majority, a runoff shall be conducted, the ballot providing for a selection between the two choices receiving the largest and second largest number of valid votes cast in the election.

(4) Nothing in this section shall be construed to prohibit the waiving of hearings by stipulation for the purposes of a consent election in conformity with regulations and rules of decision of the Board.

(5) In determining whether a unit is appropriate for the purposes specified in subsection (b) the extent to which the employees have organized shall not be controlling.

(d) Whenever an order of the Board made pursuant to section 10(c) is based in whole or in part upon facts certified following an investigation pursuant to subsection (c) of this section and there is a petition for the enforcement or review of such order, such certification and the record of such investigation shall be included in the transcript of the entire record required to be filed under section 10(e) or 10(f), and thereupon the decree of the court enforcing, modifying, or setting aside in whole or in part the order of the Board shall be made and entered upon the pleadings, testimony, and proceedings set forth in such transcript.

(e) (1) Upon the filing with the Board, by 30 per centum or more of the employees in a bargaining unit covered by an agreement between their employer and a labor organization made pursuant to section 8(a) (3), of a petition alleging they desire that such authority be rescinded, the Board shall take a secret ballot of the employees in such unit and certify the results thereof to such labor organization and to the employer.

(2) No election shall be conducted pursuant to this subsection in any bargaining unit or any subdivision within which, in the preceding 12-month period, a valid election shall have been held.

Prevention of Unfair Labor Practices

Section 10.   (a) The Board is empowered, as hereinafter provided, to prevent any person from engaging in any unfair labor practice (listed in section 8) affecting commerce. This power shall not be affected by any other means of adjustment or prevention that has been or may be established by agreement, law, or otherwise: *Provided,* that the Board is empowered by agreement with any agency of any State or Territory to cede to such agency jurisdiction over any cases in any industry (other than mining, manufacturing, communications, and transportation except where predominantly local in character) even though such cases may involve labor disputes affecting commerce, unless the provision of the State or Territorial statute applicable to the determination of such cases by such agency is inconsistent with the corresponding provision of this Act or has received a construction inconsistent therewith.

(b) Whenever it is charged that any person has engaged in or is engaging in any such unfair labor practice, the Board, or any agent or agency designated by the Board for such purposes, shall have power to issue and cause to be served upon such person a complaint stating the charges in that respect, and containing a notice of hearing before the Board or a member thereof, or before a designated agent or agency, at a place therein fixed, not less than five days after the serving of said complaint: *Provided,* that no complaint shall issue based upon any unfair labor practice occurring more than six months prior to the filing of the charge with the Board and the service of a copy thereof upon the person against whom such a charge is made, unless the person aggrieved thereby was prevented from filing such charge by reason of service in the armed forces, in which event the six-month period shall be computed from the day of his discharge. Any such complaint may be amended by the member, agent, or agency conducting the hearing or the Board in its discretion at any time prior to the issuance of an order based thereon. The person so complained of shall have the right to file an answer to the original or amended complaint and to appear in person or otherwise and give testimony at the place and time fixed in the complaint. In the discretion of the member, agent, or agency conducting the hearing or the Board, any other person may be allowed to intervene in the said proceeding and to present testimony. Any such proceeding shall, so far as practicable, be conducted in accordance with the rules of evidence applicable in the district courts of the United States under the rules of civil procedure for the district courts of the United States, adopted by the Supreme Court of the United States pursuant to the Act of June 19, 1934 (U.S.C., title 28, secs. 723-B, 723-C).

(c) The testimony taken by such member, agent, or agency or the Board shall be reduced to writing and filed with the Board. Thereafter, in its discretion, the Board upon notice may take further testimony or hear argument. If upon the preponderance of the testimony taken the Board shall be of the opinion that any person named in the complaint has engaged in or is engaging in any such unfair labor practice, then the Board shall state its findings of fact and shall issue and cause to be served on such person an order requiring such person to cease and desist from such unfair labor practice, and to take such affirmative action including reinstatement of employees with or without back pay, as will effectuate the policies of this Act: *Provided,* that where an order directs reinstatement of an employee, back pay may be required of the employer or labor organization, as the case may be, responsible for the discrimination suffered by him: *And provided further,* that in determining whether a complaint shall issue alleging a violation of section 8(a) (1) or section 8(a) (2), and in deciding such cases, the same regulations and rules of decision shall apply irrespective of whether or not the labor organization affected is affiliated with a labor organization national or international in scope. Such order may further require such person to make reports from time to time showing the extent to which it has complied with the order. If upon the preponderance of the testimony taken the Board shall not be of the opinion that the person named in the complaint has engaged in or is engaging in any such unfair labor practice, then the Board shall state its findings of fact and shall issue an order dismissing the said complaint. No order of the Board shall require the reinstatement of any individual as an employee who has been suspended or discharged, or the payment to him of any back pay, if such individual was suspended or discharged for cause. In case the evidence is presented before a member of the Board, or before an examiner or examiners thereof, such member, or such examiner or examiners, as the case may be, shall issue and cause to be served on the parties to the proceeding a proposed report, together with a recommended order, which shall be filed with the Board and if no exceptions are filed within 20 days after service thereof upon such parties, or within such further period as the Board may authorize, such recommended order shall become the order of the Board and become effective as therein prescribed.

(d) Until the record in a case shall have been filed in a court, as hereinafter provided, the Board may at any time, upon reasonable notice and in such manner as it shall deem proper, modify or set aside, in whole or in part, any finding or order made or issued by it.

(e) The Board shall have power to petition any court of appeals of the United States, or if all the courts of appeals to which application may be made are in vacation, any district court of the United States, within any circuit or district, respectively, wherein the unfair labor practice in question occurred or wherein such person resides or transacts business, for the enforcement of such order and for appropriate temporary relief or restraining order, and shall file in the court the record in the proceedings, as provided in section 2112 of title 28, United States Code. Upon the filing of such petition, the court shall cause notice thereof to be served upon such person, and thereupon shall have jurisdiction of the proceeding and of the question determined therein, and shall have power to grant such temporary relief or restraining order as it deems just and proper, and to make and enter a decree enforcing, modifying, and enforcing as so modified, or setting aside in whole or in part the order of the Board. No objection that has not been urged before the Board, its member, agent, or agency, shall be considered by the court, unless the failure or neglect to urge such objection shall be excused because of extraordinary circumstances. The findings of the Board with respect to questions of fact if supported by substantial evidence on the record considered as a whole shall be conclusive. If either party shall apply to the court for leave to adduce additional evidence and shall show to the satisfaction of the court that such additional evidence is material and that there were reasonable grounds for the failure to adduce such evidence in the hearing before the Board, its member, agent, or agency, the court may order such additional evidence to be taken before the Board, its member, agent, or agency, and to be made a part of the record. The Board may modify its findings as to the facts, or make new findings, by reason of additional evidence so taken and filed, and it shall file such modified or new findings, which findings with respect to questions of fact if supported by substantial evidence on the record considered as a whole shall be conclusive, and shall file its recommendations, if any, for the modification or setting aside of its original order. Upon the filing of the record with it the jurisdiction of the court shall be exclusive and its judgment and decree shall be final, except that the same shall be subject to review by the appropriate United States court of appeals if application was made to the district court as hereinabove provided, and by the Supreme Court of the United States upon writ of certiorari or certification as provided in section 1254 of title 28.

(f) Any person aggrieved by a final order of the Board granting or denying in whole or in part the relief sought may obtain a review of such order in any circuit court of appeals of the United States in the circuit wherein the unfair labor practice in question was alleged to have been engaged in or wherein such person resides or transacts business, or in the United States Court of Appeals for the District of Columbia, by filing in such court a written petition praying that the order of the Board be modified or set aside. A copy of such petition shall be forthwith transmitted by the clerk of the court to the Board, and thereupon the aggrieved party shall file in the court the record in the proceeding, certified by the Board, as provided in section 2112 of title 28, United States Code. Upon the filing of such petition, the court shall proceed in the same manner as in the case of an application by the Board under subsection (e) of this section, and shall have the same jurisdiction to grant to the Board such temporary relief or restraining order as it deems just and proper, and in like manner to make and enter a decree enforcing, modifying, and enforcing as so modified, or setting aside in whole or in part the order of the Board; the findings of the Board with respect to questions of fact if supported by substantial evidence on the record considered as a whole shall in like manner be conclusive.

(g) The commencement of proceedings under subsection (e) or (f) of this section shall not, unless specifically ordered by the court, operate as a stay of the Board's order.

(h) When granting appropriate temporary relief or a restraining order, or making and entering a decree enforcing, modifying, and enforcing as so modified, or setting aside in whole or in part an order of the Board, as provided in this section, the jurisdiction of courts sitting in equity shall not be limited by the Act entitled "An Act to amend the Judicial Code and to define and limit the jurisdiction of courts sitting in equity, and for other purposes," approved March 23, 1932 (U.S.C., Supp. VII, title 29, secs. 101–115).

(i) Petitions filed under this Act shall be heard expeditiously, and if possible within 10 days after they have been docketed.

(j) The Board shall have power, upon issuance of a complaint as provided in subsection (b) charging that any person has engaged in or is engaging in an unfair labor practice, to petition any district court of the United States (including the District Court of the United States for the District of Columbia), within any district wherein the unfair labor practice in question is alleged to have occurred or wherein such person resides or transacts business, for appropriate temporary relief or restraining order. Upon the filing of any such petition the court shall cause notice thereof to be served upon such person, and thereupon shall have jurisdiction to grant to the Board such temporary relief or restraining order as it deems just and proper.

(k) Whenever it is charged that any person has engaged in an unfair labor practice within the meaning of paragraph (4) (D) of section 8(b), the Board is empowered and directed to hear and determine the dispute out of which such unfair labor practice shall have arisen, unless, within 10 days after notice that such charge has been filed, the parties to such dispute submit to the Board satisfactory evidence that they have adjusted, or agreed upon methods for the voluntary adjustment of, the dispute. Upon compliance by the parties to the dispute with the decision of the Board or upon such voluntary adjustment of the dispute, such charge shall be dismissed.

(l) Whenever it is charged that any person has engaged in an unfair labor practice within the meaning of paragraph (4) (A), (B), or (C) of section 8(b), or section 8(e) or section 8(b) (7), the preliminary investigation of such charge shall be made forthwith and given priority over all other cases except cases of like character in the office where it is filed or to which it is referred. If, after such investigation, the officer or regional attorney to whom the matter may be referred has reasonable cause to believe such charge is true and that a complaint should issue, he shall, on behalf of the Board, petition any district court of the United States (including the District Court of the United States for the District of Columbia) within any district where the unfair labor practice in question has occurred, is alleged to have occurred, or wherein such person resides or transacts business, for appropriate injunctive relief pending the final adjudication of the Board with respect to such matter. Upon the filing of any such petition the district court shall have jurisdiction to grant such injunctive relief or temporary restraining order as it deems just and proper, notwithstanding any other provision of law: *Provided further,* that no temporary restraining order shall be issued without notice unless a petition alleges that substantial and irreparable injury to the charging party will be unavoidable and such temporary restraining order shall be effective for no longer than five days and will become void at the expiration of such period: *Provided further,* that such officer or regional attorney shall not apply for any restraining order under section 8(b) (7) if a charge against the employer under section 8(a) (2) has been filed and after the preliminary investigation, he has reasonable cause to believe that such charge is true and that a complaint should issue. Upon filing of any such petition the courts shall cause notice thereof to be served upon any person involved in the charge and such person including the charging party, shall be given an opportunity to appear by counsel and present any relevant testimony: *Provided further,* that for the purposes of this subsection district courts shall be deemed to have jurisdiction of a labor organization (1) in the district in which such organization maintains its principal office, or (2) in any district in which its duly authorized officers or agents are engaged in promoting or protecting the interests of employee members. The service of legal process upon such officer or agent shall constitute service upon the labor organization and make such organizations a party to the suit. In situations where such relief is appropriate the procedure specified herein shall apply to charges with respect to section8(b) (4) (D).

(m) Whenever it is charged that any person has engaged in an unfair labor practice within the meaning of subsection (a) (3) or (b) (2) of section 8, such charge shall be given priority over all other cases except cases of like character in the office where it is filed or to which it is referred and cases given priority under subsection (1).

*   *   *   *   *

[Omitted: Sections 11 and 12—Investigatory powers of the NLRB.]

Limitations

Section 13. Nothing in this Act, except as specifically provided for herein, shall be construed so as either to interfere with or impede or diminish in any way the right to strike, or to affect the limitations or qualifications on that right.

Section 14. (a) Nothing herein shall prohibit any individual employed as a supervisor from becoming or remaining a member of a labor organization, but no employer subject to this Act shall be compelled to deem individuals defined herein as supervisors as employees for the purpose of any law, either national or local, relating to collective bargaining.

(b) Nothing in this Act shall be construed as authorizing the execution or application of agreements requiring membership in a labor organization as a condition of employment in any State or Territory in which such execution or application is prohibited by State or Territorial law.

(c) (1) The Board, in its discretion, may, by rule of decision or by published rules adopted pursuant to the Administrative Procedure Act, decline to assert jurisdiction over any labor dispute involving any class or category of employers, where, in the opinion of the Board, the effect of such labor dispute on commerce is not sufficiently substantial to warrant the exercise of its jurisdiction: *Provided,* that the Board shall not decline to assert jurisdiction over any labor dispute over which it would assert jurisdiction under the standards prevailing upon August 1, 1959.

(2) Nothing in this Act shall be deemed to prevent or bar any agency or the courts of any State or Territory (including the Commonwealth of Puerto Rico, Guam, and the Virgin Islands), from assuming and asserting jurisdiction over labor disputes over which the Board declines, pursuant to paragraph (1) of this subsection, to assert jurisdiction.

* * * * *

[Omitted: Sections 15, 16, 17, and 18; relating to limitations.]

Individuals with Religious Conviction

Section 19. Any employee who is a member of and adheres to established and traditional tenets or teachings of a bona fide religion, body, or sect which has historically held conscientious objections to joining or financially supporting labor organizations shall not be required to join or financially support any labor organization as a condition of employment; except that such employee may be required in a contract between such employees' employer and a labor organization in lieu of periodic dues and initiation fees, to pay sums equal to such dues and initiation fees to a nonreligious, nonlabor organization charitable fund exempt from taxation under section 501(c) (3) of title 26 of the Internal Revenue Code, chosen by such employee from a list of at least three such funds, designated in such contract or if the contract fails to designate such funds, then to any such fund chosen by the employee. If such employee who holds conscientious objections pursuant to this section requests the labor organization to use the grievance-arbitration procedure on the employee's behalf, the labor organization is authorized to charge the employee for the reasonable cost of using such procedure.

* * * * *

[Omitted: Sections 102, 103, and 104, concerning effective dates of certain changes.]

TITLE II—CONCILIATION OF LABOR DISPUTES IN INDUSTRIES AFFECTING COMMERCE; NATIONAL EMERGENCIES

Section 201. That it is the policy of the United States that—

(a) sound and stable industrial peace and the advancement of the general welfare, health, and safety of the Nation and of the best interest of employers and employees can most satisfactorily be secured by the settlement of issues between employers and employees through the processes of conference and collective bargaining between employers and the representatives of their employees;

(b) the settlement of issues between employers and employees through collective bargaining may be advanced by making available full and adequate governmental facilities for conciliation, mediation, and voluntary arbitration to aid and encourage employers and the representatives of their employees to reach and maintain agreements concerning rates of pay, hours, and working conditions, and to make all reasonable efforts to settle their differences by mutual agreement reached through conferences and collective bargaining or by such methods as may be provided for in any applicable agreement for the settlement of disputes; and

(c) certain controversies which arise between parties to collective bargaining agreements may be avoided or minimized by making available full and adequate governmental facilities for furnishing assistance to employers and the representatives of their employees in formulating for inclusion within such agreements provision for adequate notice of any proposed changes in the terms of such agreements, for the final adjustment of grievances or questions regarding the application or interpretation of such agreements, and other provisions designed to prevent the subsequent arising of such controversies.

Section 202. (a) There is hereby created an independent agency to be known as the Federal Mediation and Conciliation Service (herein referred to as the "Service") . . . . The Service shall be under the direction of a Federal Mediation and Conciliation Director (hereinafter referred to as the "Director"), who shall be appointed by the President by and with the advice and consent of the Senate. . . .

(b) The Director is authorized, subject to the civil-service laws, to appoint such clerical and other personnel as may be necessary for the execution of the functions of the Service. . . .

(c) The principal office of the Service shall be in the District of Columbia, but the Director may establish regional offices convenient to localities in which labor controversies are likely to arise. The Director may by order, subject to revocation at any time, delegate any authority and discretion conferred upon him by this Act to any regional director, or other officer or employee of the Service. The Director may establish suitable procedures for cooperation with State and local mediation agencies. The Director shall make an annual report in writing to Congress at the end of the fiscal year.

* * * * *

[Omitted: Section 202(d), which relates to the original creation of the FMCS.]

Functions of the Service

Section 203. (a) It shall be the duty of the Service, in order to prevent or minimize interruptions of the free flow of commerce growing out of labor disputes, to assist parties to labor disputes in industries affecting commerce to settle such disputes through conciliation and mediation.

(b) The Service may proffer its services in any labor dispute in any industry affecting commerce, either upon its own motion or upon the request of one or more of the parties to the dispute, whenever in its judgment such dispute threatens to cause a substantial interruption of commerce. The Director and the Service are directed to avoid attempting to mediate disputes which would have only a minor effect on interstate commerce if State or other conciliation services are available to the parties. Whenever the Service does proffer its services in any dispute, it shall be the duty of the Service promptly to put itself in communication with the parties and to use its best efforts, by mediation and conciliation, to bring them to agreement.

(c) If the Director is not able to bring the parties to agreement by conciliation within a reasonable time, he shall seek to induce the parties voluntarily to seek other means of settling the dispute without resort to strike, lockout, or other coercion, including submission to the employees in the bargaining unit of the employer's last offer of settlement for approval or rejection in a secret ballot. The failure or refusal of either party to agree to any procedure suggested by the Director shall not be deemed a violation of any duty or obligation imposed by this Act.

(d) Final adjustment by a method agreed upon by the parties is hereby declared to be the desirable method for settlement of grievance disputes arising over the application or interpretation of an existing collective bargaining agreement. The Service is directed to make its conciliation and mediation services available in the settlement of such grievance disputes only as a last resort and in exceptional cases.

Section 204. (a) In order to prevent or minimize interruptions of the free flow of commerce growing out of labor disputes, employers and employees and their representatives, in any industry affecting commerce, shall—

(1) exert every reasonable effort to make and maintain agreements concerning rates of pay, hours, and working conditions, including provi-

sion for adequate notice of any proposed change in the terms of such agreements;

(2) whenever a dispute arises over the terms or application of a collective bargaining agreement and a conference is requested by a party or prospective party thereto, arrange promptly for such a conference to be held and endeavor in such conference to settle such dispute expeditiously; and

(3) in case such dispute is not settled by conference, participate fully and promptly in such meetings as may be undertaken by the Service under this Act for the purpose of aiding in a settlement of the dispute.

* * * * *

[Omitted: Section 205, which creates a national labor-management panel to advise the Director of FMCS.]

National Emergencies

Section 206.   Whenever in the opinion of the President of the United States, a threatened or actual strike or lockout affecting an entire industry or a substantial part thereof engaged in trade, commerce, transportation, transmission, or communication among the several States or with foreign nations, or engaged in the production of goods for commerce, will, if permitted to occur or to continue, imperil the national health or safety, he may appoint a board of inquiry to inquire into the issues involved in the dispute and to make a written report to him within such time as he shall prescribe. Such report shall include a statement of the facts with respect to the dispute, including each party's statement of its position but shall not contain any recommendations. The President shall file a copy of such report with the Service and shall make its contents available to the public.

Section 207.   (a) A board of inquiry shall be composed of a chairman and such other members as the President shall determine, and shall have power to sit and act in any place within the United States and to conduct such hearings either in public or in private, as it may deem necessary or proper, to ascertain the facts with respect to the causes and circumstances of the dispute.

* * * * *

Section 208.   (a) Upon receiving a report from a board of inquiry the President may direct the Attorney General to petition any district court of the United States having jurisdiction of the parties to enjoin such strike or lockout or the continuing thereof, and if the court finds that such threatened or actual strike or lockout—

(i) affects an entire industry or a substantial part thereof engaged in trade, commerce, transportation, transmission, or communication among the several States or with foreign nations, or engaged in the production of goods for commerce; and

(ii) if permitted to occur or to continue, will imperil the national health or safety, it shall have jurisdiction to enjoin any such strike or lockout, or the continuing thereof, and to make such other orders as may be appropriate.

* * * * *

Section 209. (a) Whenever a district court has issued an order under section 208 enjoining acts or practices which imperil or threaten to imperil the national health or safety, it shall be the duty of the parties to the labor dispute giving rise to such order to make every effort to adjust and settle their differences, with the assistance of the Service created by this Act. Neither party shall be under any duty to accept, in whole or in part, any proposal of settlement made by the Service.

(b) Upon the issuance of such order, the President shall reconvene the board of inquiry which has previously reported with respect to the dispute. At the end of a 60-day period (unless the dispute has been settled by that time), the board of inquiry shall report to the President the current position of the parties and the efforts which have been made for settlement, and shall include a statement by each party of its position and a statement of the employer's last offer of settlement. The President shall make such report available to the public. The National Labor Relations Board, within the succeeding 15 days, shall take a secret ballot of the employees of each employer involved in the dispute on the question of whether they wish to accept the final offer of settlement made by their employer as stated by him and shall certify the results thereof to the Attorney General within 5 days thereafter.

Section 210. Upon the certification of the results of such a ballot or upon a settlement being reached, whichever happens sooner, the Attorney General shall move the court to discharge the injunction, which motion shall then be granted and the injunction discharged. When such motion is granted, the President shall submit to the Congress a full and comprehensive report of the proceedings, including the findings of the board of inquiry and the ballot taken by the National Labor Relations Board, together with such recommendations as he may see fit to make for consideration and appropriate action.

* * * * *

[Omitted: Section 211, which covers authorization for collection and dissemination of collective bargaining information by federal agencies, and Section 212, which exempts persons covered by provisions of the Railway Labor Act from the provisions of the LMRA.]

Conciliation of Labor Disputes in the Health Care Industry

Section 213. (a) If, in the opinion of the Director of the Federal Mediation and Conciliation Service, a threatened or actual strike or lockout affecting a health care institution will, if permitted to occur or to continue, substantially interrupt the delivery of health care in the locality concerned, the Director may further assist in the resolution of the impasse by establishing within 30 days after the notice to the Federal Mediation and Counciliation Service under clause (A) of the last sentence of section 8(d) (which is required by clause (3) of such section 8(d), or within 10 days after the notice under clause (B), an impartial Board of Inquiry to investigate the issues involved in the dispute and to make a written report thereon to the parties within 15 days after the establishment of such a Board. The written report shall contain the findings of fact together with the Board's recommendations for settling the dispute, with the objective of achieving a prompt, peaceful and just settlement of the dispute. Each such Board shall be composed of such number of individuals as the Director may deem desirable. No member appointed under this section shall have any interest or involvement in the health care institutions or the employee organizations involved in the dispute.

* * * * *

[Omitted: Section 213(b), which provides for compensation for members appointed to a Board formed under Section 213(a).]

(c) After the establishment of a board under subsection (a) of this section and for 15 days after any such board has issued its report, no change in the status quo in effect prior to the expiration of the contract in the case of negotiations for a contract renewal, or in effect prior to the time of the impasse in the case of an initial bargaining negotiation, except by agreement, shall be made by the parties to the controversy.

(d) There are authorized to be appropriated such sums as may be necessary to carry out the provisions of this section.

TITLE III

Suits by and against Labor Organizations

Section 301.   (a) Suits for violation of contracts between an employer and a labor organization representing employees in an industry affecting commerce as defined in this Act, or between any such labor organizations, may be brought in any district court of the United States having jurisdiction of the parties, without respect to the amount in controversy or without regard to the citizenship of the parties.

(b) Any labor organization which represents employees in an industry affecting commerce as defined in this Act and any employer whose activities affect commerce as defined in this Act shall be bound by the acts of its agents. Any such labor organization may sue or be sued as an entity and in behalf of the employees whom it represents in the courts of the United States. Any money judgment against a labor organization in a district court of the United States shall be enforceable only against the organization as an entity and against its assets, and shall not be enforceable against any individual member or his assets.

(c) For the purposes of actions and proceedings by or against labor organizations in the district courts of the United States, district courts shall be deemed to have jurisdiction of a labor organization (1) in the district in which such organization maintains its principal offices, or (2) in any district in which its duly authorized officers or agents are engaged in representing or acting for employee members.

(d) The service of summons, subpoena, or other legal process of any court of the United States upon an officer or agent of a labor organization, in his capacity as such, shall constitute service upon the labor organization.

(e) For the purposes of this action, in determining whether any person is acting as an "agent" of another person so as to make such other person responsible for his acts, the question of whether the specific acts performed were actually authorized or subsequently ratified shall not be controlling.

* * * * *

[Omitted: Section 302—Restrictions on payments to employee representatives.]

Boycotts and Other Unlawful Combinations

Section 303. (a) It shall be unlawful, for the purpose of this section only, in an industry or activity affecting commerce, for any labor organization to engage in any activity or conduct defined as an unfair labor practice in section 8(b) (4) of the National Labor Relations Act, as amended.

(b) Whoever shall be injured in his business or property by reason of any violation of subsection (a) may sue therefor in any district court of the United States subject to the limitations and provisions of Section 301 hereof without respect to the amount of the controversy, or in any other court having jurisdiction of the parties, and shall recover the damages sustained by him and the cost of the suit.

* * * * *

[Omitted are the following sections: Section 304—Restrictions on political contributions; Title IV—Creation of a joint committee to study and report on basic problems affecting labor relations and productivity.]

TITLE V

Definitions

Section 501. When used in this Act—

(1) The term "industry affecting commerce" means any industry or activity in commerce or in which a labor dispute would burden or obstruct commerce or tend to burden or obstruct commerce or the free flow of commerce.

(2) The term "strike" includes any strike or other concerted stoppage of work by employees (including a stoppage by reason of the expiration of a collective bargaining agreement) and any concerted slowdown or other concerted interruption of operations by employees.

(3) The terms "commerce," "labor disputes," "employer," "employee," "la-

bor organization," "representative," "person," and "supervisor" shall have the same meaning as when used in the National Labor Relations Act as amended by this Act.

Saving Provision

Section 502.   Nothing in this Act shall be construed to require an individual employee to render labor or service without his consent, nor shall anything in this Act be construed to make the quitting of his labor by an individual employee an illegal act; nor shall any court issue any process to compel the performance by an individual employee of such labor or service, without his consent; nor shall the quitting of labor by an employee or employees in good faith because of abnormally dangerous conditions for work at the place of employment of such employee or employees be deemed a strike under this Act.

Separability

Section 503.   If any provision of this Act, or the application of such provision to any person or circumstance, shall be held invalid, the remainder of this Act, or the application of such provision to persons or circumstances other than those as to which it is held invalid, shall not be affected thereby.

Index to Cases for Part One

Index to Cases for Part One *(continued)*

Index to Cases for Part One (*continued*)

Index to Cases for Part One (concluded)

Case Number and Title	Principal Issues of Case	Principal LMRA Provisions Involved
28. Refusal to Bargain over a Representation Fee in a Right-to-Work State	Union's attempt and employer's refusal to bargain over a fee for representing nonmembers in a right-to-work state.	8(a) (3), 8(b) (3), 8(d), 14(b)
29. The Union's Refusal to Process a Grievance to Arbitration	Union's refusal to process a grievance to arbitration on behalf of discharged employee.	8(b) (1) (A)
30. The Employer's Refusal to Process a Grievance to Arbitration	Refusal of employer to process grievance of employee who simultaneously filed unfair labor practice charges protesting suspension for statements and involvement in union demonstration at hospital.	8(a) (1), 8(a) (3), 8(a) (4), 8(a) (5), 8(b) (7) (C), 8(g)
31. Was the Superseniority Clause an Unfair Labor Practice?	Preferential job bidding clause negotiated for union shop stewards in labor contract.	8(a) (1), 8(a) (3), 8(b) (1) (A), 8(b) (2)
32. Was the Union Contract Proposal A "Hot Cargo" Clause?	Union effort to have owner-drivers of trucks become employees and union members.	8(b)(4)(A), 8(b)(4)(B), 8(e), 10(l)
33. Who Should Erect and Install the Metal Panels and Sheets?	Jurisdictional issue involving claims of two unions to perform disputed work.	8(b) (4) (D), 10(k), 10(l)
33. Was the Attemped Consumer Boycott Legal?	Union handbilling of customers at a shopping center to urge them not to patronize stores.	8(b)(4), 8(b)(4)(ii)(B), 10(l)

1. Discharge for Violation of the No-Solicitation Rule

Company:
>   W. W. Grainger, Inc., Niles, Illinois

Union:
>   International Brotherhood of Teamsters, Chauffeurs, Warehousemen and Helpers of America, Local 714

BACKGROUND

W. W. Grainger, Inc., was engaged in the business of wholesale distribution of electrical products and operated a distribution warehouse in Niles, Illinois. Approximately 90 people were employed.

For several years the company had experienced attempts at union organization of its employees. During the first week of April 1975, two employees, Lou Bommarito and Carlos Gomez,[1] solicited employees to sign Teamsters union authorization cards at the warehouse entrance. Bommarito and Gomez were both brothers-in-law of Martin Tolman, another employee. Their relationship to Tolman and their union activity were also known to Raymond Nolan, the company personnel manager.

On several days prior to work, Tolman gave union authorization cards to some of the employees at the warehouse, and handed out some ball-point pens imprinted with the name of the union. On several occasions, Tolman discussed the union with several employees during work time. In May 1975, Nolan indicated to Tolman that he had heard that Tolman was soliciting for the union on working time. Tolman denied the charge and stated that he was merely telling the employees that "the union was good." Nolan then warned Tolman that "any further soliciting on working time" would result in his termination. Later the same day, Nolan confronted another employee, Walt Pulsifer, with a similar accusation. Pulsifer denied that he had been soliciting for the union, and stated that it was Tolman who was soliciting. Nolan then warned Pulsifer that soliciting during working time could be punished by discharge. In neither interview did Nolan reveal any of the details concerning the alleged solicitations, or tell them who had reported that they had been soliciting during working time.

---

[1] The names of all individuals have been disguised.

On June 2, Ralph Macon, the company's warehouse operations manager, issued a written warning to Pulsifer, advising him that employee Bill Cheek had told Macon that Pulsifer had solicited Cheek during working time. Although Pulsifer denied the accusation, he signed the written warning. Pulsifer then told Macon that it was Tolman who had been soliciting. Later the same day, Macon asked Pulsifer whether Tolman had solicited others. Pulsifer said that Tolman had solicited him during the prior week in regard to a meeting to be held in June. Pulsifer further stated that Tolman had solicited employees Mort Polanski and Marty Donald, although he gave no details about this solicitation nor was he asked to do so. A couple of days later Macon handed Pulsifer a statement, which read: "I was approached during working hours by Martin Tolman. My work was interrupted by Tolman's solicitation activity. I have brought this to the attention of my supervisor."

Upon Macon's request, Pulsifer signed the statement. Macon showed the document to the company's vice president, Stanley Lincoln, with a recommendation that Tolman be fired. Lincoln remarked that this "written documentation" constituted evidence of "flagrant multiple violations" of the company's no-solicitation rule during working time.

On June 9, as Tolman was reporting for work, he was escorted by a foreman to Macon's office. Macon told Tolman that he was being terminated for soliciting for a union, and that the company had evidence in its files that he was soliciting on company time. Tolman denied the accusation and asked to see the evidence in the files. His request was refused; Tolman was escorted off the premises.

Subsequently, on behalf of Martin Tolman, the union filed unfair labor practice charges against the company, claiming that the company had violated Sections 8(a) (1) and 8(a) (3) of the Labor Management Relations Act (LMRA) by maintaining a vague, "overbroad" no-solicitation rule, and then by issuing disciplinary warnings to two employees and later discharging one of them for alleged violations of this rule.

POSITION OF THE UNION

The union claimed that Martin Tolman's open distribution of union authorization cards and ball-point pens and discussion of the union with employees, as well as his familial relationship to others doing the same, were well known to company management. According to the union, almost all of Tolman's actual soliciting occurred before and after work or during breaks and lunch periods. At the first meetings with Pulsifer and Tolman, Nolan accused the two of soliciting during working time on the basis of what he had heard. The record contained no evidence of what acts led Nolan to believe that Tolman and Pulsifer had solicited on company time. According to Tolman, he merely had been remarking to other employees that the union was good—an act that can hardly amount to soliciting, especially since company supervisors allowed virtually unrestricted discussion among employees as long as they continued to work.

With respect to the June 2 meeting between Pulsifer and Macon, Pulsifer told Macon that Tolman had solicited him on company time. Macon did not inquire of Pulsifer or anyone else as to the details concerning when, where, what was done, and so on, but rather drafted a conclusory statement, which Pulsifer later signed. Further, the substance of what Pulsifer told Macon was far from clear. According to Pulsifer, the solicitation consisted of a conversation with Tolman, lasting about five minutes during working time, which ended with his signing an authorization card and receiving a ball-point pen. According to Macon, Pulsifer told him that Tolman "solicited" about a meeting to be held at Tolman's house. After Pulsifer stated to Macon that Tolman had also solicited Marty Donald and Mort Polanski during working time, an effort was made to confirm the solicitation of Polanski. Other than the conclusion that Tolman had solicited Polanski during working time, the company offered no evidence that the facts underlying the conclusion had been investigated. Apparently no effort was made to contact Donald to check out whether Tolman had actually solicited him during working time.

In essence, the union claimed the company's no-solicitation rule was not valid, since it was "overbroad" and lacking in specifics as to intent. All of the company management's actions were a pretext to discourage union organization activity. By issuing improper warnings to Tolman and Pulsifer, the company had violated Section 8(a) (1) of the Act. By preparing a statement for Pulsifer to sign that was not supported by specific evidence, the company deliberately sought to create a reason for terminating Martin Tolman. The real reason for terminating Tolman was not for violating a no-solicitation rule, but to discourage union organizational activity.

The union requested that Martin Tolman be reinstated and made whole for all lost pay and benefits, and that the company be ordered to cease and desist from issuing warnings and attempting to enforce an invalid no-solicitation rule.

POSITION OF THE COMPANY

The company first of all claimed that its no-solicitation rule was quite valid and a legitimate management right under the Act. Company managers had clearly conveyed to employees who were sympathetic to the union that any solicitation during working time was prohibited. These employees understood that the intent of this rule was to limit any union solicitation to the employees' own time, such as breaks and during lunch periods.

The company further contended that Pulsifer and Tolman were adequately warned that soliciting on company time for the union was punishable by dismissal. Nevertheless, Tolman persisted in soliciting during working time. His discharge, therefore, was consistent with the company's right to maintain discipline at its business.

The company maintained that it had supporting evidence to show that Tolman had violated the no-solicitation rule. A fellow employee, Walt Pulsifer, signed a statement attesting to this fact. Other employees had reported that Tolman had solicited them during working time. This could not be tolerated by the company. Even though the amounts of time involved in the union solicitation on company time were small, the employees had been specifically warned that any such solicitation during working hours could lead to their dismissal. The company in discharging Tolman exercised its managerial rights in order to prevent a potential wholesale breakdown in employee discipline.

The company claimed that it had not violated the Act, and that the unfair labor practice charges should be dismissed in totality.

QUESTIONS

1. Was the company's no-solicitation rule overbroad and lacking in specifics? Why should a company be very careful in any efforts to prohibit solicitation of employees on company time?

2. Evaluate the union's argument that company management's actions in this case were a "pretext" designed to discourage union organizational activity.

3. Were the company's disciplinary and discharge actions consistent with the company's right to maintain discipline at its business?

4. Why is it unusual—and of questionable merit—for a company to try to pit one employee against another employee in gathering information related to union organizing efforts and violation of company rules?

2. Discharge of a New Employee for a "Bad Attitude"

Company:
   Salem Leasing Corporation, Hickory, North Carolina

Employee and Union:
   Sam Hanson and the International Union of Electrical, Radio and Machine Workers

BACKGROUND

Salem is a truck leasing company with eight locations in North Carolina. Sam Hanson,[1] who was hired by Salem in June 1982, worked at its facility in Hickory, North Carolina. Hanson was hired as a "tire man"; his responsibilities included changing tires on trucks, maintaining a tire inventory, and filling out the required paperwork. Hanson was also given additional duties as a "fuel man" when the fuel man quit. Hanson successfully completed Salem's 90-day probationary period for new employees. He was fired on October 26, 1982, one month after his probationary period had ended.

Hanson had previously worked from 1973 to 1981 for General Electric at its unionized plant near Hickory, but he was laid off because of economic conditions. While employed at General Electric, Hanson was a member of the International Union of Electrical, Radio, and Machine Workers, AFL-CIO, a membership that he maintained while working for Salem. None of Salem's employees was represented by a labor organization.

Hanson was fired one week after a company-sponsored and -financed fishing trip to a campground in South Carolina, which took place on October 17 and 18, 1982. On the evening of October 17, during a poker game in Hanson's room, Hanson responded to questions from fellow employees regarding his employment at G.E. and his union membership. He described his pay and benefits at G.E. and the amount of his union dues. He expressed a desire to return to G.E., because his pension there would vest in six months. He stated, however, that given current economic conditions, he probably would not be rehired for a couple of years. At one point during the game, Hanson commented on a

---

[1] The names of all individuals are disguised.

pot won by another player saying, "Take that little bit of change; it's just chicken feed, like what I'm making."

Also participating in the poker game was a Salem vice president, George Scalia. A day or two after the fishing trip, Scalia called Marcus Newman, president of Salem, and told him that Hanson had a "bad attitude." Newman then called Arnie Donner, operations manager at the Hickory facility, and told him that Hanson had a "bad attitude." Donner fired Hanson a few days later.

On October 29, 1982, Hanson, with the assistance of Larry Kitchen, business representative of the union, filed charges with the NLRB alleging that Hanson's discharge was in violation of Sections 8(a) (1) and 8(a) (3) of LMRA. Hanson and the union urged that Hanson should be reinstated and made whole for all lost pay and benefits, and that the company should be ordered to cease and desist in any and all activities designed to discriminate against employees and discourage membership in a labor union.

POSITION OF THE EMPLOYEE AND THE UNION

Counsel for Sam Hanson and the union argued that there was no credible evidence that Hanson was an inadequate employee. Hanson had successfully completed the 90-day probationary period and had even been assigned additional responsibilities. Thus, the firing of Hanson shortly after he had made favorable comments about General Electric, a unionized employer, in front of a Salem vice president was quite indicative that the real motive for discharging Hanson was his pro-union remarks, to which the company management objected.

In this regard, an office employee named Melanie Smith testified that in late September 1982, Arnie Donner told several employees including herself that they "ought to be thankful that there wasn't any union organization because all the union places were going broke . . . ."

Another employee, Willie Carol, submitted a notarized affidavit claiming that on the same day that Hanson was fired, he heard Arnie Donner tell another supervisor, Timothy Bunges, that the company "should not have hired a union man." Carol acknowledged that he didn't know whether Donner was referring to Sam Hanson by this remark.

In summary, counsel for Sam Hanson and the union claimed that Hanson's discharge was motivated primarily by the company's desire to "thwart and chill" any pro-union organizing efforts and pro-union sentiments among Salem's employees. The company had clearly violated Sections 8(a) (1) and 8(a) (3) of the Act, and the NLRB should order the requested remedy accordingly.

POSITION OF THE COMPANY

Several company managers testified vigorously that Sam Hanson's discharge in October of 1982 would have occurred irrespective of any pro-union comments that Hanson had made. Even though Hanson had completed his probationary period, his work performance was marginal at best, and it was poorer than most of his fellow-employees. Economic conditions during the fall of 1982 necessitated terminating several employees, and Hanson was one of those who was terminated. Arnie Donner testified that he had chosen to terminate those employees with the least job tenure and the poorest work performance. In his view, Hanson was "among the worst of the lot." The company felt that Hanson's comments in front of Vice President Scalia showed that Hanson was very disloyal to the company, and this was what Scalia meant when he reported to the company president that Hanson had a "bad attitude" that could not be tolerated. The company's motives in discharging Hanson had nothing to do with discriminating against Hanson because of his pro-union sentiments. Hanson was an "at-will" employee who could be terminated at any time by the company, and the company chose to discharge him for his poor work performance and bad attitudes.

Concerning alleged "anti-union" comments that union witnesses ascribed to Arnie Donner, the company claimed that these were isolated statements of just one manager that were taken out of context. None of Donner's statements nor the discharge of Hanson were intended to interfere with any employee's protected legal rights to attempt to join a labor union if this was their desire.

In summary, the company claimed that the unfair labor practice charges were without foundation; they were a misguided attempt by Hanson and the union to embarrass the company and to regain employment for Hanson, who was an unsatisfactory employee. The company urged that the unfair labor practice charges should be dismissed in their entirety.

QUESTIONS

1. Why is this type of case difficult for the NLRB to decide?
2. Did Sam Hanson's comments reflect disloyalty and a "bad attitude" toward the company? Why, or why not?
3. Does the fact that several other employees were terminated at about the same time as Hanson for economic and other reasons prove that Hanson's discharge would have happened irrespective of any of his pro-union sentiments? Discuss.
4. Why should any manager be careful to avoid making statements such as those attributed to Arnie Donner in this case?

3. Were the LPNs Agents of the Employer?

Employer:
  St. Paul's Church Home, St. Paul, Minnesota
Union:
  Local No. 113, Service Employees Union

BACKGROUND

In 1981, the union was engaged in an intensive organizing campaign designed to gain representational rights for certain employees of St. Paul's Church Home. On August 27, 1981, the union sent a letter to James Hammer,[1] Administrator of the nursing home, which claimed that the union had secured signed authorization cards from a majority of employees, and that the employer should recognize the union as the employees' bargaining representative.

At approximately noon of the same day, a group of employees who were opposed to the union met with Administrator Hammer on the back porch of the main building. These employees were Vickie Shear, Elizabeth Dore, Brian Paul, and Magda Krantz. Shear and Dore were Licensed Practical Nurses (LPNs); Paul and Krantz were employees who served as orderlies in the care of residents and patients. The four of them discussed the union organizing campaign with Hammer and told him that they opposed having a union in a health care facility. They requested permission from Hammer to hold meetings with the employees, and they asked Hammer if he would speak at these meetings. Elizabeth Dore said that such meetings were needed to find out why so many of the employees wanted a union to represent them. Hammer gave them permission to proceed. A number of prounion employees had observed the group on the back porch, but at this time they did not know what was being discussed.

Shortly thereafter, Elizabeth Dore announced over the intercom system that there would be two employee meetings in the chapel, the first at 1 P.M. and the second at 2 P.M. She urged that all employees who could be spared from their regular duties should attend. When the first meeting began, Administrator Hammer, Elizabeth Dore, and Vickie Shear were in the front part of the chapel. Vickie Shear opened the meeting and did most of the talking.

After her opening remarks, Shear expressed her concerns about

---

[1] The names of all individuals are disguised.

the union organizing effort, and then she asked the assembled employees why they wanted a union when they were not willing to discuss their complaints with supervisors and management. At this point, a prounion employee, Betsy Conrad, stood up and said, "What gives you the right to call us here and ask us about the union? We don't have to listen to you!" Administrator Hammer then stood up and said that Conrad was right, and that the employees did not have to listen to Shear or him if they didn't want to do so. A large group of employees then left the chapel, and the meeting soon adjourned. A second group of employees assembled in the chapel at 2 P.M. Some of them had been present at the first meeting.

Vickie Shear was again at the front of the chapel with Administrator Hammer. After Hammer made several general remarks concerning the union organizing campaign, a number of prounion employees indicated their objections to having Hammer at a meeting where employees wanted to express their views; they felt that Hammer should leave. Hammer acquiesced to this request and left the chapel. Vickie Shear then assumed the role of chairperson of the meeting, and there ensued a discussion concerning the pros and cons of the employees' voting for the union to represent them. Near the end of the meeting, Vickie Shear expressed her opposition to the union and said, "If you vote for the union and the union gets in, all of the benefits that you now have will be gone, and this place will be run with a lot more rules than before."

Also in attendence at this meeting was Elizabeth Dore, who was seated near the front of the chapel. Immediately after Vickie Shear's statement, Dore stood up and said, "Vickie's right! If the union gets in, you can kiss all of your benefits good-bye!"

Shortly thereafter, the union filed unfair labor practice charges that alleged that St. Paul's Church Home had illegally interfered with the union's organizing efforts in violation of Section 8(a) (1) of the Labor Management Relations Act.[2] The union requested that the NLRB should order the employer to cease and desist in its interference with the protected activities of its employees.

POSITION OF THE UNION

The union claimed that the actions and statements of the two LPNs, Vickie Shear and Elizabeth Dore, constituted unfair labor practices, because they had served as agents of management at St. Paul's

---

[2] During the ongoing union organizing campaign in 1981, the union also filed a number of other unfair labor practice charges involving claims of interference, improper surveillance, and discrimination. These involved other incidents at the employer's facility and other personnel.

Church Home within the meaning of Sections 2(2) and 2(13) of LMRA. The union pointed out that Shear and Dore and two other antiunion employees had met with Administrator Hammer, who expressly authorized a meeting to ascertain why employees wanted union representation. At the initial meeting—which was announced over the intercom system, held on company time, and attended by Hammer—Shear asked employees why they wanted a union. This query, in the union's view, was a direct violation of Section 8(a) (1) of LMRA. At the second meeting, convened shortly after the first meeting ended, Shear and Dore both stated to the employees that they would lose their benefits if they chose the union. This, in the union's view, was an even more blatant violation of Section 8(a) (1) of the Act, since it was a threat of reprisal as prohibited under Section 8(c).

The union claimed that even though Shear and Dore were not supervisors or managers, they acted on behalf of the employer, and the employer was accountable for what they did and said. Hammer had expressly authorized the LPNs to hold a meeting to find out why the employees wanted the union. Although Hammer may not have specifically authorized their loss-of-benefits threats, these statements furthered the employer's position in opposing the union. The meetings were held under circumstances leading employees reasonably to believe that they reflected the management's position, rather than individual employee sentiment. It was only logical to conclude that Shear and Dore were agents of the employer, and as such, the employer had violated the Act by interrogating employees and threatening them with loss of their benefits if they selected the union.

POSITION OF THE EMPLOYER

The employer strongly denied that the LPNs had spoken and acted on behalf of the management of St. Paul's Church Home. Administrator Hammer acknowledged that he agreed to permit the antiunion employees to announce and hold two meetings in the chapel. At the first meeting, he told the employees that they did not have to stay and listen if they did not want to do so. At the second meeting, he left the chapel because of the sentiment of prounion employees that he should do so. When Shear and Dore made their statements about the possible loss of benefits if the union gained representational rights, Hammer was not present. Hammer testified that he had never given Shear and Dore any instructions or authority concerning what they should or would say at these meetings. Shear and Dore expressed their own personal viewpoints; what they said had not been authorized by Hammer. Further, they were LPNs, who were not supervisors or managers.

Counsel for the Church Home argued that under Section 2(13) of the Act, the responsibility of an employer for the actions of others who are alleged to be its agents has been held by the NLRB to be controlled by the application of the common law rules of agency.[3] The establishment of an agency relationship requires proof of an employer's specific bestowal of authority on the asserted agent, whether actual or apparent, and either in advance or by later agreement.

The employer in this case did not give authority to Shear or Dore, nor give them specific approval to do and say what they did. In no way were Shear and Dore acting as agents of management. Therefore, the unfair labor practice charges filed by the union were devoid of any substance and should be dismissed.

QUESTIONS

1. Were the LPNs acting as agents of the employer? Why, or why not?

2. In connection with the first question above, what inferences—if any—should be drawn from the fact that: (a) Administrator Hammer was seen with a group of antiunion employees shortly before the meetings were called and held; (b) the Home's intercom system and chapel were used; (c) Hammer was present at some time during both meetings?

3. Could the unfair labor practice charges involved in this situation be of sufficient consequence to move the NLRB to order the employer to recognize the union, or at least for the Board to direct a representational election? Discuss.

4. Why should both employers and labor organizations be careful in regard to the interpretation and application of Sections 2(2), 2(5) and 2(13) of LMRA? Discuss.

---

[3] The primary case citation here was Electric Motors & Specialties, 149 NLRB 1432, 57 LRRM 1513 (1964).

4. Should the Department Managers, Security Receivers, and Bookkeepers be Included in the Bargaining Unit?

Company:
  Big Y Foods, Inc., Springfield, Massachusetts
Union:
  Retail Clerks Union, Local 1459

BACKGROUND

The company operated a chain of 16 retail food stores. Eleven of these stores, employing approximately 850 to 900 people, were involved in the case at hand. The other 5 stores had been organized in whole or part by the Meat Cutters Union, which also was involved in efforts to organize the remaining 11 stores. A representational campaign to organize the remaining 11 stores was conducted by the Retail Clerks Union and the Meat Cutters Union beginning in 1976. A number of questions and issues developed concerning the appropriate storeswide bargaining unit and who should be included in this unit. These issues had not been fully resolved at the time of this case in early 1978. However, the NLRB had determined that the 11 stores constituted an appropriate collective bargaining unit.

In the course of filing for a representational election to be conducted by the Regional Office of the Board and the litigation that arose out of the petition for an election, three separate disputes arose between the Retail Clerks Union and the company concerning the appropriate status of the stores' department managers, security receivers, and bookkeepers.

THE DEPARTMENT MANAGERS

The company's entire chain of stores was centrally operated. Personnel policies were developed and administered by the central office. Full-time employees were hired by the central office. All stores had the same job classifications, such as store managers, department managers, head meatcutters, meatcutters, wrappers, and clerks, which covered the same job functions.

Each store was divided into five departments: front-end, grocery, meat, delicatessen, and produce. Consequently, there were five classifications of department managers at each store, that is, front-end manager, grocery manager, meat manager, delicatessen manager, and produce manager. All of these department managers reported directly to the overall store manager of each store.

Additionally, the central office employed specialists for each department who coordinated purchasing. The specialists also visited the stores in order to supervise merchandising, and in general to oversee the operations of the various departments. In this respect, the specialists worked in support of and in conjunction with the department managers and store managers.

The company claimed that the department managers were supervisors, while the Retail Clerks Union claimed that they were employees under the Act.[1] In seeking to determine whether these positions were supervisory within the meaning of Section 2(3) and Section 2(11) of the Act, testimony and evidence were presented concerning the actual responsibilities assigned to the department managers and not on their job titles.

In the case of the produce department managers and delicatessen department managers, their respective departments were quite small. For the most part, other employees, either full- or part-time, were not present when these managers were at work. Produce department and delicatessen department managers did prepare the work schedule for employees who worked when the department managers were not present. However, these managers could participate in disciplining of unit employees. On one occasion, a delicatessen manager was involved in the discharge of an employee who had failed to report for work. The company argued that these department managers were responsible for decisions concerning their respective products and the profitability of each department. However, other evidence showed that the central office department specialists were primarily responsible for these functions for the produce and delicatessen departments.

Concerning the grocery department managers, their responsibilities were similar to the produce department and delicatessen department managers. However, the grocery departments were considerably larger in size; normally other grocery department employees were present at the same time that the grocery department managers would be working. Similarly, the meat department managers and the front-end managers directed a substantial number of employees in

---

[1] During the proceedings at hand, the Meat Cutters Union took the position that the meat department manager was a supervisor under the Act. The Meat Cutters Union expressed no view on the status of the other department managers at issue, nor concerning the security receivers and bookkeepers.

their departments. The meat department managers supervised the head meatcutters, meatcutters, apprentice meatcutters, and meat clerks. These managers could impose discipline, interview prospective employees, adjust grievances, attend supervisory meetings, and prepare schedules. Similarly, the front-end managers supervised the cashiers, summoned additional employees from other parts of the stores when help was needed to package customers' purchases, and disciplined employees regarding shortages.

The union argued that all of the department managers were really "working straw bosses" or "lead people," not supervisors within the meaning of Section 2(11) of the LMRA. In reality, the department managers were tightly controlled by the store specialists, and the store managers and could exercise little independent judgment. Similarly, the central office specialists and the store managers were responsible for most of the stores' operating results, not the department managers. The union urged that the department managers should be included in the bargaining unit and be eligible to vote in the representational election. The company, however, claimed that all of the department managers exercised supervisory authority as defined under Section 2(11) of the Act, and that they should thus be excluded from the proposed bargaining unit as specified in Section 2(3) and be ineligible to vote in the representation election.

THE SECURITY RECEIVERS

The company and union also disputed the status of the security receivers. The company argued that they were guards, and pursuant to Section 9(b) (3) of the Act, they should not be included in the bargaining unit.[2] The Retail Clerks Union argued that the security receivers were not guards, and they should appropriately be included in the unit and be eligible to vote in the representational election.

Testimony indicated that security receivers spent approximately 60–70 percent of their time actually receiving goods. This involved determining the quantity of each item that the store received each week and completing a computer form with that information. During

---

[2] Section 9(b) (3) of the Act states in relevant part: "(b) The Board shall decide in each case whether, in order to assure to employees the fullest freedom in exercising the rights guaranteed by this Act, the unit appropriate for the purposes of collective bargaining shall be the employer unit, craft unit, plant unit, or subdivision thereof: *Provided,* that the Board shall not . . . (3) decide that any unit is appropriate for such purposes, if it includes, together with other employees, any individual employed as a guard to enforce against employees and other persons rules to protect property of the employer or to protect the safety of persons on the employer's premises."

their remaining time at work, security receivers performed such tasks as opening and pricing goods, sweeping and washing floors, pulling cardboards from shelves, and picking up carriages from the parking lots, in addition to delivering and recording merchandise. Security receivers were not uniformed or armed, did not wear badges, and did not have police powers. Security receivers were paid according to a separate wage schedule, but they had the same benefits as other company employees. The company engaged an outside security service to provide surveillance related to shoplifting and parking lot checks during the business day as well as at night and on Sundays. This outside security service also had responsibility for apprehending employees suspected of thefts.

The union claimed that the security receivers were little more than inventory control clerks who performed clerical and physical job functions. The company, however, claimed that the security receivers primarily were involved in protecting the property of the company, and thus they were properly classified as guards as defined in Section 9(b)(3) of the Act.

THE BOOKKEEPERS

A third disagreement between the company and union concerned whether the bookkeepers in each store should be included in the storeswide bargaining unit. The company would exclude them, and the Retail Clerks Union would include them.

Under the union's petition for a representational election, the Regional Office of the Board had determined that central office clerical employees employed by the company were not to be included in the storeswide unit of 11 stores sought by the union. However, under Section 9(b) of the Act, the status of each store's bookkeeper came into dispute. Each store had a courtesy booth, where a bookkeeper worked along with a "booth person," but each in separate rooms. The bookkeepers received the same pay and benefits as cashiers. Some of the stores trained a regular cashier to serve as a backup bookkeeper whenever the regular bookkeeper was absent. Bookkeepers wore the same smocks as cashiers, and they occasionally substituted for the cashiers. Job progression was normally from cashier to bookkeeper. Bookkeepers took their breaks in the same area as other employees, and they reported to the store manager for supervision. Technical problems were handled over the telephone by the main office. The bookkeepers' primary responsibility was to handle money and process lottery tickets and money orders that were received by the front end of the store. They also had to be familiar with the operation of a cash register.

The company contended that these employees primarily performed an accounting function, since they were responsible for maintaining the financial records for each store. The company stressed the financial and clerical nature of the bookkeepers' job and argued that they should be excluded from a unit of store employees. The company claimed that store bookkeepers could be included in a separate clerical employees' bargaining unit along with central office clerical employees in the eventuality that these employees sought some form of union representation. But store bookkeepers should not be included in a storeswide unit of store employees whose primary functions were associated with the selling of merchandise to customers in stores.

The Retail Clerks Union, however, argued that the bookkeepers were merely "senior experienced cashiers and booth persons" who were responsible for one facet of front-end store duties. Their jobs were essentially store- and customer-related, and thus bookkeepers should be included and eligible to vote in the stores' representational election.

QUESTIONS

1. Which—if any or all—of the department managers should be classified as supervisors within the meaning of the Act? Discuss.

2. Were the security receivers guards within the meaning of the Act? Discuss.

3. Should the bookkeepers be excluded from the proposed storeswide bargaining unit? Why, or why not?

4. Why is the resolution of the status of these persons of crucial significance to both the company and the union?

5. Election Interference, or Permissible Campaign Propaganda?

Company:
Cafe Tartuffo, Inc., and Fiorello's Roman Cafe, Inc., New York, New York

Union:
Local 6, Hotel and Restaurant Employees Union

BACKGROUND

In late 1980, Local 6 of the Hotel and Restaurant Employees won a representational election to represent certain employees at Fiorello's Roman Cafe, Inc. In the spring of 1981, Fiorello's Roman Cafe and the union signed a collective bargaining agreement covering employees of Fiorello's Roman Cafe.

Fiorello's was owned by the same management that operated Cafe Tartuffo, another restaurant, located several blocks from Fiorello's on the west side of New York City. In 1981, the union began an organizing campaign among employees of Cafe Tartuffo, and an election was ordered by the regional office of the NLRB to be held on July 9, 1981.

Prior to the election date, the company on June 25, 1981, sent a letter to the home address of all its employees. This letter contained the following statements (which are designated for reference purposes by paragraph numbers):

Dear Fellow Employees:

1. As you know, there will be a Union Election on July 9. At that Election each of you will have the opportunity to vote to determine whether or not you want to be represented by the restaurant workers' union.

2. You are much luckier than the employees at Fiorello's, our restaurant on the west side. Some time ago those employees voted to be represented by the restaurant workers' union. They were led down the primrose path by union promises of increased wages and benefits. In fact, after the election the Union negotiated a contract with the restaurant management which, in my opinion, gave the employees at Fiorello's no more than they would have gotten had there been no union—and probably gave them less. In addition, I believe many of these employees will be hurt by the inflexibility of the Union contract.

3. On the other hand, you know from the experience of the Fiorello's employees exactly the kind of contract the Union would negotiate if it became your collective bargaining representative. A contract which produces nothing more than you would expect to receive were there no union in the picture. For that, you are afforded the privilege of paying Union dues.

Paragraph 6 of the letter stated:

6. The restaurant does not want a union at Fiorello's! Our experience on the west side has shown that we can negotiate an agreement with the Union which does not cost us any more in wages and benefits than without the Union and may even cost less. But our experience on the west side has also shown us that the presence of the Union results in a tense working relationship with extreme disharmony among the employees. This is a real cost to everyone. It can result in a loss of customers and a loss of income to our employees who serve those customers, as well as to the restaurant itself. The Union benefits no one but itself.

The union lost the representational election at Cafe Tartuffo. Immediately thereafter, the union filed unfair labor practice charges and exceptions to the election under Section 9(c) of the Labor Management Relations Act, requesting that the results of the election be set aside.

POSITION OF THE UNION

The union contended that the company letter of June 25, 1981, went far beyond permissible employer statements allowed by Section 8(c) of LMRA.

First of all, with respect to paragraph 2 of the letter, there was reference to the election and the union's collective bargaining agreement with Fiorello's Roman Cafe. While the letter indicated that Fiorello's employees had "probably" received "less" with the union, Fiorello's Roman Cafe employees had in fact gained a wage increase that was greater than that obtained previously and also had acquired various additional benefits. Similarly, paragraph 6 of the letter and that paragraph's second sentence stated that the company could negotiate an agreement with the union that would not cost the company any more money than without a union and might cost it less. The language in paragraphs 2 and 6 of the letter thus meant that the company was saying it would provide its employees with the same planned benefits whether or not they chose a union. And taken together, paragraphs 2 and 6 constituted a promise of benefit if employees rejected the union and suggested the futility of selecting a union.

The union also protested the language in paragraph 3 of the letter to the effect that the company could negotiate "a contract which produces nothing more than you would expect to receive were there no union in the picture. For that you are afforded the privilege of paying union dues." This language conveyed the impression that not only would no new benefits come to the employees with a union, but that the employees would lose benefits because they would have the additional requirement of paying union dues.

Finally, the union protested the language of paragraph 6, which indicated that the "presence of the union results in a tense working relationship" and "this is a real cost to everyone," which "can result in a loss of customers and a loss of income to our employees." The union claimed that this was an obvious threat to employees designed to put employees in fear of losing money and possibly their jobs if they voted for the union.

In summary, the union claimed that since the company letter contained both promises of benefits and threats of loss of benefits, the company had violated Section 8(c) of the Act and thus had coerced and interfered with employees' rights in violation of Section 8(a) (1) and Section 7 of the Act. The union requested that a new election should be held, and that the company should be ordered to cease and desist in interfering and coercing employees in their selection of a collective bargaining representative.

POSITION OF THE COMPANY

The company claimed that all of the language within its letter of June 25, 1981, was legitimate and permissible "campaign propaganda" within the protected limits of Section 8(c) of the Labor Management Relations Act.

Concerning paragraph 2 of the letter, the company claimed it simply was stating its opinion relative to a union contract at its other location. The letter cannot be read fairly to state or imply that the company acting independently would grant the same wages and benefits to its employees that were negotiated at Fiorello's Roman Cafe. In this regard, the company claimed that it had held a general meeting with its employees on June 15, at which time it distributed copies of the collective bargaining agreement between the union and Fiorello's Roman Cafe. At this meeting, company management informed the employees that a union business agent had made management an offer to sign the same basic agreement for Cafe Tartuffo employees if the company would agree to forgo an election; alternatively, if the election were held, the union was willing to negotiate a collective bargaining agreement for Cafe Tartuffo based on the one formulated for Fiorello's Roman Cafe.

Similarly, the company contended that paragraph 6 of the letter did not constitute or contain a promise of benefits. It was only the company's opinion of the outcome of negotiations at Fiorello's Roman Cafe, and the company's further opinion that based on those negotiations the union would likely be willing to negotiate a contract that would not result in significant increases for employees at Cafe Tartuffo. Such comments are protected by Section 8(c) of the Act.

For essentially the same reasons, the company argued that there were no impermissible statements in paragraph 3 of the letter. Here, too, the company reiterated its perception of the contract that the union had negotiated at Fiorello's Roman Cafe. The paragraph did not indicate what the company's position would be if the union won the election; it only indicated management's interpretation of what the union's position in negotiations would be. The company was not prohibited from making such statements. Further, the company did not say that voting for the union indicated to the employees that a union would be futile. The company did not indicate that it had a fixed position with regard to what it would offer in negotiations and only expressed an opinion of what the union would seek in negotiations.

Finally, the company contended that the last four sentences of paragraph 6 were not designed to place employees in fear of losing money or possibly their jobs if they voted for the union. These statements constituted nothing more than an employer's permissible predictions of the effects of unionization. Nor did the company's statements correlate unionization with a loss of job security. The statements were devoid of any implications that the company would take adverse actions against employees if they selected the union. The company also explained that the tension mentioned in its letter referred to its earlier filing of objections to the election at Fiorello's and to the union's filing of unfair labor practice charges against that restaurant. Such charges and countercharges could reasonably be expected to occur at Cafe Tartuffo as well.

The company requested that the union's exceptions to the election and the unfair labor practice charges filed by the union should be dismissed, and that the NLRB should certify the results of the representational election.

QUESTIONS

1. Evaluate the union's contentions that the company letter went far beyond the permissible employer statements allowed by Section 8(c) of LMRA.

2. Evaluate the company's contentions that its letter was legitimate and permissible within Section 8(c) of LMRA.

3. Some companies hire management attorneys or consultants to conduct their campaigns prior to a union representational election. Why is the final decision in this type of case (irrespective of which side prevails) an extremely "close call" with important precedent implications?

6. Were the Employees Laid Off in a Discriminatory Manner?

Company:

Webb Furniture Enterprises, Inc., Galax, Virginia

Union:

Furniture Workers, AFL-CIO

BACKGROUND

In 1981, the union waged a vigorous representational campaign that culminated in an NLRB-conducted election on October 14, 1981. The election result was 188 votes for and 204 votes against the union, with 20 challenged ballots. After resolution of the challenged ballots, the union still had lost the election.

Immediately thereafter, the union filed certain charges and objections with the NLRB concerning the election.[1] The union also distributed leaflets after the election that announced that the union would continue its efforts to organize the company's workers. On February 5, 1982, while the union's election objections were still pending, the company laid off 24 employees, allegedly for economic reasons.

On February 23, 1982, the union filed additional unfair labor practice charges against the company claiming that the layoff of at least eight of the employees was precipitated by discriminatory antiunion motivations of the company in violation of Sections 8(a) (3) and 8(a) (1) of LMRA.

Eventually these charges focused upon the layoffs of four employees, Scott Hahn,[2] Ed Pelayo, Laura Valli, and Steve Mortimer. The union claimed that each of these employees had been laid off in a disparate, discriminatory manner; that the company was guilty of unfair labor practices; and that the company should be ordered to reinstate these employees and make them whole for all lost pay and benefits for the periods that they were discriminatorily laid off.

---

[1] Among these were unfair labor practice charges concerning the company's no-solicitation rule and the interrogation of an employee concerning his union activities. The union was upheld on these charges, but the NLRB did not direct that a new election be held as part of its remedial order.

[2] The names of all individuals are disguised.

The company denied that its layoffs were motivated by antiunion considerations. The company claimed that: (1) all of the layoffs were economically necessary because of severely reduced business; and (2) that the criteria used in laying off the employees were related to business performance and were applied in a uniform, nondiscriminatory manner. In this regard, the company claimed that it considered job performance, versatility, physical condition, and attendance in deciding which employees would be laid off. If these factors resulted in a tie, then management claimed that it relied on seniority as the deciding factor.

Scott Hahn

Scott Hahn was employed in the machine room at the time he was laid off. Before the October 14, 1981, election, Hahn had signed union literature on several occasions, signed a union card, attended union meetings, wore union T-shirts and buttons daily, and passed out union literature before work on numerous occasions. Plant Superintendent Artis Reinhold acknowledged in testimony that Hahn was an "experienced machinist and a good man." Hahn testified on his own behalf that he had received "a lot of compliments" on the quality of his work before the layoff.

Nearly all of the company's supervisors had observed Hahn passing out union literature. Plant Superintendent Reinhold admitted that he had examined union literature that was posted on a bulletin board to determine which employees had signed it. Reinhold also stated that he was in frequent contact with supervisors to determine the strength of the union's support in the various departments.

At the same time, Plant Superintendent Reinhold strongly maintained in his testimony that Scott Hahn was laid off because Hahn originally was hired as a "spare hand," and because the department's assistant foreman could readily assume Hahn's job duties. Hahn's job function was to fill in for absentees in the department. Other employees were assigned to a specific machine eight hours a day. Reinhold testified that he could do without Hahn easier than without any of the other employees in the machine room, because the assistant foreman could take Hahn's place. Further, a primary basis for Hahn's being laid off was that he was the least senior employee in this department.

The union maintained that Hahn had been singled out for layoff because of his strongly and highly visible activities on behalf of the union. The company's reasons for laying off Hahn were merely a pretext designed to disguise the antiunion motivation of the company.

Ed Pelayo

Ed Pelayo was employed as a ripsaw operator in the rough-end department when he was laid off. He had signed certain posted union literature and wore a union T-shirt and buttons several days a week before the election. He also solicited for the union and distributed union cards. Several of the company's supervisors acknowledged that they had observed Pelayo wearing a union T-shirt and soliciting on behalf of the union.

Company managers claimed that Pelayo had been laid off principally because of his attendance record, which was "among the worst in the department." Moreover, the company claimed that Pelayo was "not versatile," that is, he could handle only one machine, and the company needed to retain those employees who could be assigned to different machines in the interests of efficiency and economy, particularly during a severe business decline such as occurred in early 1982.

The union introduced attendance records that showed that two other employees in the same department who were not laid off had poorer attendance records than did Pelayo. Kaye O'Keefe and Adam Nolan had been absent $45\frac{1}{2}$ days and $26\frac{1}{2}$ days, respectively, in 1981; Pelayo had been absent 25 days during this same period. Neither O'Keefe nor Nolan had ever signed union literature or worn union buttons on the company's premises. The union claimed that there was no evidence to indicate that either O'Keefe or Nolan was more versatile than Pelayo, since both O'Keefe and Nolan normally operated only one machine in this department.

Laura Valli

Laura Valli was employed in the company's cabinet room at the time she was laid off. She had signed union literature on several occasions, and her name appeared in a union advertisement in a local newspaper on September 21, 1981. This advertisement had listed employees who supported an ongoing strike by one of the union's locals at another facility. Valli also had worn union buttons at work.

Plant Superintendent Artis Reinhold conceded that he had read posted union literature to determine who had signed it, and that he also had read the newspaper in which the union advertisement appeared and that included Laura Valli's name. But Reinhold maintained that Valli's layoff had nothing whatsoever to do with her support of the union. Rather, Valli was laid off primarily because (1) her absenteeism record was among the worst in the cabinet department and (2) her job could easily be divided up among other employees who were retained. The company stressed its need to be more efficient in a time of economic duress.

The union again introduced attendance records that showed that two other employees in the same department who were not laid off had poorer attendance records than did Laura Valli. Hadley Perkins and Margaret Hunter had been absent $56\frac{1}{2}$ days and $37\frac{1}{2}$ days, respectively, in 1981; Valli had been absent 34 days during this same period. The union acknowledged that Perkins' job could not be divided up readily among remaining employees, but the union claimed that Margaret Hunter's job was essentially the same as Laura Valli's and could have been divided up just as easily if Valli had been retained and Hunter had been laid off. The union pointed out that neither Perkins nor Hunter had ever signed union literature or worn union buttons on the job.

Steve Mortimer

Steve Mortimer was employed in Department 3 of the company's facility before being laid off. He signed union literature on two occasions, but he did not wear union buttons to work at any time. Plant Superintendent Reinhold testified that Mortimer was laid off solely because of his high absenteeism rate. Although Reinhold acknowledged that he probably was aware that Mortimer had signed some union literature, this had nothing to do with Mortimer's layoff. The union's claim of a discriminatory layoff of Mortimer was just an effort to have Mortimer reinstated from layoff and was a claim totally devoid of any merit.

The union once again introduced attendance records to show that another employee in the same department who had not been laid off had a worse attendance record than did Steve Mortimer. Wes Pritzell had been absent 29 days in 1981, while Mortimer was absent 20 days during that year. The union further pointed out that Wes Pritzell had never signed any union literature or worn union buttons on the job.

QUESTIONS

1. Under settled NLRB case law, if there is sufficient (i.e., prima facie) evidence to suggest that an employer's actions were motivated in part by antiunion (i.e., discriminatory) considerations, the employer then has the primary burden of showing that its actions would have occurred irrespective of any antiunion motivation or interference with the protected activities of the employees. With this in mind,

evaluate the layoffs of each of the employees in this case to determine whether or not the layoffs were or were not discriminatory in violation of LMRA.

2. Why are these so-called dual motivation cases often difficult for the NLRB to resolve? Discuss.

3. Why should employers be very careful if they use absenteeism of an employee as a major justification for some type of adverse personnel action (e.g., layoff, discharge)? Discuss.

7. Discharge for Lying, or a Pretext for Terminating a Union Organizer?

Company:
   Industrial Label Corporation, Omaha, Nebraska
Union:
   Local No. 520, Graphic Arts Union

BACKGROUND

Martin Dalton[1] worked as a press operator on the company's day shift. The company operated eight presses; 18 employees worked on the day shift, and 6 employees at night. Dalton was sometimes required to complete press runs on jobs that a night-shift operator had started. On June 19, 1980, a night-shift operator, Alice Higgins, had left a job for Dalton to run. Dalton ran the job, but it was discovered that a significant error had been made, and the run had to be repeated. On the same day, Dalton saw Higgins when she reported for the night shift. She told Dalton that she heard that the morning job had had to be rerun. She then asked Dalton whether he had obtained supervisory approval to run the job. He responded that he had done so. On the following day, June 20, Dalton was called to President Robert Fishman's office and was asked in the presence of Vice President Carl Neilson and an office secretary whether he had obtained supervisory approval for the previous day's press run. Dalton acknowledged to Fishman that he had not received supervisory approval. Fishman then asked Dalton whether he had told Higgins that he had received approval. Dalton then admitted that he had lied to Higgins, explaining his action as being prompted by Neilson's earlier caution to avoid arguing with night-shift employees. Fishman then discharged Dalton, stating that his dishonesty violated a company policy and that Dalton had been warned earlier that if he lied again he would be discharged.

Shortly thereafter, the union filed unfair labor practice charges on behalf of Martin Dalton against the company. The union claimed that Dalton's discharge primarily was motivated by Dalton's union organizing efforts, and his discharge thus violated Sections 8(a) (3) and 8(a) (1) of the Labor Management Relations Act.

---

[1] The names of all individuals have been disguised.

POSITION OF THE UNION

The union pointed out that in March 1980, Martin Dalton had openly undertaken a one-person organizing campaign for the union among company employees. Dalton distributed union literature, carried a notebook bearing the union's logo, left the notebook in plain view at his work station, and placed union decals prominently on his automobile. In May 1980, the union formally notified company management that an organizing campaign was underway.

Martin Dalton testified that during his morning break on June 18, 1980, he telephoned the union's president, Otis Strong, from company Vice President Carl Neilson's office to report on the status of the campaign. Dalton told Strong that based on the number of signed authorization cards, the union would win an election. However, Carl Neilson had come to the doorway of the office, and he overheard Dalton's part of this conversation. Upon being observed by Dalton, Neilson shook his head and walked away. Later that day, Neilson told Dalton to keep the "damn union crap" for his own personal time.

Concerning the incident that the company claimed precipitated his discharge, Martin Dalton testified that his so-called lying to Alice Higgins was a response to a direct order by the company vice president, Carl Neilson. Dalton noted that he worked as a day-shift press operator, and Higgins operated the same press during the night shift. In February 1980, they had a very heated argument regarding the cleanliness of their shared work area. Shortly thereafter, Carl Neilson told Dalton to "take any steps necessary" to avoid arguments with Higgins. Dalton did not deny that he told Higgins on June 19, 1980, that he had obtained supervisory approval to run the job in question. But he said that he was just trying to avoid an argument with Higgins, as he had been told to do.

The union contended that the real reason that the company discharged Martin Dalton was Dalton's union activities. Company management was aware of Dalton's conspicuous union activities and discovered on June 19 that Dalton thought the union could win an election. Dalton was discharged the very next day after the company learned of the apparently successful union campaign.

In the union's view, the company chose to magnify an insignificant event into one of major proportions in order to justify discharge. The so-called lying incident was not the actual reason for the discharge of Dalton. The company was not harmed by Dalton's lie to Higgins. But by claiming that Dalton's lie was a violation of the company's dishonesty policy—despite a previous warning—the company seized upon this opportunity to discharge Dalton. This exaggeration of a minor event cast serious doubt as to the company's asserted motivations for the discharge.

In summary, the union claimed that the company had seized upon Dalton's lie to Higgins as a pretext for terminating the chief union organizer among its employees, and thereby violated Sections 8(a) (3) and 8(a) (1) of LMRA.

The union requested that the company be ordered to reinstate Martin Dalton with full back pay and restoration of all benefits, and that the company be ordered to cease and desist in its discriminatory actions and interference with the union organizing efforts.

POSITION OF THE COMPANY

The company maintained that it had discharged Martin Dalton for lying to a fellow employee about a work-related matter, and that this was the third such incident involving dishonesty on Dalton's part.

The company first introduced its employee policy manual—which Dalton acknowledged having received—which specifically included a statement to the effect that dishonesty in company matters would be considered ground for automatic dismissal.

Company president Robert Fishman testified that he had had two prior confrontations with Dalton involving dishonest statements. In July 1976, Dalton was accused of lying about the nature of certain work instructions previously given to him by a supervisor. Since the company could not definitely determine who was lying, Fishman only warned Dalton that he would be disciplined if the company later determined that he had lied.

In December 1979, Dalton suffered a back injury and was hospitalized. The attending physician recommended that Dalton rest for 8 to 10 weeks before returning to work. Fishman requested that Dalton seek a second opinion from his own personal physician. Dalton consulted a local clinic physician, who confirmed the original diagnosis. Dalton then reported this information to Fishman but presented it as the opinion of his own doctor. Fishman, however, spoke to Dalton's personal physician and determined that Dalton was lying. He confronted Dalton with this knowledge. After some discussion, Fishman told Dalton that he would be terminated if he ever lied about a company matter again.

The lying incident by Dalton on June 19, 1980, was in the company's view sufficient ground in itself for terminating Dalton. But when he terminated Dalton on June 20, Fishman reminded Dalton that he had been warned twice before about lying, and he was being discharged for his cumulative acts of dishonesty, which represented direct violations of company policy.

The company maintained that it had the right to discharge Dalton for his repeated dishonesty, which could no longer be tolerated, and that this discharge action had nothing to do with Dalton's union organizing activities. The company urged that the unfair labor practice charges filed by the union should be dismissed in their entirety.

QUESTIONS

1. Was the company's discharge of Martin Dalton justified, or was it a pretext to terminate a union organizer in violation of LMRA? Discuss.
2. Was Martin Dalton's past record relevant in concluding that his pattern of "dishonesty" justified his termination? Discuss.
3. Why is it difficult for the NLRB to determine the employer's true motive in a situation of this sort?
4. Compare the issues in this case with those in Case 16, "Suspension for Absenteeism, or Retaliation for Union Activities and Giving Testimony?"

8. The Union's Demand for Recognition and Bargaining Rights

Company:
   First Lakewood Associates, Chicago, Illinois
Union:
   Janitors Union, Local 1

BACKGROUND

The employer owned and managed an apartment building and townhouse complex, where it employed a number of janitorial workers. On December 5, 1975, the union held an organizing meeting with these workers and obtained signed authorization cards from 6 of the employees in a proposed unit of 11 employees. One other employee in the unit was already a member of the union. On December 8, 1975, Orval Schimmel,[1] a union organizer, advised Thomas Hall, the employer's property manager, that the union represented a majority of the employer's janitorial employees and requested recognition and bargaining rights. Hall responded that he had nothing to do with union matters, and that the appropriate person with whom to speak was vice president Carl Alton.

On December 8, 1975, after the union had first requested recognition, maintenance supervisor Larry Melton telephoned employee George Thompson at his home and asked if any union people had contacted him. Thompson replied that none had. The next morning Melton entered the maintenance office, where the janitorial employees reported for work, and asked employee Alice Coleman, "What has the union done to you?" Coleman did not reply. Melton then entered his own office and called in employee Theo Ewing. Melton told Ewing that he knew that the employees had brought in an organizer and wanted to organize a union. He then asked Ewing whether he had attended the meeting and whether he knew who sent for the organizer. When Ewing denied attending the meeting and any knowledge about who sent for the organizer, Melton repeated the questions and told Ewing not to

---

[1] The names of all individuals have been disguised.

sign anything or talk to any organizer and to keep him informed of any such activities.

On the evening of December 9, 1975, Melton again telephoned George Thompson and asked whether he had spoken to any union people. Thompson admitted that he had, but refused to offer any further information. Melton continued to question him about why he was doing this and who attended the meeting. After several unsuccessful attempts to elicit additional information, Melton said to Thompson, "You are either on my side of the fence or your side of the fence. . . . You always had it good. I have given you . . . you got a nice job, you got an apartment. . . . This is your last chance." Thompson still refused to answer.

That same evening, December 9, Melton telephoned Gloria Greer, another employee, and asked why she had not told him about the union meeting. Greer denied knowledge of the meeting. Melton then telephoned Ewing and then asked who brought in the organizer. He repeatedly attempted to elicit this information, but Ewing said he did not know. Melton ended the conversation by telling Ewing to keep his ears and eyes open and to let him know if he heard anything. He also told him not to sign anything.

On December 10, 1975, Melton called Al Holt, an employee, into his office and asked, "So you want to join the union, huh?" Holt responded, "Who told you that?" Melton said, "The union man." Holt then left, and Melton called in Cecil Snow and asked him whether he had joined the union. Snow responded that it was none of his business. Melton told him that he just wanted him to know that there were no hard feelings, and that he would probably do the same thing if he were in Snow's position.

On December 24, 1975, supervisor Larry Melton was terminated by the company, and he was replaced by Leo Nord. At about this same time, the company announced that it was improving its sickness and health benefits program for employees, including a new benefit to cover maternity medical expenses for employees and/or their spouses.

On January 30, 1976, the morning of the representational election, supervisor Leo Nord told employee Cecil Snow that if the union won the election, the employer would take the rent-free apartments away from the janitors' helpers and charge the head janitors for the second bedroom in their apartments.

On January 30, 1976, the union lost the representation election 6 to 4. The union filed numerous unfair labor practice charges, claiming that these violations had dissipated the union's majority status as established by the authorization cards. These violations, in the union's view, were so serious and widespread that they made a fair rerun election unlikely. The union requested that the company be ordered to recognize the union and bargain with the union on the basis of the prounion majority previously established by the signed authorization cards, which it had secured in early December 1975.

POSITION OF THE UNION

The union filed unfair labor practice charges against the company, claiming that the company had violated Section 8(a) (1) of the LMRA by:

a. repeatedly interrogating employees concerning their union activities;
b. threatening employees with deprivation of benefits if the union should be selected to represent them;
c. threatening an employee for refusing to reveal the identities of employees who attended a union meeting;
d. informing an employee that it knew (or heard) that the employee had joined the union;
e. promising to pay and paying employees for certain medical benefits to discourage them from supporting the union.

The union urged that the company should be found in violation of the Act accordingly and ordered to cease and desist from these practices. Further, because the company's violations were so severe and pervasive, a valid union majority status had been dissipated, and it would be impossible to have a fair rerun election in the climate created by the company's actions. The union requested that the company should be ordered by the NLRB to recognize the union's majority status as of December 8, 1975, and to bargain with the union as the authorized representative of a bargaining unit of janitorial employees.

POSITION OF THE COMPANY

The company presented a number of contentions in urging that the union's unfair labor practice charges be dismissed.

First of all, company management claimed that it was unaware of the telephone calls and other questioning of employees conducted by former supervisor Larry Melton. Regardless, most of Melton's statements and questions to employees were not coercive, but they were legitimate inquiries necessary to determine whether the union had the majority status that it claimed. Melton never specifically threatened employee George Thompson on December 9; his statement to Thompson was very vague and inconclusive in nature.

Concerning the granting of improved sickness and health benefits in late December 1975, the company contended that these improved

benefits were part of the company's annual review of its benefit program. The company announced the benefit change to coincide with the
Christmas season, and this had nothing to do with the union representational campaign.

The company pointed out that supervisor Larry Melton was terminated by the company on December 24, 1975, and the election was not
held until January 30, 1976. Thus Melton's influence on the election, if
any, had "totally evaporated" and was no longer a factor. The statement of new supervisor Leo Nord to employee Cecil Snow on that day
did not constitute a threat, but it was a legitimate prediction and
Nord's own personal opinion concerning what unionization logically
would bring to the company. This was "free speech" protected by
Section 8(c) of the Act.

Finally the company claimed that even if the Board held that the
company had violated the Act in any way, such violations were minor
and did not influence the outcome of the representational election,
which the union lost. The union's claim to a majority status in December 1975, based on signed authorization cards, was never accepted
by the company or verified by the NLRB. The union was promulgating
unfair labor practice charges against the company in an effort to gain
representational rights after losing an NLRB election. The election
was a true determination of the majority of the employees' feelings,
and the Board should allow the results of the election to stand.

QUESTIONS

1. Evaluate the various claims made by the union and counterclaims
   made by the company regarding the unfair labor practice charges.
   Which of the arguments are most persuasive?
2. Was the statement of supervisor Nord to employee Snow on the date
   of the representational election a threat or a legitimate prediction
   and personal opinion protected by the free speech provisions of the
   Act?
3. Was the company obligated to accept the union's majority status
   claim based on authorization cards submitted by the union?
4. If the company is found to have violated the Act, what would be the
   appropriate remedy, a bargaining order or a new election?

9. The Supervisors Who Wanted a Labor Union

Employer:
> Wright Memorial Hospital, Trenton, Missouri

Union:
> Service Employees International Union, Local No. 50

BACKGROUND

At the time of this case, Wright Memorial Hospital was a 78-bed facility in Trenton, Missouri, located in a one-story building with a basement. The main floor was divided into three wings with a nursing station in each wing. Each nursing station had a registered nurse in charge on each of three shifts. Fifteen registered nurses so assigned were called charge nurses.

On October 8, 1980, the union filed a petition to be certified as the bargaining representative of certain employees, including the charge nurses at the hospital. On October 22, 1980, the NLRB's Region 17 office (Kansas City) conducted a hearing on the representation petition. At the hearing, the hospital contended that the charge nurses were supervisors within the meaning of Section 2(11) of LMRA, and thus they could not be part of the bargaining unit (Section 2(3) of LMRA). The union urged the inclusion of the charge nurses. The Regional Director for the NLRB rejected the hospital's arguments and decided that the charge nurses were professional employees rather than supervisors. Under Sections 2(12) and 9(b) of the Act, professional employees may be included in a bargaining unit with nonprofessionals, if the majority of the professionals vote for inclusion in that unit.

On November 17, 1980, the hospital, pursuant to Section 9(c) of the Act, filed a timely request for review of the Regional Director's decision. The hospital, however, did not request a stay of the election. While the hospital's request for review was pending before the NLRB, the election campaign proceeded. A number of charge nurses campaigned actively on behalf of the union. The nurses wore union buttons to work, attended union meetings, handed out union buttons, passed out authorization cards, and responded to questions at union meetings.

On December 4, 1980, the Board conducted a secret-ballot election. The ballots were subsequently impounded, and the ballots of the charge nurses were segregated from the others pending disposition of the hospital's request for review. Five months after the election, on

May 5, 1981, the NLRB overruled the Regional Director and held that the charge nurses were supervisors. While acknowledging that the charge nurses did not hire, fire, or interview potential employees, the Board held that the charge nurses were supervisors because they had the authority to "hold employees over to work overtime, release employees from work, assign work and set priorities for employees, call in off-duty employees to work, resolve complaints or grievances, evaluate employees in writing, give written reprimands, send employees home on disciplinary suspension without pay, and recommend harsher discipline up to and including discharge." The Board remanded the case to the Regional Director for the purpose of opening and counting the ballots of the eligible voters.

On June 11, 1981, the ballots of the eligible voters were opened and counted. Of the 147 ballots cast, 87 were in favor of the union, 55 were against representation by the union, and 5 were challenged.

On June 18, 1981, the hospital filed objections to the election. The hospital argued that: (1) the union had recruited a large number of the hospital's charge nurse supervisors, and those supervisors had solicited support and campaigned on behalf of the union throughout the election campaign; (2) a number of the union's organizational and strategy meetings, which were attended by employees, were held in the homes of supervisors; (3) charge nurse supervisors actively solicited employees to sign authorization cards on behalf of the union and to vote in favor of the union; and (4) three supervisors served as principal organizers on behalf of the union. On July 9, 1981, a hearing was held on those objections, and the hearing officer subsequently recommended that the objections be overruled in their entirety and that the union be certified. On March 10, 1982, the NLRB adopted the hearing officer's recommendations and certified the union.

On July 16, 1982, the union requested that the hospital bargain with it. By letter dated July 22, 1982, the hospital refused to bargain with the union. On August 11, 1982, the union filed unfair labor practice charges against the hospital, alleging that the hospital had violated Sections 8(a) (5) and 8(a) (1) of the Act by refusing to recognize and bargain with the union. The hospital admitted its refusal to bargain but argued that the union was improperly certified.

POSITION OF THE UNION

The union argued primarily that there was no evidence whatsoever to show that the charge nurse supervisors' activities on behalf of the union had been coercive upon the employees, nor had the supervisors caused any employees to vote for the union because they feared future retaliation by the supervisors if they did not support the union. The union acknowledged that most of the charge nurses (12 or 13 of 15) signed authorization cards and wore union buttons. But such activity in itself was not coercive, nor did it have any tendency to imply retaliation upon employees who did not want a union to represent them.

Several of the charge nurses acknowledged in testimony that they had spoken to other employees about benefits of the union, but they maintained that nothing was stated by any charge nurse that was threatening or coercive.

The union admitted that three charge nurses actively participated in the union campaign. But, contrary to the hospital's assertion, the union claimed that they did not hold leadership positions in the campaign. Two of the three charge nurses were members of an 18-member union campaign committee,[1] but they had no more influence than any other committee members. The union business agent controlled and directed the campaign, chaired all meetings of the committee, and acquired the majority of the 140 authorization cards signed by hospital employees. Further, the meetings attended by the three charge nurses were informal discussions in which all individuals in attendance could and did participate. The charge nurses' participation was limited to answering a number of questions directed to them.

In summary, the union argued that there was nothing in the record to indicate that the employees did not exercise their free choice in the union representational election. There was no evidence whatsoever that the charge nurse supervisors ever threatened or in any way implied retaliation upon employees who did not support the union. Nor was the active union campaigning of a number of the charge nurses of such a magnitude as to significantly taint the outcome of the election. The union had won a clear majority without counting any of the charge nurses' ballots. In the union's view, the hospital was raising objections primarily in an effort to avoid its statutory obligation to recognize and bargain with the union. The union urged that the hospital should be found in violation of Sections 8(a) (1) and 8(a) (5) of the Act and should be ordered to recognize the union and bargain with it accordingly.

POSITION OF THE HOSPITAL

The hospital relied primarily upon its continuing objections to certification of the union because of the charge nurses' active participation in the union organizing effort when they were actually supervisors. In the hospital's view, the charge nurses (the overwhelm-

---

[1] The union campaign committee was composed of two charge nurses, two licensed practical nurses, two paramedics, and representatives of the aides, lab technicians, and medical records, dietary, and housekeeping staff. The members of the committee were selected by the union business agent and employees.

ing majority of whom supported the union) had immediate and virtually complete control over their employees' working lives.

The cumulative effect of the prounion activities of the supervisors should require that the election be overturned. The supervisors engaged in almost every type of prounion activity, and the evidence should support a finding that the supervisors' actions interfered with the employees' free choice to such an extent that the supervisors' actions materially affected the results of the election.

The hospital also argued that the hospital was unfairly deprived of its right to utilize its charge nurse supervisors against the union in the campaign. The hospital engaged in an aggressive antiunion campaign. The hospital organized an antiunion committee, distributed handouts two to three times a week, and held mandatory meetings at which the hospital's antiunion position was clearly stated. But the charge nurse supervisors were not part of this antiunion campaign, although the hospital had a right to expect them to be as agents of management.

In summary, the hospital contended that the representational election was so tainted that the NLRB was in error when it certified the union as bargaining agent for the employees. Because of this error and the serious questions that the hospital had concerning whether the majority of the employees really wanted the union to represent them, the hospital rightfully refused to recognize and bargain with the union until its appeal concerning the representational election was decided. In the hospital's view, the results of the first election should be set aside, and the Board should conduct a second election that would be free of the taint and coercive actions and influence of the charge nurse supervisors. Therefore, the unfair labor practice charges were without merit and should be dismissed.

QUESTIONS

1. Evaluate: *(a)* the hospital's position that the charge nurse supervisors' prounion activities were coercive in nature; and *(b)* the union's position that these activities were not coercive and did not taint the outcome of the election.

2. What inferences—if any—should be placed upon the fact that the charge nurses wanted a union to represent them?

3. Should the NLRB have ordered a new representational election in May or June of 1981 when the Board decided that the charge nurses were supervisors and not professional employees under LMRA? Why, or why not?

4. Why would the hospital refuse to recognize and bargain with the union while its objections to the certification of the union were still pending? Discuss.

10. Was the Franchise Barbecue Restaurant in Interstate Commerce Under the Act?

Company:

Love's Barbecue Restaurant, Hayward, California, and Love's Enterprises, Inc.

Union:

Hotel, Motel, and Restaurant Employees and Bartenders Union, Local 50

BACKGROUND

Love's Enterprises operated and franchised a number of restaurants on the west coast. In December 1973, Love's Enterprises took over the direct operation of a Hayward, California, restaurant from a prior franchise operator. Earlier in 1973, a memorandum agreement had been signed between the Hayward restaurant franchise operator and Culinary Workers and Bartenders Union, Local 823, of the Hotel and Restaurant Employees and Bartenders International Union, AFL-CIO. Under the terms of this agreement, the restaurant agreed to recognize Local 823 as the sole collective bargaining representative for a bargaining unit to consist of "all employees at the Hayward restaurant engaged in the preparation, handling, and serving of food and/or beverages, excluding office clerical employees, guards, and supervisors as defined in the Act." The agreement also provided that: "The Employer agrees to accept, adopt, and observe all of the wages, hours, and other terms and conditions of employment contained in the Collective Bargaining Agreement between the Union and the East Bay Restaurant Association, Inc., California Licensed Beverage Association, Inc., or its successors" as well as "the Restaurant and Tavern Health Fund Trust Agreement, the Southern Alameda County Restaurant and Tavern Pension Trust Agreement, the health and pension plans established thereunder, and all amendments to said Trust Agreements and plans." When Love's Enterprises took over the Hayward restaurant in December 1973, the Hayward restaurant continued to adhere to the memorandum agreement with the union.

In 1975, by virtue of a merger of three unions, Local 50 of the Hotel, Motel, and Restaurant Employees and Bartenders Union succeeded Local 823 and became the Hayward employees' collective bargaining representative.

On September 26, 1977, Love's Enterprises closed its Hayward restaurant and terminated all of the employees who had been working there. On October 20, Lester Coleman[1] opened the Hayward restaurant for business under a franchise agreement, equipment lease, and real property sublease with Love's Enterprises. Coleman operated the restaurant as Love's had done using the same equipment for the same customer market at the same location under the name, "Love's Barbecue Restaurant." Coleman, however, did not hire any of the employees who previously had been employed by Love's at Hayward. Nor did he recognize the union or adhere to the memorandum agreement. Instead, Coleman began nonunion operations with an entirely new complement of approximately 30 employees. On October 21 the union commenced picketing at the Hayward restaurant to protest the restaurant's failure to reemploy any of the former employees and its failure to recognize the union as the collective bargaining representative.

Subsequently, the union filed unfair labor practice charges against Love's (Hayward) Barbecue Restaurant and its parent, Love's Enterprises, Inc., claiming that the company had violated Sections 8(a)(1), 8(a)(3), and 8(a)(5) of the LMRA.

POSITION OF THE UNION

The union first of all claimed that when Lester Coleman reopened on a franchise basis Love's (Hayward) Barbecue Restaurant on October 20, 1977, this in fact was a successor employer to the restaurant that had been operated directly by Love's Enterprises, Inc. All of the factors that the NLRB has determined for finding successorship were present here except for the fact that former employees of the restaurant were not retained. The Board has also ruled, however, that successorship exists in such circumstances if the new owner fails to hire a predecessor's employees because of their affiliation or possible affiliation with a union.[2] In the union's view, Lester Coleman refused to hire the former employees of Love's Hayward restaurant for discriminatory reasons.

---

[1] The names of all individuals have been disguised.

[2] According to a number of NLRB precedent decisions, an employer who purchases or otherwise acquires the operations of another may be obligated to recognize and bargain with the union that represented the employees before the business was transferred. In general, these bargaining obligations exist—and the purchaser is termed a *successor employer*—where there is a substantial continuity in the employing enterprise despite the sale and transfer of the business. Whether the purchaser is a successor employer is dependent on several factors, including the number of employees taken over by the purchasing employer, the similarity in operations and product of the two employers, the manner in which the purchaser integrates the purchased operations into its other operations, and the character of the bargaining relationship and agreement between the union and the original employer. See the following precedent cases: *NLRB v. Burns International Security Service*, 406 U.S. 272 (1972), and *Potter's Drug Enterprises, Inc. d/b/a Potter's Chalet Drug and Potter's Westpark Drug*, 233 NLRB No. 15 (1977).

The union presented evidence to show that after entering into the franchise agreement with Love's Enterprises, Lester Coleman reserved two rooms at the Vagabond Motel, located several miles away from the Hayward restaurant, to be used for interviewing job applicants. He placed advertisements in the *Oakland Tribune* and the *Hayward Daily Review*, which stated that a "new restaurant" was hiring and that applications should be made in person at the Vagabond Motel. The name of the restaurant did not appear in the advertisements. Coleman conducted interviews at the motel for two and a half days starting on October 12, and he subsequently hired 30 individuals through this process who had never worked at Love's Hayward restaurant previously. In the union's view, this entire hiring procedure was carefully calculated to virtually ensure that former Hayward union employees would not know about the job interviews.

To further support its claim that in hiring an all-new employee work force Coleman was motivated by discriminatory intentions against former union employees, the union cited a number of specific instances:

a. When former union employees began picketing at the restaurant, Coleman had an assistant manager take pictures of every union picket. The union claimed that this was illegal surveillance.

b. Several of these persons did fill out application forms for jobs. Coleman told one of them, former waitress Mary Peters, "If you put down your picket sign, we might rehire you at your old job. But this restaurant will be nonunion." Two others, George Pranschke and Carlos Kuvacka, applied for cook positions that they formerly held. Coleman told both of them that he might be able to offer them jobs "at some future date" but only as a busboy or as a dishwasher. The union claimed that this was designed to discourage Pranschke, Kuvacka, and other former union employees from seeking positions at their former job levels, which they had held or achieved through prior union seniority.

c. Coleman was heard on one occasion to remark to several union pickets, "I had a choice to make, and I chose to operate nonunion."

In summary, the union claimed that by (1) expressing his intention not to have the union in his restaurant, (2) unlawfully photographing union pickets, (3) conducting his initial job interviews under conditions that virtually ensured that most former union Hayward employees would not know of the interviews, and (4) avoiding hiring former Hayward employees because of their affiliation with the union, Coleman and his company had violated Section 8(a) (3) of the Act by refusing to hire the former Hayward employees of Love's. Further, these employees had been represented by the union in an appropriate unit. If it were not for this unlawful conduct, the union's status as the exclusive collective bargaining representative would have survived Coleman's takeover of the Love's (Hayward) restaurant. This, together with Coleman's continued operation of the restaurant at the same location and in substantially the same manner as before, made the restaurant under Coleman a legal successor with respect to the company's bargaining obligation to the union. Thus, the union claimed that Coleman and Love's (Hayward) restaurant had violated Sections 8(a) (5) and 8(a) (1) of the Act by disavowing the company's bargaining obligation to the union.

The union requested that all former Hayward employees be reinstated to their former jobs and be made whole for all lost pay and benefits with full previous seniority rights. Further, the union requested that the company should be ordered to recognize the union as the employees' bargaining representative and to bargain with the union as it would have if the union's lawful status had been acknowledged on October 20, 1977.

POSITION OF THE COMPANY

Lester Coleman, in denying that he and the company had engaged in unfair labor practices, offered a number of explanations of his actions.

First of all, he claimed that when he franchised the Hayward restaurant, he felt he could not operate it profitably unless he had a new complement of employees. Since he was under no legal obligation to hire the former Hayward personnel employed by Love's Enterprises, he decided to interview all new people whom he could hire at an acceptable wage level and whom he could train the way he wished. In fact, Coleman had been informed by several managers of Love's Enterprises that the Hayward restaurant had been closed down in September 1977 for economic reasons, including the high wage rates being paid to the union employees.

When the former union employees began picketing the restaurant, he ordered their pictures taken in case there was trouble and disruptive behavior that might require calling the police.

Coleman stated that he had been reluctant to hire former Hayward employees, such as Pranschke and Kuvacka, into their old jobs because the kitchen when he took over the restaurant was dirty and in disorder, which reflected the old employees' poor job attitudes.

Coleman could not recollect making the statements that the union alleged he made to Mary Peters and several other union pickets. Even if he had made such statements, they were "isolated" in nature, and they had occurred after he had hired an entirely new complement of employees. Because his work force was entirely new and these new employees had not expressed a preference for or voted for a union to represent them, Coleman claimed that he had no legal obligation to bargain with the previous union. That union only represented employees who had been dismissed by the previous operator of the restaurant, that is, Love's Enterprises, Inc.

Regardless, counsel for the company claimed that the entire set of unfair labor practice charges should be declared moot, because Love's Barbecue Restaurant in Hayward, California, was not engaged in interstate commerce at the time the charges were filed. The NLRB's standard to claim jurisdiction over a retail enterprise is gross annual sales of over $500,000.[3] In the previous year of operations under Love's Enterprises, the Hayward restaurant did have gross sales in excess of $500,000. But in the first year of operation under Coleman's franchise arrangement, gross sales at the Hayward restaurant were projected to be under the $500,000 level. Coleman testified that he attributed this drop in revenue in part to the union's picketing, which had interfered with his business to some degree.

In summary, the company denied committing unfair labor practices. But even if the NLRB should find on behalf of the union position, the NLRB had no jurisdiction over a restaurant that in the applicable period was not engaged in interstate commerce under the NLRB's standards for interstate determination.

QUESTIONS

1. At the time of the unfair labor practice charges, was the restaurant in interstate commerce within the meaning of the LMRA? Why, or why not?

On the assumption that the NLRB would claim jurisdiction in this case:

2. Was Lester Coleman obligated under the Act to hire all, some, or none of the former unionized Hayward employees? Why is the answer to this question crucial in regard to determination of the employer's motivations (i.e., discriminatory or nondiscriminatory intent)?

3. Evaluate the union's contentions and proposed remedies.

4. Evaluate Coleman and the restaurant's explanations in urging the Board to dismiss the unfair labor practice charges.

5. Compare the issue of "successorship" in this case with that involved in Case 17, "Was the Picketing to Protect Jobs, or for Recognition by a 'Successor' Employer?"

---

[3] This is required under Sections 2(6) and 2(7) of LMRA. See footnote 4 on page 7 in the Introduction to the LMRA for a list of NLRB jurisdictional standards.

11. The Objectionable Union Statement During a Representational Campaign

Company:
   Miller's Pre-Pared Potato Company, Inc., Blue Island, Illinois
Union:
   International Brotherhood of General Workers

BACKGROUND

This case involved an objection raised by the company concerning certain statements in a letter sent by the union to company employees just four days prior to a union representational election. On that election, the union won representation rights for bargaining unit employees by a vote of 21–17. The company filed objections to the election under Section 9(c) of the LMRA requesting that the election results be set aside.

The company's objections primarily focused upon a letter sent by the union to its employees four days before the election. That letter stated in relevant part:

> The Union will negotiate for better pay and benefits. The members of this Union get salaries between $3.90 and $200 an hour.

POSITION OF THE COMPANY

At the time of the election in late 1978, newly hired unskilled laborers were paid $2.85 per hour by the company. While the lower wage figure mentioned in the union letter was apparently accurate, the company asserted the higher figure was totally misleading. Because the company did not learn of the statement of the union to the employees until after the election, the company was unable to respond to the union's misleading claims.

The company contended that the union statement implied that the union had negotiated wages in the range cited for employees in bargaining units represented by the union. In fact, the union office simply had acted as a talent agency in arranging a number of performance dates for certain persons who were entertainers at salaries that exceeded $200 per hour. But the union could not prove that those entertainers were its members. Similarly, while some members of the union who were also entertainers received salaries in excess of $200 per hour,

107

108

the union had not negotiated such wages for those individuals. These union members typically negotiated their own fees with individuals, groups, and others who employed them. Thus, the union had substantially misrepresented its success in negotiating high wages for employees.

The company presented evidence that prior to the election, two or three employees had asked the union business agent about the union's statement in the letter. The business agent admitted that the $200 per hour salary applied only to a number of "entertainer members" of the union. However, apparently only these several employees received this clarification; other employees were not so informed and thus were conceivably misled.

The company contended that this "material misrepresentation" could have swung the balance in the close election. Under its election standards, the NLRB has held that material misrepresentation is grounds for setting aside election results. The company urged that the election results be voided, and a new election held.

POSITION OF THE UNION

The union claimed that it did not interfere with the representation election, when four days before the election it sent a letter to certain employees stating that its members get salaries of "between $3.90 and $200 an hour." This statement was neither literally untrue nor within the range where it was likely to mislead employees.

The union pointed out that the claim in the letter was technically accurate. The union represented employees in a number of bargaining units involving differing crafts and skills. Some union members were actually entertainers who earned over $200 an hour at times. Misrepresentation could arise only through drawing an inference that the union meant to claim that it had negotiated the union members' entertainers' salaries, but circumstances did not warrant such an inference. The fact that the statement was vaguely worded and subject to different interpretations could not establish such misrepresentation as to require setting aside the election. Additionally, the fact that some employees may have inquired about the higher wage figure in the statement should not mandate the conclusion that the statement had a tendency to mislead.

The union claimed that the company was merely using this objection as a means to avoid the results of the election. The union argued that the election be certified, and that the company be ordered to recognize the union as its employees' bargaining unit representative and to bargain with the union accordingly.

QUESTIONS

1. Evaluate the union's letter sent to the employees. Was this "material misrepresentation" as claimed by the company?

2. Since a number of employees inquired about the union letter, does this indicate that the union letter was confusing and/or misleading?

3. Why would the union send a letter of this nature to employees if its purpose was not to influence employee opinion?

4. Even if the union's letter was improper, was it serious enough to cause the NLRB to order a new election?

12. The Union's Threat to Discipline Its Members During an Organizing Campaign

Company:
> S & M Grocers, Inc., Silver Spring, Beltsville, and Hyattsville, Maryland

Union:
> Amalgamated Meat Cutters and Allied Workers of North America, Local 593, affiliated with the Amalgamated Meat Cutters and Butcher Workmen of North America

BACKGROUND

The company operated three supermarket-type grocery stores in three separate locations. In March 1976, the union began an organizational drive at these three supermarkets. On May 12, 1976, the union held an organizing meeting with the employees. At this meeting, a number of employees stated that some of the union's members who worked for the company were not participating in the organizational effort.

Many of the company employees also held part-time or full-time jobs in other stores, which already were under contract with the union. They were union members pursuant to a union security clause in collective bargaining agreements with their other employers.

On June 21, 1976, the vice president of the union, on behalf of the union's Executive Board, wrote a letter to those union members who were employees of S & M Grocers. In relevant part, this letter stated as follows:

> All members are hereby requested to assist and cooperate with the organizing committee of this union.
> Any member of this union that does not support, when so requested, or actively opposes the organizing activities of this union, will be called before the Executive Board and shall suffer such disciplinary action as the Board deems necessary including but not limited to expulsion from this union.

A number of S & M employees complained to company management about this letter from the union. Jointly with the company, they subsequently filed unfair labor practice charges against the union claiming that the union had violated Section 8(b) (1) (A) of the LMRA

110

by threatening disciplinary action upon certain employees in violation of their rights guaranteed by Section 7 of the Act.

POSITION OF THE COMPANY AND ITS COMPLAINANT EMPLOYEES

The principal arguments presented by the company and certain employees generally focused upon the contention that the union had violated Section 8(b) (1) (A) of the Act by threatening to discipline members who did not support or participate in or who actively opposed the organizing drive at the company's stores.

Although the proviso to Section 8(b) (1) (A) preserves a union's "right . . . to prescribe its own rules with respect to the acquisition or retention of membership therein," it is well established that this proviso does not permit union actions which undermine an overriding public interest, or which conflict with Section 7 rights guaranteed under the Act. Thus, while a union ordinarily has the right to discipline members for failing to obey internal rules aimed at solidarity, employees at the same time have a long-established statutory right to be free of coercion in the process of choosing a collective bargaining representative. During union organizing campaigns, employees are guaranteed rights to have full freedom to exchange views and ideas on the subject of union representation with other employees as well as having the right to make their own decision on whether to vote for or against the union.

It would be quite understandable and reasonable for an employee to choose union representation at one employer and decide to reject it at another—because of differing circumstances in the employment relationships the employee had with his or her respective employers. Further, some employees become union members primarily because of union security agreements already in place as a condition of their employment. At a different employer, they might choose to reject union membership if they had the option to exercise their free choice.

In this situation, the union sought to prevent full discussion by employees because it threatened that any criticism of or opposition to the union would subject employees who already were union members to discipline or expulsion from the union.

And while the employee might be free to vote against the union in an election, that freedom was substantially inhibited by the effects of the union's coercion of employee members' preelection activities. Therefore, the union's threatened disciplinary action constituted improper and unjustified restraint or coercion of employees in the selection of their collective bargaining representative.

The union should be held in violation of the Act, and be ordered to cease and desist and to refrain from its unfair labor practices accordingly.

POSITION OF THE UNION

The union claimed that its letter of June 21, 1976, to employees of S & M Grocers who already were union members because of being employed by other employers, did not violate the LMRA. The union argued that union discipline does not violate the Act unless the disciplinary action either reaches an employee's employment status or infringes on certain other rights under the Act. The union's letter of June 21 was in furtherance of its legitimate desire for solidarity in its drive to organize the company's employees. While the letter may have sought to restrict certain members' exercise of free speech during an organizational drive, the purpose was to require them to act only in a manner consistent with their membership status in the union. As members, they participated in the election of officers and in the other internal affairs of the union that led to the decision to organize particular employees. They could resign the union at any time if the union set out on a course they did not agree with.[1] Having resigned, they would be totally free to campaign against the union. Thus, there was no coercion in such a setting, as maintained by the company and the complainants. However, as long as they remained members, the union had a right to expect their support, including actual participation in the union's organizational efforts. Moreover, although the members were subject to the discipline if they did not support the union's campaign and did not in the alternative resign, they were still free to make their own determination as how to vote at S & M Grocers on the issue of union representation. Thus, the union's effort at member discipline was a valid enforcement of a legitimate internal regulation that did not contravene an overriding policy of labor law.

The union pointed out that the NLRB and the courts have long held that labor organizations have the right to promulgate reasonable rules and regulations and to discipline members in order to carry out their duty and responsibility to organize and represent employees. The union urged that the unfair labor practice charges should be dismissed.

QUESTIONS

1. Evaluate the arguments presented in support of the unfair labor practice charges. Which of these arguments is most compelling?

---

[1] The union constitution permitted this. Under union security clauses in effect, resigned members would still be obligated to meet their financial obligations (i.e., dues or a dues equivalent) to the union as a condition of employment.

2. Was the union's letter primarily aimed at "union solidarity" or to coerce certain employee members improperly?

3. Evaluate the union's contention that there was no coercion, since the members involved could resign the union if they wished.

4. Why is the issue in this case important from a broad public labor policy point of view?

13. Were the Job-Enrichment Work Teams Labor Organizations?

Company:
    General Foods Corporation, St. Anne, Illinois
Union:
    Local No. 70, American Federation of Grain Millers

BACKGROUND

The company operated a large manufacturing plant at St. Anne, Illinois, near Kankakee, where it produced dog food and other varieties of pet food. Production and maintenance employees were organized and represented by Local No. 70 of the American Federation of Grain Millers. Adjacent to the production plant was a research and testing facility known as the Gaines Nutrition Center; about 25–30 workers were employed at this site. The research and testing facility housed about 500 dogs and 250 cats, which were used for testing the food produced by the company and for research related to the production of new and different kinds of pet foods.

In 1974, the union attempted to organize the Gaines Nutrition Center. An NLRB representation election was held on August 15, 1974; the union lost by a vote of 10 to 13.

Employees at the Nutrition Center were salaried, and in 1975 they became covered by the terms and conditions of a compensation system designed for General Foods Administrative and Technical Group (ATG). This plan provided for a rather elaborate and involved method of evaluating and compensating salaried employees. It had been developed at the company's headquarters in White Plains, New York, and was administered uniformly throughout all General Foods plants in the United States. The plan applied to all supervisory and nonsupervisory employees who were salaried and who were not covered by collective bargaining agreements.

In the early 1970s, General Foods had embarked upon a job-enrichment program for certain groups and classifications of employees. The job-enrichment program was based upon premises derived from behavioral psychology. One such premise, for example, is that employees desire to have a larger and more meaningful role in their day-to-day work activities than normally would be assigned to them in a production-line operation. Job enrichment also assumes that employees desire to make a significant contribution to the business organizations of which they are a part.

At the Gaines Nutrition Center, the company decided to enlarge the responsibilities of its rank-and-file employees and to give them certain authority or controls over their job situations that normally were not assigned to the workers. Employees were divided into four teams. Each team, acting by a consensus of its members, was to make certain job assignments to individual team members, assign job rotations, and schedule overtime as needed. A team had no disciplinary authority, however. From time to time, individuals would be drawn from the teams to conduct job interviews with applicants for vacancies at the Nutrition Center.

Before the ATG program and the job-enrichment efforts began, there were two teams or work crews employed at the Nutrition Center called "acceptability teams." Their basic functions were to provide for the feeding and sanitation of the animals and the maintenance of buildings and grounds. Because animal care requires daily attention, the two acceptability teams, supervised directly by foremen Karl Dayley[1] and Ray Dooley, worked 10 straight days and then were off 4 days in a row. Thus, a team or crew was present every day of the year to attend to the needs of the animals. These teams included relatively unskilled workers called "kennelmen." Beginning in mid-1974, however, the work at the kennels became such that two additional teams, called the "methodology team" and "the nutrition team," were formed to handle more specific functions. The methodology team, supervised by Ann Perry, became responsible for testing of dogs' and cats' food preferences. Team members used specialized equipment designed for that purpose. This team was composed of semiskilled employees. The nutrition team, supervised by Jane Hildebrand, charted the growth of animals when fed certain kinds of foods, gave grooming and first aid to injured or sick animals, and tested samples of blood and feces. The nutrition team also was primarily composed of semiskilled employees. It was these four teams that, in 1975, became the subject of union unfair labor-practice charges.

In the fall of 1975, the company implemented its ATG compensation plan at the Nutrition Center. In December 1975, Ollie Musgrove, personnel director of the General Foods operation at St. Anne, held several meetings with members of the four teams in the Nutrition Center for the purpose of explaining and outlining the plan and how it would operate. He explained the basic compensation plan, the incentive (or merit) system, the promotion system, the so-called Chairman's Award (an incentive award), and the method of evaluating employee performance that the plan required. Each covered employee was sup-

---

[1] The names of all individuals are disguised.

posed to discuss and arrive at a "contract" with his or her supervisor, in which the employee outlined in writing what the supervisor expected of the employee, what the employee expected from the supervisor, and certain job goals. These goals amounted to suggestions by the supervisor concerning how the employee's own performance or the departmental operation could be improved. As a part of this process, employees would write (on a form provided by the company) their own job descriptions—which identified regular and recurring assignments. Each employee's performance would be compared periodically against the terms of the "contract" the employee had agreed to with the supervisor in order to determine eligibility for a merit increase. At the meetings conducted by Ollie Musgrove with employees to be covered by this system, discussions took place for the purpose of clarifying the requirements and components of the ATG plan. Subsequently, Musgrove also met separately with the various teams to discuss the implementation of the ATG compensation system for each group. The objectives of a team or group of employees were discussed at these team meetings.

At about the same time, the company retained Dr. Melody Whitaker, a professor of organizational psychology at a nearby university, as a consultant to assist in the job-enrichment program. Beginning in mid-1974, Dr. Whitaker held periodic meetings with the teams in an attempt to improve internal communications among team members and to build "trust levels" among them by conducting "team-building" exercises. Some of these meetings were held away from the company's premises, while other meetings took place at the Nutrition Center. First-line supervisors normally attended these meetings along with the employees. By mid-1975, Dr. Whitaker expressed her opinion to higher management that her efforts in building "trust levels" were "bearing fruit" with three teams but not with the acceptability team supervised by Ray Dooley.

At a team meeting in the fall of 1975, Gus Harmon (a kennelman who worked for Ray Dooley's team) outlined to team members, to Dr. Whitaker, and to Dr. Evan Percy (the director of the Center, who was in attendance) an idea for a more equitable rotation of overtime within his crew. Dr. Percy asked for opinions from other team members about Harmon's suggestion. Because a number of team members did not agree with Harmon, Dr. Percy did not put Harmon's suggestion into effect. At another meeting, Harmon asked Ollie Musgrove whether the ATG compensation plan would mean more money for employees, since he felt it was a waste of time to prepare detailed job descriptions and documents for manual laborers. Musgrove replied that it "would mean more money."

At various times, other employees besides Harmon voiced opinions at team meetings concerning what they liked or disliked about their jobs. On one occasion, Harmon registered a complaint to the managers in attendance about a raise that had been given to a female employee. He complained that supervisors were "catering to female employees" and were not assisting other employees enough in performance of the chores that they were supposed to do. Additional complaints about lack of promotions were aired. Several supervisors agreed that they would try to address these issues. At one meeting, employees complained about the job expectations that were a part of the "management contract" each employee had to reach with his or her supervisor; they especially criticized the job descriptions they had prepared. As a result, the practice of requiring employees to write up job descriptions was discontinued.

On occasion, Dr. Percy designated certain employees from each of the four teams to act as a safety committee and to tour the Nutrition Center to observe and report safety violations. A committee of employees drawn from the teams was also designated to prepare a list of new procedures for the feeding and sanitation of dogs. Another group collectively wrote up a job description for a "Grade 6 Kennelman," which was to be applied to a number of employees. In the course of these meetings, employees made recommendations to management concerning snow removal, collaring dogs, separation of animals in the habit of fighting, and other similar matters. At a meeting that took place in August 1975, Miller Hartke, a kennelman, asked Dr. Whitaker if employees could take their vacations one day at a time rather than on consecutive days. Dr. Whitaker looked up the vacation provision in the company's personnel handbook; she told them that it was permissible under the handbook procedure to take five days of vacation at different times so long as another five days were taken consecutively. At a meeting of Dooley's acceptability team late in October 1975, Dr. Whitaker discussed a list of grievances that had previously been submitted to the director of the Nutrition Center and to the personnel manager by employee Milburn Cravens.

On still another occasion in late 1975, employee representatives of the four teams met with Dr. Percy, director of the Nutrition Center, to talk about the work schedule during the Christmas and New Year's holiday season. They requested changing the schedule to provide a greater amount of free time. Dr. Percy agreed to change the holiday schedule in accordance with the recommendations of the teams.

In February 1976, the union filed unfair labor practice charges against the company, alleging that the company was in violation of Section 8(a) (2) of the Labor Management Relations Act. The union claimed that the four employee teams at the Nutrition Center were labor organizations within the meaning of Section 2(5) of the Act; and that the company had unlawfully assisted, interfered with, and dominated the administration of these organizations of employees. The union urged that the company should be ordered to cease dominating and interfering with the employee groups and that the Board should issue an order to disestablish the teams as the bargaining representatives of their members.

POSITION OF THE UNION

The union claimed that the so-called job-enrichment work teams at the Nutrition Center of the company were labor organizations within the meaning of Section 2(5) of the Act. This section defines a labor organization as:

> Any organization of any kind, or any agency or employee representation committee or plan, in which employees participate and which exists for the purpose, in whole or in part, of dealing with employers concerning grievances, labor disputes, wages, rates of pay, hours of employment or conditions of work.

Section 8(a) (2) of the LMRA makes it an unfair labor practice for an employer:

> to dominate or interfere with the formation or administration of any labor organization or contribute financial or other support to it.

The union pointed to numerous examples of team meetings during which employees discussed terms and conditions of employment, enumerated their complaints, and suggested changes of various kinds with management. These discussions on occasion caused managers to respond by changing or resolving the issues brought to their attention. The union thus claimed that the work teams had acted as labor organizations, but the teams had been formed and dominated by company management. The union suggested that the company in part had implemented the ATG and job-enrichment programs with these work teams in an effort to "control" the employees, who otherwise might vote for the union to represent them in their employment relationships with the company.

The union urged that the company should be found in violation of the Act and that the NLRB should issue the appropriate "cease and desist" remedies.

POSITION OF THE COMPANY

The company contended that the four work teams at its Nutrition Center were merely work crews and administrative subdivisions of the employees, which did not constitute labor organizations within the meaning of Section 2(5) of the Act. The company also maintained that it had the legal right to communicate with employees at team meetings in the manner in which it did by virtue of the proviso to Section 8(a) (2) that states:

> that subject to rules and regulations made and published by the Board pursuant to section 6, an employer shall not be prohibited from permitting employees to confer with him during working hours without loss of time or pay;

The company claimed that its original purpose in establishing the crews or teams had nothing to do with labor relations as that term is generally understood. The first two teams were created for the purpose of performing various jobs that had to be done in the Nutrition Center. As new jobs and new functions arose at the Center, two new teams came into existence. Thus, the four teams were not established to head off organizing drives by outside unions, nor did they come into existence in response to any proposed bargaining unit which had been rejected by the majority. The four teams at the Nutrition Center represented the company's view that this was the best way to organize the work force to get the work done.

Concerning the team meetings themselves, the company claimed that they enabled the work teams to discuss certain matters of concern to the teams and to management. Some individual employees did on occasion voice complaints to management representatives who were present, but there was no evidence that any team ever acted as an agent on behalf of any dissatisfied employee to assist him in pressing his case. In the words of the company's counsel, a work team "lacked sufficient internal functional cohesiveness to be regarded as a unit or an entity separate and apart from its membership." A team could not be a bargaining agent, because it lacked any structure or capacity to be an organization or an agent of any kind. No team had a designated spokesman. At team meetings, those who spoke did so primarily on their own behalf and in their own individual capacities. If this constituted the existence of a labor organization, no employer could ever have a conference or meeting of employees without being accused of having a labor organization in its midst. The Act never intended or provided for such an unrealistic, unworkable result.

In summary, the company argued that the union's unfair labor practice charges were without merit, and the work teams clearly were not labor organizations within the meaning of the Act. The unfair labor practice charges should be dismissed.

QUESTIONS

1. In recent years, many companies have implemented quality circle (QC), quality-of-worklife (QWL), and labor-management participation programs similar to the job-enrichment approach described in

this case. Why are these programs often attacked by labor unions as being in violation of Section 8(a) (2) of LMRA? Discuss.

2. Evaluate the various aspects and incidents described in the factual body of this case. To what degree would each of them support the union's position and the company's position?

3. Discuss the company's argument that a ruling by the NLRB in favor of the union in this case could expand the Act in an unrealistic and unworkable manner?

4. On what crucial point(s) should the Board decide this case? Discuss.

14. The Hospital's Withdrawal of Recognition and Refusal to Bargain with a Nurses' Union

Employer:
> Windham Community Memorial Hospital, Windham, Connecticut

Union:
> Registered Nurses Unit 62, Connecticut Nurses Association

BACKGROUND

On August 7, 1975, nonsupervisory nurses employed at the Windham Community Hospital voted in a union representational election. On the date of the election, the hospital employed 65 nonsupervisory nurses. A two-thirds majority of those voting selected the Connecticut Association as their collective bargaining representative. The actual vote was 38–19 in favor of the union, with eight employees not voting.

The union was certified by the NLRB on August 15, 1975, and negotiations commenced on November 6, 1975. After several negotiating sessions, major issues remained unresolved and the union voted to engage in an economic strike. After giving the hospital and the Federal Mediation and Counciliation Service (FMCS) due notice as required by Section 8(g) of the LMRA, the union commenced its strike on April 21, 1976. Negotiations continued for a time, but were suspended on June 9, 1976.

On August 23, 1976, Marjorie Mueller,[1] a union agent, called Richard Stone, the hospital's attorney and a member of the negotiating team, and told him that the union would like to resume bargaining. The substance of this conversation was later disputed. Stone claimed that he was told that resumption of negotiations was preconditioned on reinstatement of 23 employees and on the union's "getting something to show for the strike."

Mueller claimed that she merely indicated the union's willingness to make certain concessions, such as reducing the number of employees to be immediately rehired from 42 to 23 and altering wage demands.

Stone immediately contacted the hospital's administrator, Fred Richter, and communicated the union's desire to resume negotiations.

---

[1] The names of all individuals have been disguised.

At that time, Richter told Stone that the hospital would no longer negotiate with the union, because he felt that the union no longer had the support of a majority of the hospital's nurses. Later that day, the union was notified that the hospital had refused to resume bargaining and had withdrawn recognition from the union.

Statistically, it was established that at the time of the walkout, 72 nurses were employed in the bargaining unit.[2] Of these, 57 employees initially engaged in the strike, while 15 employees did not strike but continued working. Nine striking employees returned to work, and another six employees resigned the union and returned to work by August 23, 1976. The hospital also had hired 42 replacement employees by August 23, 1976.

Both the quality and quantity of picketing had gradually diminished over the months. Such activities had been officially terminated by the union on August 8, 1976.

POSITION OF THE UNION

The union contended that the hospital's withdrawal of recognition and refusal to bargain with the union were unlawful for several reasons.

First of all, the union pointed out that it is settled labor law that except under unusual circumstances, a union's representative status is presumed to continue during the first year following certification, so that the collective bargaining relationship has the opportunity to become established. Withdrawal of union recognition by management during this period is an unfair labor practice and violates the Act. Following the expiration of the certification year, the presumption of union recognition remains in effect unless an employer can either show conclusively that on the date recognition was withdrawn, the union in fact did not have majority support; or present sufficient evidence that a refusal to bargain was based on a serious good faith doubt of the union's majority. In this case situation, neither of the above had occurred.

The union contended that the hospital had failed to establish that as of August 23, 1976, the union was in fact no longer supported by a majority of the hospital's employees. The union pointed out that of the 57 original strikers, only 9 employees returned to work and only 6 other employees resigned the union and returned to work before August 23, 1976; this left a total of 42 strikers who obviously supported

---

[2] Apparently, a total of seven additional nursing employees had been hired beween August 7, 1975, and April 21, 1976.

the union. For purposes of determining majority status of the union, all of these remaining 42 strikers retained their legal rights under the Act as employees and must be considered members of the bargaining unit in support of the union.[3]

Concerning the 15 nonstrikers and the 9 strikers who did not resign the union but who returned to work before August 23, 1976, the union maintained that many of them still strongly wanted the union to represent them. Among these employees were nurses who felt that they could not afford economically to go out or stay out on a strike and/ or who felt that a strike by nurses was inappropriate to their profession. The union claimed that of these 24 employees, it could be approximated that two thirds (or 16) of them supported the union—the same 2-to-1 ratio by which the employees originally voted for the union.

This meant that on August 23, 1976, a total of 58 employees favored the union: 42 strikers plus 16 of the 24 nonstrikers and returnees. Thus, even if it were assumed that the 42 replacement employees did not support the union, a majority of employees still did so; that is, 58 of the 114 employees in the applicable employee bargaining unit should be counted as being for the union.

The union contended that its reduction of picketing activity during the summer months of 1976 was attributable to the combination of several different factors: summer vacations, family responsibilities

---

[3] The union relied on NLRB policy, labor case law, and court decisions in making these assertions. In general, employees who strike for a lawful object fall into two classes—economic strikers and unfair labor practice strikers. Both classes continue as employees, but unfair labor practice strikers have greater rights of reinstatement to their jobs.

If the object of a strike is to obtain from the employer some economic concession such as higher wages, shorter hours, or better working conditions, the striking employees are called economic strikers. They retain their status as employees and cannot be discharged, but they can be replaced by their employer. If the employer has hired bona fide permanent replacements who are filling the jobs of the economic strikers when the strikers apply unconditionally to go back to work, the strikers are not entitled to reinstatement at that time. However, if the strikers do not obtain regular and substantially equivalent employment, they are entitled to be recalled to jobs for which they are qualified when openings in such jobs occur if they, or their bargaining representative, have made an unconditional request for their reinstatement.

Employees who strike to protest an unfair labor practice committed by their employer are called unfair labor practice strikers. Such strikers can be neither discharged nor permanently replaced. When the strike ends, unfair labor practice strikers, absent serious misconduct on their part, are entitled to have their jobs back even if employees hired to do their work have to be discharged.

If the Board finds that economic strikers or unfair labor practice strikers who have made an unconditional request for reinstatement have been unlawfully denied reinstatement by their employer, the Board may award such strikers back pay starting at the time they should have been reinstated.

engendered by school vacations, and the strikers' feelings that additional picketing was no longer necessary because the continuation of the strike itself was sufficient to notify the hospital that the union was still pressing its claims.

Thus, the union argued that on August 23, 1976, it was still the legally constituted representative of the nursing unit employees. Since the hospital unlawfully withdrew its recognition of the union and refused to bargain with the union as required by Section 8(d) of the Act, the hospital had caused the nurses' economic strike to become an unfair labor practice strike. The real motive of the hospital was its determination to destroy the union. The union was willing to negotiate concerning reinstatement of certain strikers, but the hospital refused to bargain at all.

The union urged that the hospital be found to have violated Sections 8(a) (5) and 8(a) (1) of the Act. As remedies, the hospital should be ordered to: *(a)* cease and desist from unfair labor practices; *(b)* recognize and bargain, on request, with Windham Community Memorial Hospital, Registered Nurses Unit 62, Connecticut Nurses Association (the union); and *(c)* reinstate with back pay, or otherwise to make whole, all striking employees.

POSITION OF THE HOSPITAL

The hospital claimed that it had not violated the Act because it was justified in concluding that the union no longer had a majority status among the nursing employees on August 23, 1976.

First of all, the hospital claimed that the union itself had abandoned the strike in August 1976. The diminution in enthusiasm for picketing indicated loss of support for the union by the employees.

Secondly, the hospital contended that its failure to return to the bargaining table in response to the union's August 23 initiative did not constitute a "refusal to bargain" within the meaning of Section 8(a) (5) of the Act. The union's offer was preconditioned with a demand by the union to reinstate 23 strikers. Neither the Act nor NLRB policy required the hospital to accept such an offer as a condition for bargaining.

But most importantly, the hospital argued that the union had lost its majority status. By the union's own statement, only 23 of the 42 strikers wanted their jobs back on August 23, 1976; the other 19 strikers who did not ask for their jobs back should not be counted as being part of any applicable bargaining unit. Thus, the union no longer had a majority status, since the conceivable bargaining unit consisted of only 95 employees, not 114 employees as claimed by the union. Of these 95 employees, the 42 replacement employees and the 15 nonstrikers should clearly be presumed to be against the union, plus the 6 striking employees who resigned the union and who returned to work.

The hospital thus asserted that it had good faith doubt about the union's majority status in August 1976, and its objective data supported its decision to withdraw recognition of the union accordingly. The hospital urged that the unfair labor practice charges should be dismissed in their entirety.

Alternatively, the hospital argued that if the Board should conclude that the company erred in not bargaining with the union in August 1976, then the appropriate remedy should be a new NLRB representation election to determine whether the union had a majority status. The hospital contended that nothing in the record would justify the union's extraordinary claim that strikers should be reinstated and/ or made whole for lost pay and benefits.

QUESTIONS

1. Evaluate the union's statistical contention that it still represented a majority of employees at the time of this case.
2. Evaluate the hospital's statistical contention that the union no longer represented a majority of employees.
3. Was the union's statement to the hospital on August 23, 1976, a precondition for bargaining, or merely a bargaining position that was negotiable?
4. If the hospital is found to have violated the Act, is the appropriate remedy a reinstatement and making whole of employees, or a new representational election to determine the union's representational status?

15. Discharge for Failure to Pay Union Dues

Company:
   R. H. Macy & Co., Inc., Bronx, New York
Union:
   Local 3, International Brotherhood of Electrical Workers
Individual:
   Alan Gomez[1]

BACKGROUND

Since 1978 until his discharge on January 8, 1981, Alan Gomez had been employed by Macy's as an electrician. In that capacity, Gomez was covered by a collective bargaining agreement containing a union security clause. This clause required that, as a condition of employment, all bargaining unit employees become and remain members of the union after 30 days of employment. As the contract did not contain a dues-checkoff provision, unit employees submitted their dues directly to the union. From April 1978 to September 1979, Gomez paid his dues on a quarterly basis. However, because of personal financial difficulties, Gomez did not remit any dues for the last quarter of 1979, and until December 17, 1980, he had remitted no dues for any quarter period in 1980.

In late December 1980, Gomez feared that he might be discharged pursuant to the terms of the union security agreement if he did not correct his union dues delinquency. On December 17, 1980, Gomez forwarded a check to the union for $252.80 covering dues owed for the four quarters of 1980; he believed that this amount was all he owed the union. However, Gomez had not paid dues for the last quarter of 1979, and he was therefore still in arrears for that quarter.

On December 22, 1980, the union's executive board met to discuss the dues status of various members, including that of Gomez. A form letter dated December 30, 1980, was thereafter mailed out to Gomez advising him that he had been listed as a "ceased" member,[2] and that

---

[1] The names of all individuals have been disguised.

[2] A member was classified as "ceased" when his dues were in arrears for six months or more. A "lapsed" member was one whose dues were in arrears for only three months. Although a lapsed member was still considered a union member, a ceased member was not.

if he wished to remain a member he would have to pay the sum of $66.70, which represented dues owed for the last quarter of 1979, plus a reinstatement fee of $30. According to the letter, such payments would assure him "good standing in the union until December 31, 1980." Gomez did not receive that letter until several days after the December 30 date. Upon receipt of the letter, Gomez (believing that his dues had been brought up to date by his December 17 check) phoned the union office. After questioning the contents of the union's letter, Gomez was told that if he paid the amount stated in the letter, he would no longer be a "ceased" member but would be reinstated.

However, prior to this, on December 22, 1980, George Hulser, a Macy's manager, had informed Macy's vice president for labor relations Bernice Wambles that union business representative Tony Mataya had requested that Gomez be discharged for failing to pay union dues for a long period of time. Wambles advised Hulser that such a request must be made in writing. Thereafter, a letter dated December 26, 1980, and signed by Mataya was mailed to Wambles stating that according to the union's records Gomez was not a member in good standing, having failed to pay his dues since September, 1979; the union requested that Gomez be discharged from his position as of the date of this letter. Wambles did not receive this letter until January 5, 1981.

Upon receipt of the union's letter, Wambles reviewed the collective bargaining agreement to insure that the union's request for Gomez' discharge was proper. After doing so, she notified Macy's personnel manager, Alice Kelso, of Gomez' apparent dues delinquency and instructed that, in accordance with the union-security agreement, Gomez be discharged. On January 8, 1981, Kelso summoned Gomez into her office, and informed him that at the union's request, he was being terminated for failing to pay dues as required under the union contract. Although Gomez protested that a mistake had been made, he was advised by Kelso that he would have to take the matter up with the union. Gomez responded that the union was out to get him because of an earlier discrimination suit he had filed against the union concerning job assignments.

Immediately after leaving Kelso's office, Gomez went directly to the union's office, where he tendered a check postdated for the following day, January 9, 1981, in the amount of $225 covering the amount requested by the union in the December 30 letter plus an advance payment of dues for two additional quarters. Gomez then returned to Kelso's office later that afternoon in an effort to get reinstated, but he was denied reinstatement because of his failure to produce a receipt indicating his union dues had been paid.

Subsequently, Alan Gomez filed charges with the NLRB against the company alleging a discriminatory discharge in violation of Sections 8(a) (3) and 8(a) (1) of the Labor Management Relations Act. Gomez filed similar charges against the union alleging violations of Sections 8(b) (1) (A) and 8(b) (2) of the Act.

While these charges were still being litigated, Gomez was reinstated to his former position in late May 1981.

POSITION OF ALAN GOMEZ

Although Alan Gomez acknowledged that he had fallen behind some 15 months in his dues payments to the union, his failure to make any payments during that period did not result from a willful and deliberate attempt on his part to avoid his financial obligations to the union. Rather, his failure to keep up with his payments resulted from his personal financial difficulties and by the union's own inattention to the matter. On his own initiative, Gomez had mailed a check to the union, before any request for his discharge had been made, in an amount that he in good faith, but erroneously, believed was sufficient to cover all of his dues obligations. Gomez claimed that his failure to include his dues for the last quarter of 1979 in his December 17, 1980, check did not result from an intentional act, but from a lack of knowledge as to the extent of his dues delinquency, which primarily was the fault of the union.

Alan Gomez claimed that by failing to inform him specifically of his 1979 dues obligations and by failing to give him an opportunity to clear up his dues account prior to seeking his discharge, the union had discriminated against him in violation of Sections 8(b) (1) (A) and 8(b) (2) of the LMRA. In part, Gomez felt that the union was retaliating against him for his having filed an employment discrimination suit against the union a year or so previous, a suit that he subsequently dropped. And since the company had unlawfully discharged him upon the request of the union, the company too, had violated Sections 8(a) (3) and 8(a) (1) of the Act. Alan Gomez requested that his discharge of January 8, 1981, should be rescinded, and that he should be made whole by the union and/or the company for the period between his termination and his reinstatement.

POSITION OF THE COMPANY

The company claimed that it simply acted on the request of the union to terminate Alan Gomez for his failure to pay dues, as required by the collective bargaining agreement. The company had no reasonable basis whatsoever to believe that the union's request was either improper or unlawful. The union's dues problem with Alan Gomez was an internal union matter. If there was anything unlawful about what happened, it was the union's total responsibility, not the company's. The company requested that the unfair labor practice charges filed against the company by Alan Gomez should be dismissed.

POSITION OF THE UNION

The union argued that it had the right both under its collective bargaining agreement with the company and under Section 8(b) (2) of the LMRA to request the company to terminate Alan Gomez for his failure to pay all of his delinquent union dues. Although Gomez did make an effort to pay most of his delinquent dues at the end of 1980, he still owed dues for the last quarter of 1979 when the union made its request to the company to have Gomez terminated. Gomez had been a "free rider" for a long period of time, and the union could not overlook his dues delinquency any longer. The union requested that the unfair labor practice charges filed against the union by Alan Gomez should be dismissed.

QUESTIONS

1. Evaluate the company's position that it simply acted upon the union's request to discharge Alan Gomez for his failure to pay union dues. Does a valid union shop clause in a negotiated labor agreement absolve the company of any responsibility in this matter?

2. Evaluate the union's position that it had the right to request Alan Gomez' discharge both under the labor contract and within the provisions of LMRA, even though Gomez did pay most of the dues he owed.

3. Was Alan Gomez discriminated against in violation of the Act? If so, by the company, the union, or both?

4. Regardless of the NLRB's findings concerning the discrimination charges, why is a case such as this "embarrassing" to both the company and the union?

16. Suspension for Absenteeism, or Retaliation for Union Activities and Giving Testimony?

Company:
   Best Products Company, Sacramento, California
Union:
   Local 588, Retail Clerks International Association

BACKGROUND

Best Products Company, a Virginia corporation, was a nationwide showroom merchandiser with two locations in the Sacramento area. In the summer of 1975, authorization cards for Local 588, Retail Clerks International Association, were distributed to employees of both Sacramento, California, showrooms. Subsequently, the union filed a petition for elections at both locations in September 1975. Employee Sally Hong[1] participated in the solicitation of cards and in the election campaigns on behalf of the union. On November 21, 1975, elections were held at both Sacramento showrooms. The union lost both elections. On December 1 of that year, the union filed post-election objections. In March 1976, hearings on those objections were held at a regional office of the NLRB. Sally Hong was present and testified at those hearings. On June 10, 1976, the NLRB's hearing officer issued a report sustaining certain objections, recommending that the November 21st elections be set aside and ordering subsequent elections for each showroom. In October of 1976, the Board adopted the hearing officer's report. However, the union subsequently withdrew its request for second elections, and the elections were never held.

During the fall of 1976, Sally Hong was frequently absent from work. During a period of approximately three months, she missed 13 full days and 4 partial days of work. These absences were primarily due to illness, and they occurred during the company's peak work period.[2] The months of October, November, and December are the

---

[1] The names of all individuals have been disguised.

[2] Hong provided the company with statements from physicians for several of her absences; these documented various ailments and illnesses that she had experienced.

industry's busiest time of year because of the holiday season: approximately 50 percent of Best's annual business occurs during those three months.

On January 10, 1977, Showroom Manager Estelle Laclede called Sally Hong into her office and read to Hong the following statement:

> SUBJECT: EXCESSIVE ABSENTEEISM
> COMMENTS: For the past three months your absenteeism has been exceptionally high again as it was last year during the same time period. This imposes a severe burden upon your department and the showroom in general. We hereby are directing you to take a two-month leave of absence to restore you to good health.
> Leave to commence 1-10-77
> Leave to terminate 3-10-77

Two days later, a statement was read to other employees of the Best showroom, stating that Sally Hong had taken a leave of absence for health reasons.

Subsequently, Sally Hong and the union filed unfair labor practice charges against the company. They claimed that her two-month suspension was in retaliation for her union activities and for her giving testimony at an NLRB hearing. Such retaliation was in violation of Sections 8(a) (3), 8(a) (4), and 8(a) (1) of LMRA.

POSITION OF THE UNION

The union claimed that the real motive for the company's suspending Sally Hong was that she had been a union activist who was openly involved in the union's representational campaign. Sally Hong had testified and participated in an NLRB hearing that resulted in the company's being found guilty of unfair labor practices during the union's representational campaign. Among the conclusions of a Board hearing officer was that the company had shown a "general antiunion animus" and had engaged in unfair labor practices including asking employees to remove union buttons while in the showroom area, questioning employees regarding union activities, and discriminatorily enforcing a no-solicitation rule.

Sally Hong's testimony was significant in this Board hearing, which resulted in an NLRB order setting aside the results of the elections (which the company had won).

In the union's view, the company's past record, coupled with the timing of the disciplinary action taken upon Sally Hong, supported the conclusion that the suspension was primarily motivated by retaliation for Hong's union activities, and not for absenteeism. The union requested that the company be ordered to rescind the suspension action, to make her whole for lost earnings, and to cease and desist in discriminatory unfair labor practices.

POSITION OF THE COMPANY

The company first presented evidence to show that Sally Hong had been frequently absent from work during the fall of 1975 and that she had been given a written warning for "excessive absenteeism." The company next showed that Hong's rate of absenteeism was the highest for any employee during the fall 1976 period. Company evidence further was introduced that showed that disciplinary action was common in cases such as Hong's. The previous year, another employee had been terminated after absences of 15 days. Other employees were routinely given warnings or suspensions when their absenteeism reached 10 days or so. Hong had not been treated differently from other employees who had unsatisfactory attendance records.

The company argued strongly that Sally Hong's two-month suspension was intended as a "leave of absence" for her to recuperate from any illness and to have her health restored. The company did not single her out for disparate, discriminatory treatment. Hong's absenteeism record during fall of 1976 was intolerable, and the company could not afford to have any employee continue such an attendance pattern without taking efforts to correct it.

The company maintained that the union's unfair labor practice charges were frivolous. The company had suspended Sally Hong for a terrible and unacceptable absenteeism record; this action was within its management judgment and for sound business reasons. The union's unfair labor practice charges should be dismissed.

QUESTIONS

1. Why is it difficult for the NLRB to establish an employer's true motivation in a case of this type?

2. Should the employer's previous record of unfair labor practices during the union representational campaign be considered as a directly relevant factor in regard to its actions toward Sally Hong? Why, or why not?

3. Was the two months' suspension of Sally Hong for absenteeism a legitimate management/business decision, or discrimination against Hong for union activity and testifying in an NLRB hearing? Discuss.

4. Compare the issues in this case with those in Case 7, "Discharge for Lying, or a Pretext for Terminating a Union Organizer?"

17. Was The Picketing to Protect Jobs, or for Recognition by a "Successor" Employer?

Company:

Don Davis Pontiac, Tonawanda, New York

Union:

United Automobile, Aerospace and Agricultural Implement Workers of America, and Its Amalgamated Local 55 (to be referred to as UAW)

BACKGROUND

The company operated an automobile dealership located on Bailey Avenue in Buffalo, New York, until June 11, 1976. At this location, some 20 service employees were represented by the UAW. The company's collective bargaining agreement with the UAW expired on March 20, 1976, but was renewed on a day-to-day basis during negotiations for a new contract until May 19, 1976. On that day, the company's final contractual offer was rejected by the union negotiators, and the UAW commenced picketing the Bailey Avenue location with signs bearing the legends: "UAW ON STRIKE FOR JUSTICE" and "UAW ON STRIKE FOR EQUITY." A strike followed at midnight, May 19, 1976.

Because of declining business conditions for some months—at least since November 7, 1975—the company had been considering the sale of the Bailey Avenue dealership and the acquisition of another that was acceptable to the Pontiac Motor Division of General Motors Corporation. In April 1976, the company was advised by Pontiac that the Al Ives Pontiac dealership in Tonawanda, New York, would probably be available, and that the company would be considered as a candidate for the purchase of that dealership. Subsequent negotiations between the managements of the Davis and Ives dealerships were substantially completed on May 20, 1976. On the day prior thereto, May 19, 1976, the company notified the UAW by letter that "we are contemplating a decision to terminate our Bailey Avenue shop operations for economic reasons."

As part of the purchase agreement with Ives, and as a condition precedent imposed at the insistence of Ives, the company was required to retain all of the Ives employees, including the unit represented by

Auto Mechanics Lodge 1053 of District 76, International Association of Machinists and Aerospace Workers (IAM), AFL-CIO, and to assume the IAM contract in its entirety. Likewise, the company agreed to purchase the Ives inventory, its equipment, fixed assets, and goodwill, along with assuming all of Ives's liabilities. The IAM had been certified as the exclusive bargaining representative of all service employees at the Ives place of business on October 14, 1975, and a collective bargaining agreement, effective February 4, 1976, continuing until February 4, 1979, was outstanding. Some 16 service employees were in the IAM bargaining unit at this time.

In response to the company's letter of May 19, the UAW advised that there was no purpose in meeting to discuss the situation, as "the closing or termination of your shop operations is solely your decision to make;" but the UAW nevertheless reserved the right to negotiate the effects of that decision.

On June 3, 1976, the company notified the UAW that it had decided to terminate the business effective June 11, 1976, but invited the UAW "to meet and discuss with you the effects of our decision." On June 14, the purchase from Ives was finalized. On the following day, June 15, 1976, the company commenced operations at the Tonawanda location, which was situated about 15 miles from the Bailey Avenue location. Also, the company and the IAM executed an agreement on June 15, 1976, carrying into effect the recognition of the existing labor agreement between Ives and IAM.

The next day, June 16, 1976, pursuant to prior telephone conversations, the company's vice president and its attorney went to the offices of UAW and met with representatives of the Local and International. The UAW was notified that operations had been terminated at the Bailey Avenue location, that the company had acquired the Ives operations on Niagara Falls Boulevard in Tonawanda; and that an agreement had been signed with IAM pursuant to the company's obligation to assume under the buy-sell agreement with Ives. A discussion was held regarding the nature of the closing of Bailey Avenue operations and whether the UAW was going to picket the Niagara Falls Boulevard operation. The UAW requested the company to hire UAW members on a preferential basis. The company attorney said that they would be considered on a nondiscriminatory basis without preferential treatment.

UAW picketing with the same legends on the signs continued at the Bailey Avenue location until June 26, although the company had closed its operations at the end of the day on June 11. On June 21, 1976, the UAW commenced picketing the Tonawanda site, again with the same legends on the signs. On June 28, by letter, the UAW made an offer to return to work at the Tonawanda facility.

The letter of June 28 stated in part:

> The Union is terminating the strike and all striking employees are ready and willing to return to work unconditionally on Tuesday morning at 8:00 A.M., June 29, 1976.

No picketing took place on June 29; but in response to the company's denial of the union offer, picketing was resumed on June 30 with picket signs carrying the legend: LOCAL 55 PROTESTS THE REFUSAL OF DAVIS PONTIAC, INC., TO REEMPLOY ITS MEMBERS.

Picketing continued until July 19, when the regional office of the NLRB requested a U.S. District Court to issue a preliminary injunction against the UAW's picketing at the Tonawanda premises.

This injunction was issued in response to company charges of unfair labor practices filed against the UAW, as well as the UAW's unfair labor practice charges against the company.

THE UNFAIR LABOR PRACTICE CHARGES

On June 30, 1976, the company filed unfair labor practice charges against the union, which specified in part:

> Since on or about June 21, 1976, and continuously thereafter, it, a labor organization, by its officers, agents, and representatives, has picketed Al Ives Pontiac (now Don Davis Pontiac, Inc.) at its premises at 2277 Niagara Falls Boulevard, Town of Tonawanda, New York, with an object of forcing or requiring Don Davis Pontiac, Inc., to recognize or bargain with United Automobile, Aerospace and Agricultural Implement Workers of America, and its Amalgamated Local 55, as the representative of his employees notwithstanding that District No. 76, International Association of Machinists and Aerospace Workers, AFL-CIO, has been certified on October 14, 1975, and a question concerning representation may not appropriately be raised under Section 9(c) of the Act.

The company requested that the UAW be ordered to cease and desist from its picketing and in its efforts to force the company to recognize and negotiate with the UAW.

On July 6, 1976, the UAW filed a petition for certification and unfair labor practice charges against the company. The charges against the company were actually signed by the union business agent on June 28, 1976, but not filed until the date noted above. The union claimed that the company had violated Sections 8(a) (1), 8(a) (2), 8(a) (3), and 8(a) (5) of the LMRA. Specifically, the UAW claimed:

> a. Since on or about May 19, 1976, the employer by its officers, agents, and representatives has dominated and assisted the formation among

its employees of a labor organization known as Auto Mechanics Lodge 1053, AFL-CIO, and, at all times since that date, has interfered with the operation and administration of the charging party.

b. Since on or about June 29, 1976, the employer, by its officers, agents, and representatives has terminated the employment of all of the members of the bargaining unit represented by the charging party by refusing the unconditional offer of each such employee to return to work and by unlawfully recognizing another labor organization to represent employees in the appropriate bargaining unit represented by the charging party because of the membership and activities of said employees on behalf of the charging party.

c. Since on or about May 1, 1976, and at all times thereafter, the employer by its officers, agents, and representatives has refused to bargain collectively with the charging party, a labor organization chosen by a majority of its employees in an appropriate unit for the purpose of collective bargaining in regard to rates of pay, wages, and other conditions of employment.

The UAW requested the NLRB to certify the UAW as the appropriate bargaining unit representative, to order the company to cease and desist in recognizing a unit of IAM employees, to bargain with the UAW, to reinstate all UAW employees to their former positions, and to make them whole for any lost pay and benefits.

POSITION OF THE COMPANY

The company argued that the sole purpose of the UAW picketing at its Tonawanda facility was to force the company to recognize and bargain with the UAW, when the company as a successor employer agreed to recognize an existing bargaining unit and labor agreement with the IAM. The union's picketing was in direct violation of Section 8(b) (7) (A) of the Act, which states:

(b) It shall be an unfair labor practice for a labor organization or its agents—

(7) to picket or cause to be picketed, or threaten to picket or cause to be picketed, any employer where an object thereof is forcing or requiring an employer to recognize or bargain with a labor organization as the representative of his employees, or forcing or requiring the employees of an employer to accept or select such labor organization as their collective bargaining representative, unless such labor organization is currently certified as the representative of such employees:

(A) where the employer has lawfully recognized in accordance with this Act any other labor organization and a question concerning representation may not appropriately be raised.

The company pointed out that it is settled labor law that a successor employer may be obligated to recognize and bargain with a duly certified representative of a predecessor owner's employees.[1] The UAW collective bargaining agreement with the company, which expired March 20, 1976, contained a successor clause that provided for the sale of the business, notice to UAW, and potential assumption by a purchaser of the bargaining agreement. The buy-sell agreement of May 20, 1976, between Don Davis Pontiac and Al Ives Pontiac, Inc., contained an express clause as follows: "Buyer shall, on the date of closing, assume all obligations of Seller, as of that date, under Seller's contract, dated February 4, 1976, with the Auto Mechanics Lodge Local 1053, International Association of Machinists and Aerospace Workers."

Don Davis Pontiac, when it acquired Ives, became in fact and law a successor to Ives. This was not a mere relocation but was, in fact, a successorship. The company took over the Ives operation; it sold the same kind of automobiles; new franchise agreements were executed; the Ives inventory parts and equipment were acquired and used by the company; and all employees (except officers) of the Bailey Avenue former operations were terminated as of the close of business on June 11, 1976.

The company requested that the unfair labor practice charges filed against it by the UAW should be dismissed; that the UAW should be found in violation of Section 8(b) (7) (A) of the Act; and the UAW should be permanently ordered to cease and desist in its picketing of company facilities.

POSITION OF THE UNION

The UAW argued that it was the company, not the union, that had violated the Act. The union's picketing of the company's facilities at Tonawanda was legitimate and protected activity, since the union was engaged in efforts to protect the job rights of its members.

In testimony, the union business representative for Local 55, UAW, pointed out that even after the company notified the UAW that it had terminated the Bailey Avenue operations, he caused the pickets to be moved to Tonawanda; and that he was still concerned with negotiating a contract for the company's employees who formerly worked at the Bailey Avenue site.

Counsel for the UAW claimed as follows: "The employer, it is our contention, had a bargaining agent; it was us. When they relocated, they still had a bargaining agent, and therefore could not recognize the

---

[1] See *NLRB v. Burns International Security Services,* 406 U.S. 272, 89 LRRM 2225, 1972.

other bargaining agent for the employees on Niagara Falls Boulevard. Our picketing was engaged in because (a) the employer failed to negotiate with us regarding the relocation, which he had an obligation to do; and (b) he relocated and recognized another bargaining agent in violation of our members' rights. So in essence, we became unfair labor picketers because at this time what the employer did was wrong and illegal; they recognized another union at a time that valid questions concerning representation existed."

In support of its arguments, the union claimed that Don Davis Pontiac was not really a successor employer to Al Ives Pontiac. The company had used the purchase device simply to "relocate its operations." This was evidenced by the fact that the company transferred considerable equipment from its Bailey Avenue location to the Tonawanda location and the officers and management of the firm did not change. Therefore, the union did not violate Section 8(b) (7) (A) of the Act by picketing at Tonawanda, since the UAW had a legitimate and legally protected right to try to preserve jobs that rightfully belonged to the Bailey Avenue employees. The only means available to the union to achieve this result was through picketing Davis at Tonawanda. Since the object of the UAW's picketing after June 16 was job preservation, the picketing at Tonawanda therefore did not violate Section 8(b) (7) (A), and the company's unfair labor practice charges against the union should be dismissed.

The union urged that its unfair labor practice charges against the company should be upheld by the NLRB, and that the company should be ordered by the Board to bargain with the UAW and to reinstate and make whole all UAW employees as appropriate.

QUESTIONS

1. What is meant by a "successor" employer in labor relations? What criteria are appropriate in order for the Board to determine whether an employer is a successor employer, or simply a former company that has relocated its prior operations?

2. Were the actions of the UAW primarily to protect jobs, or to force the company to recognize the UAW at the new location?

3. Did the company properly follow bargaining procedures with the union, or did it fail to bargain in good faith when it made its decision to purchase the new dealership?

4. What should be the appropriate disposition and remedies, if any, for the various charges and countercharges of unfair labor practices filed by the company and the union?

18. The Union's Refusal to Furnish its Membership Lists

Employers:

Apple City Electric, Inc.; J&M Electric, Inc.; and Valley Electric Service of Wenatchee, Inc.; all of Wenatchee, Washingtron.

Union:

Local Union No. 497, International Brotherhood of Electrical Workers

BACKGROUND

The three employers in this case had been signatories, as part of their membership in the National Electrical Contractors Association (NECA), to a two-year area-wide contract with the union that was to expire in June, 1984. In early 1984, the employers decided that they no longer would be part of the NECA area-wide contract. The three employers each informed NECA and the union that they would bargain for a new contract on a separate basis. On March 31, 1984, the employers notified the union of their intent to amend or terminate the expiring contract. Between April 25 and July 17, 1984, the parties met six times in efforts to negotiate a successor agreement. An attorney, Allen Rich,[1] jointly represented the three employers during the negotiations.

At the first bargaining session on April 25, Rich informed the union that the employers wanted a number of changes in the employee referral system. The expiring NECA contract contained provisions that required the employers to use the union's hiring hall as the exclusive source of applicants for employment. Rich said that the employers had experienced problems with the qualifications of certain employees referred by the union; the employers also were dissatisfied with a 48-hour provision for filling referral requests, which had caused delays in meeting their employment needs. The parties discussed a number of possible alternatives, but they did not reach any agreement on these issues.

During a bargaining session held on May 19, 1984, attorney Allen Rich made an oral request for a list of the names and addresses of all of the union members who were subject to the referral system under the

---

[1] The names of all individuals have been disguised.

then-existing NECA contract. The union refused to furnish this information. The chief spokesman for the union, Business Representative Carl Georgio, told Rich that the union's referral books could be provided for visual inspection, but they could not be copied by any of the employers. Georgio also told Rich that he (Rich) would not be permitted to see the referral books. On May 24, 1984, Rich made a written request for this information; the union again rejected this request. In his response, Georgio stated that the union had a policy of refusing to release any information about any of its members unless the particular members signed a release, or if there was a court order directing the union to furnish such information. Further, the union allowed only its own members to inspect the lists of known members and their addresses, but it did not allow any members to copy the membership lists.

Shortly thereafter, the employers jointly filed charges with the NLRB, claiming that by refusing to provide the requested information, the union was not bargaining collectively in good faith as required by Section 8(b) (3) of the Labor Management Relations Act and as is further defined within Section 8(d) of the Act.

POSITION OF THE EMPLOYERS

Counsel for the employers argued that the membership lists sought by the employers were clearly relevant to collective bargaining and should be furnished by the union at the request of the employers. The employers needed to have this information regarding the referral system for contract negotiations, since it was very relevant to the employers' concerns about union applicants' qualifications and was also related to problems with the previous contract's 48-hour provision for filling employment needs, which the employers wished to change.

Two previous NLRB cases were cited in support of the employers' position. In both of these cases, the NLRB had found that the unions had violated Section 8(b) (3) of LMRA by refusing to provide lists of their members who were covered under union hiring hall contractual provisions.[2] In both of these cases, the Board concluded that such information was "relevant and necessary to the collective bargaining process."

Concerning the union's claim that the requested information was "confidential" and would invade the union members' right to privacy, counsel for the employers argued that this claim was without any

---

[2] These cases were Asbestos Workers Local 80 (West Virginia Insulators), 248 NLRB 143, 103 LRRM 1370 (1980); and Printing & Graphic Communications Local 13 (Oakland Press Co.), 233 NLRB 994, 97 LRRM 1047 (1977).

merit. There was nothing in the employers' request or in the past conduct of the employers to suggest that the employers would use the referral lists to harass or discriminate against any union members.

Finally, it was not a sufficient response for the union just to offer the employers an opportunity to view the referral lists while denying their chief negotiator, Mr. Rich, any such opportunity. Rather, it was necessary for the employers' chief negotiator to have a copy of the referral lists in order to have time and sufficient information at hand for carrying out his role on behalf of the employer group.

The employers urged that the union should be found in violation of the Act, and that the union should be ordered to provide the requested information, which was germane to the collective bargaining process.

POSITION OF THE UNION

The union argued that any compelled disclosure of its membership lists would infringe upon the members' First Amendment rights under the Constitution. The union further contended that release of such information was precluded by the Landrum-Griffin Act,[3] which was carefully drafted to preserve the confidentiality of union membership lists by giving members themselves only a limited right to inspect such lists.

In this regard, the union cited a prior court case in which the court had been reluctant to allow even the United States Secretary of Labor to possess a copy of the union's membership lists in the absense of assurances that the lists would not be available to outsiders.[4]

The union claimed that the two previous NLRB cases cited by the employers had not considered the confidentiality and First Amendment issues, and therefore they were not applicable to this case.

Finally, the union contended that its offer to supply the requested information by allowing the employers to see the referral books was sufficient to meet its bargaining obligations under LMRA. There is nothing in the Act or in NLRB case law that requires either party to provide information in exactly the manner requested or demanded by the other side. The union offered to permit the employers to see the union's referral lists, and this inspection should have satisfied whatever needs the employers had for collective bargaining purposes. The employers' unfair labor practice charges of "bad faith" bargaining were groundless, and these charges should be dismissed by the Board.

---

[3] This is also known as the Labor-Management Reporting and Disclosure Act of 1959.

[4] Teamsters v. Goldberg, 303 F.2d 402, 49 LRRM 2968 (DC. Cir, 1962).

QUESTIONS

1. Evaluate the employer's reasons for requesting the union's membership lists.

2. Evaluate the union's reasons for refusing to permit the employers' chief negotiator to see the membership lists and also for refusing any copying of the lists by the employers themselves.

3. Should the union's First Amendment and Landrum-Griffin law arguments be considered by the NLRB in this case? Why, or why not?

4. Was the union in violation of Sections 8(b) (3) and 8(d) of the Labor Management Relations Act? Why, or why not?

19. Was the Company's Benefit Offer an Unfair Labor Practice?

Company:
   Mountaineer Excavating Company, Inc., Big Stone Gap, Virginia
Union:
   United Mine Workers (UMW), District 28

BACKGROUND

The company commenced its coal mining operations in July 1977. On July 6, 1977, the company and the union entered into a collective bargaining agreement in which the company recognized the union as the representative of its employees and agreed to be bound by the terms of the National Bituminous Coal Agreement of 1974, effective December 6, 1974, to December 6, 1977. However, the company itself did not become a member of the Bituminous Coal Operators Association (BCOA).

On July 28, 1977, the international union, acting on behalf of District 28, notified the company of the union's intention to terminate the agreement and indicated it was prepared to meet and confer with company representatives for the purpose of negotiating a new agreement and to engage in good-faith collective bargaining. On September 26, 1977, the company wrote the international union, indicating that it also desired to terminate the contract and requested that a representative of District 28 contact it when it was ready to begin negotiations on a new agreement. There were no further communications between the parties until December 1, 1977.

On December 1, 1977, Bert Colby,[1] the company president, wrote Roger Mateo, president of District 28, noting the earlier communications and commenting that the company had not heard from anyone in the union regarding the company's request to begin bargaining. Colby further noted that from the newspapers, it appeared that there would be a strike after December 6 because of the failure of the union and BCOA to reach an agreement covering the BCOA members, but that the company was not a member of BCOA. In his letter, Colby asserted that the company was not obligated to sign any agreement entered into

---

[1] The names of all individuals have been disguised.

with BCOA, and that it was willing to negotiate with the union for a new agreement between it and the union. Colby went on to state:

> If there is a strike called December 6, we understand that the health care insurance benefits under the present contract will be cut off for our miners and their families due to lack of funds. If this happens it is our intention to provide our men with a new life and health care insurance policy. We also want to negotiate a better pension plan for our men.
>
> We will be happy to answer any questions you may have about our proposed insurance and pension benefits we would like to give our men and their families. We will be happy to negotiate with you on these and other proposals at your earliest convenience.

During the evening of December 1, a previously scheduled dinner meeting of management and the employees was held. Most of the employees attended the meeting. During the course of the meeting, copies of Bert Colby's speech were distributed to the employees. Following his speech, Norris Anderhub, the company's business manager and secretary, presented the proposed health and pension plan referred to by Bert Colby in his speech. According to the printed version of the speech, Colby told the employees:

> And the worst part of it all, according to UMW officials, it looks like your hospital care may not be any good after the strike begins. From what I can read and hear, the union is saying that your health and welfare fund is almost bankrupt and they may not pay any benefits at all during the strike. If the miners walk out December 6, medical benefits will be cut off immediately.
>
> They say that pension payments could be cut from the first week in January.
>
> As you know, since the health and welfare and pension funds are financed and paid for by coal companies royalty payments, if there is no coal being produced, there will be no royalties paid into the funds during the strike. A long strike will completely bankrupt every UMW health and welfare and pension fund for future benefits.
>
> For those miners who do not work during the strike, the $100 weekly sickness and accident benefit could be lost to them. Under the law, the coal operators are not required to continue paying the insurance premiums for the $100 weekly sickness and accident benefit.
>
> We intend to keep paying this premium for every man who continues to work for us during the strike.
>
> What about your hospital and doctor bills for yourself and your family? What are you going to do about it? Unless you have enough money saved to pay these bills, they may not give you any services at the clinics except for cash.
>
> We have thought a lot about this serious problem for you and your family. We have contacted several insurance companies that provide good health care benefits for employees and their families.
>
> We have come up with what we consider to be one of the best health

care insurance programs. The beauty of this plan is that the hospital benefits are *guaranteed* to you and your family when you need them during the strike.

If your hospital and medical benefits are cut off next Wednesday, we intend to cover all of our men who continue working under this new hospital insurance plan for Mountaineer.

What will it cost you? Absolutely nothing.

On December 5, 1977, Bert Colby met with the employees at the work site. Since the contract was due to expire the next day and the UMW had called a strike for December 6, he asked the employees for a show of hands as to who would not work the next day. None of the employees raised their hands, so Colby then told them their jobs would be available. During this same meeting, employee Wally Banks handed Colby a petition signed by 10 of the 13 employees that they wished to withdraw from the UMW. Banks told Colby that he had begun circulating this petition several weeks prior to December 1, 1977. Colby had been unaware of this petition prior to his receiving it.

On December 6, 1977, the UMW commenced a nationwide strike against the BCOA, which was ultimately settled on March 27, 1978, when the UMW ratified a new contract. On December 6, the company put into effect its new hospitalization and pension plans. Approximately two weeks later, Colby granted his employees a week's vacation during the Christmas period.

On January 3, 1978, District 28 of the UMW filed unfair labor practice charges, alleging that since on or about December 6, 1977, the company had interfered with, restrained, and coerced its employees in violation of Section 8(a) (1) of the Act. Further, by unilaterally granting employees sickness, accident, and vacation benefits without negotiating these matters with the union, the company had violated Section 8(a) (5) of the Act.

Subsequently, on January 31, 1978, Drew Milliken, president of UMW District 28, wrote the company to report the unfair labor practice charges and stated that the UMW was and had been ready and willing to engage in good-faith negotiations, and offered to begin negotiations with the company. There were no further communications between the company and representatives of the UMW until March 1978, when the regional office of the Board met with the company and union representatives concerning the unfair labor practice charges.

POSITION OF THE UNION

The union claimed that the company had illegally and unilaterally approached its employees and had offered them substantial benefits without notice to or bargaining with the union at a time when the union was the bargaining representative of the employees and the union's collective bargaining agreement with the company was still in effect. Such conduct was nothing more than an attempt to bargain individually with the employees in order to discourage the employees from participating in the impending strike and to cause the union to lose its majority status.

According to the union, if the company really had been desirous of entering into negotiations with the UMW, it needed only to direct timely communications to the union requesting dates for negotiating sessions or making specific proposals to the union. The company was obligated to do either or both, but it did neither. Rather, the company played a waiting game until the bargaining at the national level reached a crisis stage, and then sent the December 1 letter to the union requesting negotiations. On that very same evening, the company met with employees, predicted dire economic circumstances, and offered them substantial economic benefits designed to induce them to abandon the union and bargain directly with the company. The union claimed that the company obviously timed the December 1 letter so as to preclude any possibility of the union's consulting with the employees, or any real or meaningful consideration by the union of the company's plan to institute certain benefits as of December 6. On December 5, the company again unilaterally offered its employees substantial economic benefits when it inquired of the employees as to whether any of them were going to strike the next day and advised them that their jobs would be available. Having precluded any meaningful response by the union by virtue of the timing of its action, the company then took the final step on December 6 by unilaterally putting into effect both the hospitalization plan and the pension plan.

The union urged that the company be found in violation of Sections 8(a) (1) and 8(a) (5) of the LMRA, that the company be ordered to cease and desist in its unfair labor practices, and that the company be further ordered to recognize and bargain in good faith with the union concerning the terms and conditions of a new collective bargaining agreement.

POSITION OF THE COMPANY

The company contended that it did not violate the Act in any way.

First of all, the company claimed that it had fulfilled its legal obligations to bargain with the union by its offers to meet with the union, which were made on September 26, 1977, and December 1, 1977. The union did not respond to either of the company's offers to negotiate. Section 8(d) of the Act imposes a "mutual obligation" upon both parties to meet and confer at reasonable times in regard to entering into a new collective bargaining agreement. It was the union, not the company, that failed in its obligation to bargain with the company. The union's offer of January 31, 1978, to begin negotiations with the company was untimely, since the previous contract had expired and the union already had filed unfair labor practice charges against the company.

Second, the company contended that after December 6, 1977, the company was free to implement whatever changes it wished, since the contractual agreement with the union had expired. The company was not a party to the BCOA negotiations, and the company was not obligated to be bound to the terms of any BCOA agreement negotiated after December 6, 1977. Since the contract had expired, and since the union had failed to respond to the company's initiatives for contract negotiations, the company was free to change the employee benefits in any way the company wanted.

Finally, the company contended that the union had lost its majority status among the employees. On their own initiative, 10 of 13 employees had signed a petition given to company management on December 5, 1977, indicating they wished to withdraw from the UMW. Thus, when the contract expired on the following day, the UMW no longer had a majority representative status among company employees, and it would have been improper for the company to recognize and negotiate with the UMW, even if the UMW had been willing to negotiate at that time.

The company claimed that the union had filed the unfair labor practice charges in an effort to offset the union's own failures to bargain in good faith, and as a pretext to regain bargaining representative status that the union had lost. The company urged that the unfair labor practice charges should be dismissed.

QUESTIONS

1. Evaluate both the company and the union arguments in regard to the unfair labor practice charges.

2. Discuss the company's position that it was the union, not the company, that had failed to meet the "mutual obligations" requirements of Section 8(d) of LMRA.

3. Did the fact that the previous contract had expired give the company the right to institute the new benefit and vacation programs? Why, or why not?

4. Is the company required to accept provisions of the new BCOA agreement since the company previously had been subject to the old agreement?

20. The Refusal to Sign and Abide by a Labor Contract

Company:

Maintenance Service Corporation, West Allis, Wisconsin

Union:

International Association of Machinists and Aerospace Workers, District No. 10

BACKGROUND

The company and the union had been parties to a series of collective bargaining agreements since 1973. The bargaining unit consisted of the company's production and maintenance employees and truckdrivers.

On February 28, 1980, the parties signed a labor agreement that was to expire on December 31, 1982. Also on February 28, 1980, the parties signed a separate "side-bar" letter,[1] which provided:

> The Company will not employ an additional number of foremen, so as to increase the number of foremen in the work force, through December 31, 1982. In the event of layoff of any bargaining unit employee, no foreman shall perform bargaining unit work. In the event that the shop is not working overtime, foremen shall not perform bargaining unit work.

The 1980–82 collective-bargaining agreement was extended until noon on February 25, 1983. On that date, the employees went on strike; during the strike, seven supervisors performed bargaining unit work. On June 16, 1983, the company sent a letter to the employees threatening to hire permanent replacements on June 27 if the employees failed to return to work by that date.

On June 22, 1982, Colin Moore,[2] the company president, and Duane Ling, the union's assistant director, met for the purpose of negotiating a new collective bargaining agreement and a strike settlement agreement. Moore commented that foremen had been performing bargaining unit work during the strike, and he indicated that the company intended that foremen would continue to do so afterwards. Ling said that he hoped the problem would disappear, since the prac-

---

[1] This type of letter is sometimes referred to as a "memorandum of understanding," and it may or may not be included as an appendix to a labor agreement.

[2] The names of all individuals are disguised.

148

tice violated the union's constitution. Neither man mentioned the "side-bar" letter.

On June 25, 1983, the parties met again and reached a tentative contract and strike settlement agreement. Neither agreement referred to the issue of foremen performing bargaining unit work or to the "side-bar" letter. On June 28, 1983, the union membership ratified the tentative contract.

On July 6, 1983, Colin Moore mailed the text of the tentative agreement to the union for review and signature. Upon receipt, Duane Ling called Moore and told him that the contract looked fine except that the "side-bar" letter was not included. Moore responded that he knew nothing about a "side-bar" agreement. Ling offered to send Moore a copy of the letter, which Moore claimed he had never seen before.

When Colin Moore received the copy of the "side-bar" letter, he discovered that it had been negotiated and signed by his father, Elton T. Moore, on February 28, 1980. The senior Mr. Moore had been president of the company at that time, and it was in June of 1981 that Elton Moore had retired and Colin Moore had become company president.

After reviewing the "side-bar" letter, Colin Moore decided not to agree to it, and he informed the union by letter of this decision. The union, by a telephone call from Duane Ling, informed the company that it would not sign the tentative contract reached June 25, 1983, because there was no agreement with respect to supervisors' not performing bargaining unit work.

In mid-July, Ling called Moore in an attempt to resolve the problem. Ling suggested that the union would sign the contract without the "side-bar" if the company would pay medical insurance for six months for employees who were still on layoff after the strike. No agreement was reached.

Because of vacation and other commitments, it was not until September 7, 1983, that Moore and Ling again met to discuss the unresolved contract matter. At this meeting, Moore stated that the company's position was that the parties had negotiated a contract with no restrictions on the amount of bargaining unit work that foremen might perform. Ling then proposed changing the dates in the "side-bar" agreement to make it effective September 30, 1983. Moore did not agree to this proposal.

On September 21, the parties met again, and Moore reiterated that he had no intention of signing the "side-bar" agreement, but he was prepared to sign the contract as negotiated with no restrictions. The parties discussed alternatives, such as restricting the amount of work a foreman could do to two or four hours a day. Moore asked if the foremen could join the union, but the union representative responded that they could not. The meeting ended with no resolution.

Shortly thereafter, each party filed unfair labor practice charges against the other alleging "refusal-to-bargain" violations of the Labor Management Relations Act. The union claimed that the company had violated Sections 8(a) (1) and 8(a) (5), as related to Section 8(d) of the Act; the company claimed that the union had violated Section 8(b) (3), also as related to Section 8(d).

After investigation, on October 19, 1983, the Regional Director of the NLRB dismissed all of these unfair labor practice charges. The Regional Director found that there had been "no meeting of the minds" on the "side-bar" letter or on the subject of foremen doing bargaining unit work. The Regional Director observed that although there was no reference to the "side-bar" letter during the negotiations leading to the June 25, 1983, tentative agreement, the union had contended that language in the strike settlement stating that "all of the items in the tentative agreement, as well as the expired labor agreement as modified, shall constitute the new agreement," was intended to include the "side-bar" letter. On the other hand, the Regional Director also noted the company's position that the "side-bar" letter was a separate document that did not modify the prior contract. The Regional Director therefore concluded he was unable to find that a collective bargaining agreement had existed between the company and union. He further directed that the parties should resume bargaining in order to resolve their dispute.

On January 3, 1984, the parties met again. Colin Moore and Andrew Burback, the company's attorney, represented the company. Charles Pickett, the union's director; Travis Unger, the union's business representative; and Alan Grier, the union's local attorney, represented the union. Colin Moore asserted that the parties had a past practice of foremen working, and the company would be willing to sign the contract with that understanding. Alan Grier replied that when the "side-bar" letter was signed, the past practice was broken. Grier then said, however, that the union would sign the contract "as is" and "take it on a case-by-case basis if a foreman did any great amount of work." Colin Moore eventually stated that he wanted a written agreement on how working foremen would be treated, because he was puzzled by the union's position regarding past practice. The company representatives stated at the end of the meeting that they would respond further by letter.

On January 4, 1984, Andrew Burback, the company attorney, wrote a letter to the union, which included the following:

> At the conclusion of our meeting yesterday, I stated that the Company would attempt to develop language concerning the issue of foremen performing bargaining unit work. As I understand the Union's position,

it does not object to foremen performing bargaining unit work unless the Company uses foremen to prevent laid-off bargaining unit employees from being recalled on a regular full-time basis. Based on our discussion, it appears that the Union has no objection to the work which is presently being performed by the foremen; this matter became an issue only after the strike, and, then, only for a short period of time.

Accordingly, in order to settle this issue and the parties' collective bargaining agreement, the Company proposes that the following be added to the contract as Article II, Section 2:

Foremen may perform work normally performed by bargaining unit employees except that, in the event of a layoff of a bargaining unit employee from a seniority list, each foreman may perform work normally performed by employees within that seniority list if such work performed by each individual foreman is less than 40 hours per week."

By a letter of January 11, 1984, Travis Unger replied for the union as follows:

Please be advised that the Union is in complete disagreement with your letter and language, dated January 4, 1984. The Union is willing to sit down and sign the contract as soon as the Company is ready.

It is the Union's understanding, as explained to the Company, that supervisors working doing bargaining unit work will not be tolerated while employees are on layoff. With that understanding the Union will sign the contract. Any cases of supervisors working will be taken on a one-to-one basis in the grievance procedure.

By a letter dated January 13, 1984, Andrew Burback replied for the company as follows:

Maintenance Service Corporation cannot sign the agreement under the conditions you have suggested in your letter of January 11, 1984, particularly in view of your comment that you are in 'complete disagreement' with our letter of January 4, 1984. In view of the comments made by the Union during our meeting of January 3, which comments I attempted to summarize in my letter, I am at a loss to explain why you are in 'complete disagreement.' It would be helpful to the progress of our negotiations if you would provide an explanation.

Burback also proposed scheduling another bargaining session and suggested that a Federal mediator be appointed.

By a letter dated January 16, 1984, Travis Unger replied for the union, stating:

In response to your most recent January 13, 1984, letter, it is the Union's position that they are willing to sign the contract without language pertaining to supervisors doing bargaining unit work. If there is no one laid off from that seniority list, or to deprive any employee of any overtime, that might be a different situation.

If this meets your approval, please contact my office and set up a date for signing.

On February 6, 1984, the union filed new refusal-to-bargain charges with the NLRB against the company, alleging that since on or about January 3, 1984, the company had refused to sign the June 25, 1983, agreement, and had made unilateral changes by ceasing dues deductions, refusing to put a wage increase into effect, and eliminating the grievance procedure. The union claimed that these actions constituted violations of Sections 8(a) (5) and 8(a) (1) of the Act, and the union urged a cease and desist order be directed at the company.

On February 28, 1984, Colin Moore wrote a letter to the union, requesting a meeting and stating that the "working foreman language of our letter of January 4, 1984 is negotiable within the general framework."

On March 6, 1984, Travis Unger sent the following letter to Colin Moore:

> Be advised that the Union will sign the contract as negotiated and ratified, without any conditions.
>
> Please contact my office at your very earliest convenience to set up a date to sign the agreement.

In response to the union's latest letter, Colin Moore wrote a letter to the union dated March 9, 1984, requesting a meeting and asking the following questions:

> 1. If the contract is signed, what is the Union's position as to foremen performing bargaining unit work?
> 2. If the contract is signed, will it be retroactive, particularly with respect to working foremen?
> 3. If the contract is signed, will the Union dispute or file a grievance concerning the work presently being performed by the foremen?
> 4. If the contract is signed, will the Union dispute or file a grievance concerning the work performed by the foremen after the strike?

The union did not respond to this March 9, 1984, letter, which led Colin Moore to write another letter dated March 28, 1984, which included the following:

> In your letter of March 6, 1984, you stated that the Union will sign the agreement "without any conditions." While I would much rather discuss face to face what "without any conditions" means, in the absence of a meeting or a written response from the Union to my March 9 letter, and based upon your representation that the Union will sign "without any conditions," the Company proposes that the parties sign the agreement with the understanding that (1) the agreement does not cover the issue of foremen performing bargaining unit work and (2) there are no other conditions which restrict the Company's right to assign foremen to bargaining unit work.

On April 6, 1984, Travis Unger sent copies of the June 25, 1983, negotiated agreement to Colin Moore and requested by an attached letter that Moore sign the agreement copies.

However, on April 12, 1984, Colin Moore replied by letter to Unger that he would not sign the June 25, 1983, agreement because of the unresolved issues. In his letter, Moore again raised essentially the same questions about the union's position that he had posed in his March 9 letter. Moore inquired whether the union agreed that the tentative contract, if signed, did not cover foremen performing bargaining unit work and that there were no other restrictions on the company's right to assign foremen such work.

By letter dated April 30, 1984, Duane Ling responded that, "The Union's answer is no."

On May 15, 1984, Moore called Ling in response to the union's April 30 letter. Moore asked Ling, "Assuming I sign the contract today or tomorrow, what would happen regarding the working foremen issue?" Ling responded that he did not know, and he could not give him an answer one way or another.

The labor agreement remained unsigned as the NLRB investigated the unfair labor practice charges that had been filed by the union.

POSITION OF THE UNION

The union primarily claimed that as of January 3, 1984, the union had accepted the company's contract offer, which previously had been agreed upon by the parties as of June 25, 1983. This contract offer had never been withdrawn by the company. At the meeting of January 3, 1984, the union indicated that it would accept the terms of the contract "as is," and without the "side-bar" letter. However, the company refused to agree to this and abide by the new contract; further, the company continued to insist upon additional contract language or commitments from the union to the effect that the union would never raise the issue of foremen doing bargaining unit work under the new contract. This the union refused to do.

The union argued strongly that there had been a standing, viable contract offer since June 25, 1983, which the union agreed to accept as of January 3, 1984. The company's refusal at that time and thereafter to agree and abide by it was clearly bad-faith bargaining that violated Sections 8(a) (5) and 8(a) (1) of the Act as these are related to Section 8(d). The union urged that the company should be directed to sign and implement the terms and conditions of the new contract, and that employees should be made whole as appropriate for any lost wages and benefits that might have been denied them since January 3, 1984, because of the company's violations of the Act.

Alternatively, the union argued that if there was some question concerning whether the January 3, 1984, meeting constituted a firm understanding of the union's acceptance of the contractual offer, then March 6, 1984, and thereafter should be considered as the period of the company's unfair labor practices. On March 6, 1984, the union, by letter, accepted the contract offer without conditions. All of the union's arguments were applicable in regard to this date and in regard to the union's requested remedies.

POSITION OF THE COMPANY

The Company asserted that throughout the periods in contention, the company had bargained in good faith with the union and had not violated the LMRA. According to the company, there was no agreement at any time between the company and the union over the issue of foremen performing bargaining unit work. The company pointed out that the union first raised the issue of the "side-bar" letter on July 6, 1983, after the June 25, 1983, tentative agreement had been reached; the union declined to sign the contract because there was no agreement regarding supervisors' performing bargaining unit work. Subsequent negotiations between the parties in September produced no common understanding on the issue. The Regional Director of the NLRB dismissed each party's unfair labor practice charges in October of 1983, recognizing the parties' failure to agree.

Similarly, the company maintained that there was no agreement between the parties over this same issue during the January 3, 1984, meeting, or during any of the subsequent communications and correspondence between the parties including the union's March 6, 1984, letter. Just because the union offered at these times to sign a contract did not mean that the company had to sign such a contract when there was still a substantive issue over which there was no agreement. The company was not obligated to sign a contract that contained only the matters upon which the company and union had agreed, while a major issue remained unresolved.

The company urged that the unfair labor practice charges filed by the union should be dismissed.

QUESTIONS

1. Was the company in violation of LMRA after the meeting of January 3, 1984? Why, or why not?
2. Was the company in violation of LMRA following the union's offer by letter of March 6, 1984? Why, or why not?

3. Does the dismissal by the NLRB, in October 1983, of the previous unfair labor practice charges filed by both parties have any bearing upon the positions of the parties in 1984? Discuss.

4. Discuss why "side-bar" letters and other such agreements that are not included in the labor contract can become difficult obstacles in the ongoing relationships between a company and a union.

21. Must the Union Notify the State Department of Human Resources?

Company:
Wilhow Corporation operating Town & Country Supermarkets,
Baxter Springs, Kansas

Union:
Retail Store Employees, Local 322

BACKGROUND

Wilhow Corporation owned and operated Town & Country Supermarkets as a Kansas corporation engaged in retail sale and distribution of groceries and related products at various facilities, including one in Baxter Springs, Kansas. The company's annual gross volume of business in the state of Kansas in 1977 exceeded $500,000, and it purchased directly from points outside the state of Kansas goods, products, and materials valued in excess of $10,000 for use in its Kansas facilities. Retail Store Employees, Local 322 represented certain employees in an appropriate bargaining unit.

The company and union had negotiated several prior collective bargaining agreements, the most recent of which was to expire on August 3, 1977. On May 4, 1977, the union sent a notice to the company indicating that it sought to negotiate modifications and changes in the collective bargaining agreement. Notice on an appropriate form was simultaneously sent to the FMCS, but no notice of any type was sent to any agency of the state of Kansas concerning this matter.

Following the May notice, representatives of the union and the company met on five occasions to negotiate a new collective bargaining agreement. The parties were unable to reach final agreement, and on August 12, 1977, the union struck the company.

Shortly thereafter, the company filed unfair labor practice charges against the union, charging that the union had violated Section 8(b) (3) of the LMRA because it had failed to give notice to an appropriate state mediation agency as required by Section 8(d) (3) of the Act.

After receipt of these charges, the union on August 24, 1977, did notify the Kansas Department of Human Resources concerning the labor dispute and strike. But the union claimed that this was not a state agency to which a Section 8(d) (3) notice was required under the Act.

POSITION OF THE COMPANY

The company claimed that the Kansas Department of Human Resources was a state mediation agency within the meaning of Section 8(d) (3) of the Act. By failing to give it notice before engaging in a strike, the union committed an unfair labor practice within the meaning of Section 8(b) (3) of the Act.

It was factually stipulated that in 1976 the Kansas state legislature reorganized the government and created cabinet departments. Certain functions formerly performed by a State Labor Commissioner were transferred by statute to the Department of Human Resources. The statute that was material to the issue involved here read as follows:

> K.S.A. 44-817. Mediators; appointments; functions; compensation. The secretary of human resources shall have the power to appoint any competent, impartial, disinterested person to act as mediator in any labor dispute either upon his own initiative or upon the request of one of the parties to the dispute. It shall be the function of such mediator to bring the parties together voluntarily under such favorable auspices as will tend to effectuate settlement of the dispute, but neither the mediator nor the secretary of human resources shall have the power of compulsion in mediation proceedings. The secretary of human resources shall provide necessary expenses for such mediators as may be appointed under reasonable compensation not exceeding fifty dollars ($50) per day for each such mediator, and prescribe reasonable rules of procedures for such mediators.

Milton Pasquale,[1] an employee of the Department of Human Resources, testified that he had been with this agency since 1970. During this period, the agency had not been involved in any mediation matters, either formally or informally.

However, as further testified to by Pasquale, the state agency did have personnel available to perform mediation services, had the funds to do so, and routinely proffered its services to parties who were involved in contract negotiations. Pasquale said that the agency made 11 such offers in 1977.[2] He indicated that if the parties had requested

---

[1] The name has been disguised.

[2] Pasquale explained that his state agency received periodic screenout lists from the FMCS, on which the FMCS indicated which employers were too small to justify its intervention. From this, the state agency made its determination to proffer its services.

mediation assistance, his agency would have been available to assist accordingly.

The company contended, therefore, that the Kansas Department of Human Resources was a state mediation agency to which notice was required to be sent within the meaning of Section 8(d) (3) of the Act.

Therefore by striking on August 12, 1977, without having given the state agency notice as required by Section 8(d) (3), the union had engaged in an unfair labor practice within the meaning of Section 8(b) (3).

The company requested that the union be issued a cease and desist order dissolving the strike and requiring the union to fulfill its statutory requirements for bargaining in good faith as mandated by the Act.

POSITION OF THE UNION

The union contended the Kansas Department of Human Resources by its own admission had not, for at least seven years, exercised any authority to mediate disputes, did not view its function as including mediation of contract negotiations, and had no funds directly earmarked for mediation. Accordingly, this agency should be found not to meet the statutory definition of Section 8(d) (3). Thus, the union's failure to give notice to an effectively nonexistent state agency was not an unfair labor practice on the part of the union.

In any event, the union claimed that the alleged violation of Section 8(d) (3) by the union was a mere technicality of little importance. The union did give the required statutory notice to the FMCS, and the union and the company had bargained for several months before the union initiated a strike on August 12, 1977.

Further, the company's charges were beyond remedy, since the union did on August 24, 1977, notify the Kansas Department of Human Resources concerning the labor dispute, even though the union believed it was unnecessary as a matter of complying with the Act.

The union claimed that the company was trying to undermine the union's lawful right to strike through the filing of trivial unfair labor practice charges. The union argued that these charges should be dismissed or alternatively, the charges should be declared moot, given all the circumstances of the case.

QUESTIONS

1. Was the Kansas state agency, which had not mediated any labor disputes in seven years previously, a state mediation agency within the meaning of Section 8(d) (3) of LMRA? Why, or why not?

2. Is this a trivial, technical issue as claimed by the union? Discuss.

3. If the union was found to have violated Section 8(b) (3) of the Act in this case, what could be the potential consequences to the union and its membership for having struck the company?

4. Since the union eventually did notify the Kansas state agency— even though the union believed it was unnecessary—does this alter and/or mitigate the findings/remedies open to the NLRB?

22. The Union's Request for Access to an Employee's Confidential Personnel File

Employer:

Salt River Valley Water Users' Association, Phoenix, Arizona

Union:

International Brotherhood of Electrical Workers, Local Union No. 266

BACKGROUND

The Association and the union were parties to a collective bargaining agreement that included procedures for grievance processing and arbitration of grievances arising under the agreement. In early 1984, a dispute arose when two bargaining unit employees, Charley Dennis[1] and Julio Garza, were caught sleeping on the job. The Association fired Garza but only suspended Dennis. The union filed a grievance on behalf of Garza, requesting that he be reinstated with back pay. The union notified the Association that it was prepared to arbitrate the grievance, if necessary, to resolve the dispute.

In order to determine whether Garza had been the victim of disparate treatment, the union sought access to Charley Dennis' personnel file. The union filed a request to obtain three categories of information in Dennis' file: performance reviews, disciplinary records, and any other record upon which the company might rely in the grievance and arbitration proceedings. The Association responded by letter that in accordance with its established personnel policy, the requested information would not be released without Dennis' consent.

The relevant portion of the Association's personnel policy (identified as "HR 305"), which management cited in denying the union's request, included the following:

1. Accessibility of employee records is as follows:
   a. SRV employee—has a right to review or correct his/her personal records.
   b. SRV management—has the right to review employee record information for job-related reasons.
   c. Outside agencies—accessible with employee consent.
   d. Instances covered by law—accessible with legal documents.

---

[1] The names of all individuals are disguised.

The union then filed unfair labor practice charges against the Association, alleging violations of Sections 8(a) (1) and 8(a) (5) of the Labor Management Relations Act. The union urged that the Association should be compelled to release the requested information to the union.

POSITION OF THE UNION

The union pointed out that the NLRB has often held that under Sections 8(a) (1) and 8(a) (5) and as further defined under Section 8(d), the failure of an employer to provide a union with the information necessary to intelligently evaluate grievances may constitute an unfair labor practice.[2] The union is this case needed to examine Charley Dennis' personnel file in order to determine whether another employee who was grieving his discharge had been singled out by management in a disparate or discriminatory fashion. The Association's confidentiality policy permitted its managers to have access to the records of a nongrieving employee in connection with grievance proceedings. In letters to the union and in meetings, the Association had relied on Dennis' employment history in responding to Garza's grievance. To explain the less severe punishment given to Dennis, management representatives had claimed that Dennis had an "unblemished record," and that his file showed him to be an "exceptionally reliable employee who rarely took days off or used sick leave."

The union argued that it was not appropriate or equitable that management should be permitted to refer to such information in its own defense, while at the same time denying the grievant's bargaining representative access to this and other relevant information.

The union pointed out that arbitrators routinely consider employee work records in deciding grievance cases and in determining whether employers have applied disciplinary actions in a consistent, evenhanded, and nondiscriminatory manner. Without access to Charley Dennis' personnel file in this case, the union would be unable to determine whether or not Julio Garza—a Hispanic employee—had been discharged in a manner that was arbitrary or discriminatory in nature.

The union emphasized that its sole objective in requesting access to Dennis' personnel file was in order to carry out its statutory responsibility (under Section 8(b) (1) (A) of LMRA) to represent Garza in processing his grievance. The union would not use any of this informa-

---

[2] Among the cases cited were: NLRB v. Truck Drivers Local Union No. 449, 353 U.S. 87, 96, 39 LRRM 2603 (1957); and Pfizer, Inc., 268 NLRB 916, 115 LRRM 1105 (1984).

tion to harass or embarrass Dennis, or publicize it in any forum other than in weighing the merits of and processing Garza's grievance.

In summary, the union argued that the Association's concern about confidentiality of Dennis' personnel file was misplaced, and that the Association had a statutory obligation to provide the requested information to the union.

POSITION OF THE EMPLOYER

The Association argued that it had an across-the-board, uniform policy to protect confidential employee records, which contained sensitive information. Included in an employee's personnel file were: disciplinary records, which described infractions and the discipline imposed; performance reviews; and evaluations by the employee's supervisors.

Release of such information to any outside party, without an employee's consent, could result in significant invasions of an individual's privacy, and possibly lead to abusive consequences.

The Association argued that some NLRB and court decisions have ruled that in certain situations, it is not necessary to provide confidential information to the union if there is no evidence that the employer is attempting to interfere with the union's obligations and rights in representing its members.[3] In this situation, the Association had informed the union concerning the general nature of Charley Dennis' work record and the reasons for discharging Garza but not Dennis. The union could also obtain information about Dennis' performance record by other procedures, such as by interviewing his supervisors. Therefore, the Association was not withholding relevant information from the union; the Association only was preserving its uniform policy of protecting confidential information about employees and protecting their privacy.

In the Association's view, the unfair labor practice charges of the union were without merit and should be dismissed.

QUESTIONS

1. Why have the NLRB and the courts interpreted Sections 8(a) (5) and 8(d) of LMRA to include the obligation of an employer to furnish certain types of relevant information to a labor organization?

---

[3] The case primarily cited here was Detroit Edison Co. v. NLRB, 440 U.S.301, 100 LRRM 2728 (1979).

2. Compare this case with Case No. 18, in which an employer representative was seeking certain information from a union and filed unfair labor practice charges under Section 8(b) (3) of the Act.

3. Why is it often difficult for the NLRB to weigh statutory rights of the parties under LMRA against concerns that parties have for maintaining confidentiality of sensitive information, including the privacy rights of individuals?

4. Does it make any difference in this case that the employer informed the union concerning Dennis' work record without permitting the union to inspect his personnel file? Why, or why not?

23. Was the Employee's Walkout Protected Concerted Activity?

Company:
    Ontario Knife Company, Franklinville, New York
Individual Employee:
    Mary Costello[1]

BACKGROUND

Ontario Knife Company was a knife manufacturer, which at the time of this case employed about 300 persons on day and night shifts. The plant was nonunion.

Mary Costello was first hired in 1976 as a riveter; she was assigned to the second shift (3:30 P.M. to midnight) with two other employees, Veronica Thorp and Julie Moore. Their basic work was to rivet wood or plastic handles to knives. For several years, they had encountered major difficulties and problems in the riveting of handles to machetes, one of the company's major products. These difficulties adversely affected their additional incentive pay. Also, the work was dirtier than on other knives; in the six months preceding the incident in this case, the machete blades had been dipped in oil to retard rusting.

Mary Costello, Veronica Thorp, and Julie Moore frequently brought complaints about the situation to their leadman, George Wilson; the night foreman, Carl Saunders; and the plant manager, Marvin Schwartz. In response to these complaints, management took a number of steps to adjust the incentive pay problem. Further, employees who performed the riveting work were placed on rotating schedules with respect to machete production. However, the three night shift employees continued to complain, and in mid-1978 their major grievance was that the burden of machete work was unfairly distributed between the day and the night shifts.

In June 1978, the complaints of the night shift employees became particularly vocal because no first shift operator had worked on machetes on June 20 when Costello did, on June 21 when Moore did, or on June 22 when Thorp was scheduled to do so. This imbalance was explained by Schwartz as due to the fact that Ontario was behind

---

[1] The names of all individuals have been disguised.

schedule in its machete deliveries. Blades, handles, and special rivets often did not arrive until the afternoon; therefore, the night shift was obligated to start the work to get the production out. The day shift foreman normally made out the night shift production schedule.

On arriving for work on Thursday, June 22, Mary Costello looked at the day foreman's desk for the night shift instructions and found that machetes were on the list. It was Veronica Thorp's turn to do that work that night, with Costello's turn to come the next night if machetes should again be scheduled. On the previous day Costello had complained to George Wilson about the unequal distribution of the machete work between day and night shifts. While she and Veronica Thorp were complaining to each other on the afternoon of June 22, Wilson came through their department. Costello asked him what he had found out in the office about her complaint of the previous day. Wilson said nothing, but he then reported to the night foreman, Carl Saunders, that "Costello and Thorp are upstairs griping again about the machines and doing the machetes." Saunders and Wilson then went upstairs, brought Costello and Thorp into another room, and asked them what the problem was. Costello answered that Wilson was supposed to find out from someone why the night shift employees were doing machetes when the day crews had not done any. Saunders responded that Wilson had no reason to go to the front office, since he (Saunders) was the boss and it was his place to decide the schedules. After more discussion, the two employees said that the next time it was their turn to work on machetes, they were going to refuse. Saunders responded that the employees were bound to do whatever work was described on the day foreman's list, and that if they didn't like the type of work so described, they should get out and the employer would find other people. Looking directly at Costello, Saunders said, "If there is a thing on there (the day foreman's list) that says you have to kiss my ass, that is what you are going to do!" Costello retorted, "I don't need this garbage!" She walked to her machine, shut it down, packed her belongings, left the job, and punched out, crying as she left.

Saunders and Wilson then went to the office in order to report the incident to Marvin Schwartz. Not finding him there, Saunders contacted Ivan Kilgore, the personnel manager. The next day Costello telephoned Kilgore, told him her story, and asked if she was to come to work that evening. Kilgore replied that he didn't know and asked why she had walked off the job. Costello answered that she was upset by the unfair work assignments; that she felt Saunders was not concerned about the employees' complaints; and his offensive, insulting remark had caused her to become angry. She offered to get a doctor's slip to verify her nervous condition. Kilgore advised against this and said he would have to discuss the matter with Schwartz. On Monday, June 26, Kilgore called Costello to tell her that she was being terminated for "walking off the job."

Shortly thereafter, acting with the assistance of legal counsel, Mary Costello filed unfair labor practice charges against the company claiming that her discharge had violated the Labor Management Relations Act as amended.

POSITION OF THE EMPLOYEE

Counsel for Mary Costello argued that Ontario's discharge and refusal to reinstate Mary Costello violated Section 8(a) (1) of the Act, which makes it an unfair labor practice "to interfere with, restrain, or coerce employees in the exercise of the rights guaranteed in Section 7." That section gives employees the right "to engage in . . . concerted activities for the purpose of collective bargaining or other mutual aid or protection." Employees Mary Costello and Veronica Thorp, in registering their complaints with management over the discrimination against the second shift in the recent assignments of machete work, were engaged in a "concerted activity" for the purpose of "mutual aid or protection."

Citing a precedent NLRB decision,[2] it was a well-established Board policy that a concerted walkout of employees in a nonunion situation to protest job conditions could be activity protected by the LMRA. This is particularly supported where employees have no other recourse open to them; where there has been no prior work stoppage involving the employees' refusal to perform work; where the employees have not made specific demands on an employer; and where a decision to walk out is for a single day and not designed to be continued in future plans of the employees.[3]

Mary Costello and Veronica Thorp had been acting together— along with Julie Moore—in protesting working conditions at the Ontario Company. The precipitating incident of June 22 found both Costello and Thorp jointly registering their complaints to management. The night foreman was not really listening to their complaints, and after direct, offensive provocation by this foreman, Mary Costello refused to perform any work that evening. Even though she was not joined in her refusal to work by Veronica Thorp, Mary Costello was acting on behalf of and in concert with her coemployees. Since the employees did not have a labor union to represent them, this was

---

[2] NLRB v. Washington Aluminum Company, 370US9, 50–50 LRRM 2235 (1962).
[3] NLRB v. Polytech Incorporated, 195 NLRB No. 126 (1971).

precisely the type of protected and concerted activity within the meaning of Section 7 of the LMRA.

Counsel for Mary Costello argued that the company should be found guilty of violating Section 8(a) (1) of the Act, and that Mary Costello should be reinstated and made whole for all lost earnings accordingly.

POSITION OF THE COMPANY

The company strongly contended that Mary Costello was terminated for walking off the job on the evening of June 22, 1978. This action by Ms. Costello was in direct defiance of legitimate management authority. She chose to leave the company plant on her own volition, and she was not accompanied by anyone else in this unauthorized behavior. Even her fellow complainant, Veronica Thorp, did not join Mary Costello in her temperamental refusal to perform her job that evening. Costello's walkout could not be condoned by management; if not dealt with severely, such insubordination could lead to a wholesale breakdown of discipline among company employees. Management justly terminated Costello's employment for her gross misconduct.

As to the unfair labor practice charges, the company characterized these charges as being a desperate effort by Mary Costello to be reinstated to her job. In the company's view, Costello walked off the job by herself, and no one joined her in doing so. This behavior by Costello alone could hardly be identified as "mutual" or "concerted" activity.

The company urged that the unfair labor practice charges filed by Costello should be dismissed.

QUESTIONS

1. Discuss the meaning of the terms, "concerted activities" and "mutual aid or protection" within Section 7 of LMRA. Why are these terms difficult to define in nonunion work situations?
2. Was Mary Costello's walkout under the case circumstances entitled to protection within the meaning of Section 7 of the Act? Why, or why not?
3. Does it make any difference that Mary Costello left the plant by herself and was not joined in her walkout by any other employees?
4. Why does company management view Costello's behavior as being in defiance of management authority with the potential for a wholesale breakdown of employee discipline?

24. The Distasteful and Offensive Definition of a "Scab"

Company:
Southwestern Bell Telephone Company, Houston, Texas
Union:
Communications Workers of America, Local 12222

BACKGROUND

On a Monday morning in early September, 1984, Jan Betheda,[1] an equipment technician, reported to two of her supervisors that there was a "distasteful and offensive" memorandum on two union bulletin boards located in the plant and office complex of the company. The supervisors, Art Laclede and Debbie Lynkirk, investigated this report and discovered on both union bulletin boards a printed memorandum entitled, "Jack London's Definition of a Scab."[2] In pertinent part, the memorandum included the following:

Jack London's Definition of a Scab

After God had finished the rattlesnake, the toad, and the vampire, he had some awful substance left with which he made a SCAB. A SCAB is a two-legged animal with a corkscrew soul, a water-logged brain, and a combination backbone made of jelly and glue. Where others have hearts, he carries a tumor of rotten principles.

When a SCAB comes down the street, men turn their backs and angels weep in Heaven, and the devil shuts the gates of Hell to keep him out. No man has the right to SCAB, so long as there is a pool of water deep enough to drown his body in, or a rope long enough to hang his carcass with. Judas Iscariot was a gentleman . . . compared with a SCAB; for betraying his master, he had the character to hang himself—a SCAB hasn't.

Esau sold his birthright for a mess of pottage. Judas Iscariot sold his

---

[1] The names of all individuals are disguised.

[2] Jack London (1876–1916) was an American adventurer and writer. He wrote a number of adventure books and also wrote several books that dealt with poverty and social injustice. The source of the "Definition of a Scab" attributed to Jack London was not identified on the posted memorandum.

Savior for thirty pieces of silver. Benedict Arnold sold his country for a promise of a commission in the British Army. The modern strikebreaker sells his birthright, his country, his wife, his children and his fellow men for an unfulfilled promise from his employer, trust or corporation.

Esau was a traitor to himself. Judas Iscariot was a traitor to his God. Benedict Arnold was a traitor to his country.

A strikebreaker is a traitor to himself, a traitor to his God, a traitor to his country, a traitor to his family and a traitor to his class.

THERE IS NOTHING LOWER THAN A SCAB . . . .

After discussing their findings with the company's Director of Human Resources Management, Laclede and Lynkirk removed the two identical memoranda from the union's bulletin boards. They then informed all of their employees in several meetings of their actions. They further told employees than any re-posting of this "Definition of a Scab" memorandum was prohibited, and that any individuals found doing so would be subject to discipline, including suspension.

Shortly thereafter, the union filed unfair labor practice charges with the NLRB, alleging that the company had violated Section 7 and Section 8(a) (1) of the LMRA by removing the memorandum from the union's bulletin boards and by threatening disciplinary action toward the employees.

POSITION OF THE UNION

The union claimed, first of all, that there never had been any company rules concerning what could or could not be posted on union bulletin boards located on company premises. The union had negotiated with the company for the right to have these bulletin boards, and there were no specific negotiated restrictions placed on this privilege.

In the union's view, the "Definition of a Scab" memorandum was an expression of opinion that was not disruptive to employee work performance or discipline. Just because someone considered it to be distasteful or offensive did not justify the company's actions and threats to discipline employees. There had been no work disruption; even though employees were observed in groups discussing the memorandum, this was not unusual or threatening to anyone. Therefore, the company violated Sections 7 and 8(a) (1) of the Act by interfering with the union's protected rights and by attempting to coerce and restrain the union and the employees in their expression of those rights. The union requested that the company should be ordered to cease and desist in this and any other actions that would tend to interfere with the union's statutory rights and negotiated privileges.

POSITION OF THE COMPANY

First of all, the company pointed out that the posting of the "Definition of a Scab" memorandum had occurred only several days following the end of a several weeks' strike during which some one third to one half of the employees had crossed the union's picket lines in order to work. In the company's view, the memorandum was primarily aimed at these employees, who had exercised their personal freedom of choice in a difficult situation. Not only was the memorandum offensive to them, but it was likely to contribute to further animosity, internal dissension, and strife that could lead to wholesale disruptions in employee discipline and work performance. An employer cannot afford simply to wait until a breakdown in discipline occurs. In this situation, company management decided that for the sake of avoiding further deterioration in workplace harmony and employee morale, the very "provocative and inflammatory" memorandum should be removed. The company did not interfere with any of the union's protected rights in this matter when it removed this offensive and "sacrilegious" memorandum.

In support of its position, the company cited a Supreme Court decision that employers have an "undisputed right . . . to maintain discipline in their establishments," which under some circumstances may limit the exercise of employee rights guaranteed by Section 7. [Republic Aviation Corp. v. NLRB, 324 U.S. 793, 797–798, 16 LRRM 620 (1945)].

Similarly, the NLRB has found "special circumstances" can exist that would justify an employer's ban on otherwise protected activity in the workplace if "objective evidence supports the employer's belief that the ban was necessary to main decorum and discipline among its employees." [Midstate Telephone Corp., 262 NLRB 1291–1292, 110 LRRM 1533 (1982)]. In the company's view, this was a "special circumstance" that fully justified the company's position. The unfair labor practice charges should be dismissed.

QUESTIONS

1. Was the "Definition of a Scab" memorandum a real threat to maintenance of employee decorum and discipline? Why, or why not?

2. Does it make any difference in this case that the company and union had not negotiated any specific limits or rules concerning what could be posted on the union bulletin boards? Discuss.

3. Why does a situation of this type pose a major dilemma for a

company management? Were there other alternatives that the company might have pursued? Discuss.

4. Was this situation a "special circumstance" under the NLRB's rulings that would justify the company's position? Why, or why not?

25. The Consumer Boycott Signs on the Company Parking Lot

Company:
  Firestone Tire & Rubber Company, Pottstown, Pennsylvania
Union:
  United Rubber Workers (URW), Local 336

BACKGROUND

At the time of this case in 1978, the company's production and maintenance workers were represented by a local of the United Rubber Workers Union, and they were engaged in an economic strike against the company as a result of their inability to reach agreement on a new contract. As part of this strike activity, a lawful consumer boycott had been organized by the United Rubber Workers Union against Firestone products. In order to publicize this boycott, bumper stickers and posters had been prepared, and they were displayed—among other places—at the picket line patrolling the company's main entrance.

Carla King,[1] a union shop steward, was employed by the company at this time and was represented by URW Local 336, a unit of technical employees. Local 336 was a sister local to the URW local that represented the production and maintenance employees. The technical employees continued to work during the strike of the production and maintenance unit employees, and King continued to cross the picket line and perform her assigned duties. However, King also was a participant in the union's consumer boycott activities off the company premises, and she had marched in a parade with a boycott sign shortly after the start of the strike. In order to emphasize her support of the boycott, King affixed to her car several prominent signs stating, "Support URW" and "Don't Buy Firestone Products." Thereafter, King and her family continued to use this car as they had done previously, for example, to go shopping and as transportation to and from the plant. After arriving at the plant, King would normally leave her car in a lot containing approximately 800 spaces. This lot was used primarily by employees, but other persons parked there as well, and there were a number of spaces designated as visitor spaces. After King had placed

---
[1] The name has been disguised.

the signs on her car, she attempted to continue to park her vehicle where she previously had parked. But on July 15, 1978, and thereafter, company supervisors informed her that as a condition for her continued use of the lot, King would have to remove these signs. She refused, and as a result she was told to remove her vehicle from the parking lot and was issued a written reprimand for her "disloyal conduct." On behalf of King, the union subsequently filed unfair labor practice charges against the company.

POSITION OF THE UNION

The union claimed that by denying King the right to use the company parking lot because of the signs affixed to her car, the company had violated Sections 8(a) (3) and 8(a) (1) of the LMRA.

The union claimed that except for the fact that the parking lot was located on the company's premises, King was clearly engaged in protected concerted activities. The union cited a number of previous NLRB and court decisions that held that actions taken in sympathy with other striking employees fall within the protection of Section 7 of the Act. Such actions may even include the advocacy of a boycott of the employer's product, as long as the boycott is tied to a labor dispute and does not disparage the employer's product.[2]

The consumer boycott signs displayed by King on her car were related to the strike of the production and maintenance unit employees, particularly in view of the fact that similar signs were located among the picketing production and maintenance workers positioned at the main entrance to the company plant. Further, these signs did not in any way disparage or criticize Firestone products. Most importantly, the signs in no way interfered with production or otherwise disrupted company operations.

In summary, the union argued that by denying Carla King the use of the company parking lot because of the boycott signs affixed to her car, and by reprimanding her, the company had discriminated against her in regard to a "term or condition of employment"—an 8(a) (3) violation—and had interfered in and coerced her in the "exercise of rights guaranteed in Section 7" of the Act—an 8(a) (1) violation. The union requested that the NLRB issue a cease and desist order upon the company.

---

[2] The union here cited several previous NLRB cases in which this principle had been enunciated by the Board.

POSITION OF THE COMPANY

The company argued that its actions toward King were legitimately a part of its property rights and its normal managerial rights to maintain decorum and order. Employees do not have any legal or statutory rights to display prounion, anticompany posters on an employer's property. King brought her automobile on the company parking lot with offensive, anticompany posters. Uncontrolled, this could lead to arguments and possible fights between union adherents and individuals such as visitors, customers, and nonunion personnel who were not sympathetic to the union strike and consumer boycott.

In summary, the company claimed that its actions toward King were not discriminatory or coercive against her in violation of her protected rights under the Act. The company exercised only its usual and customary property and managerial rights, which were legally protected. The unfair labor practice charges should be dismissed.

QUESTIONS

1. Compare the issues at dispute in this case with the issues in Case 24, "The Distasteful and Offensive Definition of a 'Scab'." What similarities and differences are apparent?

2. Which is superior under law: a company's property rights, or protected employee rights under the LMRA? Discuss.

3. Does it make any difference that this case involved a single employee rather than numerous employees? Discuss.

4. Would it have made any difference if Carla King had been a member of the production and maintenance workers local union of URW? Of an entirely different union, for example, the Teamsters? Discuss.

26. A Commendation for Excellence, or an Unfair Labor Practice?

Employer:

United States Postal Service, Cleveland, Ohio

Union:

Branch No. 40, National Association of Letter Carriers

BACKGROUND

Midpark Branch is one of numerous branch facilities of the United States Postal Service serving the greater Cleveland, Ohio, metropolitan area. In July 1979, acting upon the recommendation of Midpark Branch Manager John Canterra,[1] the Cleveland Postal Service office decided to issue a Certificate of Excellence to the staff of 10 postal clerks employed at the Midpark Branch facility. On July 12, 1979, the 10 postal clerks and the 64 letter carriers were gathered together for the presentation ceremony. Supervisory personnel read copies of the certificate to the assembled group and gave each of the 10 postal clerks a copy. A copy was also placed in each clerk's personnel file. The certificate, signed by Midpark Branch Manager Canterra and Cleveland Postmaster Leslie Spiegel, stated as follows:

> This Certificate of Excellence is presented to the Clerical Staff at Midpark Branch of the Cleveland Ohio Postal Service for Outstanding Achievements during the Fiscal Year of 1979 in the categories listed below:
>
> 1. Outstanding Public Relations
> 2. Outstanding Productivity
> 3. Very Satisfactory Audit
> 4. Minimum Time Lost Due to Sick Leave Usage (Of 20,800 scheduled clerk hours, only 189 Sick Hours or 0.9 percent were used.)
> 5. No Lost Time Due to Injury on Duty (I.O.D.)
> 6. No Registered Complaints or Grievances
> 7. No Registered E.E.O. Complaints

---

[1] The names of all individuals have been disguised.

I would like to commend each employee in this group for his productivity, devotion to duty, dependability, and professionalism. All of you have demonstrated that the key to a successful operation is teamwork: congratulations!

After a number of meetings between the parties about this matter, the union, in January 1980, filed unfair labor practice charges against the employer. The union claimed that the Postal Service management had interfered with employee rights guaranteed under Section 7 of LMRA and in violation of Sections 8(a) (3) and 8(a) (1) of the Act.

Several weeks later, in February 1980, the employer issued and posted the following notice—signed by Cleveland Postmaster Leslie Spiegel—on several bulletin boards at the Midpark Branch facility:

NOTICE TO EMPLOYEES: Branch 40, National Association of Letter Carriers, AFL-CIO, filed an unfair labor practice charge with the National Labor Relations Board on January 8, 1980, which alleges that the Postal Service is attempting to induce the Letter Carriers from not filing grievances by giving nonmonetary awards to members of another craft, who do not file grievances. This allegation has to do with a July 12, 1979, Certificate of Excellence presented to the clerical staff at Midpark Branch of the Cleveland Post Office. In our view it would be indeed ironic that what we first considered as an innocent and simple form of employee recognition for employees' cost consciousness and productivity would ultimately result in potential litigation for the Postal Service. We did not intend the Certificate to be considered as an inducement to our employees to relinquish their rights to file or process grievances. Moreover, I wish to take this opportunity to reiterate the Postal Service's policy that all our employees be free to file and process grievances without interference, restraint, or coercion. To the best of my knowledge no employee at Midpark Branch has ever been discriminated against because of his grievance filing activity and no one will be discriminated against in the future either. We believe that the language of the Certificate is protected by the First Amendment and Section 8(c) of the National Labor Relations Act and sincerely hope that this clarifies the matter for all concerned.

POSITION OF THE UNION

The union pointed out that the Certificates of Excellence were given only to the clerical employees at the Midpark Branch who were members of a different independent and separate employee organization. These certificates were based in part upon the fact that the clerical employees had not filed any grievances. Such certificates thus rewarded the clerical employees for not filing grievances and encouraged them not to file grievances and also attempted by direct implication to induce the letter carrier employees to refrain from filing grievances and to avoid utilizing the union's grievance machinery under its labor contract with the employer. By issuing the award and by placing it in the employees' personnel files, the employer was thus discriminating against those employees who chose or who in the future might choose to exercise their Section 7 rights to file grievances, thereby discouraging union activity in violation of Sections 8(a) (1) and 8(a) (3) of the Act.

The union requested that the employer be found in violation of the Act as stated above, and that the employer be ordered to (a) disavow the Certificates of Excellence it had issued, (b) cease and desist from issuing any similar awards in the future, and (c) post a notice to this effect.

POSITION OF THE EMPLOYER

The Post Office management contended that the unfair labor practice charges filed by the union were trivial in nature and designed to harass the employer in its efforts to recognize good employee performance and to promote positive and constructive employer/employee relations. In this regard, the employer argued that the issuance of the Certificates of Excellence was protected communication under Section 8(c) of LMRA—the so-called free speech provisions—since the certificates contained no "threat of reprisal or force or promise of benefit."

Concerning the unfair labor practice charges, the employer contended that there was no evidence whatsoever that the employer had discriminated or would in the future discriminate against any employee for filing a grievance. Thus, the 8(a) (3) allegations were totally without foundation and should be dismissed. And even if the Certificate of Excellence contained some wording that by broad (although incorrect) inference might have been construed as a technical violation of Section 8(a) (1) of the Act, the fact that the employer issued and posted an explanatory notice in February 1980 was "ameliorative action" that should have been sufficient to eliminate any finding of an unfair labor practice and remedial order from the NLRB. The employer urged that all of the unfair labor practice charges should be dismissed.

QUESTIONS

1. Evaluate the union's contentions that the Certificates of Excellence were an inducement to employees not to file grievances and/or exercise their Section 7 rights under LMRA.
2. Evaluate the employer's contentions that the Certificates of Excellence did not violate the Act, and that the union's charges were trivial and harrassment tactics.

3. Did the employer's explanatory notice of February 1980 absolve the employer of any technical violation of LMRA? Why, or why not?

4. Why should any notice or letter of commendation—such as the one in this case—be carefully worded so as to avoid possible unfair labor practice charges (and also possible charges of discrimination under the Civil Rights Act)?

27. Did the Employee Have the Right to Have a Union Representative Present?

Company:
    Eagle Discount Supermarkets, Midwestern Food Division of Lucky Stores, Inc., Glen Ellyn, Illinois
Union:
    Food and Commercial Workers, Local No. 1540

BACKGROUND

On May 1, 1982, the company acquired several grocery stores from another retail chain, Kohl's. The employees working at Kohl's were represented by the Food and Commercial Workers Union. As part of the transfer-of-ownership agreement, the company and the union agreed to continue in effect most terms of the collective bargaining agreement. One major change, however, was the elimination of a provision concerning "just cause" for discharge during a 30-day probationary period for store personnel. Under the transfer-of-ownership agreement, an employee could be terminated during the 30-day probationary period at the sole discretion of the company. Of approximately 450 employees affected by this transfer of ownership, about 40 were terminated under the new probationary provision.

Pamela Golden[1] first began working for Kohl's in 1977. By March 1979 she had attained the position of deli manager of the Hanover Park store. Despite the title of "deli manager," this was a bargaining-unit position and Golden was included within the unit represented by the union. She held this position until the Hanover Park store closed late in 1981. Following the closing of that store, her next job placement became the subject of dispute. Her permanent assignment remained unsettled until February 1982, when certain grievances were resolved on her behalf. Golden was on maternity leave from mid-February until August 1982. During her leave, Eagle Discount Stores had acquired ownership of the stores in which Golden had worked, and her assignment upon her return to work again became the subject of controversy. She once more grieved the issue. On August 11, 1982, Golden began

---

[1] The names of all individuals are disguised.

working at the Glen Ellyn store under manager Elmer Ellis. Golden was subject to a 30-day probationary period at this time.

Scheduling arose almost immediately as a problem. Golden told Ellis that her child-care responsibilities made it inconvenient for her to have to open the deli in the mornings. Ellis agreed to keep her situation in mind when arranging the schedule. Golden was not scheduled to work on August 12, and she was out sick on both August 13 and 14. When she returned to work and saw the posted schedule, Golden objected to the number of successive workdays she was given. The schedule was then revised. On August 19, she again raised objections to the following week's schedule. This led Ellis to respond that she would have to abide by the schedule. Golden in turn responded that she probably would have to "take my problem to the union."

On August 20, 1982, Pamela Golden worked until 9:30 P.M., one-half hour past her scheduled quitting time, because she had to serve a late customer. She did not put the deli in good order before she left. When Elmer Ellis arrived the next morning, he discovered that the deli case was in disarray, some unwrapped cheese had been left out on the counter, and the refrigerator door was ajar. When Golden came in to work, Ellis gave her a written reprimand about the condition of the deli. The writeup contained admonishments about Golden's "poor attitude and work habits."

On August 24, Golden was scheduled to begin work at 1 P.M. At noon she called Ellis and told him that she was unable to get a babysitter. She asked if it would be all right not to report as scheduled. Ellis replied that it was not all right in view of the difficulty he would have trying to find a replacement, but he also said that, "If you cannot come in, you cannot come in."

Midway through her shift on August 26, Golden was called to Ellis' office. He told her he wanted to discuss her attendance with her. Assistant Manager Christine Kuroski was present in Ellis' office. When Golden arrived, she asked that she be permitted to have a union representative present as her witness. Ellis, however, handed her a written warning concerning her absences on August 13 and 14 and her having called off work on short notice on August 24. Golden looked at the writeup and said that she refused to sign it. Ellis stated he would read the warning to her, whereupon Golden began to leave the room, stating that she wanted her union representative present. At that point Ellis pointed to the telephone on his desk and said, "Here, call and we can set up a meeting whenever you want to talk." Golden did nothing. Ellis then attempted to read the warning aloud, and Golden left the office and walked down the hall. Ellis followed her, reminding her that he was her boss and that it was important that they talk. He told her she could either return to his office or punch out and leave.

Golden followed Ellis back into his office. Ellis again attempted unsuccessfully to have her read the warning or to listen to him read it to her. At that point Ellis told her to punch out and that she was suspended. Ellis than called District Manager Tony Carbo to inform him about what had happened. Upon Carbo's instructions, Ellis telephoned Golden later that day and told her she was fired.

Shortly thereafter, the union filed unfair labor practice charges against the company, claiming that the company had violated Sections 7, 8(a) (1), and 8(a) (3) of LMRA by denying Pamela Golden her right to have a union representative present at the meeting of August 26, 1982, and by discriminatorily reprimanding and later discharging her in retaliation for her asserting her protected rights. The union requested that Pamela Golden should be reinstated to her job position and made whole for all lost pay and benefits.

POSITION OF THE UNION

The union claimed, first of all, that the first written reprimand given to Pamela Golden on August 20 was in major part a retaliation for her statement that she would probably seek the union's assistance in her scheduling dispute with Manager Elmer Ellis.

The union's primary charges, however, focused on the incidents of August 26, 1982, during which Pamela Golden requested that a union representative be present during her meeting with two company managers. The union claimed that the company had clearly violated Golden's statutory right under the well-known NLRB Weingarten[2] decision, which was upheld by the U.S. Supreme Court. This right, which is well-established law, required the company to permit Golden to have a union representative present at an investigatory interview that she reasonably believed could result in disciplinary action.

The company's illegal refusal to permit her to have her union representative present was the primary cause for the subsequent behavior of Pamela Golden in her refusal to listen to Ellis read a warning to her. Golden was not being insubordinate to Ellis; rather, she was asserting her rights under LMRA to have a representative present in a meeting that she believed was disciplinary in nature. The union concluded that Golden was suspended and discharged because she insisted upon her right to a representative and also because she had filed grievances during the summer of 1982 concerning her assignment dispute. The union urged that the unfair labor practice charges should be upheld, and that the company should be ordered to comply with the reinstatement remedy requested by the union.

---

[2] NLRB v. J. Weingarten, 420 U.S. 251, 88 LRRM 2689 (1975).

POSITION OF THE COMPANY

Concerning the first written reprimand issued by Manager Ellis on August 20, the company argued that this reprimand had nothing to do whatsoever with any retaliation upon Golden for her seeking help from the union with her work schedule. Ellis issued the reprimand solely because of the unsatisfactory condition in which Golden had left the deli area the evening before.

The company contended strongly that it had not violated Golden's statutory (i.e., Weingarten) rights. Elmer Ellis had called Pamela Golden into his office on August 26 for the purpose of delivering to her a disciplinary write-up concerning her poor attendance and to advise her orally of the necessity of improving her attendance. He was taking a firm disciplinary step based upon what he had concluded was an unacceptable record. In this type of meeting, an employee does not have a statutory right to have a union representative present. The company stressed that the NLRB had held that when an employer has reached a decision to levy certain discipline upon an employee, no Section 7 right to union representation arises if the meeting is held simply to inform or to impose that discipline upon the employee.[3]

Pamela Golden refused in this meeting to permit her manager to administer that discipline to her. She became totally insubordinate and therefore was suspended. After review of her entire work and attendance record, she then was discharged as an unsatisfactory probationary employee, as the company contractually had the right to do.

In summary, the company claimed that the unfair labor practice charges should be dismissed, since they primarily were an effort by Golden and the union to obtain reinstatement for her to which she was not entitled under either LMRA or the labor agreement.

QUESTIONS

1. Why is a decision in this type of case a "close call," which causes difficulties for all parties concerned?
2. Distinguish between the Weingarten case cited by the union and the Baton Rouge Water Works case cited by the company. Is there a clear demarcation between the major considerations in these cases? Discuss.

---

[3] The key NLRB case cited here was Baton Rouge Water Works, 246 NLRB 995, 103 LRRM 1056 (1979).

3. Should an employer permit an employee to have a union representative present in a meeting whenever an employee requests this? Why, or why not?

4. Under Section 7 of LMRA, which speaks of protected "concerted activities" and "mutual aid or protection," the NLRB in 1982 held that an unrepresented employee had the right to have a co-worker present during an investigatory interview that the employee reasonably believed could lead to disciplinary action. In 1985, however, the NLRB reversed itself and held that only employees represented by a labor union had the (Weingarten) right to representation during an investigatory interview. Why is this area of "unsettled" labor law apt to become a major judicial issue at some time in the future? Discuss.

28. Refusal to Bargain Over a "Representation Fee" in a "Right-To-Work" State

Company:
> International Paper Company, Natchez, Mississippi

Union:
> Local No. 681, International Union of the United Association of Journeymen and Apprentices of the Plumbing and Pipefitting Industry of the United States and Canada

BACKGROUND

At the time of this case in 1977, pipefitters at company plants in Springhill, Louisiana; Panama City, Florida; Natchez, Mississippi; and Camden, Arkansas, belonged to union locals in these four states. Costs of union administration were borne by the locals; costs of negotiating a contract traditionally had been split between the locals and the international union.

In 1974, the union (including Local 681 in Natchez, Mississippi) had added a yearly assessment of 2 percent of wages to the existing union dues of $8.25 per month. Many pipefitters at the Natchez, Mississippi plant quit the union rather than pay the assessment. In 1977, Local 681's membership in Natchez declined from 38 to 1, the last member being the shop steward, who by virtue of his position was not required to pay dues. But as required by the Labor Management Relations Act, Local 681 and the union remained obligated to represent the Natchez employees even though none of them paid dues.

The other locals in the other states did not have similar problems. Two locals retained all of their members, and only 2 of 29 pipefitters represented by the third local refused to pay dues.

When the union opened contract negotiations with the company in May 1977, it proposed clauses levying "representation fees" on non-member pipefitters. The union's final draft of the clauses was:

> The cost and expenses of representing all members of the bargaining unit, without regard to union affiliation or lack of same, must be borne by all bargaining unit employees.
>
> Those unit employees who voluntarily choose not to become union members shall be required to contribute a pro rata share of the costs and expenses incurred by the union that are directly related to enforcing and servicing the collective bargaining agreement. The representation fee

will apply only when a collective bargaining agreement is in effect. Furthermore, in no case will the fee exceed the dues and assessments required of union members.

Failure of any *permanent* employee to make payment of the representation fee each month and to maintain the payments during employment shall be cause for dismissal after 10 days' written notice to the employee and the company.

The amount of the representation fee will be based upon an independent audit to determine those services performed by the union directly related to the collective bargaining process.

The union and the company reached agreement on all other contract provisions. But on September 28, 1977, the company rejected the representation fee clauses on the ground that they violated the right-to-work laws of Arkansas, Florida, Mississippi, and Louisiana—states in which the company operated plants. On October 17, the union wrote to the company to insist on the clauses, and to announce that picketing would commence at Natchez on October 31. The company then filed unfair labor practice charges against the union, claiming that the union had violated Section 8(b) (3) of LMRA by its insistence on bargaining for these representation fees in right-to-work states.

POSITION OF THE COMPANY

The company acknowledged that in non-right-to-work states, representation fees of the type proposed by the union were probably permissible under Section 8(a) (3) of the Act. However, the company claimed that under Section 14(b) of LMRA,[1] states were authorized to prohibit union shops and other arrangements that required employees to pay dues or fees to a union as a condition of their employment. The state of Mississippi passed its right-to-work statute in 1947; in pertinent part, it reads:

> No employer shall require any person, as a condition of employment or continuation of employment, to pay any dues, fees, or other charges of any kind to any labor union or labor organization.

The right-to-work statutes in Georgia, Louisiana, and Arkansas contain similar provisions. For the union to insist that the company must bargain over and agree to a contractual provision that would violate

---

[1] Section 14(b), the so-called right-to-work provision, reads as follows: "Nothing in this subchapter shall be construed as authorizing the execution or application of agreements requiring membership in a labor organization as a condition of employment in any State or Territory in which such execution or application is prohibited by State or Territorial Law."

such state right-to-work statutes was, in the company's view, a clear violation of Section 8(b) (3) as clarified under Section 8(d) of LMRA, requiring good-faith bargaining. The company requested that the union should be ordered to cease and desist in all of its efforts to negotiate and attain a representation fee contractual provision.

POSITION OF THE UNION

The union claimed that its proposed representation fees were necessary, appropriate, and legally permissible under the Labor Management Relations Act in order to carry out its required representational functions.

In regard to the situation at Natchez, the union pointed out that Local 681 continued to represent employees at the Natchez mill long after it ceased to have any dues-paying members at that location. Between May 1976 and June 1978, the union's business agent traveled to Natchez once a week to handle grievance, insurance, pension, vacation, and other matters and to attend safety meetings. The union prosecuted 19 grievances; negotiated a new contract after frequent bargaining sessions, resulting in wage increases and other added benefits for the Natchez employees; and hired an attorney to represent Local 681 in a Title VII civil rights action. In the fiscal year ending June 30, 1977, Local 681 expended approximately $10,700 in order to represent the employees at the Natchez mill.

The union attempted to remedy this erosion of its financial resources by proposing the "representation fee" clause to the company during contract negotiations in May 1977. The clause would have required collection from each nonunion employee "a pro rata share of the costs and expenses incurred by the union that are directly related to enforcing and servicing the collective bargaining agreement," with a provision for "an independent audit to determine those services performed by the union directly related to the collective bargaining process." The initial representation fee required of the 38 employees at the Natchez mill would have been $5 a week, allowing the union to collect approximately $9,900 a year, or somewhat less than the $10,700 expended by Local 681 in representing those employees. The clause specifically stated that in no event would the representation fee exceed the dues and assessments required of union members. Had the Natchez employees remained in the union and paid all their dues and assessments under the preexisting dues structure, the union would have collected a total of $14,200—which would have provided approximately $3,500 in additional income that it could have used for institutional expenses.

As to the legal issues involved, the union claimed that the core question to be determined was whether the Mississippi law banning payment of "charges of any kind" constituted a prohibition of "membership" that was within the scope of Section 14(b) of LMRA.

In the union view, the fee-for-service (or representation fee) charge provision that it was attempting to obtain was not within the meaning of the term "membership in a labor organization" as specified by Section 14(b). Section 14(b) was aimed only at allowing states to prohibit union shop or agency shop labor contracts that are based upon membership dues. But the Mississippi law went far beyond these limits. Since the Mississippi law was in conflict with and outside the scope of the LMRA, the union was within its legal rights under the LMRA to bargain and to take actions to secure a representation fee that otherwise was permissible under Sections 8(a) (3) and 8(d) of the Act.

The union argued that the differences between membership dues and representation fees were more than a matter of dollars alone. Representation fees are payments for services rendered; membership dues support an institution. All the union was trying to achieve was a pro rata share for representation expenses incurred by the union in order for the union to carry out its legally mandated duty to represent all employees in a bargaining unit.

Common sense and fundamental fairness should support the concept that a labor organization can attempt to collect expenses it incurs on behalf of nonmembers (called free-riders) that the union by law must represent. Even in a right-to-work state, nonunion employees in a bargaining unit benefit directly from union efforts on their behalf. Letting unions recoup these costs of representation does not constitute coerced "membership" within the meaning of Section 14(b) of LMRA.

For all of these reasons, the union claimed that it was well within its rights to bargain to impasse and to take other actions in its effort to secure a representation fee provision. The union requested that the Section 8(b) (3) unfair labor practice charges filed by the company should be dismissed.

QUESTIONS

1. Evaluate the union's arguments concerning the need for representation fees to cover the union's expenses to represent nonmembers in the bargaining unit. Why is this problem at the core of any union's efforts to attain a union shop in those states where union shops are not prohibited by state law?

2. Why did the company file unfair labor practice charges against the union rather than bargaining over the representational fee issue? Discuss.

3. Why was this case an important one in the continuing controversy of union representation and security rights in so-called right-to-work states?

4. Discuss the pros and cons of Section 14(b) of LMRA from the standpoint both of this case as well as of labor relations in general. Why will Section 14(b) likely continue to be a controversial issue?

29. The Union's Refusal to Process a Grievance to Arbitration

Company:

Leshner Corporation, Hamilton, Ohio

Union:

Local Union 148T, Amalgamated Clothing and Textile Workers

BACKGROUND

On April 18, 1979, employee Ruth Kesten[1] was involved in two separate physical altercations during worktime—one with employee Arlene Walker, the other with employee Elaine Davis. All three employees were fired pursuant to an employer rule against fighting. Thereafter the union on behalf of Kesten and Walker filed grievances protesting their "unjust" discharges. (Elaine Davis obtained employment elsewhere, and she did not choose to have the union file a grievance on her behalf.)

At a first-step grievance meeting, plant manager Jess Jones stated that the company was willing to reinstate Ruth Kesten but not Arlene Walker. The company's position was based on its belief that Kesten had not been the aggressor in either fight and merely had defended herself. Union representatives, especially Carol Monday, the union's financial secretary, responded to this company "offer," stating that if it was company policy to discharge all employees involved in a fight or none, then both grievants should be reinstated or neither. At a second grievance meeting, Jess Jones again stated that the company would reinstate Kesten but not Walker, whom Jones termed a "troublemaker." Union representatives again insisted that both grievants or neither be reinstated. Because Walker could not attend the second-step meeting, a third meeting was held so that she could give her version of the events. During that meeting, Tom Wozik, the union's business representative, requested again that both Kesten and Walker be reinstated. Carol Monday added that the company should reinstate both grievants if it were going to reinstate one. Jess Jones, plant manager, replied that he earlier would have brought Kesten back, but now he would "have to take it up to corporate management." Subsequently the union was notified in writing that both grievances were denied. The union did not process either grievance to arbitration.

---

[1] The names of all individuals have been disguised.

Shortly thereafter, Ruth Kesten filed unfair labor practice charges against the union, claiming that the union had violated Section 8(b) (1) (A) of the Labor Management Relations Act by failing to properly represent her.

TESTIMONY OF THE COMPANY

Although the company was not charged in this matter, plant manager Jess Jones testified that at all times the company's "offer" to reinstate Kesten was conditioned upon the union's acceptance of the company's refusal to reinstate Walker. At no time did any company representative offer to reinstate Kesten without adding that the company would not reinstate Walker. Jones further testified that the company was willing to reinstate Kesten and continue processing Walker's grievance to arbitration. But he also testified, "When they said both or none, we said if we couldn't take just Kesten back, we would take none." The company claimed that it did not need the union's approval before it could unilaterally reinstate Kesten without reinstating Walker. But since the union rejected the company's "offer," it was up to the union to decide whether or not to process either or both of the grievances to arbitration on behalf of Kesten and Walker. The union unilaterally decided not to do so.

POSITION OF RUTH KESTEN

Ruth Kesten claimed that the union had failed to properly represent her, in violation of the union's statutory obligation to do so under Section 8(b) (1) (A) of LMRA. Since the union refused to accept the company's offer to reinstate her to her job but not Arlene Walker, Ruth Kesten was denied her job by a discriminatory decision of her union. Further, after having rejected the company's offer, the union decided not to process either her or Walker's grievances to arbitration. This union decision, too, closed off whatever chance Ruth Kesten might have had to get her job back through the arbitration process. In total, Ruth Kesten claimed that the union had discriminated against her and had violated its obligation under LMRA to represent her fairly. Ms. Kesten requested that the union be required to make her whole in an equitable amount for the loss of earnings she had incurred as a result of her loss of employment and the union's failure to represent her fairly in this matter.

POSITION OF THE UNION

The union cited a previous NLRB and court decision in claiming that it had not violated Section 8(b) (1) (A) of LMRA. According to this prior decision, a union breaches its statutory duty of fair representation when its conduct toward a member of the collective bargaining unit is arbitrary, discriminatory, or in bad faith.[2] The union argued that there was no evidence or contention that the union's actions regarding Ruth Kesten's grievance were the result of bad faith or hostility toward Kesten. Nor was there any evidence of disparate treatment. The union leaders in processing the grievances had tried diligently to have both Kesten and Walker reinstated. Further, in processing the grievances the union actively advocated its position, but the company adamantly refused to reinstate both grievants.

A number of union officers testified that at a regular union meeting, the grievances of Kesten and Walker had been discussed. This discussion included the pros and cons of the likelihood of winning either or both grievances in arbitration. After the discussion, the union membership present voted by a large majority not to process either case to arbitration. On the basis of this vote, the union leaders decided to drop the grievances. This, too, demonstrated that the union did not act arbitrarily, unreasonably, or in any way that was discriminatory to Ruth Kesten. The fact that Ruth Kesten did not agree with the union's decision does not indicate that the union failed to represent her in a manner required by the LMRA. The union urged that Kesten's unfair labor practice charges should be dismissed.

QUESTIONS

1. Why does a case such as this place the union in an extremely difficult position both legally and politically?

2. Was the company's offer a "squeeze play" on the union designed to place the union in an untenable position? Discuss.

3. Did the union fail to properly represent employee Ruth Kesten? If so, what type of remedy should the NLRB order, since employment at the company no longer is open to Ms. Kesten?

4. Evaluate the union's contentions that it did not act in an arbitrary, discriminatory, or unreasonable manner in this case.

5. It is widely recognized that labor union leaders often process some grievance cases to arbitration primarily to avoid unfair labor practice (i.e., failure to properly represent) charges such as occurred in this case. Why is this (a) understandable, and yet (b) not necessarily desirable? Discuss.

---

[2] Truck Drivers, Helpers, Taxicab Drivers, Garage Employees, and Airport Employees Local Union No. 335, affiliated with International Brotherhood of Teamsters, Warehousemen, and Helpers of America (Monarch Institutional Foods), 229 NLRB 1319, 95 LRRM 1232 (1977), affd. 597 F.2d 388, 101 LRRM 3142 (4th Clr. 1979).

30. The Employer's Refusal to Process a Grievance to Arbitration

Employer:
> St. Joseph Hospital Corporation, Flint, Michigan

Union:
> Local 2635, State, County, and Municipal Employees and Council 25, State, County, and Municipal Employees, AFL–CIO.

BACKGROUND

Since 1973, the St. Joseph Hospital Corporation had collective bargaining agreements for certain service, housekeeping, and other employees with Local 2635 and Council 25 of the American Federation of State, County, and Municipal Employees, AFL–CIO. In early May 1978, Council 25 was engaged in efforts to organize some of the hospital's technical employees. In an attempt to aid Council 25 in its organizational drive, Marie Kraft,[1] president of Local 2635, sought out the assistance and participation of other unions in a "demonstration" to be conducted on the hospital's premises. In conjunction with other union leaders, Marie Kraft had published under her name an article in the May 10 edition of the Flint UAW News–Local 599 newspaper "Headlight Edition." In addition to seeking the support of UAW members in the upcoming demonstration, the article was highly critical of hospital management. Kraft wrote in the article that "the hospital administration has continually lied to, harassed, and even threatened to jail the union representatives at St. Joseph Hospital."

On May 13, the hospital's director of personnel and labor relations, Elliott Sternberg, obtained a copy of this newspaper article. After consulting with the hospital president and its legal counsel, Sternberg sent Kraft a mailgram advising her that the demonstration scheduled for May 23 was unlawful under Section 8(g) of the Labor Management Relations Act. Further, Sternberg indicated that Kraft's appeal for a mass demonstration was "an irresponsible act," and that the hospital would "take appropriate action" to ensure that quality patient care would continue to be provided. On May 20, a local newspaper, the *Flint*

---

[1] The names of all individuals have been disguised.

Journal, published an article on the upcoming demonstration that identified Marie Kraft as being a leader in the demonstration.

On May 23, the hospital was picketed by union members as well as by several other labor organizations at various hospital entrances and on the hospital parking lot. Among those engaged in the picketing on behalf of Local 2635 were Kraft and employees Dan Slovic and Theresa Kolb. Both Slovic and Kolb, like Kraft, were union officials. The hospital shortly thereafter filed unfair labor practice charges against both Local 2635 and Council 25 of the union, claiming that the union had violated Section 8(g) of LMRA.

On May 25, 1978, a union representation election was held. A majority of employees in a proposed technical employees bargaining unit voted against having Council 25 represent them.

On May 26, the day after the election, Elliott Sternberg advised Kraft, Slovic, and Kolb that he was considering taking disciplinary action against them. He told them that when he returned from his vacation and had reviewed the facts and consulted legal counsel, he would inform them what disciplinary action, if any, would be taken. Upon his return from vacation on June 5, Sternberg reviewed the matter with the hospital's attorney and president. They decided to discipline only Marie Kraft, because they were not sure whether Slovic or Kolb had helped organize or had been leaders in the picketing.

At a meeting held on June 7, 1978, Sternberg handed Kraft a letter advising her that she was being suspended for two weeks for having been a leader and organizer in an illegal picketing demonstration and for having violated a hospital rule that prohibited employees from making "vicious, false, or malicious statements about employees of the hospital." Because of Kraft's good work record, however, she was not required to serve out the two-week suspension, but a record of the disciplinary action was placed in her personnel file. Kraft requested that the hospital remove from her file the record of the action taken against her, but the hospital declined to do so. She then filed a grievance pursuant to the grievance-arbitration procedure in the parties' collective bargaining agreement. At the same time, Kraft and the union also filed a charge with the NLRB on June 27, alleging her suspension as being in violation in Section 8(a) (3) and 8(a)(1) of the Act.

By a letter dated July 5, the hospital advised Kraft and the union that by filing a charge with the NLRB, Kraft had elected to pursue "a legal or statutory remedy." Accordingly, under Article V, Section 5, of the collective bargaining agreement, she was barred from further processing her grievance, and the hospital considered the grievance matter closed. Article V, Section 5, in part provided that, "The sole

194

remedy available to any employee for any alleged breach of this agreement shall be pursuant to the grievance procedure, provided, however, that nothing herein shall prevent an employee from electing to pursue a legal or statutory remedy providing such election will bar any further or subsequent proceedings for relief under the grievance procedure."

Subsequently, the union filed amended charges against the hospital, claiming that by refusing to process Marie Kraft's grievance, the hospital was discriminating against Kraft in violation of Sections 8(a) (4) and 8(a) (1) and refusing to bargain in violation of Sections 8(a) (5) and 8(a) (1) of the Act.

POSITION OF THE EMPLOYER

The hospital claimed, first of all, that the union's picketing of hospital premises was a direct violation of Section 8(g) of LMRA, as amended, which requires that a union in a health care institution must give a written notice to the hospital and the Federal Mediation and Conciliation Service at least 10 days prior to "engaging in any . . . picketing . . . at any health care institution." The hospital requested that the union be ordered to cease and desist from any such unlawful activities in the future.

Concerning its disciplinary suspension action upon Marie Kraft, the hospital claimed that it was well within its rights to discipline Ms. Kraft for her unlawful conduct and for her false and malicious statements in a published article. These statements were a direct violation of a published hospital rule. The hospital's rule prohibiting employees from making false statements about other hospital employees had been in effect for many years, and it had nothing to do with interfering with legitimate union activities and efforts.

The two-week disciplinary suspension was not excessive by comparison to Ms. Kraft's gross misconduct.

Finally, the hospital argued that it was not obligated to process Marie Kraft's grievance protesting her suspension, because Article V, Section 5 of the hospital's labor agreement with the union specifically barred an employee from pursuing both a grievance and a statutory legal remedy simultaneously. The union had negotiated this provision in good faith with the hospital; therefore the hospital was well within its rights to refuse to process Ms. Kraft's grievance when she filed unfair labor practice charges at the same time with the NLRB. The hospital urged that all of the unfair labor practice charges filed against it should be dismissed.

POSITION OF THE UNION

In regard to the Section 8(g) charge filed against the union by the hospital, the union claimed that the union's "demonstration" or "picketing" of the hospital on May 23, 1978, was only informational in nature and of the type specifically permitted under Section 8(b) (7) (c) of LMRA. The union and its supporters were merely informing other employees about the representation election to be held, and there was no attempt to disrupt deliveries or services. Therefore, the hospital's unfair labor practice charge was without merit and should be dismissed.

The union made various contentions concerning the numerous unfair labor practice charges it had filed against the hospital. First of all, the union claimed that the hospital's rule concerning so-called false statements was in itself a violation of Section 8(a) (1) of the Act. The union pointed out that the rule even prohibited employees from inadvertently making false statements; the NLRB long has held that such statements are protected within the context of concerted activity. Further, the hospital rule was so broad as to prohibit employees from making any such statements, even during an employee's nonworking time and while off company property. The union urged that the hospital be ordered to cease and desist from promulgating and enforcing such an unlawful rule.

The union claimed that the hospital's two-week disciplinary action upon Marie Kraft was a direct retaliation for her having engaged in lawful, protected activity on behalf of her union. The union requested that the hospital be found in violation of Section 8(a) (3) for this discrimination against her, be ordered to remove the two-week disciplinary suspension from Marie Kraft's file, and be ordered to cease and desist from any such unlawful actions in the future.

Finally, the union contended that by refusing to process Marie Kraft's grievance, the hospital was directly retaliating against Ms. Kraft because she and her union had filed unfair labor practice charges against the hospital. This was a direct violation of Section 8(a) (4) of LMRA. Further, the hospital was also in violation of Section 8(a) (5) of the Act, since the hospital was refusing to carry out its required obligations under the negotiated labor agreement. In the union's view, Article V, Section 5 did not preclude an employee from pursuing both a legal as well as a contractual remedy for the company's numerous discriminatory and unlawful actions taken against her. The union requested that the hospital be ordered to process Marie Kraft's grievance under the required steps of the contractual grievance procedure, and be further ordered to cease and desist from refusing to carry out its obligations to bargain in good faith and live up to the terms of its negotiated agreement with the union.

QUESTIONS FOR DISCUSSION

1. Was the union "demonstration" or "picketing" a violation of Section 8(g) of the Act, or was it permissible under Section 8(b) (7) (c)? Discuss.

2. Was the hospital rule concerning "making false statements" a violation of Section 8(a) (1) of LMRA? Why, or why not?

3. Evaluate the contentions pro and con made by the union and the hospital concerning the other unfair labor practice charges filed by the union.

4. Was the hospital within its contractual rights to refuse to process Marie Kraft's grievance? Why, or why not?

31. Was the Superseniority Clause an Unfair Labor Practice?

Company:
   Preston Trucking Company, Toledo, Ohio
Union:
   Teamsters International Union, and Teamsters Local 20

BACKGROUND

This case involved unfair labor practice charges filed by an individual employee against both the company and the union. Specifically, the issue focused upon whether the company and union had violated LMRA by negotiating a superseniority clause, which gave preference to union shop stewards that went beyond layoff and recall privileges.

Preston Trucking Company was an interstate shipper, and it was one of approximately 9,800 companies engaged in multiemployer bargaining with the Teamsters International and its various local unions, including Local 20. The company and Local 20 were parties to a contract effective from April 1, 1976, to March 31, 1979, called the National Master Freight Agreement and Central States Area Over-the-Road Local Cartage Supplemental Agreement.

As part of this agreement, a new superseniority provision for shop stewards had been negotiated. This superseniority clause provided, in pertinent part,

> Stewards shall be granted superseniority for all purposes, including layoff, rehire, bidding, and job preference, if requested by the local union within sixty (60) days after the effective date of this Agreement; but only one (1) steward shall have superseniority for such purposes.

Under this clause, the shop steward, Albert Ross,[1] was assigned a route that he bid on in April 1977. Another employee, Willie Chang, would have secured that route assignment if Local 20 had not requested superseniority for Ross. The route selected by Ross returned him to Toledo three times each week, whereas his previous schedule had returned him to Toledo only once each week.

Subsequently, employee Willie Chang filed unfair labor practice charges against the company, the international union, and the local union, claiming that the superseniority clause violated Sections 8(a)

---

[1] The names of all individuals have been disguised.

(1) and 8(b) (1) (A), respectively. Further, by implementing the super-seniority clause on behalf of shop steward Albert Ross, the company and the local union had violated Sections 8(a) (3) and 8(b) (2) of the Act, respectively.

POSITION OF THE EMPLOYEE

In arguments presented on behalf of employee Willie Chang, counsel for the employee claimed that the superseniority clause in the applicable labor agreement went far beyond what was necessary for a union shop steward to carry out his representational responsibilities.

Maintaining a contractual clause that grants superseniority to stewards for "all purposes" unlawfully encouraged union adherence. The union did not justify the need for maintaining such a broad superseniority clause.

Counsel for the employee acknowledged that it was settled labor law that superseniority for union stewards that was limited to layoff and recall rights was legal.[2] But any superseniority privileges for union stewards beyond layoff and recall must be justified by representational necessity.

In this case, shop steward Ross had adequately performed his union duties while scheduled on his previous route. In Willie Chang's view, Ross had exercised his superseniority bidding rights under the disputed clause in order to secure a preferred route; it was not because of union-mandated requirements.

In summary, counsel for employee Chang argued that the super-seniority clause and its application in the company conveyed to employees that special contractual benefits were open only to union stewards. This type of treatment was discriminatory to employees who were not interested in union activities or in serving as shop stewards. Counsel urged that all of the unfair labor practice charges should be sustained, that the contractual clause and its application in this company should be voided, and that a cease and desist order should be issued accordingly.

POSITION OF THE COMPANY AND THE UNION

First of all, the international union, although supporting Local 20's contentions, claimed it was not properly a party to this matter because the international union was not a signatory to the contract between the company and Local 20. Further, the disputed clause specifically made superseniority a local union option.

---

[2] In this regard, counsel referenced the *Dairylea* case, 219 NLRB 658, 89 LRRM 1737 (1975).

The company acknowledged that it was a party to the agreement with Teamsters Union Local 20. The company had to permit shop steward Ross to exercise job bidding rights over employee Chang as provided for in the superseniority clause in the agreement. The company claimed that the superseniority clause was essentially an internal union matter. The company had agreed to the clause and its application because of union demands. The company felt that the unfair labor practice charges against the company should be dismissed, since the superseniority clause was strictly a union matter that the company did not control.

Local 20 of the union defended the superseniority clause for "all purposes" as not being overly broad, since the collective bargaining agreement afforded no benefits based on seniority other than those mentioned in the disputed clause. As regards the express benefits of "bidding and job preference," the union claimed that they were one and the same, since all of the employees are drivers, and the only "preferences" involved route assignments that were bid for. Enforcing the clause with respect to job bidding was justified because the route chosen by shop steward Ross best enabled him to perform his duties by being present to process grievances and attend to necessary business at the union hall. The union claimed that Ross could have chosen an assignment permitting his return to Toledo five times each week instead of three, but did not since it would leave insufficient time for him to transact union business after allowing for commuting and sleeping time. The union also pointed out that the route that Ross selected (and which Chang also desired) did not result in increased earnings for Ross as compared to his previous route.

In summary, the union contended that the superseniority clause and its application at the company were lawful, since the objective was the furthering of the effective administration of the bargaining agreement at the local level by permitting the continued presence of the shop steward on the job. The union urged that the unfair labor practice charges should be dismissed.

QUESTIONS

1. Was the superseniority clause "overbroad," as contended by employee Willie Chang?
2. Could the international union properly claim that it was not a party to this matter, since the superseniority clause was in effect a local union option?
3. Evaluate the contentions made by the union to justify the superseniority clause and its application at the company.
4. Why does a case such as this place the company in an awkward position?

32. Was the Union Contract Proposal a "Hot Cargo" Clause?

Company:
   Helmkamp Construction Company, Wood River, Illinois
Union:
   Chauffeurs, Teamsters, Warehousemen and Helpers, Teamsters
   Local Union No. 525

BACKGROUND

Helmkamp Construction Company, a general contractor, had maintained a fleet of trucks to fulfill its hauling needs and occasionally perform contract hauling for others. Truck drivers employed by Helmkamp were covered under a collective bargaining agreement with Teamsters Union Local No. 525, due to expire April 30, 1983.

Late in 1982, Helmkamp decided to close down its trucking division and sell its trucks, because the trucking operation was no longer profitable. Future trucking needs would be satisfied by independent owner-contractors.

In January 1983, Helmkamp's president, Farley Duncan,[1] met with the union business representative, Milton Murphy, and disclosed Helmkamp's plans. Murphy neither protested the decision nor requested bargaining over the effects of closing the trucking division. Murphy did express his regrets and noted the growing nationwide problem of owner-operators replacing union drivers.

Helmkamp's attorney wrote an official letter about this matter, which was delivered to Murphy on February 28. The letter confirmed the plan to close the trucking operation, terminate the existing collective bargaining agreement upon at its expiration on April 30, 1983, and thereafter utilize lease agreements with independent owner-operators to satisfy Helmkamp's trucking needs. Subsequently, Duncan agreed to a request from Murphy to meet with Barclay Jones, president of the Illinois Conference of Teamsters.

In early March, Duncan, Jones, and Murphy met at a local hotel. Duncan reiterated Helmkamp's intentions and offered to bargain over the effects of the impending closure of its trucking operation. In April, however, Jones wrote Duncan to request negotiations to continue or

---

[1] The names of all individuals are disguised.

replace the existing collective bargaining agreement. Duncan responded by letter on April 18, 1983, that Helpkamp still intended to eliminate its trucking division and saw no need to enter into a new collective bargaining agreement since the company no longer would employ any truck drivers. Duncan again indicated his willingness to bargain over the effects of the termination. He received no response from the union.

Duncan called Murphy again in May to remind him that liquidation of Helmkamp's trucks was nearing completion. Murphy requested that Helmkamp postpone sale of the last few trucks pending a later meeting.

Duncan and Murphy next met on August 18, 1983. Murphy presented Duncan with two contracts and demanded that Helmkamp sign one. Both contained contractual clauses that would require Helmkamp to carry owner-drivers on the company's payroll and further require these owner-drivers to join the union as a condition of being employed by Helmkamp.[2] Duncan refused to sign, because Helmkamp would no longer own any trucks nor have need for its own drivers. Murphy said it made no difference, and they would "both have to get [their] best hold and see what would happen."

On August 19, Duncan received a telegram from Barclay Jones, stating that Helmkamp had the union's last and best offer, and if Helmkamp refused to sign, the union would "take all legal economic recourse that was deemed necessary."

Helmkamp sold or leased its remaining trucks and laid off the last of its drivers on August 23. Helmkamp thereafter began to utilize independent owner-contractors for its trucking needs. On August 26, the union struck Helmkamp and began to picket. The picketing expanded to various construction sites.

Shortly thereafter, the company filed unfair labor practice charges with the NLRB, claiming that the union had violated Sections 8(b) (4) (A) and 8(b) (4) (B) of LMRA, by picketing and threatening to picket Helmkamp to force self-employed owner-drivers to join the union and force Helmkamp to enter into an agreement prohibited by Section 8(e) of the Act.

Responding to this complaint and as required under Section 10(l) of the Act, the Regional Office of the NLRB petitioned the district court for the Southern District of Illinois to issue an injunction to stop the strike and picketing. Accordingly, the court on September 7 issued a temporary restraining order upon the union to stop the strike and picketing; the union complied with this order.

---

2 The contractual provisions in dispute are included at the end of the case.

Subsequently, Helmkamp signed a new collective bargaining agreement with the union on September 21, 1983, containing the disputed union membership clause requirements. In return, the union agreed not to enforce the disputed clauses pending determination of their legality.

POSITION OF THE COMPANY

The company cited Section 8(e) of LMRA—(the so-called hot cargo provision)—which prohibits:

> any contract or agreement . . . whereby [an] employer ceases or refrains or agrees to cease or refrain from handling, using, selling, transporting or otherwise dealing in any of the products of any other employer or to cease doing business with any other person.

The company attorney noted that the Board and the courts have held that agreements that limit an employer to subcontracting only with businesses that recognize a union or have a union contract violate Section 8(e).[3]

The clauses at issue here, which would force independent owner-operators to join the union by requiring them to be carried on the company payroll as employees, were union signatory clauses that focused on the union affiliation of a subcontractor or subcontractor's employees. That is to say, they restricted subcontracting work solely to those who had union membership. In the company's view, such clauses were a blatant violation of Section 8(e).

Further, Section 8(b) (4) (A) of the Act prohibits strikes by labor organizations designed either to force a self-employed person to join a labor organization or to force an employer to enter into an agreement prohibited by Section 8(e).

Similarly, Section 8(b) (4) (B) of the Act prohibits a labor organization from engaging in secondary types of strikes and other forms of coercive action for the purpose of "forcing or requiring any person to cease using, selling, handling, transporting, or otherwise dealing in the products of any other producer, processor, or manufacturer, or to cease doing business with any other person . . ." It was apparent that the union's strike and picketing were aimed at forcing the independent owner-drivers to join the union and to force Helmkamp to enter into an agreement that, in the company's view, violated Section 8(c). Since the union's objectives were in violation of the Act, therefore, the union's actions also violated Sections 8(b) (4) (A) and 8(b) (4) (B) of the Act. The

---

[3] See Local 814, International Brotherhood of Teamsters v. NLRB 546 F.2d 989, 93, LRRM 2800 (D.C. Cir. 1976), cert denied, 434 U.S. 818, 96 LRRM 2512 (1977).

company urged that the union should be found guilty of the unfair labor practices as charged, that the disputed contractual provisions should be permanently voided, and that the union should be ordered to cease and desist from any efforts to obtain such contractual provisions in the future.

POSITION OF THE UNION

The union claimed that its objectives and actions were all taken in an effort to preserve jobs and work for its members. The company had long recognized the union as the collective bargaining agent for the truck drivers employed by Helmkamp. In early 1983, the company had unilaterally decided to sell its fleet of trucks and use independent contractors for its trucking needs. Therefore, the union acted in an effort to preserve jobs and work for the displaced truck drivers. The proposed new union contracts, which contained the "owner-driver" provisions (see end of the case) would enable some of the displaced truck drivers who could afford to own their own trucks to retain their jobs with Helmkamp and also retain their collective bargaining rights under a union contract. Other owner-drivers to be utilized by the company would have similar contractual protection and rights that long had been afforded to drivers employed by Helmkamp.

The union claimed that the only real change would be that the truck drivers to be employed by the company would have to own their own trucks.

In summary, the union reiterated its position that the disputed contractual clauses were legitimately designed to preserve work for its members. The NLRB previously has held that if a union's primary objective is to preserve work for its members, such actions as are necessary to achieve this objective are not necessarily violative of LMRA.[4] The union urged that the unfair labor practice charges should be dismissed, and that the collective bargaining agreement that had been negotiated between the company and union should become valid and placed into effect.

THE DISPUTED CONTRACTUAL PROVISIONS

The two contracts, one a multi-employer agreement between the Illinois Conference of Teamsters and the Associated General Contractors of Illinois, the other between the Teamsters and individual em-

---

[4] See National Woodwork Manufacturers Ass'n v. NLRB, 386 U.S. 612, 634, 64 LRRM 2801 (1967).

ployers covering three local union jurisdictions, contained the following pertinent clauses:

ARTICLE XXIV
OWNER-DRIVER

24.1 The Term "Owner-Driver" means an individual, who, in addition to being employed to perform services covered by this Agreement is also the owner and operator of the equipment. Legal or equitable title must be in the name of the driver. The following provisions shall apply to all Owner-Drivers engaged to perform work.

24.2 The Owner-Driver shall be carried on the payroll of the Employer as an employee and as such, all the terms and conditions of the Agreement, including Article IV, Procurement of Labor, shall be applicable to him. A separate referral list will be kept for Owners-Drivers.

ARTICLE III
UNION SECURITY

3.1 It is understood and agreed by and between the parties hereto that as a condition of continued employment and effective after the seventh day following the beginning employment on the execution date of this Agreement, whichever is the later, all persons hereafter employed to work within the bargaining unit which is the subject of the Agreement, as well as all persons presently so working but who are not members of one of the Local Unions referred to herein, shall become members of the particular Local Union having jurisdiction for representation purposes over the geographical area within which such persons then work. It is further understood and agreed that as a condition of continued employment all persons who are presently members in good standing of one of the Local Unions referred to herein or who hereafter become such shall be required to pay the periodic dues of the local Union having jurisdiction for representation purposes over the geographical area within which such persons work a majority of the time figured on a month by month basis.

3.3. The failure of any person to become a member of a Local Union in the manner and within the time above provided for shall obligate his Employer, upon written notice from the Union to such effect and to the further effect that Union membership was available to such person on the same terms and conditions generally available to other members, to forthwith discharge such person. Further, the failure of any person to pay the monthly periodic dues required shall, upon written notice from the Union to his Employer to such effect, obligate his Employer to discharge him forthwith.

QUESTIONS

1. Does it make any difference in this case that this company is in the construction industry? (Suggestion: Closely scrutinize the entire text of Section 8(e) of LMRA on pp. 44–45.)

2. Why is a determination of the primary objective of the union in this type of case crucial to the question of unfair labor practice charges? Discuss.

3. Why have the NLRB and the courts often had difficulty in defining union and employer actions that may violate the so-called secondary boycott and hot cargo provisions of LMRA? Discuss.

33. Who Should Erect and Install the Metal Panels and Sheets?

Company:

The Lathrop Company, Clyde, Ohio

Union:

Sheet Metal Workers International Association, Local Union No. 107, and Iron Workers Local No. 55

BACKGROUND

In 1985, Lathrop was the construction manager for the Whirlpool Corporation for the construction of a distribution center and conveyor enclosure at Whirlpool's Clyde, Ohio, facility. Lathrop performed no construction work, and it did not employ construction workers at the site. Under its contract with Whirlpool, Lathrop was to award contracts for the construction work to the lowest responsible bidder.

The work in dispute involved siding and decking. The siding work was the installation of field-assembled insulated panels. The siding generally arrived at the job site in crates or bound in straps. The inner panel was installed with clips, screws, or bolts or in some cases by welding. Insulation was then inserted, and the exterior panel was installed on top of that. The installation of roof decking involved welding or screwing metal sheets to steel or wood framing.

On April 4, 1985, Lathrop awarded the siding portion of the work to Christen Corporation, whose bid of $1,485,186 was approximately $60,000 lower than the next lowest responsible bid. Lathrop also awarded the decking portion to Christen on June 7 for an additional $42,000. Whirlpool approved the decision to award the contract to Christen pursuant to the contract between Lathrop and Whirlpool.

Christen had had a continuing bargaining relationship with Sheet Metal Workers Local Union No. 6. Christen was a signatory to an area association collective bargaining agreement with Sheet Metal Workers Local 6, effective July 1, 1984, through June 30, 1986. Christen also was a signatory with Sheet Metal Workers Locals No. 6 and No. 107 to the "Specialty Contracting Agreement of the Sheet Metal Industry"; this agreement, too, was effective from July 1, 1984, through June 30, 1986. The Clyde, Ohio, job site was outside Local 6's jurisdiction, but within Local 107's jurisdiction. Sheet metal contractors were allowed under their contracts with their "home" locals to perform work within the jurisdiction of other Sheet Metal Workers locals and were permitted to employ two employees from their home area. All additional labor, however, had to come from the local in whose jurisdiction the work was being performed. Local 107 began supplying employees to Christen for the Whirlpool job on May 1, 1985.

Christen had no collective bargaining relationship with Iron Workers Local 55, which had a collective bargaining agreement with Lathrop as part of an area agreement with the Associated General Contractors. Under this contract, there was a provision that required Lathrop to subcontract work within Local 55's jurisdiction to employers who had signed agreements with Local 55.

Near the end of April, Ted Harvey,[1] Iron Workers Local 55 business manager, called Charley Woolf, president of Christen, and informed Woolf that he "could have a problem" if Christen used Sheet Metal Workers–represented employees to perform the work.

During the week of April 22, Harvey called Max Wilson, Lathrop's executive vice president and general manager. He asked Wilson whether the siding contract had been awarded to Christen. Wilson said it had been, and Harvey replied that the work was the Iron Workers' work. Harvey further said that he would have to do everything he could to see that Iron Workers got the work. Harvey then said that he understood the roof deck also was going to be awarded to Christen, but that he would not "make an affair out of the roof deck" if he could get some resolution on the siding.

After this conversation, Wilson called Charley Woolf to discuss with him the possibility of withdrawing the contract from Christen. Woolf's position was that the Christen company had bid successfully for the job, was qualified, and the job was within its line of work. Woolf told Wilson that if Lathrop attempted to reaward the contract, "we will have to resort to legal action."

On May 21, 1985, Ted Harvey, the Iron Workers business representative, wrote a letter to the Associated General Contractors, requesting implementation of the grievance procedure, and alleging that Lathrop had violated article I, paragraphs 5 and 6, and article XXVI, paragraph 197, of the agreement between Lathrop and Local 55. Paragraphs 5 and 6 are broad jurisdictional claims to metal construction work. By letter dated May 23, Harvey amended the grievance to remove the references to paragraphs 5 and 6. Paragraph 197 was an agreement by Lathrop to use Iron Workers–represented employees to perform the work claimed by Iron Workers on jobs where Lathrop was the employer, or to subcontract such work to other employers who would use Iron Workers–represented employees.

---

[1] The names of all individuals are disguised.

On May 28, 1985, Lathrop filed an unfair labor practice charge against Iron Workers Local 55 based on the filing of this grievance. Lathrop accused the Iron Workers of unfair labor practices in violation of Section 8(b) (4) (D) of LMRA.

On learning about the possibility that Christen might be removed from the job, Sheet Metal Workers Local 107's business manager, Angelo Futrillo, wrote a letter to Lathrop dated May 30, 1985, stating in part:

> Local #107 has reason to believe that your firm has been and is being pressured by representatives of the iron workers craft to have this work withdrawn from Christen Corporation and reawarded to a subcontractor who will perform the same using employees in the iron workers craft. You are hereby advised that if your firm withdraws from Christen Corporation the work awarded under these subcontracts, or any of it, and reassigns or rewards it so as to be performed by iron workers or employees in any other craft, Local #107 will take appropriate action to protect its interest including, but not limited to picketing at the Whirlpool plant in Clyde, Ohio, to advise that your firm is unfair to employees in the sheet metal trade.

On June 3, 1985, Lathrop filed unfair labor practice charges against Local 107, alleging that the object of Futrillo's letter was to force Lathrop not to withdraw the subcontract from Christen. Lathrop accused Local 107 of the Sheet Metal Workers of violating Section 8(b) (4) (D) of LMRA.

Pursuant to Sections 10(k) and 10(l) of the Act, the Regional Office of the NLRB expeditiously investigated the charges filed by Lathrop against the Iron Workers and the Sheet Metal Workers. On June 19, 1985, the Regional Director dismissed the unfair labor practice charges against Iron Workers Local No. 55 on grounds that the filing of a grievance alone, without picketing or threat of picketing, did not constitute force or coercion within the meaning of Section 8(b) (4) (D) of the Act. The Board then proceeded to take testimony and evidence in regard to the charges filed by Lathrop against Sheet Metal Workers Local No. 107, and to make a determination concerning which labor union was entitled to perform the disputed work.

POSTITION OF THE SHEET METAL WORKERS

The Sheet Metal Workers, first of all, pointed out that Christen was party to a collective bargaining agreement between the Toledo Area Sheet Metal and Roofing Contractors Association and Sheet Metal Workers Local 6, effective July 1, 1984, through June 30, 1986, and that article I of that agreement covered the disputed work. Christen's agreement with Local 6 covered work within Local 107's jurisdiction. Christen was also signatory to the Specialty Agreement with Locals 6 and 107, which also covered the work in dispute. Christen was not signatory, however, to any collective bargaining agreement with Iron Workers Local No. 55.

The Sheet Metal Workers stressed that Christen had assigned the disputed work to Sheet Metal Workers–represented employees and had indicated satisfaction with their performance. Since 1934, Christen had always assigned such work to Sheet Metal Workers–represented employees.

Local 107 presented evidence of hundreds of assignments of siding and decking work to Sheet Metal Workers–represented employees in Ohio, Michigan, West Virginia, Pennsylvania, and New York. Local 107 acknowledged, however, that the work in dispute had also been performed by employees represented by Iron Workers.

Business Manager Futrillo testified that Christen employees represented by Sheet Metal Workers Local 107 and Local 6 possessed sufficient skills to perfrom the disputed work. Christen, Lathrop, and Whirlpool were satisfied with Sheet Metal Workers–represented employees' work quantity, productivity, and efficiency. The work could be done by any sheet metal worker who had completed his apprenticeship, and the work did not require any skills above that level of training.

Finally, Sheet Metal Workers Local 107 introduced evidence of a number of Impartial Jurisdictional Disputes Board[2] decisions awarding siding and decking work similar to the disputed work to Sheet Metal Workers–represented employees. The IJDB based the roof decking awards on a Joint Board "decision of record" of August 21, 1948, and the siding awards on trade practice. Iron Workers Local 55 did not present evidence of any Joint Board decisions in favor of Iron Workers–represented employees.

The Sheet Metal Workers urged that all of the disputed work

---

[2] This refers to the Impartial Jurisdiction Disputes Board of the AFL–CIO. For many years, labor organizations affiliated with the Building and Construction Trades Department of the AFL–CIO and various employer associations who employed their members signed a stipulation to be bound by decisions of the Impartial Jurisdictional Disputes Board. In essence, when there was a dispute or potential jurisdictional dispute regarding an assignment of work, either the contractor(s) or labor union(s) involved could refer the issue to the Impartial Jurisdictional Disputes Board for a decision. There was a rather detailed procedure for both filing complaints and appealing rulings of the Board.

However, in June, 1981, the IJDB was ended, and it was not until June, 1984, that it was replaced by a new internal jurisdictional disputes procedure, which provides for arbitration as the final and binding step for settlement of certain jurisdictional disputes. See *Procedural Rules and Regulations for the Plan for the Settlement of Jurisdictional Disputes in the Construction Industry* (Building and Construction Trades Department, AFL–CIO).

should be awarded to employees represented by Local 6 and Local 107 of this union. Further, the unfair labor practice charges filed against it should be dismissed.

POSITION OF THE IRON WORKERS

The Iron Workers pointed out, first of all, that the National Labor Relations Board had never certified either Sheet Metal Workers Local 107 or 6, or Iron Workers Local 55, as the collective bargaining representative of Christen's employees. However, Iron Workers Local 55 did have a collective bargaining agreement with Lathrop to subcontract work within Local 55's jurisdiction to employees who had signed agreements with Local 55. Lathrop should have adhered to its labor agreement with the Iron Workers by subcontracting the work at Whirlpool to a contractor who employed Iron Workers members and by withdrawing the work from Christen Corporation.

Business Manager Ted Harvey acknowledged that companies under labor agreements with the Iron Workers union generally used Iron Workers–represented employees, and companies under labor agreements with the Sheet Metal Workers union generally used Sheet Metal Workers–represented employees to do the siding and decking work in dispute. He claimed that Iron Workers journeymen had all of the requisite skills to perform this type of work. Industry data showed that there was no difference between the overall productivity, efficiency, and quality of work done by Iron Workers and that done by Sheet Metal Workers.

Concerning the previous awards by the Impartial Jurisdictional Disputes Board presented by the Sheet Metal Workers, Ted Harvey pointed out that the IJDB had ceased to function in 1981, and therefore its prior awards could not be considered as being binding or precedential upon the parties.

The Iron Workers urged that all of the disputed work should be awarded to employees represented by its Local 55.

QUESTIONS

1. Study carefully the provisions of Sections 8(b) (4) (D), 10(k), and 10(l) of LMRA. Discuss why the NLRB was directed by these parts of the Act to give priority handling and determination of disputes involving Section 8(b) (4) (D) violations.
2. When required to make a jurisdictional determination, the NLRB typically will consider the following aspects in order to decide which union is to be awarded jurisdiction over disputed work: (1) certification and collective bargaining agreements; (2) company preference

and past practice; (3) area and industry practice; (4) relative skills; (5) economy and efficiency of operation; and (6) any prior jurisdictional awards or agreements concerning the type of work in dispute. Weigh each of these in this case concerning the claims of the Sheet Metal Workers and the Iron Workers in order to make an overall determination of which union should be awarded the siding and decking work.

34. Was the Attempted Consumer Boycott Legal?

Company:

The Edward J. DeBartolo Corportion, Tampa, Florida

Labor Organization:

Florida Gulf Coast Building Trades Council, AFL–CIO.

BACKGROUND

At the time of this case in 1980, the DeBartolo Corporation owned and operated East Lake Square Mall, a shopping center in Tampa, Florida. Approximately 85 tenant-merchants occupied the shopping center under conditions set forth in a standard lease with DeBartolo. Under this lease agreement, each tenant paid DeBartolo a set minimum rent. The standard lease further provided that each tenant's minimum rent would automatically increase 10 percent upon the date each additional department store of a certain size or larger opened for business. In addition to the minimum rent, each tenant paid DeBartolo a percentage rent based upon a percentage of the tenant's adjusted gross sales in excess of a set yearly figure.

The standard lease also provided that all tenants would pay a proportionate share of the costs of operating, maintaining, and repairing the common areas of the shopping center. Arrival of a new tenant in the shopping center would reduce each tenant's proportionate share. Additionally, tenants had to join and pay dues to a merchants association, the purpose of which included joint advertising projects. DeBartolo, through the standard lease, exercised control over its tenants' construction work, business hours, signs, and equipment. Each tenant agreed not to use its premises in any way that might injure the reputation of the shopping center or interfere with the operations of the other tenants.

Wilson's Department Store was to become a tenant of DeBartolo's when it agreed to construct a department store that would connect to and become part of East Lake Square Mall. Wilson's contracted with the High Construction Company to build its store. High Construction Company was a nonunion general contractor that paid wages considerably lower than those paid to union building tradesmen in the area. The Florida Gulf Coast Building Trades Council was an association of AFL–CIO building trades unions in the area that had a continuing dispute with the High Company—as well as with several other nonunion contractors—concerning what the unions claimed were substandard wages and benefits paid by the nonunion contractors.

In early January 1980, several individuals hired by the Building Trade Council appeared at all four entrances of East Lake Square Mall to distribute handbills to everyone who was willing to accept them. The following was the message contained on each handbill:

**PLEASE DON'T SHOP AT EAST LAKE SQUARE MALL.
PLEASE.**

The FLORIDA GULF COAST BUILDING TRADES COUNCIL, AFL–CIO, is requesting that you do not shop at the stores in the East Lake Square Mall because of the Mall ownership's contribution to substandard wages.

The Wilson's Department Store under construction on these premises is being built by contractors who pay substandard wages and fringe benefits. In the past, the Mall's owner, The Edward J. DeBartolo Corporation, has supported labor and our local economy by insuring that the Mall and its stores be built by contractors who pay fair wages and fringe benefits. Now, however, and for no apparent reason, the Mall owners have taken a giant step backwards by permitting our standards to be torn down. The payment of substandard wages not only diminishes the working person's ability to purchase with earned, rather than borrowed, dollars, but it also undercuts the wage standard of the entire community. Since low construction wages at this time of inflation mean decreased purchasing power, do the owners of East Lake Mall intend to compensate for the decreased purchasing power of workers of the community by encouraging the stores in East Lake Mall to cut their prices and lower their profits?

CUT-RATE WAGES ARE NOT FAIR UNLESS MERCHANDISE PRICES ARE ALSO CUT-RATE.

We ask for your support in our protest against substandard wages. Please do not patronize the stores in the East Lake Square Mall until the Mall's owner publicly promises that all construction at the Mall will be done using contractors who pay their employees fair wages and fringe benefits.

IF YOU MUST ENTER THE MALL TO DO BUSINESS, please express to the store managers your concern over substandard wages and your support of our efforts.

We are appealing only to the public—the consumer. We are not seeking to induce any person to cease work or to refuse to make deliveries. FLORIDA GULF COAST BUILDING TRADES COUNCIL, AFL–CIO.

The DeBartolo Corporation filed unfair labor practice charges with the NLRB, claiming that the labor organization's handbilling, which requested that consumers cease doing business with all tenants of DeBartolo in its East Lake Square Mall, violated Section 8(b) (4) (ii) (B) of the LMRA. Pursuant to Section 10(l) of the Act, the Regional

Office of the NLRB shortly thereafter petitioned the federal district court to issue an injuction to stop the handbilling pending final adjudication of the Board with respect to the matter. An injunction was issued by the Thirteenth Judicial Circuit, Hillsborough County, Florida, and the handbilling ended at that time.

POSITION OF THE COMPANY

The DeBartolo Corporation first noted that Section 8(b) (4) (ii) (B) of LMRA makes it an unfair labor practice for a labor organization to threaten, coerce, or restrain any person with the object of forcing or requiring any person to cease doing business with any other person. In the company's view, the Building Trades Council violated Section 8(b) (4) (ii) (B) of the Act when, in furtherance of its primary dispute with the High Construction Company, it distributed handbills calling for a total consumer boycott of DeBartolo and the tenant employers leasing space at East Lake Square Mall. The DeBartolo company acknowledged that as a result of High's construction of a department store for Wilson's, the union could urge a total consumer boycott of Wilson's as well as High. This was true because the labor organization had a primary labor dispute with High involving the payment to its employees of alleged substandard wages and fringe benefits. But High was not a tenant of DeBartolo, did not operate department stores, and had no contract or business relationship with DeBartolo or any tenant other than Wilson's. Therefore, DeBartolo and the tenant employers other than Wilson's had no relationship to High and, as neutral persons, were protected by Section 8(b) (4) (ii) (B) from any secondary activity by the AFL–CIO labor organization.

The company then addressed that provision of Section 8(b) (4) of the Act that exempts from the secondary boycott prohibitions

> publicity, other than picketing, for the purpose of truthfully advising the public, including consumers and members of a labor organization, that a product or products are produced by an employer with whom the labor organization has a primary dispute and are distributed by another employer, as long as such publicity does not have an effect of inducing any individual employed by any person other than the primary employer in the course of his employment to refuse to pick up, deliver, or transport any goods, or not to perform any services, at the establishment of the employer engaged in such distribution

The company claimed that this so-called publicity proviso—which allows a union to request consumers of secondary employers who in some way have a relationship to the primary employer in a labor dispute to bring pressure on the secondary employer to cease doing business with the primary employer—does not encompass activity against secondary employers who have no relationship with the primary employer. There was no "producer-distributor" relationship between High and DeBartolo or between High and the tenant employers other than Wilson's. In a previous NLRB case,[1] the Board held that unless there was a producer-distributor relationship, the publicity proviso of Section 8(b) (4) did not apply.

In summary, the DeBartolo company maintained that the AFL–CIO labor organization's handbilling constituted a secondary boycott that was not protected by the publicity proviso within the Act. The union should be found guilty of an unfair labor practice and ordered to cease and desist permanently from this type of activity.

POSITION OF THE LABOR ORGANIZATION

The Building Trades Council pointed out, first of all, that the handbilling was conducted in an orderly manner without any picketing or patrolling. The handbilling did not have the effect of inducing any individual employed by any person other than the High Company to refuse, in the course of employment, to pick up, deliver, or transport any goods, or to perform any services. Since the labor organization had a continuing primary dispute with the High Construction Company, any effect of the handbilling was of a primary, not secondary, nature with the High Company.

The major argument of the Building Trades Council was that the handbilling was publicity (e.g., informational in nature) that was protected activity under the proviso to Section 8(b) (4) of the Act. The labor organization, citing the same precedent NLRB case as did DeBartolo, asserted that the mall tenants were connected with the "product" produced by the High Company for Wilson's store, because the tenants (including Wilson's) derived substantial benefit from each other's presence, and that this benefit was enhanced by the existence of the Wilson's store. DeBartolo, in turn, was related to its tenants, because DeBartolo was dependent upon their commercial success, which it attempted to secure by exercising certain controls over its tenants through leases. The labor organization contended that distribution of handbills directed at DeBartolo as owner of the mall was consistent with the Section 8(b) (4) proviso, and that including the tenants was legal because the mall and the tenants were perceived as one and the same by the public.

Finally, the labor organization urged that the Board should con-

---

[1] The case cited was United Steelworkers of America, AFL–CIO–CLC, (Pet, Incorporated), 244 NLRB No. 6, 102 LRRM 1046 (1979).

strue the Section 8(b) (4) proviso to protect this type of handbilling in order to avoid generation of a substantial First Amendment issue under the U.S. Constitution.

The Building Trades Council argued that the unfair labor practice charges filed by DeBartolo Corporation were without merit and should be dismissed.

QUESTIONS

1. Why is the question of a producer-distributor relationship crucial to the NLRB's decision in this case? Discuss.

2. Evaluate the labor organization's assertion that the case could involve a First Amendment issue under the U.S. Constitution. Should this be a consideration of the NLRB in deciding this type of case? Why, or why not?

3. Study the provision within Section 8(b) (7) (C) of LMRA that protects certain types of union informational picketing and publicity. What are the similarities and differences in this provision as compared with the publicity proviso within Section 8(b) (4)? Discuss.

PART TWO

Case Problems in Union-Management Relations

Cases From Grievance Arbitration

CONFLICT RESOLUTION, GRIEVANCE
PROCEDURES, AND ARBITRATION

SELECTED BIBLIOGRAPHY

INDEX TO CASES FOR PART TWO

THE CASES

Conflict Resolution, Grievance Procedures, and Arbitration*

The potential for conflict exists within every organization. This is true of families, business organizations, social groups, or government agencies. Conflicts may range from minor differences of opinion to open hostility resulting in physical violence. Yet, humane democratic institutions attempt to resolve intraorganizational and interpersonal conflicts in an orderly manner. While conflict can be destructive, and it often is, it need not be so. Differences of opinion, when openly confronted and fully aired, can and often do lead to new understandings and subsequent improved relationships on the part of those involved.

The avoidance of conflict is important; its resolution is critical to personal, group, and organizational viability. Conflict creates within both individuals and organizations tensions and diversions that hinder or prevent the attainment of goals. Further, striving to attain goals in itself creates tension and conflict. It is imperative that conflicts be resolved in such a manner that attainment of goals of the organization will not be thwarted. It may be hoped that resolution of conflict will produce new understanding and harmony, which will help move the organization toward its goals at an increased pace.

While an organization is concerned with the attainment of its goals and objectives, individuals within the organization are also concerned about the attainment of their own goals and objectives. Hence, the potential for conflict between an organization and the individuals within it arises. For example, a company's need for higher productivity may come into conflict with an individual's need for security in advancing years. As a consequence, differences may develop over the

---

* This section provides a brief introductory overview of major considerations and issues inherent in the grievance-arbitration process. It does not include, however, a discussion of the sizable body of law that has developed on the subject of labor arbitration. This topic usually is covered fully in major texts with which these cases are normally used. A selected bibliography is included at the end of this section.

relative importance of productivity and length of service in determining layoffs.

Not all individuals within an organization share the same objectives. For example, young employees place less importance on length of service in determining promotions than do older employees. Interpersonal and intergroup conflict within the work force may develop from such differences.

Ours is a democratic society that places a high value upon justice and upon the protection of individual rights. Democratic ideals are consistent with the concept of participation in organizations. Values attached to protection of human rights have stimulated the development of various mechanisms that aim to promote the administration of laws, policies, rules, and procedures in a humane and equitable manner, giving full consideration to human dignity and welfare.[1]

APPROACHES TO CONFLICT RESOLUTION

Concern for human rights in our society has resulted in the development of various means whereby injured parties may appeal decisions made by those exercising power over them. In fact, almost every type of organization has developed one or more appeal procedures.

Most government agencies have appeal procedures that enable employees to seek redress from acts of agency administrators. Labor unions have internal procedures for the protection of members from harassment within their own ranks. For example, the International Union of United Automobile, Aerospace and Agricultural Implement Workers of America has expended unusual effort to provide its members a fair opportunity for defense against union decisions concerning them, and has provided well-defined and speedy avenues of recourse in the event of unjust acts by officers and administrators. Religious institutions have developed appeal procedures that provide members with avenues of recourse against the clergy. For example, the Roman Catholic Church has formulated internal procedures that members may employ to seek redress.

Many business organizations also have appeal procedures, which exist in both union and nonunion companies. Many nonunion organizations have developed formalized problem-solving or grievance procedures that guarantee employees the right to appeal decisions made

---

[1] For a brief but excellent discussion of the historical background of grievance-arbitration development in labor relations, see Paul Prasow and Edward Peters, *Arbitration and Collective Bargaining—Conflict Resolution in Labor Relations*, 2d ed. (New York: McGraw-Hill, 1983), pp. 1–18.

concerning them by their supervisors. In most instances, recourse may be sought all the way up through the organization to the president. Some nonunion employers are even providing opportunities for "juries" of employees to render final decisions in complaints that have gone through a number of steps without resolution.

Formalized appeal procedures seem to become more necessary as organizations become larger and more institutionalized. Further, the more demanding and urgent the goals and objectives of the organization, and the more that they press upon individuals, the less freedom an individual is able to exercise. The hierarchical and authoritarian nature of some organizations tends to produce dependency of the subordinate on the superior. Dependency, in turn, tends to create frustration in the individual seeking freedom of self-expression on the job. Inability to exercise freedom of self-expression, in turn, may block the individual in a search for satisfaction through work.

Thus, appeal procedures provide an opportunity for individuals to exercise greater control over their environment and may expand the opportunities for them to achieve their personal goals through work. But even more significantly, such procedures give individuals a chance to contest those decisions or actions of management that employees feel are unfair and that violate their rights and the obligations of the employer.

GRIEVANCE PROCEDURES

Appeal opportunities are generally formalized in unionized organizations in grievance procedures that are included in the collective agreement. These formalized procedures vary considerably from organization to organization. Typically, however, they provide that, at the first step, the employee takes the grievance to either the immediate supervisor or the union steward.[2] The supervisor, the steward, and the employee discuss the issue and, in the best circumstances, arrive at an amicable settlement. Most grievances are settled on an informal basis at this first step. If the parties are unable to agree, either because the supervisor disagrees with the request of the employee or because the supervisor lacks authority to make a decision, the grievance is appealed to the second step of the grievance procedure. Typically, the

---

[2] A distinction customarily is drawn in labor relations between a *complaint* and a *grievance*. A complaint refers to any feeling of injury or injustice, real or imagined, expressed or unexpressed. A grievance is a complaint that has been formally presented to the supervisor, union steward, or some other union official under the provisions of a grievance procedure, alleging a violation of the labor agreement.

grievance committee of the union and the plant superintendent or office manager attempt to reach a settlement. However, grievances that are not settled at the first step of the grievance procedure may not be settled at the second step either; they are then usually appealed to the third step of the grievance procedure. At this level, the handling of the grievance is quite formalized; the parties involved may include members of top management of the company and members of the national office of the union. An estimated 97 percent of all collective agreements in the private sector provide that if the parties are unable to arrive at a decision at the third (or fourth) step of the grievance procedure, either party may petition for arbitration of the dispute by a third party.

The following is a quite typical grievance procedure that shows the various steps to be followed in processing a grievance to ultimate resolution.[3]

Article XIX—Grievance Procedure

Section 19.1 Should differences arise between the Company and the Union, or between the Company and employees of the Company, or should trouble of any kind arise in the plant, such differences shall be handled through the Grievance Procedure as set forth elsewhere in this Agreement.

Section 19.2 Except as set forth below, no grievance or differences shall be processed under the Grievance Procedure set forth herein unless presented by the employee, or the Union, to the Company in the First Step within three (3) days from the time the aggrieved acquires knowledge of such grievance.

Section 19.3 No grievance involving discharge, suspension or discipline shall be processed unless presented in writing to the Company within seven (7) working days from the date of which the Union receives notice of such discharge, suspension or discipline.

Section 19.4 No other grievance and/or claims involving back pay shall be effective retroactively beyond thirty (30) days prior to the filing of the grievance and/or the claim. This shall not apply to claims for back pay involving general wage increases or regular allowances, such as clothing changing time.

Section 19.5 Grievances shall be processed as follows:

STEP ONE: The employee with or without the Union Steward, may present the grievance to the Foreman. The Foreman shall reply within twenty-four (24) hours.

---

[3] From 1983–86 Agreement between FDL Foods, Inc., Dubuque, Iowa, and Local 758, International Union of Operating Engineers, AFL–CIO, pp. 20–22.

STEP TWO: In case the employee, or the Union, is dissatisfied with the decision of the foreman in the First Step, the Union representative, with or without the aggrieved employee, may present the grievance to the Department Supervisor, or any representative appointed by the Company within forty-eight (48) hours. The grievance presented by the Union in Step Two shall be in writing, and the Company shall reply in writing within forty-eight (48) hours after the Company receives such written grievance. The answer will be given to the Steward.

STEP THREE: In case the employee, or the Union is dissatisfied with the decision in the Second Step, the Union must notify the Company within seventy-two (72) hours after receipt of the Second Step response, in writing, of their desire to move the grievance to Step Three. Third Step grievance meetings will be held on the first Wednesday of each month if there are any grievances pending. This date and time may be changed by mutual agreement between the Union and the Company. The Grievance Committee of the Union, composed of not more than three (3) Union Representatives, together with the Local Union Business Agent and Recording Secretary or their representatives, shall meet with the Department Supervisors and other representatives appointed by the Company for the purpose of discussing the grievance involved. In grievances involving particularly complex or controversial problems, the Union shall be allowed to have an employee from the department of the aggrieved employee serve on the grievance committee as an additional member of the group. The grievance in Step Three shall also be in writing and the Company shall reply in writing within seventy-two (72) hours after the hearing. The answer will be given to the Union Business Agent or his representative.

STEP FOUR: In case the Union is dissatisfied with the decision in the Third Step, the Union must notify the Company within five (5) days after receipt of the Third Step response, in writing, of their desire to move the grievance to Step Four. The grievance will be presented to the Plant Manager and one other person designated by the Company and the Local Union President and one other local Union representative and/or the International Union Representative, or their designated deputies, for discussion and settlement.

STEP FIVE: If no satisfactory settlement is reached in Step Four within five (5) days, then either party may request arbitration. Within five (5) days after such request is made, the Company and the Union may request the Federal Mediation and Conciliation Service to submit a list of seven (7) names, and the Union and the Company shall select one to arbitrate the grievance. The arbitrator shall render his decision as soon as possible after the hearing is concluded, but no later than thirty (30) days after the closing of the hearing, unless time is extended by mutual agreement. Both parties may call witnesses and present written and oral evidence to support their respective positions. The decision of the Arbitrator shall be final and binding upon all parties. The Arbitrator shall have no right to modify, amend, or add to the terms of this Agreement, or to require of the Company, of the Union, or of the employee, any act which is not required by law or by this agreement to be performed.

The time limits stated in the grievance procedure exclude Saturday, Sunday and holidays. Forfeiture of a grievance due to the time limits reverts back to the last position in the grievance procedure either Company or Union. Forfeiture is considered a settlement on a no precedent basis.

Section 19.6 The fees of the Arbitrator, as well as all other costs incidental to the arbitration, shall be borne equally by both parties.

Although grievance procedures are used for numerous reasons, the following are among the most important purposes that grievance procedures serve. First, they serve to locate problems that exist in the relationship between the union and the company, and also to locate problems that exist within both organizations. Second, they tend to open the channels of communication between employees and management. They are especially helpful in stimulating communication upward from employees to management, often to the discomfiture of the managers! Third, the grievance procedure is the instrument that enables the parties to initiate action, to interpret provisions of the collective agreement, and to apply the contract to new and changing aspects of daily relations between the employees and management. Finally, it serves as valuable source of information and data at contract negotiation periods.

ARBITRATION

Arbitration constitutes the final step in most grievance procedures for settling disputes. It begins where the other procedures leave off, since the parties are presumed to have explored alternatives of settlement and compromise before resorting to an arbitrator. When the parties turn to arbitration, they voluntarily agree to refer their dispute to an impartial third person. The arbitrator's determination will be made on the basis of the evidence and arguments presented by the disputants, who agree in advance to accept the decision of the arbitrator as final and binding.

In the United States, grievance-arbitration is essentially a voluntary system. Federal labor law does not require the parties to include an arbitration clause in their collective agreement. However, the NLRB and the federal courts normally will defer to private arbitration those disputes that occur during the life of a labor agreement, provided that there is no dispute involving a legal statute. Thus, grievance-arbitration is considered as a voluntary process in the United States, since an arbitration clause is the result of negotiations between management and a labor union.[4]

Arbitration is usually viewed as a judicial process. However, the parties do influence this process by the internal policies that each has adopted with respect to it. For example, either the company or the union may follow a policy of carefully screening disputes that are referred to arbitration. Their objectives may be to present to arbitration only those cases that have merit and that the appealing party believes it has a good chance of winning. On the other hand, one or both parties may operate on a percentage basis. If they adopt this approach to arbitration, they may elect to appeal doubtful cases on the theory that arbitrators will tend to compromise. According to this reasoning, they expect to win certain points that they might otherwise have conceded. Of course, this approach to arbitration can be short-sighted; the theory that arbitrators will split decisions is generally not valid, since most arbitrators try to judge each case on the specific issues involved in the case. Thus, while the arbitration process is essentially a judicial one, in certain respects it is an extension of collective bargaining.

Arbitration has become an important means for the resolution of conflict. First, it has prevented open conflict, which tends to be very costly in terms of income lost to workers and profits lost to companies. Second, arbitration creates a better climate for the resolution of conflict. The parties resolve, as a matter of principle, to settle their disputes amicably. It can promote a spirit of cooperation that tends to pervade the entire grievance-handling process. Third, the parties know in advance that if they do not settle a dispute between themselves, it will ultimately be settled by a third party. While this may, in a few instances, prevent the parties from behaving in a mature and responsible manner, as a general rule arbitration has helped to develop mature dispute settlements. Finally, no-strike and no-lockout provisions in a collective agreement are possible only if an alternative means for ultimate settlement exists. If a union gives up the right to strike and if a company gives up the right to lock out employees over a grievance during the life of the agreement, both must be assured that some other method for settlement of disputes is available.

---

[4] Arbitration of a grievance as the final step of a grievance procedure is referred to as "rights arbitration," meaning arbitration of rights already established within a collective bargaining agreement. If an arbitrator is asked to render a decision that specifies contractual language, that is, that in effect establishes new terms of a contract, this is referred to as "interest arbitration."

Many years ago, Harry Shulman, former dean of the Yale School of Law and a distinguished labor arbitrator, summarized the role of arbitration and of the arbitrator in a classic statement as follows:

> The arbitration is an integral part of the system of self-government. And the system is designed to aid management in its quest for efficiency, to assist union leadership in its participation in the enterprise, and to secure justice for the employees. It is a means of making collective bargaining work and thus preserving private enterprise in a free government.

* * * * *

> The important question is not whether the parties agree with the award but rather whether they accept it, not resentfully, but cordially and willingly. Again, it is not to be expected that each decision will be accepted with the same degree of cordiality. But general acceptance and satisfaction is an attainable ideal. Its attainment depends upon the parties' seriousness of purpose to make their system of self-government work, and their confidence in the arbitrator. That confidence will ensue if the arbitrator's work inspires the feeling that he has integrity, independence, and courage so that he is not susceptible to pressure, blandishment, or threat of economic loss; that he is intelligent enough to comprehend the parties' contentions and empathetic enough to understand their significance to them; that he is not easily hoodwinked by bluff or histrionics; that he makes earnest effort to inform himself fully and does not go off half-cocked; and that his final judgment is the product of deliberation and reason so applied on the basis of the standards and the authority which they entrusted to him.[5]

LIMITS AND OBJECTIONS TO ARBITRATION

Voluntary arbitration is a valuable device for settling disputes during the life of a contract, when the arbitrator's function is primarily that of interpreting the language or intent of the parties. Both management and unions generally reject arbitration as a method for determining the language of the contract. The contract is "law," since it represents critical areas of managerial and union decision making. Matters in dispute often are considered by the parties to involve issues of principle, rights, or prerogatives. Neither management nor unions wish to permit an outside third party to resolve such important issues. Not only do they fear losing control over their destinies, but they also fear that a provision of an agreement determined by arbitration could

---

[5] Harry Shulman, "Reason, Contract, and Law in Labor Relations," *Harvard Law Review*, vol. 68, 1955, p. 999.

never be changed. This apprehension is in contrast to their belief that if an arbitrator's ruling on a clause of an existing contract indicates to a party that the clause is unsatisfactory, that party can hope to change or eliminate that clause in the next contract negotiation.[6]

Arbitration is most useful when the parties resort to its use sparingly and only as a last resort. Constructive conflict can lead to new insights and understandings by the parties. Agreements reached after serious negotiation also tend to be more acceptable than those imposed from outside. Serious negotiation further helps to develop maturity and responsibility. If the parties turn to an arbitrator as a means to escape a serious confrontation or to save face, they reduce their potential for developing their collective bargaining skills and the maturity essential for a satisfactory relationship. In fact, arbitrators often make comments about unsatisfactory grievance handling such as the following: "This case should never have gotten to arbitration," or "The parties should have been able to resolve this case themselves."

ARBITRATION PROCEDURES

Arbitration clauses in collective agreements usually are individually tailored to meet the needs of each union-management relationship. The American Arbitration Association many years ago developed a broad standard arbitration clause, which provided a very basic framework for those parties who were willing to utilize and rely upon the AAA's services at that time.

> Any dispute, claim or grievance arising out of or relating to the interpretation or the application of this agreement shall be submitted to arbitration under the Voluntary Labor Arbitration Rules of the American Arbitration Association. The parties further agree to accept the arbitrator's award as final and binding upon them.[7]

However, the overwhelming majority of collective agreements now in existence are much more detailed and specific than the preceding type of general clause. For example, the following arbitration provisions specify both the issues subject to arbitration and the authority of the arbitrator.[8]

---

[6] See Frank Elkouri and Edna Asper Elkouri, *How Arbitration Works*, 4th ed. (Washington, D.C.: Bureau of National Affairs, Inc., 1985), pp. 342–65.

[7] American Arbitration Association, *Labor Arbitration, Procedures and Techniques* (New York, 1960), p. 7.

[8] From Agreement between Associated Garment Industry of St. Louis (Dress Branch) with the Missouri-Mississippi River Valley District Council of the International Ladies Garment Workers Union, AFL-CIO, September 4, 1982—August 31, 1985, pp. 44–46.

27.1 Any disputes, complaints, controversies, claims or grievances (except in the settlement of piece rates which shall be settled exclusively as provided in the Article entitled WAGES AND STANDARDS) between the Union or any employees and the Association or the Employer, which directly or indirectly arise under, out of, or in connection with or in any manner relate to this agreement or the breach thereof, shall be adjusted as follows:

* * * * *

(c) Any award or decision of the arbitrator shall be final and binding and shall be enforceable by appropriate proceedings in law or in equity. The arbitrator shall not have the right to add to, subtract from, modify, or disregard any of the provisions of this agreement.

2. It is intended and agreed that the procedure herein established for the adjustment of disputes shall be the exclusive means for the determination of all disputes, complaints, controversies, claims or grievances, including those involving the arbitrability of any dispute or claims based upon any breach of the no-strike, no-stoppage pledges of this agreement or upon other breach of this agreement.

* * * * *

Neither party shall institute any action or proceedings in a court of law or equity, state or federal, other than to compel arbitration, as provided in this agreement or with respect to the award of an arbitrator. This provision shall be a complete defense to and also ground for a stay of any action or proceeding instituted contrary to this agreement.

Both the American Arbitration Association and the Federal Mediation and Conciliation Service have developed policies and procedures to govern arbitration cases that they administer.[9] More specifically, the arbitration section of a collective agreement usually will contain a statement of policy indicating what types of disputes may be arbitrated and will outline other rules governing the conduct of arbitration proceedings. Issues that must be met in the arbitration clause or by agreement by the parties include:

1. What is arbitrable? Most agreements provide that any dispute arising out of or relating to the interpretation or application of the agreement may be submitted to arbitration. On the other hand, the parties sometimes wish to exclude certain matters from arbitration, such as wage rates or determination of production or piece rate standards.

---

[9] See pamphlets: *Voluntary Labor Arbitration Rules of the American Arbitration Association,* (New York: American Arbitration Association); and *Policies, Functions, and Procedures of the Office of Arbitration Services,* (Washington, D.C.: Federal Mediation and Conciliation Service).

2. How is the arbitrator appointed, and what procedures shall be followed if the parties are unable to agree upon an arbitrator? Shall the parties appoint a permanent arbitrator to hear all disputes, or should an ad hoc arbitrator be appointed for each dispute? Most arbitrators are certified and obtained through either the Federal Mediation and Conciliation Service or the American Arbitration Association.

3. What are the rules and procedures governing the conduct of an arbitration? This issue includes methods for initiating an arbitration, time and place of hearings, swearing of witnesses, representation by legal counsel, recording of the proceedings, filings of briefs, rules of evidence, time within which an award will be made, and to whom it shall be delivered. Most of these issues will be determined by the parties themselves, but sometimes the arbitrator will be asked to rule on such procedural matters.

4. Who bears the cost of an arbitration? Typically, but not always, the parties will agree to share equally in these costs.

Disputes are brought to arbitration by one of two routes: either by a "submission" from the parties or by a "demand for arbitration" filed by either party. A submission agreement is a statement signed by both parties indicating the specific nature of the issue under contention and the specific relief that the injured party is seeking. A demand for arbitration is a formal request made by either of the two parties to the other for arbitration of an issue in dispute.

Among the major types of evidence and testimony presented and considered by arbitrators are:

1. The language of provisions of the agreement.

2. The intent of the parties in negotiating agreement provisions.

3. Past practice or precedents in handling similar or parallel matters.

4. Practices at other plants in the same industry or in other industries.

5. Equity or fairness in certain matters, "just cause" in disciplinary cases.

6. Arbitration rulings and precedents established by other arbitrators.

7. Industrial relations practices accepted as desirable or undesirable.

The American Arbitration Association has identified 10 common errors committed by parties in arbitration.[10]

1. Using arbitration and arbitration costs as a harassing technique.

---

[10] American Arbitration Association, *Labor Arbitration, Procedures and Techniques* (New York, 1960), pp. 20-21.

2. Overemphasis of the grievance by the union or exaggeration of an employee's fault by management.

3. Reliance on a minimum of facts and a maximum of arguments.

4. Concealing essential facts; distorting the truth.

5. Holding back books, records, and other supporting documents.

6. Tying up proceedings with legal technicalities.

7. Introducing witnesses who have not been properly instructed on demeanor and on the place of their testimony in the entire case.

8. Withholding full cooperation from the arbitrator.

9. Disregarding the ordinary rules of courtesy and decorum.

10. Becoming involved in arguments with the other side. The time to try to convince the other party is before arbitration, during grievance processing. At the arbitration hearing, all efforts should be concentrated on convincing the arbitrator.

The parties to a dispute seek an award from the arbitrator. The purpose of the award is to provide a final and conclusive decision with respect to the controversy. The arbitrator must not exceed the authority given him or her under the terms of the collective agreement. Most agreements, for example, state in some way that the arbitrator may not add to, detract from, or otherwise modify any part of the collective agreement. Even if this is not specifically stated in a collective agreement, this restriction is generally implied in the submission of a dispute to the arbitrator. The award of the arbitrator is to be accepted by both parties, and it will be upheld in the courts unless the arbitrator exceeds the authority granted him or her by the parties, fraud or some other breach of ethics is proved, or the result is contrary to law (e.g., an arbitrator enforces an illegal union security provision).

Expedited Arbitration. Expedited arbitration is a fairly recent and in some situations still an experimental approach designed to simplify and speed up the arbitration process. A typical arbitration may require several months or more to complete and cost each side thousands of dollars, when costs of personnel, lost time, and attorneys' and the arbitrator's fees and expenses are calculated. In fiscal year 1987, according to FMCS data, an arbitrator's fees and expenses alone averaged about $1,500 per case. In 1971, 10 of the country's largest steel companies and the United Steelworkers Union agreed to a three-year experiment that they named "expedited arbitration" or "mini-arb." The experiment was successful, and they subsequently incorporated this procedure into their collective agreements. Numerous companies and unions are currently utilizing this procedure.

Expedited arbitration system is not a substitute for regular arbitration. It is usually employed to settle certain types of disputes at some agreed-upon step of the grievance procedure after the parties have not settled at a previous step, and then only after a joint labor-management committee agrees to the abbreviated procedure.

This arbitration technique is marked by informality. The hearing is usually conducted in the office or shop, sometimes at the workplace rather than in a hotel room or other neutral site. The arbitrator may interview witnesses on the spot. The more legalistic rules of evidence often employed in arbitration proceedings are considerably relaxed. The arbitrator normally renders his or her decision within 24 to 48 hours of the hearing. Sometimes the arbitrator renders it the same day, on occasion within minutes after the conclusion of the hearing. This is called a bench decision.

The procedure is more applicable to some cases than others. It has been most useful in settling minor disciplinary cases, although it has also been employed to decide nondisciplinary issues, including compensation and employee rights questions. It is less useful in resolving issues involving interpretation of the meaning of an important contractual clause or questions of principle. Some disputes involve issues so fundamental to the parties that one or both may refuse to submit them to an expedited arbitration. For example, questions involving the meaning of management or union "rights" provisions in the contract, subcontracting, or production standards are more appropriately resolved by means of a more thorough arbitration procedure.[11]

Although expedited arbitration normally is associated with settlement of rather minor grievances, some companies and unions are utilizing the concept for discharge and other selected cases where the parties wish to bring the arbitration process to a swift conclusion. Here the parties may well have a very thorough and formal arbitration hearing of the case matter, but the selection of the arbitrator, the scheduling of the hearing, and the rendering of the arbitrator's decision are all accomplished within a specified and relatively short period of time. The following "Expedited Procedure" is representative of this type of approach.[12]

---

[11] For a brief, but balanced, view of this topic, see Lawrence Stessin, "Expedited Arbitration: Less Grief over Grievances," *Harvard Business Review,* no. 1 (1977): 128–34. Also see pamphlet, *Expedited Labor Arbitration Rules of the American Arbitration Association* (New York: American Arbitration Association).

[12] From Agreement between Anheuser-Busch, Inc., of St. Louis, Missouri, and Bottlers Local Union No. 1187, affiliated with the International Brotherhood of Teamsters, Chauffeurs, Warehousemen, and Helpers of North America, effective 1985 through 1987, pp. 7–10.

Section 4(a). If a grievance involving the discharge of an employee shall have been submitted but not adjusted under Step 3, the following Expedited Procedure shall apply unless the Employer and the Union mutually agree to waive any of these provisions:

1. If the Union wishes to proceed to arbitration, it must give written notice to the Employer of its demand for arbitration within five (5) days after its receipt of the Employer's written reply following the Step 3 meeting.

2. The Employer will promptly notify the appropriate arbitrator selected as set forth below and schedule a hearing which is to take place within the five-day period following the Employer's receipt of the Union's demand for arbitration.

3. The arbitrator shall render a written decision within ten (10) days following the close of the hearing, and within sixty (60) days following the close of the hearing, the arbitrator will render a written opinion explaining the reasons for the decision.

In conjunction with any Expedited Arbitration hereunder, either party may, at its option, submit a pre-hearing brief. And, either party may, at its option, request a court reporter for the hearing at its own cost, unless both parties request a transcript in which case the cost of the court reporter will be shared equally.

The decision of the arbitrator shall be final and conclusive on both the Employer and the Union. The arbitrator shall have no power to add to, detract from, or alter this agreement in any way. Pending final decision by the arbitrator, there shall be no action taken by either party to the controversy. Any expense incidental to and arising out of the arbitrations shall be borne equally by the Employer and the Union except as otherwise provided in this Article.

(b). Expedited Arbitration Panel—Within thirty (30) days following the effective date of this Agreement, and annually thereafter, the Employer and the Union shall select a panel of five (5) arbitrators designated to decide Expedited Arbitration cases under this Article. The panel of five (5) arbitrators shall be selected as follows: The Federal Mediation and Conciliation Service will be asked to provide five (5) lists of arbitrators with each list containing names of seven (7) names from the Midwest area comprised of the states of Michigan, Illinois, Indiana, Iowa, Arkansas, Kansas, Nebraska, and Missouri. One arbitrator will be chosen from each FMCS list by the procedure of alternating strikes—the party having the first strike on the first list will be determined by a coin flip and thereafter the party having the first strike on the remaining lists will alternate. The five (5) arbitrators thus chosen will constitute the Expedited Panel for proceedings under this Article.

(c). Selection of an Arbitrator from the Expedited Panel—The arbitrator for an Expedited Arbitration shall be selected from the Expedited Panel as follows: The five (5) arbitrators on the Expedited Panel shall be listed in alphabetical order and cases will be referred to the arbitrators in that sequence until a new Expedited Panel is chosen (for example, the first expedited arbitration will be referred to arbitrator No. 1, the second will be referred to arbitrator No. 2, the fifth will be referred to arbitrator No. 5, the sixth will be referred to arbitrator No. 1, the seventh will be referred to arbitrator No. 2, the tenth will be referred to arbitrator No. 5, and so on). However, in the event the arbitrator designated by this procedure is unable to schedule a hearing within the five-day time period provided for above, the case will be referred to the next arbitrator in sequence and so on until an arbitrator is designated who can schedule the hearing within the appropriate time period, and any arbitrator thus bypassed will not be designated again until his name comes up in the regular sequence. Provided further that in the event none of the arbitrators on the Expedited Panel is able to schedule a hearing within the five-day time period described above, then that case will be referred to the arbitrator on the Expedited Panel who is able to schedule the earliest possible hearing, and again the sequence of selection of arbitrators for subsequent cases will start with the next arbitrator on the list and any bypassed arbitrator will not be designated again until his name comes up on the regular sequence.

It is likely that expedited arbitration in one form or another will become more commonplace in future years. Expedited arbitration that serves the mutual interests of the parties thus represents another form of conflict resolution that can foster a more constructive atmosphere in union-management relationships.

SELECTED STATISTICS ON ARBITRATION AS REPORTED BY THE AMERICAN ARBITRATION ASSOCIATION AND THE FEDERAL MEDIATION AND CONCILIATION SERVICE

The American Arbitration Association reported that of some 9,000 case awards issued through its services in calendar year 1986, 51 percent of the grievances were denied, 32 percent were upheld, and 17 percent were partially upheld and partially denied by the arbitrators. At the arbitration hearings themselves, 77 percent of the employers and 52 percent of the unions were represented by attorneys. Transcripts were taken at 22 percent of the hearings, and post-hearing briefs were filed by the parties in 59 percent of the cases.[13]

According to the Federal Mediation and Conciliation Service, in fiscal year 1987 its Office of Arbitration Services assigned some 32,000 arbitration panels, from which arbitrators were appointed in about one

---

[13] From a letter to members of AAA Labor Panels by Robert Coulson, President of the American Arbitration Association, New York, N.Y., January 20, 1987.

third of the case panels assigned. However, the FMCS actually closed only 4,145 cases in FY87, a number that was considerably lower than during several previous years. The predominant issues involved in the cases closed were: discipline/discharge (48 percent); seniority issues (12 percent); and work assignment issues (6 percent). FMCS sample data for FY87 indicated that the average elapsed time between the date of the filing of a grievance and the date on which the parties requested an FMCS arbitration panel was 104 days. The average elapsed time between the date an FMCS arbitration panel was requested and the date of the arbitrator's award was 242 days.[14]

DECIDING ARBITRATION CASES FROM AN ARBITRATOR'S POINT OF VIEW

The cases included in this section all resulted from actual disputes that were processed through grievance procedures in collective bargaining agreements, that remained unsettled, and that then were subsequently submitted to arbitration. In a condensed form, these cases provide the essential information available to the arbitrator. By studying the issues in such cases, one has the opportunity of experiencing actual arbitration situations and of arriving at one's own decisions with respect to the disputes. In so doing, however, it is desirable to follow certain principles that most arbitrators and practitioners of labor relations have come to understand as being appropriate to an arbitrator's decision-making responsibilities.[15]

In general, the three major aspects that an arbitrator must consider, in order of importance, are as follows:

1. What does the labor agreement say?
2. What is the role of past practices or precedents?
3. What standards of fairness or equity should be applied?

1. What Does the Labor Agreement Say?

It usually is recognized by the parties that a labor agreement is essentially a general outline for handling many problems and situations that arise during the course of an agreement, and that no contract could possibly cover all of them. Nevertheless, an arbitrator is

---

[14] From *Memorandum to FMCS Arbitrators—Fiscal Year, 1987* (Washington, D.C.: Federal Mediation and Conciliation Service, August 1988).

[15] Parts of this section were excerpted from Raymond L. Hilgert, "An Arbitrator Looks at Grievance Arbitration," *Personnel Journal* (October 1978), pp. 556–59, 578.

first of all bound to the wording and general interpretation of the agreement itself. As a rule, most arbitrators take a somewhat restrictive view when applying and interpreting a labor agreement. That is to say, they normally do not expand upon the meaning of a clause in the agreement unless there is some reasonable evidence that this is what the parties had intended.

2. What Is the Role of Past Practices or Precedents?

If a clause in a labor agreement is not clear, or if it is subject to ambiguous interpretation, most arbitrators will look to past practices or precedents for guidance to determine the intent of the parties. Past practices or precedents can become an extension of a labor agreement almost as if the parties had negotiated additional contract language accordingly. This does not mean that a past practice or precedent always is a permanent fixture and cannot be changed for good reasons. But if the parties have handled a certain problem or parallel problems along consistent lines on a number of occasions, an arbitrator usually is reluctant to make a ruling contrary to such a practice, just as an arbitrator would not choose to change the wording of a labor agreement.

3. What Standards of Fairness and Equity Should Be Applied?

The third and probably most subjective area of the arbitration process involves standards for fairness and equity to be applied in certain types of cases. This is especially true in discipline and discharge cases, since most labor agreements specify that a company may discipline or discharge an employee for "just cause" or "proper cause."

Over the last several decades, the majority of arbitrators have adopted in one form or another the "Seven Tests for Just Cause," which were first formulated by arbitrator Carroll R. Daugherty in the *Enterprise Wire Company* case, (46 LA 359, 1966). These seven tests were posed in the form of questions that could be applied to the facts of any case involving discipline or discharge. A "no" answer to one or more of these questions presumably would signify that a standard of just (or proper) cause was not met, and the arbitrator, therefore, probably would set aside or modify the employer's disciplinary or discharge action. The seven tests for just cause are as follows:

1. Did the company give to the employee forewarning or foreknowledge of the possible or probable disciplinary consequences of the employee's conduct?

2. Was the company's rule or managerial order reasonably related to: *(a)* the orderly, efficient, and safe operation of the company's business; and *(b)* the performance that the company might properly expect of the employee?

3. Did the company, before administering discipline to an employee, make an effort to discover whether the employee did in fact violate or disobey a rule or order of management?

4. Was the company's investigation conducted fairly and objectively?

5. At the investigation, was there substantial evidence or proof that the employee was guilty as charged?

6. Has the company applied its rule, orders, and penalties even-handedly and without discrimination to all employees?

7. Was the degree of discipline administered by the company in a particular case reasonably related to: *(a)* the seriousness of the employee's proven offense; and *(b)* the record of employee in his service with the company?[16]

One aspect that often is crucial in regard to the above tests is the matter of burden of proof in presentation of evidence. Most arbitrators believe that in discipline and discharge cases, the primary burden falls upon management to demonstrate from the preponderance of evidence available that what it did in a particular matter would be considered a reasonable course of action by a neutral or impartial person. Thus, in discharge and disciplinary matters, the cases most likely to go to arbitration, it becomes prudent for management to ask itself how a reasonable, neutral person would view what was done.

---

[16] For an expanded discussion of these tests, see Donald S. McPherson, "The Evolving Concept of Just Cause: Carroll R. Daugherty and the Requirement of Disciplinary Due Process," *Labor Law Journal* (July, 1987), pp. 387–403.

Selected Bibliography

Allen, Robert E., and Timothy J. Keaveny. *Contemporary Labor Relations*. 2d ed. Reading, Mass.: Addison-Wesley Publishing, 1988.

Baer, Walter E. *Discipline and Discharge under the Labor Agreement*. New York: American Management Association, 1972.

Begin, James P., and Edwin F. Beal. *The Practice of Collective Bargaining*. 7th ed. Homewood, Ill.: Richard D. Irwin, 1985.

Brand, Norman. *Labor Arbitration: The Strategy of Persuasion*. New York: Practising Law Institute, 1987.

Carrell, Michael R., and Christina Heavrin. *Collective Bargaining and Labor Relations: Cases, Practices, and Law*. 2d ed. Columbus, Ohio: Charles E. Merrill Publishing, 1987.

Code of Professional Responsibility for Arbitrators of Labor-Management Disputes. Published jointly by the National Academy of Arbitrators, American Arbitration Association, and the Federal Mediation and Conciliation Service, November 1974.

Colosi, Thomas R., and Arthur Eliot Berkeley. *Collective Bargaining: How It Works and Why*. New York: American Arbitration Association, 1986.

Davey, Harold W.; Mario F. Bognanno; and David L. Estenson. *Contemporary Collective Bargaining*. 4th ed. Englewood Cliffs, N.J.: Prentice-Hall, 1982.

Dilts, David A., and Clarence R. Deitsch. *Labor Relations*. New York: Macmillan, 1983.

Elkin, Randyl D., and Thomas L. Hewitt. *Successful Arbitration—An Experiential Approach*. Reston, Va.: Reston Publishing, 1980.

Elkouri, Frank, and Edna A. Elkouri. *How Arbitration Works*. 4th ed. Washington, D.C.: Bureau of National Affairs, 1985.

Fairweather, Owen. *Practice and Procedure in Labor Arbitration*. 2d ed. Washington, D.C.: Bureau of National Affairs, Inc., 1983.

Fossum, John A. *Labor Relations: Development, Structure, Process*. 4th ed. Homewood, Ill.: BPI/Irwin, 1989.

Grievance Arbitration in the Federal Service. Huntsville, Ala.: Federal Personnel Management Institute, Inc., 1987.

Hill, Marvin, Jr., and Anthony V. Sinicropi. *Evidence in Arbitration*. 2d ed. Washington, D.C. Bureau of National Affairs, Inc., 1987.

Imundo, Louis V. *The Arbitration Game*. Cincinnati: South-Western Publishing, 1982.

Kagel, Sam. *Anatomy of a Labor Arbitration*. 2d ed. Washington, D.C.: Bureau of National Affairs, Inc., 1986.

Labor Arbitration Awards. Chicago: Commerce Clearing House.

Labor Arbitration Reports. Washington, D.C.: Bureau of National Affairs, Inc.

McPherson, Donald S., with Conrad John Gates and Kevin N. Rogers. *Resolving Grievances: A Practical Approach*. Reston, Va.: Reston Publishing, 1983.

Mills, Daniel Quinn. *Labor-Management Relations*. 3d ed. New York: McGraw-Hill, 1986.

Mills, Daniel Quinn, and Janice McCormick. *Industrial Relations in Transition*. New York: John Wiley & Sons, 1985.

Pops, Gerald M. *Emergence of the Public Sector Arbitrator*. Lexington, Mass.: D. C. Heath, 1976.

Prasow, Paul, and Edward Peters. *Arbitration and Collective Bargaining— Conflict Resolution in Labor Relations*. 2d ed. New York: McGraw-Hill, 1983.

Repas, Robert. *Contract Administration: A Guide for Local Stewards and Officers*. Washington, D.C.: Bureau of National Affairs, Inc., 1984.

Robinson, James W.; Wayne L. Dernoncourt; and Ralph H. Effler. *The Grievance Procedure and Arbitration: Text and Cases*. Washington, D.C.: University Press of America, 1978.

Sandver, Marcus Hart. *Labor Relations: Process and Outcomes*. Boston: Little, Brown, 1987.

Sauer, Robert L., and Keith E. Voelker. *Labor Relations: Structure and Process*. Columbus, Ohio: Charles E. Merrill Publishing, 1987.

Scheinman, Martin F. *Evidence and Proof in Arbitration*. Ithaca, N.Y.: New York State School of Industrial and Labor Relations, 1977.

Sloane, Arthur A., and Fred Witney. *Labor Relations*. 6th ed., Englewood Cliffs, N.J.: Prentice-Hall, 1988.

Trotta, Maurice S. *Arbitration of Labor-Management Disputes*. New York: American Management Association, 1974.

Index to Cases for Part Two

Case Number and Title	Management Rights	Union Rights and Activities	Seniority and Employee Rights	Discipline and Discharge	Work Assignments and Job Bidding	Work Performance	Technological Change/Past Practices	Wages and Benefits	Employee Health, Safety, and Security	Discrimination
35. Stolen Kisses	X			X		X				X
36. Impaired Performance	X			X	X	X			X	
37. No More Coffee or Bottled Water	X	X	X				X			
38. The Bypassed Senior Clerk	X	X	X		X	X	X	X		
39. The Disabled Blower Motor	X	X	X				X			
40. The Subcontracted Heaters	X	X			X	X				
41. The Rescheduled Lunch Period	X		X		X	X	X			
42. A "Horns of a Dilemma" Situation	X		X	X		X				
43. The Right to Work on a Birthday Holiday	X				X		X	X		
44. Sunday Is the Sabbath Day	X		X		X		X			X

Index to Cases for Part Two (continued)

Index to Cases for Part Two (continued)

Case Number and Title	Management Rights	Union Rights and Activities	Seniority and Employee Rights	Discipline and Discharge	Work Assignments and Job Bidding	Work Performance	Technological Change/Past Practices	Wages and Benefits	Employee Health, Safety, and Security	Discrimination
58. Emergency Leave Pay	X						X	X		
59. The Disputed Test	X		X		X	X				X
60. The Forbidden Nuptials	X			X			X			
61. The Frustrated Bus Drivers	X		X		X	X	X	X		X
62. No Bread in the Store				X	X	X				
63. One Last Chance	X			X	X	X			X	
64. The Payroll Error	X			X				X		
65. The Unrecorded Purchase	X			X		X	X			
66. Do New Hires Include Rehires?	X	X	X					X		
67. The Right to Work Overtime	X		X	X	X	X	X	X		
68. The Revised Payroll Period	X	X					X	X		
69. The Pregnant Laboratory Analyst			X		X			X	X	X

Index to Cases for Part Two (concluded)

Case Number and Title	Management Rights	Union Rights and Activities	Seniority and Employee Rights	Discipline and Discharge	Work Assignments and Job Bidding	Work Performance	Technological Change/Past Practices	Wages and Benefits	Employee Health, Safety, and Security	Discrimination
70. The Police Detective's Request for a Switch of Shifts			X		X					
71. The Lunch-Time Tipplers	X			X		X			X	
72. Vacation Time After Recall?	X		X				X	X		
73. "Restructured" Out of the Company	X	X	X		X		X			
74. COLA Takes a Dip	X	X						X		
75. The "Rehabilitated" Employee	X		X	X		X	X		X	X
76. No Smoking in the Restrooms	X		X				X			
77. Too "Punk" to Work?	X		X	X						

35. Stolen Kisses

Company:
   Williams Brothers Markets, Santa Maria, California
Union:
   Retail Clerks Union, Local 899

At 11:00 A.M., October 5, 1974, Henry Hampton,[1] vice president of Williams Brothers Markets, discharged Joyce Stephens and George Folsom for "unbecoming conduct." In a letter of discharge addressed to them jointly, Mr. Hampton stated:

> We believe that two adult married people are morally wrong when they kiss (on many occasions) at their place of employment. We believe that this is not socially acceptable and therefore is unbecoming conduct.

The company claimed that the employees' activities were in violation of Section A of Article III of the collective bargaining agreement, which reads:

> The Employer shall have the right to discharge an employee for good cause, such as dishonesty, insubordination, incompetency, intoxication, unbecoming conduct, failure to perform work as required, and excessive absenteeism.

Joyce Stephens immediately filed a grievance in which she asked for reinstatement to her former position, payment for lost wages, and restoration of all rights and benefits.

BACKGROUND

Joyce Stephens was a checker at Store 3 in Arroyo Grande, California, a position she had held since February 1974. At this same time George Folsom was employed as a produce manager in the same market. On September 17, 1974, Folsom confided to Arnold Singleton, produce merchandiser, that he was in love with Stephens. Singleton told him that the company could not tolerate "two married people playing around on the job." He also advised Folsom to terminate the relationship. Singleton immediately reported his "confidential" conversation to store manager Daniel Vandenberg, who indicated that he

---

[1] The names of all individuals have been disguised.

had already been aware that Folsom had a "greater than average attraction to Stephens."

On September 23, Willis Goode, an auditor for the company, was at the store investigating a money shortage problem. He noted that both Stephens and Folsom had gone into the produce processing room, and that Folsom acted "very excited." Goode followed them into the room, where he observed them kissing.

Goode, Vandenberg, and Hampton agreed that if any disciplinary action was to be taken, they should catch Stephens and Folsom in the act of kissing. They set up a "blind" in the produce processing room, and on October 5 confronted them in the act of embracing and kissing. It was at this point that Hampton discharged them "on the spot."

POSITION OF THE UNION

The union contended that Stephens had been observed kissing on only two occasions, on neither of which was she on duty. No customer or employee had observed the kissing or embracing, nor had any customer or employee complained. On the two days in question, Stephens had not "clocked in." In other words, she had not started work. It was customary for her to arrive about 15 to 20 minutes early to check the produce department for recent price changes and to check for new price changes and specials throughout the store. It was her practice to check the price lists and then go into the produce processing room to have a cup of coffee before starting work.

The union also contended that Stephens did not encourage Folsom's "amorous antics." She admitted that he was kissing her when they were discovered. She claimed, however, that she was not returning the kiss, and that in fact, she was attempting to discourage his advances. She said that they were good friends, they had a number of acquaintances in common, that they had a similar approach to problems, and that on their breaks they spent time discussing matters of mutual interest.

The union also pointed out that Stephens was a good employee. Her performance appraisals described her as a "good checker," "better than average," and "competent." She had never received any warnings or complaints, either written or oral, regarding her work. While both Singleton and Vandenberg had warned Folsom about having an "amorous relationship" with another employee, no such warnings had ever been given Stephens.

The union added that the company had never adopted any standards defining unbecoming conduct. It was not until October 5, after this incident, that a policy had been decided upon. The company had acted arbitrarily in discharging the employee without warning and without prior notice of what constitutes unbecoming conduct.

The union requested that Joyce Stephens be returned with no loss of seniority to her position as checker, and that she be made whole for all loss of pay and benefits while she was off work because of her improper discharge.

POSITION OF THE COMPANY

The company contended that the conduct of Stephens and Folsom was detrimental to the conduct of business. In the company's view, the public is sensitive to the behavior of employees in retail organizations. Customers who disapprove of amorous public behavior between married adults will trade elsewhere if the company condoned such behavior on the part of its employees.

The company also argued that it is commonly accepted that an employer cannot tolerate married employees kissing and embracing others than their spouses at their place of employment. It is not necessary to spell out this type of behavior as specifically constituting unbecoming conduct.

The agreement specifically gives the company the right to discharge employees for unbecoming conduct. The company exercised this right appropriately in this matter, and the grievance should be dismissed.

QUESTIONS

1. Was the behavior of the female employee in relationship to the produce manager "unbecoming conduct"? Was it conduct of sufficient gravity to justify discharge in this case? Discuss.

2. Did management under the agreement have the right to determine standards for defining "unbecoming conduct"? Why, or why not?

3. Should conduct of employees in a retail supermarket be of a higher standard than in a factory situation, where employees do not come into regular contact with the public?

4. If the arbitrator should return employee Joyce Stephens to her position, would the company be obligated also to return the produce manager to his position? Why, or why not?

36. *Impaired Performance*

Company:
Public Service Electric and Gas Company, Burlington, New Jersey

Union:
Public Utility Construction and Gas Appliance Workers, Local 274

BACKGROUND

Having satisfied the job requirement of typing 50 words per minute and meeting the other application prerequisites, Nancy Bell[1] was hired as a general clerk, second class, by the company on December 22, 1969. She began work in the Burlington district office, and in December 1971 she was promoted to general clerk, first class, a job that principally required strong typing skills. She was regarded as an excellent worker; periodic management appraisal reviews noted her good typing and quickness to learn and rated her as an above-average to excellent performer.

On December 6, 1972, Nancy Bell suffered serious head injuries in a three-car accident. She remained comatose for two weeks, and then began to slowly recover from a spastic left hemiplegia. In mid-January, 1973, she began receiving occupational therapy at Thomas Jefferson Hospital and was eventually released from the hospital on January 28, 1973. Following her hospitalization, Bell remained under close medical supervision until August 29, 1973. She was then discharged from full care, and she returned to her job on September 4, 1973, with her doctor's approval and opinion that she was physically capable of such work.

Bell still had difficulty walking, as her left-side coordination was weak. Following an examination on September 26, her physician at Thomas Jefferson Hospital reported that "she still has evidence of a very mild organic brain syndrome with periods of emotional liability." However, he, too, concluded that she was capable of returning to work.

After her return, Bell's work did not match her former level of performance, either in quality or quantity. Her typing was slow and often contained many errors. Initially management chose to overlook her poor performance, attributing it to her long absence and physical

---

[1] The names of all individuals have been disguised.

problems. On January 31, 1974, however, she was advised that her work performance had been very poor, and that if she did not improve within three months, she would face "more severe disciplinary actions." Bell's typing, nevertheless, remained below the minimum requirement of 50 words per minute, and she continued to perform her other tasks at an unsatisfactory level. On February 25, 1974, her supervisor again reviewed her poor performance with Bell, and informed her that if her work did not improve to a level satisfactory to the company by April 30, 1974, the company would consider her discharge.

Recognizing her difficulty, Nancy Bell enrolled in an evening typing course at a local high school in an attempt to improve her speed and accuracy. She reported that she had increased her productivity from 37 words per minute with five errors to 55 words per minute with no errors by the end of May. Management, however, did not notice any significant improvement in her performance on the job. Subsequently, in June 1974 management reassigned her to the dispatch office as a general clerk, second class, although she continued to be paid as a general clerk, first class. In this position, Bell was primarily responsible for receiving emergency telephone calls, logging information, and preparing service orders, a job to which most persons adapted within a few days. Nevertheless, Bell's work over the next few months continued to be rated "unsatisfactory" by her supervisor, principally because of her slowness, and in early October 1974 she was transferred back to the district office.

Again, her work did not show any improvement, and on October 24, 1974, the division superintendent requested that the company physician examine her to determine if she was "capable of improving her work output to acceptable levels." She was examined by Charles Wallace, M.D., on November 14, 1974. He concluded that Bell had suffered a "cerebral contusion with posttraumatic cerebral edema and partial left hemiparesis." He went on to conclude in his report:

> In my opinion, this young woman has reached a point of recovery which will not progress any more. I also feel that her recovery has been nothing short of remarkable considering the severity of her accident. She has lost some mental facility because of the prolonged coma secondary to the cerebral edema and brain damage. It is my feeling that this facility will never be regained. Without specific psychological testing, it is impossible to precisely pinpoint her main areas of deficiency. However, one gets the impression that her ability to think automatically and relate one thing to another is somewhat impaired. She must study everything, make a decision, and then go ahead. Apparently, when she does this, she performs adequately, but obviously this process is quite slow. It is my medical opinion that she can do the type of job she is now assigned to, but

management must accept the fact that her work will be slow and her output less than that of someone who has not had a severe brain injury.

Several weeks after receiving Dr. Wallace's report the company decided to terminate Bell. She was placed on a six-month disability leave beginning December 10, 1974, and was then terminated.

The union filed a grievance on Bell's behalf, alleging that the company lacked "just cause" (see Appendix to this case for Article II of the agreement) for its discharge of Bell and seeking her reinstatement to active service with the firm.

UNION POSITION

The union contended that the company had not done all within its power to determine whether Nancy Bell's work could be further improved. The union maintained that she was fully capable of performing at an acceptable level, based upon Bell's assertion that she could perform "adequately." She argued that she was, at the time of arbitration, capable of performing nearly as well as she was doing before the accident, and she felt she would continue to improve. For these and for humanitarian considerations, the union requested full reinstatement of Bell to her former or to an equivalent position.

COMPANY POSITION

The company maintained that it had given Nancy Bell ample opportunity to achieve an "acceptable" level of productivity. Management maintained that it regretted her inability to perform adequately, and pointed out that it had allowed her an extensive period of readaptation to her work routine. However, it contended that Bell had demonstrated that she was unable to achieve acceptable levels of performance, and management was well within its rights to discontinue her from its service. The discharge action should be sustained.

APPENDIX

Relevant Provisions of the Agreement

Article II—Union-Employer Relationship

It is specifically agreed that the management of the plant and the direction of the working forces shall be vested exclusively in the Employer. This right shall include but not be limited to, the right to hire and discharge (for just cause), the right to suspend from duty (for just cause), and the right to transfer personnel from one position to another (for just cause), provided, however, that the foregoing shall not impair any of the rights of the Union or the employees granted by other provisions of the Agreement.

QUESTIONS

1. Did the company give the employee reasonable time and opportunity to achieve an acceptable level of performance following her accident? Discuss.
2. Is a company obligated to assist an employee in a rehabilitation program following a serious physical and mental injury?
3. Evaluate the union's argument in asking for reinstatement of employee Nancy Bell that humanitarian considerations should be taken into account.
4. Why is a case of this sort difficult for all parties involved, including the arbitrator who is asked to decide the issue?

37. No More Coffee or Bottled Water

Company:

Ametek California Spring Company, Pico Rivera, California

Union:

United Automobile, Aerospace and Agricultural Implement Workers of America, Local 509

On April 7, 1975, a directive was issued by the company plant manager informing employees that (1) coffee was no longer to be prepared during company working hours and (2) the bottled-water stations scattered throughout the plant had been replaced by water fountains in the course of a new plumbing installation. Martin Adams,[1] an employee of the company for over 20 years, immediately questioned his supervisor, John Willis, concerning the memorandum. He reminded Willis that he had been preparing a 36-cup pot of coffee in his department every working day for the previous 19 years. He noted that the practice had been initiated at the request of a foreman who was no longer with the firm, and that it took only five minutes of his time each morning unless a second pot was required later in the day. The coffee was available to anyone in the plant during break periods, and the only limitation was that each person pay 10 cents for each cup in order to pay for supplies. Adams further noted that the company had acknowledged and supported the practice several years before by installing a water outlet in the first-aid room. This enabled Mary Miller to obtain water for the coffee when Adams was on vacation, since Adams normally obtained water from the faucet in the men's room. Willis listened to Adams' protest but informed him that the order came from the plant manager and it had to be enforced.

The union then filed a grievance protesting the company's unilateral action in terminating the coffee-making privilege and removing six bottled-water stations in the plant. The union maintained that the company had violated past practice and Section 3 of Article XIII of the Agreement, which stated:

> The Company shall not take away any privileges that are now enjoyed by the employees.

The question eventually reached the arbitration level, where the parties agreed that the issue to be resolved by the arbitrator should be:

---

[1] The names of all individuals have been disguised.

Did the Company violate Article XIII by removing the bottled water and refusing to allow employees to make coffee on Company time?

POSITION OF THE UNION

At the hearing, Martin Adams related the background and procedure of his daily coffee brewing, just as he had commented to Willis on the day of the directive. He particularly noted the long duration of the practice and the apparent company acquiescence in allowing it to continue and even promoting the brewing by installing the water faucet in the first-aid room. The union acknowledged that several times in the previous three or four years management had mentioned discontinuation of the practice, but that no serious effort had been made prior to April 17, 1975, actually to effectuate that policy.

The union maintained that both the coffee brewing and bottled-water stations, which had been located in the plant for approximately 10 years, were established past practices that could not be unilaterally discontinued by management. It argued that the company had acquiesced to the coffee brewing for over 19 years and had provided bottled water since the plant facility's inception. The union cited Section 3 of Article XIII of the agreement and alleged the company had violated these provisions.

The union requested the arbitrator to order the company to restore the coffee-making privilege and the bottled-water stations in the plant.

POSITION OF THE COMPANY

Alfred Perry, general manager of the plant, testified that after joining the company in his present position in 1969, he had become aware of the practice of making coffee on company time. Perry stated that over a period of three or four years he had instructed supervisors approximately a dozen times to stop the practice, and each time he was informed that the directive had been enforced.

Management representatives further argued that the preparation and drinking of coffee on company time wasted a considerable amount of time and interfered with efficiency. Management claimed that it had the right to abolish the coffee making under Section 1 of Article II of the contract, which read:

> It is the responsibility of the management of the company to maintain discipline and efficiency in its plant.

Perry and the plant manager, Jerome Epps, also testified concerning the bottled water. They affirmed that the company had provided bottled drinking water in the plant over the years. They maintained that it had done so because in the past the company had had inadequate drinking fountains. However, the remodeling completed in the spring of 1975 provided plumbing facilities so that water fountains could be installed at various points in the plant. The company argued that the need for bottled water no longer existed, and that it had acted legitimately in terminating the bottled-water system.

Finally, management contended that the installation of drinking fountains constituted an improvement in working conditions, as well as being more efficient.

The company urged that in the interests of maintaining efficiency in the plant, its position in prohibiting the preparation of coffee on company time and the installation of drinking fountains be upheld.

QUESTIONS

1. Was the coffee drinking privilege a well-established practice in the plant? Was the providing of bottled-water stations a well-established past practice? Evaluate.

2. To what degree are Section 3 of Article XIII and Section 1 of Article II of the agreement contradictory? Which of these provisions is "superior" in the circumstances of this case?

3. What standards should an arbitrator utilize to determine whether something is a well-established past practice, or whether something is within the province of management rights to handle as appropriate to efficient operation? Discuss.

38. The Bypassed Senior Clerk

Company:
   Marion Food Towne, Incorporated, Marion, Illinois
Union:
   Retail Clerks International Association, Local 896

BACKGROUND

In June 1975, Raymond White,[1] co-owner of Marion Food Towne, Charles Ridgeway, manager of the store, and Frank Costilli, assistant manager, unanimously concluded that because of increased business it was necessary to hire an additional full-time clerk at the store. At that time, seven part-time clerks were employed at the store, and the managers decided to consider first the three part-time clerks with highest seniority for the new position.

Robert Sharp, who was in his early 50s, had worked several years in a part-time position and held highest seniority among the part-time clerks. He had been passed over several times during those years by management in hiring full-time clerks because he was considered to be too slow in carrying out his duties. In spite of this, however, the managers considered him valuable for stocking in the evening, when he normally worked. James Moran, 20, having been hired on April 29, 1974, was second in seniority among the part-time stock clerks. John Anthony, having been hired on June 17, 1974, also 20, was third on the seniority list. He worked on essentially the same jobs as Moran.

The managers again decided in this instance that Sharp was too slow to be promoted, although he requested the job. They then evaluated the work performance of Moran and Anthony in an attempt to determine the best man for the position. Although they considered seniority in arriving at their decision, White, Ridgeway, and Costilli were primarily concerned with hiring into the full-time position the person with the best performance record who gave promise of having most long-run value to the store.

After considering both Moran and Anthony for the promotion and consulting with White, Costilli, and other store employees, Ridgeway awarded the full-time position to Anthony, who held least seniority among the three part-time clerks. The three managers had generally agreed that Anthony was superior to Moran in handling his duties

---

[1] The names of all individuals have been disguised.

around the store. Costilli had commented that in observing both Moran and Anthony stocking shelves, Anthony was consistently quicker, neater, and more conscientious in handling his aisles. The head checker had told Ridgeway that Anthony was usually "much quicker" in coming to the checkout counter to assist in bagging, in reporting prices on unmarked items, and in assisting customers, and that Anthony was more efficient, helpful, and friendly than Moran. Ridgeway also took into consideration several customer comments he had received in March and April of 1975, complaining of Moran's "lack of friendliness." Ridgeway had discussed those complaints with Moran, and Moran's behavior had improved somewhat following that meeting. Ridgeway concluded, however, that Anthony was more interested in his work and in the store, and that he was the best man available for the promotion. Anthony was given the full-time position in mid-June 1975.

Following Anthony's appointment, Moran filed a grievance with the union on June 23, 1975, complaining that the company had hired a part-time employee of lower seniority to the full-time position without first offering the job to him. On June 25, 1975, Virgil Neickhorn, president of Local 896, sent a letter to the company, the relevant part of which stated:

> This is to advise that James Moran has filed a grievance with this office contesting the Company's action of hiring a less senior employee for a full-time job. Mr. Moran was not offered the full-time job opening.
> We feel this is in violation of the Agreement: Article 9—Seniority.[2]

The company and the union failed to resolve their differences in the first three steps of the grievance procedure. The two parties submitted the following issue to an arbitrator on October 9, 1975:

> Did the Company violate the Agreement when it offered a full-time clerk's position to part-time employee John Anthony rather than offering the position to James Moran, another part-time employee who had about two months seniority over Mr. Anthony?

POSITION OF THE UNION

Counsel for the union interrogated store manager Ridgeway at great length during the arbitration hearing. Ridgeway related the considerations involved in promoting Anthony to the full-time position, including the consultations he had had with other personnel in the store and his own observations, which led him to conclude that

---

[2] See Appendix to this case.

Anthony was superior to Moran in his work and the "best man" for the full-time position. Ridgeway testified that he wanted the "best man" regardless of his seniority, and that his decision rested largely on the person's ability to do the job. He noted that in the past the company's policy of promoting the "best man" had provided the basis for promoting lower seniority part-time employees instead of Robert Sharp into full-time positions. He also stated that he regarded a full-time position as a promotion from a part-time status.

Ridgeway stated that analysis of work performance had shown Anthony's work aisle was consistently in "much better shape, neater, and had less back stock" than did Moran's. Under questioning, Ridgeway also testified that he had discussed with Moran several customer complaints regarding Moran's friendliness, but had never given him any written reprimand or report to help improve his performance. The company had an "Employee Corrective Action Notice" form to be used to note for an employee any deficiencies, but Moran had never been given one of these reports. Ridgeway stated that he considered Moran to be a "satisfactory employee" but that there were significant differences between that and an "excellent" employee.

Union president Virgil Neickhorn then testified that Article 9, Section A, of the contract had remained the same throughout the past 12 years, during which he had first been a business agent for the union and, for the last 2 years, president of the local. He stated that at no time during that period had a similar grievance been filed by any union member.

In the course of his testimony on his own behalf, Moran related that he was presently working approximately 24 hours per week and was being paid about $3.10 per hour. He stated that he "did not remember" anyone in management ever criticizing his work, nor did he recall ever being advised by Ridgeway concerning his lack of friendliness toward customers. He stated that he performed essentially the same work as Anthony. He pointed out, however, that Anthony's aisles were located closer to the checkout stations than his own, and that this probably explained why it took him longer than Anthony to respond to requests for help from the checkers.

In summary arguments, the union contended that a change from part-time to full-time employment status did not constitute a promotion but rather a straight seniority claim to additional hours of work. The union noted that under Article 9, Section A, seniority was defined as "the length of continuous employment within the bargaining unit" and that "all circumstances being reasonably equal, length of service shall be the controlling factor." The union noted that Moran had seniority over Anthony, and that the company manager admitted Moran was capable of performing the clerk's work. Moran had never been formally counseled or reprimanded, and from this it must be concluded that Moran was fully capable of performing the clerk's tasks. The union cited several arbitration decisions holding that in situations in which an employee had the ability to do a job and was a satisfactory employee, seniority should be the controlling factor in determining advancement.

The union argued that despite the fact that Article 9, Section A, did not expressly state that a senior part-time employee who was satisfactory should be offered a full-time position in preference to a lower seniority part-time worker, the provision should be interpreted in that manner. It maintained that the spirit of the agreement implicitly led to that interpretation, and that the company should have followed that guide. Ability to do the job should have been the criterion for selecting the full-time clerk. As shown by the testimony, Moran was satisfactory in his work, and the "best-man" criterion should not have entered into management's consideration. The union argued that the company's admitted general disregard for seniority in choosing a part-time employee for a full-time position was a violation of the agreement.

Counsel for the union requested that the grievance be sustained. As a remedy, counsel for the union suggested the following: (1) The grievant, James Moran, should be assigned to a 40-hour work week schedule; (2) he should be made whole for the difference in pay that he would have received having worked a 40-hour schedule since approximately June 23, 1975, to the present time; (3) the number of additional hours that he should have been employed as a full-time employee should be credited appropriately and payments made correspondingly to the pension fund; and (4) he should have full-time seniority status effective as of June 23, 1975.

POSITION OF THE COMPANY

The company referred to the testimony provided by store manager Ridgeway during interrogation by the union counsel and cross-examination by company counsel concerning the criteria employed by the company in deciding to promote Anthony instead of Sharp and Moran. The company emphasized its long-standing policy and practice of hiring full-time employees who indicated that they possessed outstanding ability and a very good attitude. For example, in September 1974 and again in April 1975 management promoted less senior part-time men to full-time clerk positions over Sharp. In 1971 management hired a full-time clerk "off the street," bypassing all the part-time clerks, who had been considered unqualified to fill the full-time position.

Frank Costilli, the assistant manager, testified that he had been employed at the store for six years, and that he had been the assistant manager for the last 18 months, though he still retained membership in Local 896. As assistant manager his job involved supervising and directing stock work by the clerks. He stated that, on the basis of numerous observations, Anthony was consistently quicker, neater, and more efficient in his stocking work than was Moran. In fact, on average, Anthony stocked 35–40 cases per hour, while Moran stocked 20–25 cases per hour. This was true despite the fact that Moran stocked the glass aisles, traditionally easier and quicker than the cereal, coffee, and tea aisles handled by Anthony, which required stock rotation, facing out, and other special operations. Anthony was also willing to "look for other jobs when he was done with his aisle" while Moran would only "just do his aisle."

Costilli stated that he never discussed Moran's poorer performance with him because he felt that the employees might consider his observations to be "spying." He noted, too, that the Employee Corrective Action Notice form for employee evaluation had been introduced in the store in May 1975, only a month before the incident in question.

Raymond White, co-owner of the store, testified that he maintained a philosophy of management that full-time employees should be the best employees, and that such persons must be "the most conscientious people who have the store's best interests at heart and who seek a future in the business." He noted management's previous disregard of Sharp's seniority and hiring of people "off the street" as evidence of its consistent policy of hiring the "best person" for full-time positions.

White related the decision of management to employ another full-time clerk in June 1975. He testified that he normally was in the store two or three days each week, and that he took the place of one of the managers who was on vacation. During those times he was able to make comparative observations of the work of Anthony and Moran. He stated that it was his "considered opinion" that Anthony was "head and shoulders above Moran" in all aspects of work performance. When Ridgeway recommended Anthony for the full-time position, White fully concurred that he was the best man for the job, regardless of his seniority position.

In its closing arguments, the company contended that its selection from among the three highest seniority part-time employees was proof of its concern for seniority, even if it had not promoted the most senior person. The company noted that Section 9 of the agreement required only that the company "give consideration" to part-time employees in selecting full-time personnel, and that it was not required to promote the most senior part-time employee. Since the company was not prohibited by the agreement from hiring someone "off the street," the company should not be more severely constrained in considering part-time personnel than it was in hiring outsiders to full-time positions. The company maintained that the provisions of Section A of Article 9 required the management to follow seniority only in instances of layoffs and rehiring.

The company stated that it regarded the move to full-time status as a "promotion" because of health and benefit provisions and additional available hours of work. It refuted the union assertion that Anthony's new position was merely an increase in hours, which should have been given to the part-time employee of highest seniority. Management also stated that the matter was not a disciplinary action requiring it to give notice to Moran of his deficiencies in order to provide him with full opportunity to improve his performance. The company maintained that having given consideration to seniority, it had the right to choose the person whom it considered best suited for the position.

Counsel for the company requested that the grievance be denied.

APPENDIX

Relevant Provisions of the Agreement

Article IX—Seniority

A. In layoffs and rehiring the principle of seniority shall apply. Seniority shall be defined as the length of continuous employment within the bargaining unit, with regard to an employee's experience and ability to perform the work. All circumstances being reasonably equal, length of service shall be the controlling factor. In the event a layoff, not in accordance with length of service is contemplated, the Employer shall first contact the Union and an attempt shall be made to arrive at a mutual solution. Part-time or casual employees shall not accumulate seniority over full-time employees. It is further agreed that part-time employees shall be given consideration for full-time job vacancies. Seniority shall prevail among employees in each store and shall apply to part-time and full-time employees respectively. In the event of transfer it is agreed that store seniority shall prevail. Any employee so transferred shall retain his seniority previously accumulated from the store from which he was transferred for a period of one (1) year. In the matter of promotions or transfers from one type of work to the other or from one store to the other, the Employer shall have the right to exercise his final judgment after giving due regard to seniority. Agreed upon seniority lists shall be established and maintained and such records shall be available to the Union at all times.

QUESTIONS

1. Evaluate the union contention that a change from part-time to full-time employment status was not a promotion but rather a straight seniority claim to additional hours of work.

2. Even though employee Moran was not the "best man" for the full-time position, should the fact that he was a "satisfactory" employee entitle him to the full-time position because of his seniority? Discuss.

3. To what degree is the company's claim of previous practice persuasive in support of its position?

4. To what degree is the fact that the union had never grieved this particular type of situation a relevant factor?

5. Evaluate the provisions of the agreement that require the company to "give consideration" in moving employees from part-time to full-time status and to "give regard to seniority" in promotions or transfers.

6. Compare the issues in this case with those in Case 49, "To Promote, or to Hire from the Outside?"

39. *The Disabled Blower Motor*

Company:
> Goodyear Atomic Corporation, Piketon, Ohio

Union:
> Oil, Chemical and Atomic Workers International Union, Local 3-689

On Monday, January 26, 1976, one of the three 50-horsepower electric motors powering high-pressure blowers developed a short circuit and required rewinding. The chief engineer estimated that 32 labor-hours would be required to rewind the motor. The company sent the motor to an outside contractor, the National Coil Company, for repair. No standby motor was available while the repairs were made.

Before the motor was sent out, union steward Hugh Benfield[1] questioned the company's decision to have the work performed by an outside contractor rather than by employees of Department 711, Electrical Maintenance. He called the new contract language to the attention of the line foreman, George Lemson. He also told him that the union would file a grievance charging violation of Article XVI, Section 12,[2] if the work was not performed in Department 711.

The union's grievance was rejected by the company through all three steps of the grievance procedure. The company's reply to the union at the third step read as follows:

> This grievance challenges the Company's interpretation of new contract language, Article XVI, Section 12.
>
> The Union's position is that "fully utilized" as used in Section 12 means the use of overtime on all work which could be performed on plantsite that meets the criteria established in Section 12, rather than contracting out.
>
> The Company does not agree that it negotiated any such concept in regard to Section 12. No member of the Company Negotiating Team can recall any conversation between the parties which could lead to such a conclusion.
>
> As reviewed at the hearing, the Company notes reflect the following: "Union representatives asked if the Company's opinion of offering as much work as possible to Goodyear Atomic Corporation employees is 40 hours a week." The notes further reflect that the Union representatives

---

[1] The names of all individuals are disguised.

[2] See Appendix to this case.

at one point stated, "they wanted full utilization of employees plus some overtime."

As stated in Section 12, the Company will give "full consideration to using bargaining unit employees whenever possible."

The union and the company agreed that the issue to be submitted to the arbitrator should be, "Did the company violate Article XVI, Section 12, when it contracted out the rewinding of the electric motor in question?"

NEGOTIATING BACKGROUND

The company and union negotiated a new collective agreement in May 1975. In its original proposal on April 15, the union suggested the following language for the contracting-out provision:

The Company reserves the right to subcontract work specifically, but without limitation for new construction, installation, and structural repair thereto. They will not, however, subcontract normal maintenance normally performed by the bargaining unit.

The company countered on April 24, 1975, with the following proposal:

The Company recognizes the desirability of full utilization of bargaining unit employees where sufficient qualified personnel are present, where time limits for job completion will permit, and where resources are available.

In response, the union resubmitted its original proposal on April 25, 1975, with a slight change in the second sentence as follows:

They will not, however, subcontract work normally performed by the bargaining unit.

The company countered on April 27, 1975, with the following proposal:

The Company reserves the right to subcontract, except that it will not subcontract work normally performed by the bargaining unit, for the express purpose of causing a reduction in force.

The company on the following day offered the provision that was adopted by both parties as the current Article XVI, Section 12.

While Article XVI, Section 12, is silent on the question of overtime, the parties briefly discussed overtime during their negotiations on April 23, 1975:

Henry Jenkins (company representative):
"I am not adverse to overtime to get a portion of the work done rather than let it out to contractors."

John Robertson (union representative):
"Our objective is to maintain our work even on an overtime basis as long as no law is violated."

Henry Jenkins:
"Hiring more people and adding them to the payroll for short periods of time to handle peak work loads and then laying them off could be a headache to both sides."

POSITION OF THE UNION

The union contended that employees of the electrical maintenance department daily and routinely rewound motors; that no special fixture for holding the motor was needed; and that the department possessed the space, equipment, and tools for doing the work.

The union pointed out that there were 135 to 140 electricians in the department, and that none was working overtime. The union argued that these employees, while working overtime, could have completed the repairs to the motor as quickly as the outside contractor. In fact, the disabled motor remained on the shop floor for two days before the outside contractor picked it up.

The union further contended that this case involved only one motor. The work did not require a large amount of extra work extending over a long period of time.

Finally, the union pointed out that the company, on occasions in the past, had assigned work on an overtime basis to electricians in cases such as this one. The contract anticipated that employees would be called upon to work overtime from time to time, as provided in Article X, Section 3(h) (see Appendix to this case).

The union petitioned that those electricians in Department 711 who would have been assigned the rewinding of the blower motor be reimbursed for 32 hours work at the overtime rate of time and one half.

POSITION OF THE COMPANY

The company replied that none of the electricians in Department 711 was on layoff and that all were working a full 40-hour week. Under terms of the contract, this constituted the customary workweek and represented "full utilization" of all personnel.

All qualified electricians were at that time assigned priority rewinding jobs, utilizing all rewinding stands and equipment. It was not desirable to delay any of the priority work, nor was it possible to delay the repairs to the blower motor. For these reasons, the company made the decision to send the motor to an outside contractor for rewinding.

The company argued that while Article XVI, Section 12, permitted the company to utilize overtime in order to avoid contracting out work, the company was not required to do so in order to keep the work within Department 711. The company cited Article IV of the contract to support its right.

Finally, the company argued that it contracted out the work in good faith and that its actions were reasonable under all the circumstances. It urged that the grievance be denied.

APPENDIX

Relevant Provisions of the Agreement

ARTICLE XVI
Section 12 (Utilization of Work Force)

The Company recognizes a responsibility to fully utilize all its employees; and will not subcontract work without giving full consideration to using bargaining unit employees whenever possible where time limits for job completion will permit, where sufficient qualified personnel are present and where resources are available.

ARTICLE IV
(Management Rights)

The direction of the work force, the establishment of plant policies, the determination of the processes and means of manufacture, the units of personnel required to perform such processes, and other responsibilities incidental to the operation of the plant are vested in the Company. The exercise of such authority shall not conflict with the rights of the Union under the terms of this Contract.

ARTICLE X
Section 3(h) (Hours of Work)

The provisions of this Contract shall not be considered as a guarantee by the Company of a minimum number of hours per day or per week or pay in lieu thereof, nor a limitation on the maximum hours per day or per week which may be required to meet operating conditions.

QUESTIONS

1. To what degree is the negotiating background information surrounding Article XVI, Section 12, germane to the arbitration issue?
2. What is meant by the term *fully utilize* within Article XVI, Section 12? Does this provision require the company to work bargaining unit personnel on an overtime basis, rather than to subcontract?
3. Different arbitrators have utilized varying standards in applying provisions such as Article XVI, Section 12. What types of standards might be appropriate for interpreting this and similar clauses?
4. Compare the circumstances of this case with that of "The Subcontracted Heaters" (Case 40 that follows).

40. *The Subcontracted Heaters*

Company:
> Tecumseh Products Company, Somerset Compressor Division, Somerset, Kentucky

Union:
> International Brotherhood of Electrical Workers, Local 2360

On November 22, 1974, 29 employees of Tecumseh Products Company filed the following grievance:

> The Company is in direct violation of Article XIX, Paragraph 138, of the current labor agreement. Adjustment desired—maintenance department employees be paid for all hours worked by outside plumbing contractors; and electrical employees be paid for all hours worked by outside electrical contractors. Plus this action be stopped immediately.

The company denied the grievance, charging that it had not been properly filed because part of the work identified in the grievance had not been contracted out until after the grievance had been filed. It also argued that even if the grievance had been properly filed, the company was within its rights to contract out the work under terms of the contract.

BACKGROUND

The Compressor Division manufactures small compressors for air conditioners, water coolers, and dehumidifiers. The company engaged two subcontractors in November 1974 to perform certain plumbing and electrical work in the plant. One of them, Brown Brothers, was engaged to install two industrial-type wash basins in the washroom (each basin is about six feet in diameter and can serve about 10 persons simultaneously). It also contracted to install a new rest room for truckers and a drinking fountain and waste disposal basin in the cafeteria.

The second subcontractor, Whitaker Electric Company, completed the installation of large high-voltage, industrial-type electric heating units in the heating ducts servicing the office area.

The union protested that all of this work should have been performed by the maintenance department employees and should not have been subcontracted.

TIMELINESS OF THE GRIEVANCE

Position of the Company

The company argued that the union's grievance referred to work that had not been contracted out at the time the grievance was filed on November 22, 1974. The company offered in evidence a copy of purchase order SA18845, dated December 13, 1974. This purchase order completed the contract between Whitaker Electric and the company to install electric heaters. The company cited Paragraph 31 of the contract, which stated in part:

> All grievances must be presented at this step within five (5) days of occurrence, otherwise it shall be deemed not to exist and shall have no merit.

Position of the Union

The union argued that various employees had observed preparations to perform certain plumbing and electrical work about the middle of November. One employee, Ronald Blanton,[1] working on the second shift, asked his foreman about the preparations. His foreman told him that the work was being subcontracted to Whitaker. At that point, the union filed a grievance. The union claimed that it would be unrealistic to expect it to undertake a complete study of the company's records and then make a legal determination of when a contract had been agreed upon before filing a grievance. The union requested that the filing date of the grievance be ruled timely, and that the grievance apply to all the plumbing and electrical work described above.

THE RIGHT TO CONTRACT OUT WORK

Position of the Union

The union contended that maintenance employees were qualified to perform the plumbing and electrical work contracted out. They had on prior occasions performed such work and had already completed some of the work in question before the subcontractors came in and took over the jobs. They had, in fact, redone some of the work on both the electrical and plumbing contracts after the outside contractors left.

The union also maintained that if the company had originally assigned the work to the maintenance employees, they could have

---

[1] The names of all individuals have been disguised.

completed it within the company's time requirements, especially if they had been assigned the work on an overtime basis. The company could have completed both projects at less cost employing maintenance employees on an overtime basis than by contracting out the work.

The union further argued that the company violated Article XIX, Paragraph 138, which restricts Article III, Paragraphs 17 and 18 (see Appendix to this case).

The union asked that the 29 employees signing the grievance be reimbursed for all hours worked by outside contractors and that such subcontracting cease.

Position of the Company

The company argued that the work performed by the subcontractors was not "standard production work regularly performed by Bargaining Unit employees."

The company further argued that the necessary personnel were not "readily available" to complete the work "within the projected time limits" (see Appendix to this case, Article XIX, Paragraph 138). The normal work of the maintenance employees was first and foremost to maintain the production machinery. If any time were left, it might be utilized on other projects, including those of the type performed by these two subcontractors.

The company pointed out that the plumbing work was done to satisfy employee complaints that the washroom facilities were inadequate. The work had been scheduled to be performed by maintenance employees, but it did not progress fast enough because top priority was always given to the maintenance of production machinery and equipment. As the end of the budget year, December 31, approached, it became urgent to finish the job. Such installations could not be characterized as "regular" because there are not that many commodes and wash basins to be installed in a plant.

The installation of the heaters was urgent as the winter season approached. The two old gas heaters that had previously provided heat for the offices had failed. The work had to be performed after the regular office hours because of the noise in the heating ducts.

To have taken maintenance men from their regular work to finish these two projects would have resulted in down time on production lines because of failure to do necessary maintenance and repair work on production machinery.

The company further pointed out that there were no maintenance employees on layoff, and that all were working at least 40 hours per week and some were working overtime during the period the subcontractors were working.

Finally, the company contended that no provision required the company to provide any specific amount of overtime to any employees. The three employees best qualified to perform the subcontracted work all had refused or been unavailable for overtime assignment to the work in question. The first, a licensed plumber, had regularly refused overtime assignments; the second had other outside employment on Saturdays, when much of the work was performed; the third regularly worked overtime in the plant repairing machines during the time they were shut down.

The company requested that in the event the arbitrator ruled the grievance was timely, the grievance should be denied as to its merits.

APPENDIX

The Bargaining Unit, as defined by the NLRB Certification of Representation, is:

All production and maintenance employees at the Employer's Somerset, Kentucky location, excluding all office clerical employees, professional employees, guards, and supervisors as defined in the Act.

Relevant Provisions of the Contract

Article I—Recognition

Paragraph 1. The Company recognizes the Union as the exclusive representative for its employees as defined in Paragraph 2 below for the purpose of collective bargaining with respect to wages, hours, or other conditions of employment in the Bargaining Unit which they have been so certified by the National Labor Relations Board in accordance with the provisions of the applicable state and federal laws.

Paragraph 2. For the purpose of this Agreement, the term "employee" shall include factory employees employed at the Company's Compressor Division located in Somerset, Kentucky, excluding all salaried employees, office and clerical employees, plant protection employees, supervisory employees, foremen, assistant foremen, foreladies, professional employees, sales and engineering employees, and lab technicians.

Article III—Management Rights and Responsibilities

Paragraph 17. Except as expressly and specifically limited to or restricted by a provision of this Agreement, the Company has and shall retain the full rights of management and direction of the plant and its operations. Such rights of management include the right to plan, direct, control, increase, or decrease operations; to determine the products to be manufactured; to shift products manufactured, processes, or types of work or methods in and out of the plant; to subcontract work, except as in Paragraph 138, to change machinery, methods, and facilities, or introduce new methods, techniques, and/or machines and products; to establish and enforce rules and regulations; to discipline and discharge employees for just causes; to assign, change, add to, or reduce the number of shifts, the schedules to be worked, and the work force; to determine who it shall hire, the number of employees it shall employ at any time, and the qualifications necessary for any jobs; to determine policies affecting the selection and training of new employees; to assign work duties, transfer employees; to set reasonable standards in accordance with its determination of the needs of the job and the operation. The Company reserves the right to move, sell, close, liquidate, or consolidate the plant in whole or in part.

It is expressly understood and agreed that all rights heretofore exercised by the Company or inherent in the Company as the owner of the business or as an incident to the management not expressly contracted away by specific provisions of this Agreement are retained solely by the Company. Any rights granted to or acquired by the employees or the Union under this Agreement or during its life shall have no application beyond the term of this Agreement or any renewal thereof.

Paragraph 18. It is agreed that the reserved management rights as set forth in this Agreement, including the foregoing paragraph, shall not be subject to arbitration or impairment by an arbitration award under this Agreement unless expressly contracted away or modified by a specific provision of this Agreement.

Article IV

Paragraph 29. For the purpose of this Agreement, the term "grievance" shall be limited to any dispute between the Company and the Union or between the Company and an employee concerning the application or violation of the provisions of this agreement.

Article VI

Paragraph 37. The arbitrator so selected shall schedule a prompt hearing at which time he shall have the power to make determinations of fact on the questions submitted to him and apply them to the provisions of the Agreement alleged to have been violated so long as the grievance is submitted to him in accordance with the provisions, limitations, and procedures specified in this Agreement. No arbitrator shall have the jurisdiction or authority to add to, take from, nullify, or modify any of the terms of this Agreement, or to impair any of the rights reserved to Management under the terms hereof, either directly or indirectly, under the guise of interpretation; nor shall he have the power to substitute his discretion for that of Management in any manner where the Management has not contracted away its right to exercise discretion.

The arbitrator shall be bound by the facts and evidence submitted to him and may not go beyond the terms of this Agreement in rendering his decision.

No such decision may include or deal with any issue or matter which is not expressly made subject to the terms of this Agreement. The decision of the arbitrator shall be in writing and shall be final and binding upon the parties when rendered upon a matter within the authority of the arbitrator.

Article XIX

Paragraph 138.   It is the Company policy that standard production work regularly performed by Bargaining Unit employees will not be contracted to a source outside of the Tecumseh Products Company, provided that the necessary manpower, equipment, and facilities are readily available and the work can be performed in an efficient, economic, and competitive manner as related to quality, quantity, cost, and performance within the projected time limits necessary to complete the work involved.

QUESTIONS

1. Was the grievance a timely grievance that was appropriately placed before the arbitrator? Why, or why not?

2. Evaluate Article XIX in comparison to Article III. Which article is superior in nature?

3. Was the plumbing work standard production work regularly performed by bargaining unit employees? Discuss.

4. Compare the circumstances of this case with the subcontracting issue involved in the "Disabled Blower Motor" case (Case 39, preceding).

41. The Rescheduled Lunch Period

Company:
 Outagamie County, Seymour, Wisconsin
Union:
 Outagamie County Employees Union, Local 2046

BACKGROUND

On Friday, January 30, 1976, employees working in eight county offices of Outagamie County, Wisconsin, learned through an article in a local newspaper that their offices would remain open during the hours 12 noon to 1 P.M. starting Monday, February 2. On Monday morning, county supervisor Patrick Kelly[1] announced to these employees that starting immediately the offices would be open continuously each day, Monday through Friday, from 8:30 A.M. to 5 P.M. He also stated that some employees would take their lunch period from 12:30 to 1:30 P.M., instead of from 12 noon to 1 P.M., in order to accommodate the new schedule. The total number of hours worked each day was to remain unchanged at 7½.

The employees protested the unilateral change in their lunch schedule. After receiving no satisfaction from supervisor Kelly, they filed a grievance through their union, Outagamie County Employees Union, Local 2046, which eventually was carried to arbitration.

POSITION OF THE UNION

The union argued that the county had violated Article 1, Section 1.02, of the Agreement, which stated that:

> The Employer shall adopt and publish reasonable rules which may be amended from time to time. Such rules shall be submitted to the Union for its information, thirty (30) days prior to their effective date. The Employer and the Union will cooperate in the enforcement thereof.

According to the union, the altering of employee work schedules constituted a change in a work rule. The county violated the contract by failing to submit the new rule to the employees 30 days prior to the date on which the rule became effective.

The union also contended that the new work rule was unreason-

---

[1] The names of all individuals have been disguised.

able and unnecessary. Since February 2, each of the eight affected offices had averaged only about one phone call and two business transactions per week during the noon hour. The staggered lunch hour schedules had disrupted luncheon-hour social groups, and this, too, was upsetting to the employees.

The union requested that the county be required to return to the lunch period schedule existing prior to February 2, 1976.

POSITION OF THE EMPLOYER

The county asserted that the decision as to the hours during which its offices would be open to the public was a fundamental management right, and it was not a subject upon which it was required to consult or bargain with the union. The subject was one on which management could make unilateral decisions. The county cited Article 1, Section 1.01, on management rights to support its claim. This article stated that:

> Unless otherwise provided herein, the management of the work and the direction of the working forces, including the right to hire, promote, transfer, demote or suspend, or otherwise discharge for proper cause, and the right to relieve employees from duty because of lack of work or other legitimate reasons is vested exclusively in the Employer.

The county pointed out that there was no provision in the contract that restricted its power to set the hours during which its offices would be open to the public. The contract did not specify the hours of work. It only provided for a normal work day of 7½ to 8 hours. The contract was silent as to lunch periods, and it did not contain a clause requiring the county to continue any past practices. The county cited Article VIII, Section 8.01, on the workweek to support its point:

> Permanent full-time employees shall work a normal day of 7½ to 8 hours and a normal workweek of 37½ to 40 hours (1,950–2,080 hours per year.) Overtime shall be computed on any hours worked in excess of 40 hours in any one work week.

The county further contended that it had a legitimate reason to change the luncheon schedule, since its basic purpose was to provide services for the public.

The county urged that it be permitted to retain the right to change lunch schedules as necessary. The union grievance should be dismissed.

QUESTIONS

1. Was changing the luncheon schedule a reasonable exercise of management rights? Might the manner in which the schedule change was announced have had any effect upon the employees' decision to file a grievance? Discuss.

2. Did the county alter a work rule? Justify your response.

3. Evaluate the union's argument that the change in luncheon schedule was unnecessary and unreasonable.

4. Evaluate the county's claim that it had the right to change the lunch schedule without consulting the union.

42. A "Horns-of-a-Dilemma" Situation

Company:
> Diem and Wing Paper Company, Cincinnati, Ohio

Union:
> International Brotherhood of Teamsters, Chauffeurs, Warehousemen and Helpers of America, Local 100

Managing his personal finances had always been a problem for Bob Bronson.[1] His problems while working at Diem and Wing Paper Company began with several garnishments in 1975 and culminated in the following letter from the company on July 14, 1978:

> This will confirm our meeting today during which we discussed the garnishment against your wages on behalf of Thorp Financial Services.
>
> As a result of this, and other garnishment actions, you are hereby placed on a three-day suspension, without pay, beginning July 17, 1978.
>
> If we continue to receive Orders of Garnishment, it will result in discharge from the Company.

> (s) H. W. Schuler
> Plant Manager

Bronson had been well aware that if his employer received one more garnishment, disciplinary action would be taken against him. This situation was different though. He felt that he had been entangled in a series of events that inevitably had led to this three-day suspension by the company. In frustration and anger he immediately filed the following grievance:

> This grievance is against management for an unjustified three-day suspension on a garnishing which was received on July 11, at that time having an appointment at the courthouse to go on a trusteeship, which would have stopped the garnishment. I told Bill Engle about the trusteeship appointment I had on the 11th, and he refused to let me go for 1½ hours.

> (s) Robert Bronson

Bronson's grievance eventually was carried to arbitration.

---

[1] The names of all individuals have been disguised.

BACKGROUND

Robert Bronson had been hired to work at Diem and Wing Paper Company's warehouse in 1975. Shortly thereafter, he encountered serious difficulty in managing his personal finances. He received a one-day suspension on May 24, 1976, after his wages had been subject to five orders of garnishment. His difficulties continued to mount, and from November 30, 1977, through May 24, 1978, the company received an additional seven orders of garnishment against his wages. Several other court orders issued prior to May 2, 1978, did not result in garnishments of his wages because a strike that lasted from December 6, 1977, to February 13, 1978, had reduced his wages below the garnishable level.[2]

Following receipt of a garnishment on May 2, 1978, the company sent Bronson a written notice stating that further garnishments could result in discipline up to and including discharge. The company received another garnishment on June 1, 1978. Since it was the second that the company had received within 20 days, it was returned to the court in accordance with Ohio law. Nevertheless, the company again warned him orally that he could be disciplined up to and including discharge for additional garnishments.

On June 30, 1978, both Bronson and the company received the following Notice of Court Action to Collect Debt, dated June 28, 1978.

> If you do not pay within 15 days of the date of the mailing of this notice, we will go to court and ask that your employer be ordered to withhold money from your earnings and pay it to the court to satisfy your debt. This is called garnishment.
>
> It is to your advantage to avoid it because the placing of the extra burden on your employer can cause you to lose your job.
>
> You can avoid garnishment by doing one of these three things within the next 15 days:
>
> 1. Pay us the amount due;
>
> 2. Complete the attached form entitled "Payment to Avoid Garnishment" and return it to us with the payment, if any, shown due on it; or
>
> 3. Apply to your local municipal or county court, or, if you are not a resident of Ohio, to the municipal or county court in whose jurisdiction your place of employment is located, for the appointment of a

---

[2] Effective July 1, 1970, Title III of the Consumer Protection Act limited the amount of an employee's disposable earnings (compensation paid for personal services, less deductions required by law) subject to garnishment. The maximum part of the total disposable earnings that are subject to garnishment in any workweek may not exceed the lesser of (a) 25 percent of the disposable earnings for that week, or (b) the amount by which a worker's disposable earnings for that week exceeds 30 times the federal minimum hourly wage rate prescribed by Section 6(a) (1) of the Fair Labor Standards Act in effect at the time earnings are payable.

trustee to receive the part of your earnings that is not exempt from garnishment. You will be required to list your creditors, and the amount you will then pay to your trustee each payday will then be divided among them until the debts are paid off. This can be to your advantage because in the meantime none of those creditors can garnishee your wages.

Creditor
(s) Attorney for the Creditor

Note: Ohio Revised Code Section 2715.02 provides that the above demand shall be made after judgment is obtained, by delivering such demand to the debtor by personal service by the court or by sending it to the debtor by registered or certified letter, return receipt requested, at his usual place of residence at least 15 and not more than 45 days before the order of attachment against personal earnings or the order in aid of execution against personal earnings is sought.

In order to avoid another garnishment, Bronson sought out the court in order to establish a Municipal Court Trusteeship. He completed all necessary work on the trusteeship, except for a required appearance in court on Tuesday, July 11, to be sworn in.

When Bronson requested time off on July 11 to appear in court, his supervisor, Bill Engle, turned him down. The work load was particularly heavy that day, and several employees were already away on vacation. Engle not only refused Bronson's request but also warned him that because he had already been disciplined on one prior occasion for having walked off the job, he would be discharged if he left the job on this occasion. This was very serious since the court processed garnishments only on Tuesdays.

Bronson's situation was aggravated by an error made by the creditor's attorney, who "jumped the gun" and obtained the order of garnishment from the court on July 11, which was within the 15-day grace period. Although the garnishment was unenforceable until the end of the 15 days, the company was still required to comply with the court order it received on July 11, the very day Bronson was scheduled to appear before the court to establish the trusteeship that would save him from the garnishment. Release from such a court order must come from the garnisher, or the debtor must obtain a writ of prohibition as provided in Ohio statutes. It was company practice to respond promptly to court garnishment orders, which it did on July 11 by filling out the legal documents and returning them to the court.

After complying with the court order, the plant manager sent Bronson a letter advising him of the three-day suspension beginning Monday, July 17, 1978.

POSITION OF THE UNION

The union argued that Bronson had been placed in a classic "horns-of-a-dilemma" situation. He had last been counseled on June 1, 1978, concerning the many garnishments that had been filed against him. On that occasion he had again been told that if the company were to receive another garnishment order against him, he would be disciplined. His problem was doubled by the fact that he had walked off the job without permission a few weeks earlier. For that action he had been given a three-day suspension. On June 30 he received a notice of intent to garnishee from one of his creditors. He immediately set out to prevent the garnishment by applying for a trusteeship program, under the terms of which he would make payments to the court, which would distribute the money to creditors until all debts had been discharged. When he requested time off on July 11 to go to court to be sworn in and therefore meet the last requirement of the trusteeship, his employer refused to permit him to leave his job for that purpose. Mindful of his supervisor's admonition that he would be fired if he left his job that day without permission, he did not go to court that day.

To make matters even worse, the company received a notice from the court of a garnishment of wages that had been filed before the 15-day grace period had run out. The company immediately suspended Bronson because of the July 11 garnishment. That is why he ended up on the horns of a dilemma. If he were garnished, he faced disciplinary action by the company; if he prevented the garnishment by appearing in court, he would lose his job. The garnishment arrived earlier than allowed by law, but the company suspended him anyway. There was no way Bronson could have avoided suspension under these circumstances.

If Bronson had gone to court with the company's permission on July 11, the trusteeship could have been permitted. The union submitted a letter from the county trustee to support its position:

To whom it may concern:

Bronson applied for trusteeship in Hamilton County Municipal Court. He was to appear in court as of July 11, but was unable to get off work. He did appear July 18. For this reason, the garnishment could not be stopped.

(s) J. Goodman
Trustee Clerk

The union also submitted a letter from the county clerk attesting to Bronson's good intentions in applying for a trusteeship and to his conscientious effort to carry out the terms of the court's creditor repayment plan:

> To whom it may concern:
>
> This is to verify that Bronson applied for the Trustee to Prevent Garnishment on July 11, 1978, but was unable to get off work; therefore he was garnished.
> Bronson came into the plan on July 18, 1978.
> If Bronson would have entered into the plan on July 11, 1978, Thorp Finance would have been stopped from the garnishment.
> If you have any questions please give us a call at 632–8895.
> Bronson has paid into the plan each and every week and one of the best plan members we have.

> (s) Mary Ann Waldbillig
> County Clerk

The union contended that Bronson had been treated unjustly by the company and requested that it be required to compensate him for the monies lost during the three-day suspension and to remove all references to the events from his personnel files.

POSITION OF THE COMPANY

The company contended that Bronson's history of garnishments, including the excessive number of garnishments, provided proper cause for the three-day suspension. Prior to the series of garnishments in 1977 and 1978, he had received a one-day suspension for the same reason in 1976.[3] He had been counseled and warned on May 5 and June 1, 1978, including a written warning on the former occasion, that additional garnishments could result in discipline. The company suspended Bronson only after it had received the ninth order of garnishment in as many months. During all those months Bronson's behavior gave no indication that he was making any progress in separating his personal financial problems from his employment. The company's action was more than reasonable; it was lenient.[4]

The company stated that it was very sympathetic to Bronson's request to be absent from work a large part of the day on July 11; however, it also had its own problems to contend with. The work load

---

[3] See Appendix A to this case for Bronson's suspension history.
[4] See Appendix B to this case for relevant provisions of the contract.

was heavy that day, and the warehouse was already shorthanded because several employees were away on vacation. Furthermore, his application for a Municipal Court trusteeship was a "last-second" attempt to rectify many months of inaction. His failure to complete the terms of his trusteeship should not be charged to the company's actions.

Finally, the company was required to respond to the court's order of garnishment, even though it had been filed within the 15-day grace period allowed Bronson under Ohio law. The order could be lifted only by the court. And Bronson had not informed the company that the order was unenforceable on July 11. Operating in good faith, the company completed the necessary forms and delivered them to the court as required by law. Regardless of whether Bronson went to court on July 11, the company had to operate under the court's order.

The purpose of the company's garnishment rules was to avoid the cost and disruption incurred in processing garnishment orders. These costs were incurred when the orders were processed, regardless of whether those orders were withdrawn or subsequently voided in a court of law. The burden placed upon the company to respond to the garnishments included considerable clerical work, time spent counseling with the debtor employee and with the employee's creditors, extra payroll costs, and court appearances.

For the foregoing reasons, the company claimed that it had "proper cause" to issue a three-day disciplinary suspension upon Bronson. The company requested that the grievance be denied.

APPENDIX A

Suspension History

Suspensions	Length	Reason
1976:		
May 25	1 day	Garnishment
November 4, 5, 8	3 days	Excessive absenteeism
1977:		
April 4	1 day	Excessive absenteeism
1978:		
June 22, 23, 24	3 days	Walking off job without permission
July 17, 18, 19	3 days	Garnishment

APPENDIX B

Relevant Provision of the Contract

Article 18—Rights of Management

The Management of the business and the direction of the working forces including the right to . . . , hire, suspend, or discharge for proper cause . . . are vested in management, provided however, that this right shall be exercised with due regard for the rights of the employees and provided further that it will not be used for the purpose of discrimination against any employee.

QUESTIONS

1. Why do most companies consider wage garnishments issued on its employees as disciplinary matters?

2. Was Bob Bronson caught on a horns-of-a-dilemma situation that was beyond his control? Why, or why not?

3. Did the company have proper cause to give Bronson a three-day disciplinary suspension? Does Bronson's previous record have any bearing upon the arbitrator's decision? Discuss.

43. The Right to Work on a Birthday Holiday

Company:
   United Salt Corporation, Houston, Texas
Union:
   International Chemical Workers Union, Local 680

BACKGROUND

Under the previous contracts between the parties, employees were paid time and one half for working on holidays. Holidays specified under the holiday article in the labor agreement were New Year's Day, Washington's Birthday, Good Friday, Memorial Day, Fourth of July, Labor Day, Thanksgiving, Christmas Eve, Christmas Day, and four hours on New Year's Eve. An employee's birthday was also designated as a holiday. Although the contract was silent, by custom employees could choose whether to work on that day or not. The company paid time and one half to employees who worked on any holiday including their birthday holiday, and regular straight time to employees who did not work on a holiday including their birthday holiday.

On September 26, 1978, the company and the union signed a new contract that revised the article on holidays. The revised contract provided that in the future employees would receive double time, rather than time and one half, for working on holidays. During contract negotiations, there was no discussion concerning whether or not the company could require employees to take off from work on their birthday holidays. The new contract was signed September 26, 1978, and became effective as of September 1, 1978.

For the past five years, John Dow,[1] a leadman in the production department, had chosen to work on his birthday, and he had received time and one-half pay for doing so. As was his custom, Dow had informed his supervisor that again he would like to work on his birthday, which was October 18, 1978.

A production department work schedule was posted on October 1, 1978. This posted work schedule showed that Dow was to work on October 18, 1978. However, a subsequent memorandum was issued by the company's plant manager on October 9, 1978, as follows:

---

[1] The names of the individuals have been disguised.

To all supervisors:

Effective immediately all supervisors will make every effort to schedule employees off on their birthday holidays. The idea of a holiday is free time to the employee so we should do our best to see they get it. If necessary to replace the man, temporary help will be used where possible. Overtime will be used when temporary help is unavailable or unqualified.

An occasion requiring a man to work on his birthday must have prior approval by the plant manager.

C. B. Fox
Plant Manager

On October 11, 1978, Dow was told by his supervisor that he would not be allowed to work on his birthday. This angered Dow, since it meant he would receive only $40 instead of about $80 that he was expecting to earn that day. The company cited economic reasons for its actions and stood by its decision not to let him work on his birthday. Dow then filed a grievance stating he should have been allowed to work on his birthday as he had done in the past. His grievance eventually was carried to arbitration.

Although he had not been permitted to work on October 18, his birthday, Dow did work the following Thanksgiving, Christmas Eve, Christmas, and New Year and was paid double time for doing so.

POSITION OF THE UNION

Union president Karl Adam, who had been with the firm for 20 years, and John Dow both testified that they were present at the 1978 contract negotiations. They stated that the matter of requiring employees to take off work on their birthday holiday had not been discussed, although payment of double time for working on any holiday—including a birthday holiday—had been agreed upon. The union argued that lack of discussion on this matter during contract negotiations meant that Dow and all other employees must be permitted to continue to work on their birthdays, as had been the custom in the past.

The union contended that the choice of working on one's birthday was a well-established past practice. Therefore, management could not change this practice without negotiating on the matter. The union asserted that the company had violated the labor contract in the same manner as if it had unilaterally decided to change the agreed-upon leadman's wage rate of $5.77 per hour for 1979 without negotiating the matter with the union. The union noted that eight people in addition to Dow had birthdays between September 1, 1978, and October 9, 1978, and that at least two of them had worked on their birthday. Since the new contract already was in effect, those employees who had worked on their birthdays received double time. Thus, the company had been inconsistent in permitting some employees and not others to work on their birthday holiday. The company had unilaterally changed a condition of employment in violation of a long-standing practice under both the old and new contract. This the company should not be permitted to do.

In summary, the union contended that the company had violated both the contract and past practice by denying John Dow and other employees the opportunity to work on their birthdays. The union requested that John Dow and all other employees who had wanted to work on their birthdays and who were not allowed to do so should be paid the amount they would have earned had they worked.

POSITION OF THE COMPANY

C. B. Fox, plant manager, testified that he decided in late September 1978 that because of the expense of paying employees double time for working on their birthdays, he would require employees not to work on their birthdays. He felt it was the general consensus of management that the average additional cost of $20 per employee per year for employees working on their birthday was too great for the company to bear. Thus, on October 9, 1978, he issued the memorandum concerning employees' working on their birthday.

The company contended that its actions were justified under Article III, Management Rights, of the contract.[2] The company argued that this article allowed management the right to change for economic reasons any conditions of employment previously followed.

The company acknowledged that there was a past practice under previous contracts that had permitted employees the option to work on their birthday holiday at a wage rate of time and one half their normal hourly wage. But this past practice no longer could apply, since the rate of pay for working on a holiday was changed in the new contract to double time. The company could not be required to maintain a past practice that was not applicable to the new contractual condition.

In summary, the company claimed that it had every right under the management-rights clause of the contract to require John Dow and other employees to be off work on their birthday holidays. The com-

---

[2] See Appendix to this case.

pany's motivation was economic in nature, and the company claimed that the former practice could not apply to a changed contractual provision. The company urged that the union grievance should be denied.

APPENDIX

Article III—Management Rights

Section 1. The management of the business and the direction of the working force, including but not limited to the right to hire, to transfer, to promote, to demote, to discipline or discharge for cause, to lay off for lack of work, and to assign employees to work shifts are rights vested exclusively in the management of the Company.

In the event any promotion, disciplinary action, transfer, suspension, or discharge is considered discriminatory or unjust, the matter will be handled in accordance with the grievance and arbitration procedure provided for in the agreement.

Section 2. The right to plan, direct, and control plant operations; the right to introduce new or improved production methods or facilities; the right to determine the amount of supervision necessary; the right to combine or split up departments as deemed necessary; the right to determine schedules of production and to establish standards of quality; and the right to increase or decrease production or employment are vested exclusively in the Company.

Section 3. Nothing contained herein shall be intended or shall be considered as a waiver of any of the usual inherent and fundamental rights of management. Any of the rights, power, or authorities the Company had prior to the signing of this agreement are retained by the Company, except to the extent that they are specifically abridged, delegated, or modified by this agreement.

QUESTIONS

1. Which should take priority in deciding an issue of this sort, the management rights provision in the contract or the previous plant practice? Discuss.

2. Evaluate the company argument that the previous plant practice no longer was applicable because of the change in the contract regarding holiday pay.

3. Does the fact that during negotiations the parties did not discuss the question of whether or not employees could be required to take off work on their birthday holiday have a major bearing on the arbitrator's decision? Why, or why not?

3. Compare the issues in this case with those in Case 67, "The Right to Work Overtime."

44. Sunday is the Sabbath Day

Company:

General Foods Corporation, Food Products Division, Woodburn, Oregon

Union:

Teamster Food Processors, Drivers, Warehousemen and Helpers, Local 670

BACKGROUND

The Food Products Division of General Foods Corporation in Woodburn, Oregon, purchases and processes fruit and vegetable crops grown in the Willamette Valley. The food processing occurs annually during the spring to fall harvest cycle. It is necessary to process the harvested crops as rapidly as possible because they are extremely perishable.

At the time of this case (1978), 1,200 people were employed in the production department, which operated three shifts all seven days of the week except for one shift on Sunday. The production line closed down for eight hours on Sunday in order that the sanitation department could thoroughly clean the work area.

The sanitation department employed about 75 people who worked seven days a week continuously cleaning the plant. The sanitation department sanitized the work area not only to meet government health standards but also to meet the company's standards for cleanliness. The company had never experienced a case of food contamination and believed that such an incident would have a disastrous effect upon its reputation with all segments of the community, especially consumers.

Karen Lauer[1] was initially hired on April 2, 1978, as a production employee. On June 21, 1978, she bid for and received a position in the sanitation department. But during that week she informed the sanitation department supervisor, George Bergland, that she could not work on Sundays because it was against her Old Orthodox religion. Bergland explained that working on Sundays was a long-standing requirement of sanitation employees, and that it was essential that she work on that day. Bergland also pointed out that this requirement was explicitly included in the job description, which had been posted on the

---

[1] The names of all individuals have been disguised.

bulletin board and which the personnel manager had explained to her when she requested the transfer. Nevertheless, Lauer steadfastly refused to work on Sundays. Therefore, on June 26, 1978, Bergland had her transferred back to the production department, where she could be scheduled off on Sundays.

Lauer worked for several weeks in the production department. She then informed Bergland that she would work on Sundays if she would be transferred back to the sanitation department. On July 13, 1978, the company again transferred her to the sanitation department.

Once in the sanitation department, she did not work on Sundays. She offered a variety of excuses, such as a family reunion, illness, and lack of transportation. Supervisor Bergland gave her a verbal warning about being absent after she had been absent from work on the last Sunday in July. Her Sunday absences continued in August, and Bergland warned her after each incident. When her supervisor confronted her in mid-August on the subject, she admitted that she had been absent because of her religious obligation to observe Sunday as the Sabbath day.

On August 24, 1978, Lauer was again transferred back to the production department, where she could be scheduled off on Sundays. This transfer meant she took a slight reduction in pay. Under the seniority system, she could have bid for a higher paying job within the production department when a vacancy occurred. Although job vacancies were posted, Lauer chose not to utilize this route to a better paying job. Rather, on August 28, 1978, Lauer filed a grievance claiming that she had been a victim of religious discrimination. The grievance eventually was carried to arbitration. The union and the company submitted the following statement of the issue to the arbitrator:

> Whether the Company violated Article XII, Section 1(a), of the labor Agreement and Karen Lauer's rights under Title VII of the Civil Rights Act when she was transferred from the Sanitation Department to the Production Department.

POSITION OF THE UNION

The union stated that both the collective agreement and the Civil Rights Act[2] required that the company could not discriminate against an employee because of religious beliefs and practices. Further, both arbitrators and the Equal Employment Opportunity Commission (EEOC) have ruled consistently that employers must make affirmative efforts at reasonable accommodation for an employee's religious beliefs

---

[2] See Appendix A and Appendix B to this case.

when an employee's religious needs conflict with job requirements. In this instance, the company made no real effort to do so. Lauer was merely transferred back to the production department, where she was placed in work less desirable to her and where she suffered a reduction in pay rate.

Karen Lauer testified that she could not work on Sundays because she was of the Old Orthodox faith, which required its members to observe Sunday as the Sabbath. When the company transferred her back to the production department, where she could be scheduled off on Sundays, she was assigned to perform work that was routine and dull, at a lower pay rate than sanitation workers. Unlike the company, Lauer did not look upon this transfer as an accommodation to her. Rather, she felt that she had become a victim of religious discrimination.

The union claimed that the company had already accommodated to an annual turnover rate of about 300 percent in the sanitation department of 75 persons. The absence of one additional person on Sundays could not have any effect upon the effectiveness of the crew. No one in the sanitation department had complained about Lauer being absent on Sundays, since the employees knew and understood that Karen Lauer's religion required her to observe Sunday as a Sabbath day.

According to the union, the company also had violated the contract because it unilaterally changed the work rules and had promulgated a new rule requiring everyone on the sanitation crew to work on Sunday. This rule was made without prior consultation with the union, and the union had never agreed to such a rule during contract negotiations.

The union argued that the company had discriminated against Lauer because of her religion. While insisting that Lauer work on Sundays, the company for many years had accommodated other employees in the sanitation department who were absent on Sundays to attend the funerals of members of their immediate family or to be married, who were hospitalized or jailed, or were absent for other reasons. The company's past practices of approving Sunday absences proved that Lauer's presence was not necessary for the efficient conduct of sanitation department business on Sundays. Accommodation to Lauer's religious practices should and must be made within the sanitation department, as required by the agreement and also by the Civil Rights Act.

The union requested that the company be required to return Lauer to her job in the sanitation department and to accommodate to her religious practices. The union also requested that Lauer be made whole for the loss of pay and other benefits and privileges she lost because of her transfer back to the production department.

POSITION OF THE COMPANY

The company argued that it was impossible to accommodate Lauer's religious beliefs to the extent that she be excused from work on Sundays and keep her in the sanitation department. The sanitation department crew must work seven days a week but especially on Sundays, because production shut down that day. Production was closed on Sunday because most produce growers did not harvest on that day except in emergencies. The company attributed extreme importance to sanitation, which was necessary to ensure the health of the public. The company also considered its national reputation for cleanliness to be a major competitive advantage over other food processors.

The company pointed out that production workers put in extremely long hours during the harvesting season. It was not possible to count on them to volunteer to work seven consecutive days by serving as substitutes for absent sanitation employees, especially when they often worked part of a second shift during one or more of the previous six days. Further, sanitation workers must be trained; the company needed full-time sanitation crews, not an assortment of part-time substitute volunteers.

The company admitted that turnover in the sanitation department was very high; it was 300 percent in 1977. The department had been unstable, and training costs had been high. To excuse Lauer from Sunday work would add additional costs to the company to bring in additional, untrained help in her place.

The requirement that Lauer work on Sundays was a bona fide requirement according to the company. Even federal, state, and local wage and hour laws recognized that employees in the food processing industry can be required to work seven days a week because of the special harvesting and processing demands of highly perishable fruit and vegetables. Relieving Lauer of the requirement that she work Sundays would in effect create a new policy that would lift that requirement for the entire sanitation crew. To excuse Lauer from working on Sundays would be unfair and discriminatory to everyone else in the department.

The company maintained that it had not been insensitive to Lauer's religious needs. But her demand to be relieved of the requirement that she work Sundays and hold a job in the sanitation department went beyond "reasonable accommodation." Lauer's transfer to production was an administrative transfer to reasonably accommodate her demand to be off work on Sundays. It was not a disciplinary transfer and in no way affected her good standing with the company. She could bid to better and higher paying jobs in the production department if she wished to do so.

The company insisted that it had not discriminated against Lauer because of her religion in violation of either the collective agreement or of Title VII of the Civil Rights Act. Lauer had not been treated as different from other employees under similar circumstances. The company produced documents and testimony that showed that numerous employees had been transferred or terminated when they were unable to maintain regular attendance in the sanitation department. This had been the company's practice for many years.

For all of these reasons, the company asked that Karen Lauer's grievance be dismissed.

APPENDIX A

Relevant Provision of the Contract

Article XII

Section 1. In the application of this Agreement and in accordance with applicable federal and state laws, there shall be no discrimination against employees because of race, color, religion, sex, age, or national origin.

APPENDIX B

Relevant Provisions of the Civil Rights Act of 1964, as Amended in 1972, 1975, and 1978

Title VII

Definitions
    Section 701. For the purposes of this title—
    (j) The term "religion" includes all aspects of religious observance and practice, as well as belief, unless an employer demonstrates that he is unable to reasonably accommodate to an employee's, or prospective employee's, religious observance or practice without undue hardship on the conduct of the employer's business.

Discrimination because of Race, Color, Religion, Sex, or National Origin
    Section 703(a). It shall be an unlawful practice for an employer—
    (1) To fail or refuse to hire or to discharge any individual, or otherwise to discriminate against an individual with respect to his compensation, terms, conditions, or privileges of employment, because of such individual's race, color, religion, sex, or national origin; or
    (2) to limit, segregate, or classify his employees or applicants for employment in any way which would deprive or tend to deprive any individual of

employment opportunities or otherwise adversely affect his status as an employee, because of such individual's race, color, religion, sex, or national origin.

* * * * *

(g) Notwithstanding any other provision of this title, it shall not be unlawful employment practice for an employer to fail or refuse to hire and employ any individual for any position, for employer to discharge any individual from any position or for an employment agency to fail or refuse to refer any individual for employment in any position, or for a labor organization to fail or refuse to refer any individual for employment in any position, if—

* * * * *

(2) such individual has not fulfilled or has ceased to fulfill that requirement.

(j) Nothing contained in this title shall be interpreted to require any employer, employment agency, labor organization, or joint labor-management committee subject to this title to grant preferential treatment to any individual or to any group because of the race, color, religion, sex, or national origin of such individual or group on account of an imbalance which may exist with respect to the total number or percentage of persons of any race, color, religion, sex, or national origin employed by any employer . . . in comparison with the total number or percentage of persons of such race, color, religion, sex, or national origin in any community, state, section, or other area.

QUESTIONS

1. Why is a case of this nature an awkward one for both the company and the union?

2. Was Karen Lauer a victim of religious discrimination? Why, or why not?

3. Did the company attempt to reasonably accommodate Lauer's religious beliefs, or did the company fail to do so? Discuss.

4. Does the arbitrator have power to interpret and apply the Civil Rights Act under the circumstances of this case? Why are arbitrators typically uncomfortable in a case of this nature, which involves charges of violation of both the labor agreement and a federal statute?

5. Consult the EEOC's recent guidelines concerning religious discrimination and reasonable accommodation for employees' religious beliefs. Might the EEOC's decision in the case of Karen Lauer differ from that of an arbitrator? Discuss.

45. My Time is Not the Company's Time

Company:

    Alumax Foils, Inc., St. Louis, Missouri

Union:

    International Association of Machinists and Aerospace Workers, District 9

BACKGROUND

On April 5, 1978, the union filed a grievance on behalf of Andrew Warlock,[1] furnace operator at Alumax Foils. The grievance document read:

> Contract violation: I was suspended from work while not under the jurisdiction of the plant (off the clock); also in the wrong manner.
> Date and time: 3:15 P.M.—4/3/78.
> How did it happen: An argument over a lie told by Brookings.
> Demand: Back pay from the time I missed on the job.

The company's industrial relations manager, Charles Janssen, sent the following reply rejecting Warlock's complaint:

> Warlock was suspended for threatening John B. Brookings with physical violence. He was in the plant without permission and was told to leave. He not only refused to leave, but threatened harm to company representatives. This threat was made in the presence of witnesses and was repeated in a meeting which included the Chief Shop Steward and several other persons. Warlock stated, "I really intended to hurt him."
> Suspension for a threat of this nature is mild disciplinary action. He has no back pay due to him.

Before this grievance could be appealed to arbitration, Warlock became involved in another situation. He failed to attend a required crew meeting on April 17, 1978, and accordingly was discharged. He filed a grievance on April 21 requesting reinstatement with full back pay for all time missed from work and apologies from several management representatives. Warlock attached the following statement detailing his perception of the circumstances leading to his discharge:

---

[1] The names of all individuals have been disguised.

On April 16 the foreman posted the notice for a crew meeting from 3:00 P.M. to 3:30 P.M. Later the same day he went around letting everybody know about the meeting. When 3:00 P.M. came, I noticed the foreman had changed the date to the 17th. If the meeting had been held on the 16th as he first posted it, I would have attended, but on the 17th I planned to be at my son's birthday party which I felt was more important than the foreman's crew meeting. (Which brings the question to mind—why did he cancel the first meeting? Did he remember he had something to do with his family; was there a personal matter he had to attend to or *what?*) My personal life has nothing to do with the company. I have a responsibility to the company for eight hours. I was relieved properly, and I informed the foreman on the 17th that I would not be able to make his meeting, and he said, "Well, I guess we'll have to make it some other time." About two hours later he came back up to me and said, "We all have to be at that meeting." I didn't attend the meeting for the reasons stated earlier. Why should the foremen be able to change their minds and change dates of so-called very important crew meetings when they have something personal to do and the employees turn around and do the same thing and the result is suspension or termination? If this is permitted, then it means that the company controls our lives 24 hours a day. As I've said in the past, I only work for Alumax; Alumax doesn't own me. I believe the real reason for my suspension was my efforts to get Brookings fired for possession of a gun on company premises, for which I have two witnesses willing to make firsthand testimony of facts. I also think the company hasn't got sufficient grounds to fire me for not attending a crew meeting. Another thing—why did Burgess fire me and send me over to personnel without a shop steward and Janssen dropped it down to a suspension after he had to call for a steward? It seems to me if an employee is to be fired, there should be no misunderstanding between two officials of the company. The steward asked Janssen why was I fired. He said he didn't have the facts yet, and still no positive action on his part to find out. There's something other than a crew meeting behind this, and it doesn't take five days to get to the bottom of this and realize what really caused the suspension.

In a reply signed by plant superintendent Willis Burgess, the company rejected the second grievance presented by the union on behalf of Warlock.[2]

Warlock was discharged for insubordination after he refused a legitimate direction from his supervisor to stay overtime for 30 minutes, without giving a valid reason. This insubordination, following closely other exhibitions of insubordination, threats, and intemperate actions, made it impossible for the Company to continue Warlock's employment.

The union appealed both cases to arbitration. It was agreed by the

[2] See Appendix to this case for relevant clauses of the contract.

union and the company that the issues for arbitrator's determination could be framed as follows: Did the company have proper cause as required by the agreement when it first suspended Andrew Warlock and later discharged him? If not, what should be the proper remedies?

TESTIMONY AND EVIDENCE CONCERNING THE INCIDENTS

The April 3 Incident. Andrew Warlock attempted to attend a grievance meeting in the office of the personnel director, Charles Janssen, early on the afternoon of April 3. The meeting involved his brother, David Warlock, who was also an employee of Alumax. When Janssen denied him admission, he waited outside the personnel office to speak with David at the close of the meeting.

According to Andrew Warlock, his brother said that the company had fired him because he had refused to work four hours of required overtime the previous day. Andrew said that he became angry when his brother told him that a second employee, Kevin Wilson, also had not worked overtime but was not being disciplined. David claimed that John Brookings, a casting department supervisor, had reported that Wilson had worked a full 12 hours on April 2. Andrew then returned to the personnel office to speak with Janssen, but was told to leave without seeing him.

Warlock then proceeded to the time clock, where he unsuccessfully attempted to check Wilson's time card in order to determine whether Wilson had worked 12 hours the previous day. Warlock claimed that Wilson told him that he had not worked overtime that day.

Brookings was in the plant at about 3:15 P.M. on April 3, helping an employee locate a leak in the fuel line of a forklift truck. As he was working on the machine, Andrew Warlock strode up to him from the other end of the plant, accompanied by three employees and a friend who was not employed by Alumax. As he neared Brookings, Warlock cursed Brookings and accused him of lying about the overtime incident involving his brother and Kevin Wilson. They argued about it for a short while, and finally Brookings told him, "Get the hell out of the plant! You're suspended!" Warlock ignored this order. Brookings then reminded him that he was on company property, and gave both Warlock and his friend a direct order to leave the premises. Warlock replied that nobody could give him a direct order. He stepped outside a nearby door and drew back his fist as if to strike Brookings. Two employees restrained Warlock from hitting Brookings, whom he also tried to kick. Warlock observed Superintendent Willis Burgess walk into the plant at that point. Warlock left Brookings and talked with the superintendent about having been suspended. He admitted that he was very angry and that he had wanted to hurt Brookings. He stated that he knew that neither he nor his friend had permission to be in the plant,[3] but that he wanted to help his brother, whom he felt had been given a bad deal. Burgess affirmed the supervisor's suspension and extended it to seven days.

The April 17 Incident. Brookings scheduled a mandatory over-time safety meeting for Sunday, April 16. All employees had been advised on Saturday, April 15, that this half-hour meeting would take place at the end of the shift, from 3:00–3:30 P.M. Superintendent Burgess that same day asked Brookings to reschedule the meeting for the same time on Monday, April 17, in order that he might prepare additional materials for the meeting. All employees were promptly told verbally that the mandatory overtime meeting had been re-scheduled to 3:00–3:30 P.M. on Monday, and a notice also was posted on the time clock.

No one, including Warlock, said anything about being unable to attend the rescheduled meeting when told about it. However, at about noon on Monday, April 17, Warlock told Brookings that he could not attend the meeting because "he had other plans." When asked about his "other plans," Warlock was very noncommittal other than to refer to "other plans." Brookings reminded him of his duty to attend the obligatory overtime meeting at premium pay. Warlock left the plant at 3 P.M. on Monday and did not attend the meeting.

These obligatory meetings were conducted about once each month, and usually concerned safety matters. In practice, the company would excuse an employee who presented a very good reason for being absent. Everyone, except Warlock, attended the April 17 meeting.

Warlock, when asked by Brookings his reason for not attending the Monday meeting (presumably to attend his son's birthday party), replied that it was "none of the company's business." He also said that he had attended safety meetings before, and felt that anything said in a half-hour meeting could be quickly relayed to him by any of the others in attendance. But it was his personal feelings about his duty to the company that led him to be absent. He said that he felt that his own personal business was more important than that of the company, and that he had no obligation to the job beyond eight hours. Further-more, nothing in the contract required him to tell Brookings about his personal life. However, he agreed that the company had the right under the contract to require overtime on a mandatory basis.

---

[3] Andrew Warlock's shift had ended at 3 P.M., and he had already clocked out.

Warlock later told Burgess that he felt the real reason he was fired was that he had reported seeing Brookings carrying a gun on company property, a violation of company rules against bringing firearms or other dangerous weapons into the plant. In Warlock's opinion, company management unjustly used the April 17 incident as an excuse to terminate him.

Brookings originally planned to suspend Warlock for failing to attend the April 17 meeting, but Janssen and Burgess ruled that he should be terminated.

POSITION OF THE UNION

The April 3 Suspension. The union contended that a seven-calendar-day suspension was too harsh a penalty for Warlock, who was trying to defend his brother. The union acknowledged that he should have followed the appropriate grievance procedure and that he should not have lost his temper. However, the incident should be viewed in the light of one brother trying to defend another.

The April 17 Termination. The union argued that here, too, the company's action in terminating Warlock was extremely harsh. He had simply missed one half hour of required overtime, and he had a reasonable excuse. The supervisor in this situation could have excused Warlock from attending the meeting. The union agreed that the employee should have told his supervisor the reason for missing the meeting, but discharge was far too severe for the infraction. At most, he should have received a reprimand for not attending the meeting. He did not walk off the job; he simply did not attend a meeting. The discharge should be reduced to at most a reprimand.

POSITION OF THE COMPANY

The April 3 Suspension. The company maintained that Warlock was properly suspended from April 3 to April 9, 1978, for threatening a supervisor with physical violence. The seven-calendar-day suspension was very light in view of the severity of the infraction.

The April 17 Termination. The discharge of Warlock must be considered in relationship to the previous suspension, which had occurred only a few days earlier. He had been suspended from April 3 to April 9. He returned to work on April 11, and only a few days later, in the incident of April 17, he refused a direct order to attend a required safety meeting. His refusal to attend a required meeting on an over-time basis without offering any reason whatsoever for not being able to attend demonstrated his unwillingness to cooperate with the company and his direct insubordination toward company authority. The company claimed that the "arrogant, uncooperative, and insubordinate conduct of Warlock justified his suspension and discharge."

APPENDIX

Relevant Clauses of the Contract

Article II—Hours and Overtime

Section 3. It is recognized that overtime work is important and, on occasion, necessary. Once the Company has determined that employees are to do certain work at a certain time and that there will be an insufficient number of employees available to perform the work during their regular schedules, employees will be selected for overtime work in accordance with assignment rules established by the Company and the Union. No employee will be allowed to work more than fifteen (15) consecutive hours, and no more than fifteen (15) hours in any one day.

Article III—Management

It is agreed that the management of the Company's plant and works and the direction of its working forces, including the right to hire, suspend, discipline, or discharge an employee or employees for proper cause, and the right to transfer employees, and the right to relieve employees from duty because of lack of work, or for other legitimate reasons, is vested exclusively in the Company.

QUESTIONS

1. Did the company have proper (just) cause for issuing Andrew Warlock a seven-day disciplinary suspension? Discuss.

2. Did the company have proper (just) cause for discharging Andrew Warlock? Discuss.

3. Discuss the position of the union that Warlock had a "reasonable excuse" to miss the required safety meeting. In general, does a company have a right to require employees to work a certain amount of overtime?

4. Evaluate the company position that its decision to discharge Warlock should be considered in relationship to the prior suspension action. Is such a cumulative basis for discharging Warlock appropriate in this case?

46. Which Duty Calls?

Hospital:
  Monroe County Hospital, Rochester, New York
Association:
  Civil Service Employees Association, Monroe Chapter, Local 828

BACKGROUND

As Mary Moody[1] approached her apartment on Tuesday afternoon September 19, 1978, a police car pulled up in front of her door. The officers asked her to accompany them to the juvenile detention center, where her daughter, Eileen, was being held for both medical and psychological examination. Although Eileen was only 14 years of age, she had already had several encounters with the police and also had been suspended from school on several occasions because of her violent behavior toward both her teachers and fellow students.

The situation Tuesday afternoon was more serious. Earlier that day the assistant principal of Parks Junior High School had summoned police because of Eileen's threatening and potentially violent behavior toward one of the other students. She had already been suspended from school for an indefinite period and escorted to the detention center for processing and to await the arrival of her mother.

Mary Moody spent the next day at University Hospital, where both she and her daughter received counseling. The counselors strongly recommended that Mary take a leave of absence from her work so that she could devote full time and attention to the care and rehabilitation of Eileen, as well as care for her four other small children, for whom she was the sole support.

Mary Moody was a licensed practical nurse (LPN) who had been hired by the Monroe County Hospital on October 11, 1976. The hospital was a "chronic care" facility that housed nearly 600 patients, mostly geriatric, who were mostly long-term residents. The hospital was operated by the county and was required to conform to New York state staffing and patient services regulations. The hospital's need to maintain a full staff and to render high-quality service required it to insist upon prompt and regular attendance from employees.

The hospital deemed Moody's attendance record to be unsatisfac-

---

[1] The names of all individuals have been disguised.

tory and had warned her on four occasions over a period of 21 months as detailed below:

Warning	Period of Time over Which Absences and Tardiness Occurred	Date of Warning	Number of Absences	Number of Times Tardy
1	12/31/76–4/25/77	4/25/77	6	0
2	7/26/77–9/27/77	9/27/77	8	2
3	1/1/78–4/24/78	5/17/78	13	0
4	4/24/78–9/26/78	9/26/78	12	8

In addition, she had received counseling on one other occasion during this time for unrelated conduct and for continuous unsatisfactory evaluations on her performance, especially for her erratic attendance. Although she did not file a grievance to protest the four warning notices, she maintained that her absences and lateness were based upon proper and legitimate causes.

On September 21, 1978, Moody telephoned the nursing office to inform her supervisor that she was ill and could not report to work. She again called in on September 22 to report that she would be absent because of illness. She also left word for the staff coordinator of nursing to return her call.

When the staff coordinator returned the call, Moody informed her that she was requesting an unpaid leave of absence in order to take care of severe family problems that she was having with two of her children. The coordinator informed Moody that because of staffing problems at the hospital and her poor attendance record, her request probably would be denied. Moody submitted a formal request in writing for a leave of absence because of "personal family problems." The coordinator then discussed her request with the assistant personnel director, who confirmed denial of the request.

Starting September 23, Moody did not report for work, although she telephoned her supervisor on each day of her intended absence for reasons of "sickness" or "family sickness." On October 11, she was informed of a hearing to be conducted on October 13 concerning her absences. She attended the hearing with her union representative, after which she was given a termination notice based upon her "continual absence."

Mary Moody and the union immediately filed a grievance protesting her discharge, which eventually was carried to arbitration.

POSITION OF THE HOSPITAL

The hospital contended that Moody's attendance for her entire period of employment had ben extremely unsatisfactory. In both 1977 and 1978, she had been absent almost twice as many times as the second-worst LPN. Her record contrasted sharply with the average number of absences per LPN, which was four in 1977 and three in 1978 and the average number of times tardy per LPN, which was three for both these years. No matter how valid the causes or excuses for her absence, the hospital was entitled to her regular attendance. When an employee is absent as much as 10 percent of her scheduled work time, even for good reasons, her services become of little value to the hospital and she should not expect to remain in its employ. Regular and prompt attendance was especially critical in this case because of the New York state accreditation requirements as well as the safety and health of patients.

The hospital acknowledged its responsibility to assist troubled employees, but there were limits to the assistance it was able to afford. The hospital had already endured 21 months of undependable performance by Moody, and there was no indication that Moody's performance would improve in the future.

The hospital urged that the arbitrator uphold the discharge, since the hospital had ample just cause to terminate Moody as required by hospital rules and by the labor agreement for disciplining and discharging of employees.[2]

POSITION OF THE EMPLOYEES ASSOCIATION

The association (i.e., union) pointed out that the hospital's basis for terminating Moody was "continued absence" and not her past record; her past record should not be considered. Only the reasons for her present absence and its duration should be considered by the arbitrator.

The association argued that the hospital should have given special consideration to Moody's unique situation. She was the sole support of five minor children, including Eileen, aged 14, who had caused her grievous problems. On September 19, 1978, Eileen had been suspended from school for potentially violent behavior. Trained counselors had urged Moody to take a leave of absence from work so that she could devote full time and attention to the care and cure of her sick daughter. During the period of her absence from September 23, her daughter had

---

[2] See Appendix to this case for relevant clauses of the contract and sections of the hospital rules.

undergone physical and psychological tests and examinations at the University of Rochester Medical Center to determine the cause of her abnormal behavior. She had also received treatment from a private physician and a psycho-educational evaluation at the Strong Memorial Hospital, and upon the initiative of the Rochester Board of Education, Eileen had been assigned to the Neighborhood Achievement Center, where an individualized educational and counseling program had been designed for her. During this time, Mary Moody had received counseling and psychological aid for more effective supervision of Eileen.

The association argued that in cases such as this, society should recognize individual problems of employees and attempt to help resolve them. The hospital could and should help Moody by making it possible for her to minister to the special needs of her child in this time of crisis. According to the association, Mary Moody was now ready to resume her full employment responsibilities, and she would again be a responsible and dependable employee.

The association urged that Mary Moody be restored to her job and be made whole for all monies, rights, and privileges lost as a result of her unjust termination.

APPENDIX

Relevant Provisions of the Agreement

Article VII
Discipline and Discharge

1. No employee may be disciplined or discharged unless there is just cause . . . .

2. Any employee covered by this Agreement may file a grievance with the Association Steward if he or she feels that the Hospital has violated any provision of this Agreement or has been treated unjustly by the Hospital. . . .

Hospital Rules

* * * * *

13. The Hospital expects and requires that employees will report for duty at their scheduled time and shall remain at their stations until the end of their scheduled tour of duty. If an emergency requires that the employee report late or leave early, the employee must notify his/her supervisor in advance of the time he/she is scheduled to start or end the scheduled tour of duty. Approval will be given only when a genuine emergency exists.

14. The Hospital expects and requires that employees will attend regularly. Absences must be approved in advance by the employee's immediate supervisor and will be granted only for good cause.

Excessive tardiness or absence for whatever reason cannot be permitted. Employees who are late, absent, or are required to leave their stations during their scheduled tour of duty will be counseled and warned. If such excessive tardiness or absence continues, the employees with the Hospital will be terminated.

QUESTIONS

1. Did the hospital have ample just cause to terminate Mary Moody for "continual absence"?

2. Should Mary Moody's past record be considered by the arbitrator, or only the circumstances surrounding the situation leading to her discharge? Discuss.

3. To what lengths should an employer attempt to balance the stress of personal problems experienced by an employee against its own demands for work attendance?

4. Why is a case of this nature difficult from a public-relations point of view, particularly since this is a public-sector employer?

47. Terminated at 59 Days

Company:

Paccar, Inc., Kansas City, Missouri

Union:

United Automobile, Aerospace and Agricultural Implement Workers of America, Local 710

Robert Wright[1] was employed by Paccar on March 20, 1978, and was terminated on May 24, 1978, after 59 days of service. He would have completed his probationary period after his 60th day.[2] Normally, his termination would not have been subject to the grievance procedure; however, Wright was black, and the union charged that he lost his job as a result of discrimination.

BACKGROUND

Paccar, Inc., manufactured heavy equipment such as front loaders, log stackers, refuelers, and coal haulers. The company employed approximately 43 machinists in its machine shop. There were about 30 different types of machines of all sizes in the shop, including vertical and horizontal lathes, turret lathes, vertical and horizontal milling machines, drill presses, internal and centerless honing machines, and shapers. Some of the equipment was very sophisticated, being computer controlled.

Elton Davisson, the general foreman, was responsible for the machine shop. He supervised two foremen, one on the day shift and one on the night shift. Machinists were expected to perform their work with little technical supervision. Each machinist performed a variety of jobs and was required at a minimum to operate several machines. Job assignments varied in length from a half hour to a day or two, with most jobs requiring less than a day to complete. Machinists determined what operations were to be performed on a job assignment from a document known as the hard copy. In sequence, their jobs normally required them to (1) obtain the appropriate blueprints, (2) determine the machines and tools required, (3) set up the machines to perform the required operations, (4) operate the machines by setting the proper

---

[1] The names of all individuals have been disguised.
[2] See Appendix to this case for relevant clauses of the contract.

speeds and feeds, and (5) complete the required parts to specification, using micrometers and other precise measuring devices.

Davisson was responsible for interviewing applicants for machine shop positions to determine their overall knowledge, skills, and experience. After an applicant was hired, the foreman, in this instance Keith Hellwig, was responsible for the indoctrination, supervision, and performance appraisal of the new employee during the 60-day probationary period. In evaluating a new employee's performance, the foreman followed a well-developed procedure of assigning each new employee to a standard series of job assignments.

During the five years that foreman Hellwig had supervised new employees, approximately 25 probationary employees had been assigned to him. Six of these were terminated for failure to pass their probationary period. Wright was the only one of these six failing to pass the probationary period who was black; the others were white.

POSITION OF THE UNION

The union contended that the primary reason Wright was terminated during his probationary period was that he was black. The union charged that while the company had professed to subscribe to Article V of the collective bargaining agreement, in practice it had not done so.

The union held that no minority employee had ever successfully made it through the probationary period under Hellwig's supervision. According to the union, it was not unusual for the company to hire machinists "off the street" with little or no experience. Even experienced machinists made mistakes, and the company did not require all machinists in the shop to be able to perform on all the machines. The union contended that not more than two or three machinists in the shop were competent to perform job assignments on all of the machines. The union claimed that the company's allegations of lack of job abilities concerning Wright were used as a pretext against Wright because he was a black man.

The union pointed out that Wright had had about four years' prior work experience in several other metal fabricating plants working as a machine operator, machinist's helper, and assistant machine repairman. On those jobs he had operated several of the same machines on which he had been working at Paccar. In other words, he was not inexperienced at the time he came to the company, and he had performed capably for his previous employers.

The union produced three witnesses on behalf of Wright. The first was the business representative of the international union, who stated that he felt that the company did not employ enough minorities. Only one black currently was employed in the machine shop. On the other hand, the business representative had no personal knowledge of Wright's own job performance and ability. A second witness was an employee who had worked as a machinist for the company for 10 years and who was the fair employment practices chairman in the union. He stated that the company had not employed sufficient minority workers, but he did not charge that the company had discriminated against Wright. The third union witness was also a machinist and a member of the union's bargaining committee, which represented Wright at the third step of the grievance procedure. He also made no specific charge of discrimination. However, he disagreed with the company on Wright's performance, holding that his work as a probationary employee was satisfactory. He stated that though he made this evaluation of Wright's performance, he had had little occasion to observe his work. However, he said that he had spoken with several machinists in Wright's department, all of whom said that Wright's work met at least minimum standards, and some of whom said that it was about average. All three witnesses held that in their opinion, Wright was a qualified machinist who had been unjustly terminated during his probationary period for alleged "poor performance." Although none made any specific allegations of discrimination, they believed that Wright deserved to be retained as a machinist since they felt he was as capable as other men who had passed the probationary period.

Wright testified on his own behalf. He contended that he was a qualified machinist, that he met at least the minimum standards of performance on his job assignments, and that he performed as well as other probationary employees. He made no allegations of specific acts of discrimination against him, but he insisted that he was qualified to do the work of a machinist in the company. He felt that he had been unfairly terminated because he was black.

The union sought reinstatement of Robert Wright with full back pay, seniority from the date of hire, and all other benefits and rights he would have accrued, had he not been terminated discriminatorily by the company.

POSITION OF THE COMPANY

The company argued that the union had failed to prove that Wright's termination was the result of discrimination. According to the company, the union did not demonstrate that Wright's job performance satisfied the company's normal work requirements for either a probationary or permanent machinist. The company held that Wright's work performance during his probationary period was unsatisfactory. Hellwig stated that Wright was unable to take a job from start to finish and produce acceptable parts. According to Hellwig,

Wright seemed unable to operate the machines at safe speeds and with proper feeds. Wright was responsible for scrapping several valuable parts on which he had worked because he was unable to read the micrometers and work to close tolerances. Further, Wright had trouble reading blueprints, and he was unable to lay out a sequence of machine operations from a blueprint. Hellwig also stated that Wright required more help than other probationary employees in setting up his job. Wright's productivity was lower than that of other probationary employees, and more of his production required scrapping or reworking than that of other probationary workers. Because of all of this, Hellwig said that he decided that Wright could not handle the machinist's job.

The company pointed out that Hellwig had had the primary responsibility for probationary employees in the machine shop during the past five years. During that time, he had recommended termination of five white probationary employees. Wright was the first and the only black to be dismissed by Hellwig during that period. One other black had been hired into the machine shop; he had successfully completed the probationary period under a prior foreman to Hellwig.

The company introduced as evidence of Wright's unsatisfactory performance a copy of Hellwig's 25-day and 55-day written evaluations in support of the decision by Hellwig and Davisson to terminate him. These reports cited Wright's deficiencies, including his inability to read blueprints, to establish work procedures from "hard prints," a lack of ability to set up machines, a failure to operate machines at correct speeds and feeds, his inability to read micrometers and other measuring instruments accurately, and his production of abnormally large amounts of substandard work.

The company argued that its decision to terminate Robert Wright was based solely on his unsatisfactory performance as a probationary employee. Thus, the company had the right to terminate Wright under Article VI of the labor agreement. The company requested that the arbitrator deny the grievance.

APPENDIX

Relevant Provisions of the Contract

Article V—Nondiscrimination

The Company and the Union subscribe to the principles of equal economic opportunity and nondiscrimination.

The provisions of the agreement will be carried out without regard to an employee's race, color, creed, national origin, sex, handicap, or age.

When reference is made to the masculine gender in this contract, it refers to male or female, whichever is applicable.

Article VI—Seniority

Section 1. New employees shall be required to serve a probationary period of sixty (60) days during which the Company shall judge their qualifications. When an employee has accumulated sixty (60) days service with the Company, his seniority shall be established as of his original date of employment. The discharge or layoff of any employee during the probationary period shall not be subject to the provisions of the Grievance Procedure, unless during his probationary period the employee alleges the discharge or layoff was due to discrimination.

QUESTIONS

1. Evaluate the contentions of the union made on behalf of Robert Wright. Why is it sometimes difficult for a union and/or person to "prove" discriminatory intent in a case such as this?

2. Evaluate the position of the company. Why is it sometimes difficult for a company management to "prove" that it did not discriminate in a case such as this?

3. Is the fact that there was only one black machinist employee in the company a relevant factor in the arbitrator's decision? Why, or why not?

4. Might the Equal Employment Opportunity Commission (EEOC) use different standards in a case of this sort? Discuss.

5. Compare this case with Case 48, "No Date, No Job" for similarities and differences.

48. No Date, No Job?

Company:
> Paccar, Inc., Kansas City Division

Union:
> United Automobile, Aerospace and Agricultural Implement Workers of America, Local 710

BACKGROUND

Sarah Sears[1] had been hired by Paccar, Inc., on March 27, 1978, as a frame shop assembler. Paccar, Inc., manufactured heavy-duty highway trucks. The company operated a plant in Kansas City that employed about 800 hourly employees; 12 employees were frame shop assemblers.

On May 24, 1978, after 59 days of service, Sarah Sears filed a grievance claiming that she was unjustly terminated one day before the conclusion of her probationary period because she repeatedly refused to date and party with her male foreman, John Tyler, during nonworking hours.

Sears's job consisted of obtaining air tanks from a rack nearby and installing them. These tanks were attached to the frame of the trucks that passed on the assembly line in front of her.

John Tyler had been hired two weeks after Sears. His supervisor was David Keldkamp, who was the general foreman of the frame line.

Five days before the conclusion of Sears's 60-day probationary period, Tyler and Keldkamp met to discuss Sears's job performance. They agreed that Sears did not satisfactorily perform her job; and on May 24, 1978, Tyler terminated her.

In her grievance, Sears alleged that the company had engaged in sex discrimination by firing her because she had refused to date or party with her supervisor. The union asked that Sears should be reinstated to her job with back pay and all other benefits, and that Tyler should be transferred and/or ordered to stop harassing and discriminating against her.

---

[1] The names of all individuals have been disguised.

POSITION OF THE UNION

The union contended that Sarah Sears was terminated solely because she refused to socialize with foreman John Tyler after work. The union further took the position that the company had an obligation to make sure that male employees in managerial positions did not harass or exploit their female employees.[2]

Sears alleged that on several occasions Tyler telephoned her at home to make a date to go dancing or attend a movie. She always refused these requests. She added that on the day following his telephone calls, Tyler would confront her at work about her refusal to go out with him. Further, Tyler repeatedly offered to drive her home after work or tried to induce her to join him for a "quick drink" at a bar near the plant before going home. Sears said that she refused all his overtures. She stated that following each refusal, Tyler would harass her on the job. He would sometimes step on the air hose that supplied power to her tools, hide her tools, touch her body, and make suggestive sexual remarks. She charged that his behavior caused her great emotional stress and interfered with her ability to keep pace with the work.

The union stated that whenever Sears refused to go out with Tyler, he went out of his way to impede her work performance. The union called two employees to testify about Tyler's behavior, Edward Jones and Clement Tomas.

Jones worked in the frame shop with Sears and testified that he saw Tyler step on Sears's air hose, causing work problems for her on one occasion. He stated also that Tyler several times moved trucks on the assembly line while women were working in them but not when male employees were in them.

Tomas was a member of the union bargaining committee that investigated Sears's grievance. He stated that on one occasion he saw Tyler step on Sears's pneumatic hose, causing a power wrench to be pulled from her grasp. He also testified that another female employee had complained that she was "having trouble" with Tyler.

The union pointed out that neither Tyler nor Keldkamp had notified the union steward that Sears was experiencing work problems during her probationary period. The union said that this "was customary, although not required." When the union learned that Sears had been terminated, the union tried to obtain an extension of her probationary period, but this was refused.

The union urged that Sears's grievance be sustained in full by the arbitrator.

---

[2] See Appendix to this case for relevant provisions of the contract.

POSITION OF THE COMPANY

The company stated that this case involved the discharge of a probationary employee in which the company acted reasonably. It was not a case of wrongful discharge in which the company would be required to prove "just and proper" cause. The burden of proof was upon the union to show, based upon the preponderance of the evidence, that the company acted unreasonably or that the company had engaged in illegal sex discrimination.

The company contended that the evidence did not support Sarah Sears's allegation that it had discriminated against her. When Sears was questioned about the specifics, such as time, place, and circumstances concerning the proposals made to her by Tyler, she could not provide them. John Tyler testified that he was engaged to be married and was seeing his fiancee on a daily basis during the time he was alleged to have been pursuing Sears. Tyler was married one month after Sears was terminated.

The company further argued that it could not be expected to take corrective action if it were unaware of the situation. What two people did off the job was not the legitimate concern of the company. If some of the trials and tribulations of an off-the-job courtship carried over into the workplace, there was little that the company could do about it. It would be unreasonable to expect an employer to police the workplace for "all signs of a courtship gone sour or revenge by a rejected suitor." If Sears was being harassed by Tyler, she should have informed her union steward, who could have filed a grievance in accordance with the provisions of the collective bargaining agreement. This Sears had failed to do.

The company contended that the testimony of both Jones and Tomas should be dismissed. Both admitted that they had no knowledge of Tyler's ever having asked Sears for a date or having solicited her companionship in any way. While Tyler may have been guilty of some misconduct in stepping on her pneumatic hose, this should not sustain a sex discrimination charge.

The company stated that Sears was terminated because her work had been unsatisfactory. Keldkamp stated that he recommended that she be terminated because she was not mechanically adaptable. He testified that Sears had problems with the tools she was using on the job, including problems with recognition of wrench and socket sizes. She was often far behind in performing the tasks assigned her, she required frequent help to catch up, and she had caused the production line to be slowed on numerous occasions.

Finally, the company argued that under the contract, during an employee's probationary period a company could terminate marginal performers before they became regular employees with job security and seniority rights. The right of management to discharge probationary employees before they became full-time employees was protected by the labor agreement, and this was essential in order to maintain a productive labor force. This right should not be eroded because of an unsubstantiated sex discrimination charge filed by Sears.

The company requested that on the basis of the facts of the situation, the grievance be denied.

APPENDIX

Relevant Provisions of the Contract

Article V—Nondiscrimination

The Company and the Union subscribe to the principles of equal economic opportunity and nondiscrimination.

The provisions of the agreement will be carried out without regard to an employee's race, color, creed, national origin, sex, handicap, or age.

When reference is made to the masculine gender in this contract, it refers to male or female, whichever is applicable.

Article VI—Seniority

Section 1. New employees shall be required to serve a probationary period of sixty (60) days during which the Company shall judge their qualifications. When an employee has accumulated sixty (60) days service with the Company, his seniority shall be established as of his original date of employment. The discharge or layoff of any employee during the probationary period shall not be subject to the provisions of the Grievance Procedure, unless during his probationary period the employee alleges the discharge or layoff was due to discrimination.

QUESTIONS

1. Is the burden of proof on the union to "prove" Sara Sears's charge of sex discrimination? Discuss.
2. Could Sears also file charges of sex discrimination with the Equal Employment Opportunity Commission (EEOC) under the Civil Rights Act? Might the EEOC require a kind of proof different from that required by an arbitrator?
3. Why should a supervisor (in this case a male) generally avoid becoming involved in an off-the-job relationship with an employee of the opposite sex (in this case a female)?
4. Compare the issues in this case with those in Case 54, "A Weighty Problem."

49. To Promote, or Hire From the Outside?

Company:
   Rotek, Incorporated, Aurora, Illinois
Union:
   United Steelworkers of America, Local 8565

BACKGROUND

Rotek, Incorporated, employed approximately 60 bargaining unit employees at its Aurora plant and 51 employees at its Ravenna, Illinois, plant. Employees from both plants were in the same collective bargaining unit, represented by Local 8565 of the United Steelworkers of America. The company manufactured large bearings used primarily in construction equipment and other industrial applications.

Under the labor agreement, the company had a system for posting permanent job openings for bids. On September 13, 1978, the company posted an electrician (maintenance) (hereafter to be called electrician) job for bid. James Snover[1] and 18 other employees bid on this job; Snover was the most senior bidder.

Snover and two of the other bidders were classified as "general maintenance men." As a general maintenance man, Snover's primary duties consisted of piping, machinery setup, general repair, and electrical wiring. Snover had worked for the company for 10 years. Prior to that, he had been employed for two years in home construction work, three years in industrial maintenance at a plant in Pittsburgh, and one year as an electrical repairman for a small plant.

The electrician job at Rotek required knowledge and training sufficient to install and maintain sophisticated machine tools. Electricians also were required to maintain complicated heating and air-conditioning equipment and to be generally familiar with all phases of electrical work.

The job opening, as required by the job posting provisions of the agreement,[2] remained posted for three working days. Thereafter, the qualifications of all bidders were thoroughly reviewed. They were initially reviewed by Elaine Evans, personnel administrator, who pulled records of all the bidders and reviewed them for past experience

---

[1] The names of all individuals have been disguised.
[2] See Appendix to this case for relevant provisions of the contract.

311

and formal training. The records were then reviewed by David Schulman, manager of industrial relations, to determine whether there were employees who were presently qualified or who could become qualified during a 45-day training period referred to in the labor agreement. In addition, Schulman consulted with the plant engineers of both the Ravenna and Aurora plants for their advice concerning whether any of the bidders was qualified through experience they had acquired on the job. Both plant managers said that none of the bidders was qualified. As a result of the review of the records and the consultations with the plant engineers, Schulman determined that none of the job bidders was presently qualified and none was trainable.

On October 3, 1978, Schulman notified the chairman of the union's grievance committee, Herbert Dart, that the company intended to fill the opening from the outside. Two days later, the local union president, Robert Bono, was so notified by Elaine Evans. James Snover, the senior bidder, was not notified.

The company then took the necessary steps to fill the opening from the outside, including conducting job interviews and reviewing job applications. It hired a new employee, Frank Borden, to fill the electrician's job; he reported for work on October 16, 1978. Snover did not know until that time that his bid had been rejected.

On October 18, 1978, Snover submitted an oral complaint to the Aurora plant engineer, pursuant to step 1 of the grievance procedure outlined in the labor agreement. Subsequently, Snover submitted a grievance in writing on October 20, 1978, which was required at step 3 of the grievance procedure. Snover's grievance stated as follows:

> I, the undersigned feel I have been denied the opportunity according to Article 3, Section 3.3, Paragraph (b), and Article 6, Section 6.1. The company has unjustly denied me a benefit arising out of my job. The company has violated a specified, express term of this agreement.
>
> SETTLEMENT REQUESTED IN GRIEVANCE. To receive the job that was posted (electrician/maintenance) and retroactive back pay from 10/16/78 till this grievance is settled.
>
> AGREEMENT VIOLATION Article 3, Section 3.3, Paragraph (b), and Article 6, Section 6.1.

At step 2 and in all succeeding written answers, the company took the position that there had been no violation of the labor agreement, but, "In any event, the grievance was filed untimely." The grievance eventually was submitted to arbitration.

POSITION OF THE UNION

A. Timeliness

The union argued that the grievance was timely because the company's violation was a continuing one. The union contended that

Snover's grievance was filed within the five-day limitation. It cited Article VI, Section 6.1, of the agreement, which contained the phrase "after the rise thereof." The word *thereof* refers to the complaining person's "complaint." Thus, the question was: When was the "rise" of the complaint? The union maintained that the complaint arose on October 16, when Frank Borden, the new employee, reported for work; it was only then that Snover learned that his job bid had been rejected.

In contradiction of the company's claim that it was past practice not to notify employees that their job bids had been rejected, the union claimed that the company had been inconsistent on this. The union contended that the company did not always hire from the outside when it indicated that it was going to do so. Finally, the union pointed out that following the filing of this grievance, the company began posting its decisions on employee job bids.

B. Merits

As to the merits of the company decision to reject Snover's bid for the job, the union contended that the company had acted arbitrarily when it decided that Snover was not qualified and not trainable for the job opening of an electrician. Snover was the senior bidder with 10 years of service to the company. His past job experiences both with the company and prior to joining the company were similar in nature to the duties of the electrician/maintenance position. He had always been a good employee, and he had never received any disciplinary actions concerning his work performance.

The union claimed that Snover's seniority rights were being totally ignored by the company in this decision. The company had violated Snover's contractual rights by not affording him the training and trial period prescribed in the labor agreement. Snover could possibly have met the company's job requirements had he been given the right to a trial period.

The union claimed that the company should be required to promote James B. Snover to the position of electrician retroactive to October 16, 1979, and be made whole for all wages and other rights and benefits lost as a result of the company's failure to award the position to him, at least on a trial basis.

POSITION OF THE COMPANY

A. Timeliness

The company claimed that Snover's grievance was not timely, and that the matter, therefore, was not arbitrable. Schulman had notified the chairman of the union's grievance committee on October 3 that none of the candidates was qualified to fill the position of electrician, and that the company planned to hire an electrician from outside. In

addition, Elaine Evans gave the same notice to the local union president on October 5. The company had fully met its responsibility to
Snover by notifying the union of its plan to recruit an electrician from
outside the company, since none of the interested employees was
qualified or qualifiable within the 45-day training period specified in
Section 3.2(b) of the contract. Since Snover did not grieve until October
18, the grievance was not timely and should be dismissed.

B. Merits

On the possibility that the arbitrator might rule for the union on
the issue of timeliness, the company presented testimony and evidence
concerning the merits of the case. The company pointed out that
Section 3.3(a) of the labor agreement provided that a job bidder with
the greatest seniority, previously meeting the provisions of Sections
3.2(a) and 3.2(b), would be awarded the bid. Section 3.2(a) provided
that an employee was qualified for a particular job when he had
worked that job for a specified period of time. Since Snover had not
worked the electrician's job for the specified period of time, he was not
qualified. Therefore, he was not entitled to the bid under the provisions
of Section 3.3(a).

Section 3.3(b) provided that if the opening was not filled by a
qualified employee, "an opportunity to train for the job will be given to
the highest seniority employee bidding and *considered trainable for the
job*" (emphasis added). The italicized words were the key words as far
as the determination of this case on its merits was concerned. Snover
was the highest seniority employee bidding, but was he "considered
trainable for the job?"[3]

The company conceded that its decision as to whether Snover was
or was not trainable for the job was a decision that was subject to
challenge. The company attorney stated:

> It is uniformly agreed that under such language the employer has the
> right to make the initial determination subject to challenge by the union
> that the employer's decision was unreasonable, and that where the union
> challenges management's determination, it has the burden of proving
> that the employer's evaluation of abilities and qualification was incor-
> rect.

However, the company argued that the position of electrician
required an employee who was skilled in advanced applications of

---

[3] The parties agreed that this term meant trainable within the time specified in
Sections 3.2(a) and 3.2(b).

electrical and electronic principles. The job required more than just ordinary routine, elementary electrical experience. For example, the job description stated that part of an electrician's duties was to "install and wire centralized control panels." A single control panel might regulate many remote motors in different areas of the plant. The company had never permitted general maintenance personnel to wire centralized control panels. All new machines installed in the plant were equipped with solid-state circuitry, and all electricians must "get in on the ground floor" with each machine in order to learn both its basic operation and its idiosyncrasies. A high degree of sophisticated knowledge was necessary to perform both installation and maintenance work on new solid-state equipment.

The company reviewed Snover's background at the company as a general maintenance man. Part of his duties included general electrical work, such as "trouble shooting" machines for electrical problems. He had performed a variety of tasks, including some electrical work on new machines, but not on any machines involving solid-state circuitry. His experience prior to being employed at the company was as a general house contractor, in finishing and maintenance work for a furniture company, in production and maintenance work for a manufacturing concern in Pennsylvania, and in maintenance work for a feedmill. None of the jobs entailed a great amount of electrical work, and none of them entailed the kind of intricate work that Snover would need to perform at the company as an electrician.

In contrast to the kinds of work that Snover had been performing at the company, the employees who held the position of electrician had performed much more advanced work. The company gave several examples of machinery upon which electricians worked and the type of work they performed. For example, two electricians recently reworked a new German cutoff saw machine so that it would be compatible with American voltage. Another recent project of the electricians was the installation of a new air compressor. In the process of carrying out this assignment, the electricians determined that the compressor had two auxiliary pieces of equipment that were of different voltages, necessitating determining the size of a transformer able to operate all three pieces of equipment with the available 480 volts. The electricians were able to accomplish this and properly install the equipment. A third recent project involved a problem with a geartooth hardener at the Ravenna plant. The electricians were trying to assure that the machine would be more reliable and not turn out scrap material. They wanted to pick up every other tooth in the gear, and install a counter that would tell the machine that it was going to skip teeth. In order to get the machine to skip teeth, it was necessary for the electricians to cut into a circuit and put a counter into it.

The company admitted that James Snover had assisted the electricians on some of these projects. But his work on many of the machines appeared to be only peripherally involved with straight electrical work. For example, on the new German cutoff saw, he helped mount it on the floor, but it was the two electricians who determined how to rework the machine to be compatible with American voltage. In another instance, Snover helped the electricians in the addition of a 10-foot length of high-voltage line within a special raceway located in the ceiling. He helped with the installation of that because of his experience with ironworkers; his experience had made him better qualified than the electricians to ensure that certain articles adhered to the ceiling. However, it was the electricians who determined what articles were needed to complete the project and how they would actually perform the final work on the project.

Finally, the company pointed out that Snover had agreed during discussions of his grievance that it would be necessary for him to take a course at a nearby university in order to become adequately knowledgeable of solid-state circuitry and motor controls.

In summary, the company acknowledged that James Snover had been a good, dependable employee. But the company maintained that its managers had fairly assessed that Snover would not be capable of being trained to assume the electrician's job in a 45-day period. Absent any showing by the union to the contrary, the judgment of management should be affirmed and the union grievance should be denied by the arbitrator.

APPENDIX

Relevant Provisions of the Contract

Article III—Seniority,
Vacancies, Reassignments,
Layoffs, and Releases

Section 3.2(a). An employee is qualified to do a particular job or operate a type of machine if the individual has worked at the job or operated the type of machine for forty-five (45) days of the employee's continuous working days, unless the company requests another extension of forty-five (45) continuous working days to qualify. (This extension will be granted in the following classifications: Maintenance, Electrician, Induction Fabricator, and Tool Maker/Machinist.)

(b) These forty-five (45) continuous working days shall be considered a trial period. If an employee shall fail to complete such trial period, either voluntarily or because of a company decision, the employee may return to the previous job in which said employee was qualified, provided an extension hasn't been granted as the provisions of Article III—Section 3.2, Paragraph (a), are fulfilled.

Section 3.3(a).   If a permanent job opening occurs, the employee with the greatest seniority, previously meeting the provisions of Article III—Section 2, Paragraphs (a) and (b), and having bid the job, will be chosen over other bidders.

(b) If an employee bids for a permanent job opening and has not previously met the provisions of Article III—Section 2, Paragraphs (a) and (b), and such job is not filled by a qualified employee with more seniority, an opportunity to train for the job will be given to the highest seniority employee bidding and considered trainable for the job.

Article VI—Grievances and Arbitrations

Section 6.1.   A grievance is defined as a complaint by any member of the union, covered by this Agreement, or by the union in its own behalf, that the company has violated a specified, express term of this Agreement, or that it has unjustly denied any employee his/her job contrary to the terms thereof, or has denied any employee any benefit arising out of his/her job. Such a complaint shall be treated in the following manner. With one (1) exception, suspensions pending discharge, such grievances shall proceed to step 4 of the procedure, after first lodging a complaint within the five (5) day period.

Step 1.   The complaining party shall first lodge the complaint with his/her immediate supervisor within five (5) days after the rise thereof (wage claims excepted). . . . Failure to file a complaint within the time limitations set forth by this Article shall operate to nullify the complaint, without recourse.

QUESTIONS

1. Was the grievance filed in a timely fashion as required by the labor agreement? Discuss.

On the assumption that the arbitrator would rule that the grievance was arbitrable:

2. Evaluate the facts and arguments presented by the union on behalf of grievant Snover.

3. Evaluate the facts and arguments presented by the company in support of its position.

4. Some arbitrators have advocated the use of the "head-and-shoulders concept" in deciding cases such as this. This concept suggests that a senior employee should be given an opportunity to fill a higher level job, unless the junior seniority employee or an outside person is significantly superior (i.e., head and shoulders above) the senior employee in merit, ability, and/or potential. Would this concept be applicable in this case? Why, or why not?

5. Compare the issues in this case with those in Case 38, "The Bypassed Senior Clerk."

50. Who Must Pay for the Safety Shoes?

Company:

Hater Industries, Inc., Cincinnati, Ohio

Union:

United Steelworkers of America, Local 310

BACKGROUND

On May 17, 1978, Charles Mulhaney[1] filed the following grievance on behalf of Local 310 of the union:

> The United Steelworkers of America, Local 310, claim that the Company
> violated Article XV, Section 1—Safety and Health—of the Basic Agree-
> ment when it failed to furnish the safety equipment specified by OSHA.[2]

During steps of the grievance procedure, the company made the
following reply to the union:

> Due to the fact that the Union agrees there is nothing in the collective
> bargaining agreement requiring the Company to pay for shoes, and that
> the Company has never in the past paid for safety equipment which
> employees are allowed to keep for their personal use, therefore, the
> Company has no obligation to pay for the shoes.

The parties were unable to resolve their differences and submitted
the following statement of the issue to an arbitrator for final determination:

> Has the Company violated the Agreement between the parties by refus-
> ing to pay for safety shoes which employees must wear pursuant to the
> requirements of the Occupational Safety and Health Administration,
> and, if so, to what remedy, if any, are the grievants entitled?

Prior to the current agreement between the company and union,
the company had always provided employees with certain safety equipment. During contract negotiations, the company agreed to continue
this practice and to the provisions of Article XV of the agreement.

In January 1978, the Occupational Safety and Health Administration (OSHA) conducted an inspection of the company's facilities. As a

---

[1] The names of all individuals have been disguised.

[2] See Appendix to this case for relevant clause of the contract.

result of this inspection, several citations were issued to the company for violations of federal requirements. One such citation was issued because safety shoes with metatarsal guards were not worn by employees working in the abrasive blasting area as a protection against foot injury. The OSHA regulation required that "safety shoes shall be worn to protect against foot injury where heavy pieces of work are handled."[3]

POSITION OF THE UNION

The union argued that the company must furnish the safety shoes required by OSHA regulations. The company's refusal to purchase safety shoes violated Article XV of the agreement between the parties, as well as past practices in the company. The agreement required that the company "must comply with applicable state and federal laws and regulations concerning the health and safety of its employees." In order to conform to the purposes and intentions expressed in Article XV, the company must purchase for its employees the safety shoes that OSHA mandated.

The safety shoes giving rise to this dispute were required by federal regulations. To be in compliance, the company was responsible for seeing that each employee in the affected areas possessed and used the required safety apparel. An employee's refusal to wear the required shoes would give the company grounds for discipline, including discharge. However, before the company could require employees to wear the required safety shoes, the company must furnish the shoes for the employees' use.

The union claimed that the company had always provided employees with necessary safety apparel in the past. For example, the company had supplied employees with aprons, gloves, rubber boots, safety glasses, and goggles. These items were paid for by the company at no expense to the employee. Where safety equipment was necessary, the company had also provided it. In the present instance, safety shoes had become necessary by law; thus it was the company's obligation to provide the shoes consistent with the agreement and long-standing past practices.

The grievance should be sustained.

POSITION OF THE COMPANY

The company maintained that the agreement between the parties did not require it to pay for employees' safety shoes. Further, neither

---

[3] 29CFR19.0.94(a) (5) (v).

the company's past practices nor OSHA regulations imposed this financial burden upon it.

The agreement between the parties required company compliance with all federal and state laws and regulations. However, the OSHA regulation for which the company received a citation required only that the company must assure that appropriate safety shoes were worn in compliance with the standard. But OSHA did not require that the company must pay for safety shoes to be worn by employees on the job.

In this regard, the company claimed that at no time was the company ever advised by OSHA that it was required to purchase safety shoes for its employees. Nor had the law ever been interpreted to require a company's purchasing of safety shoes. The company had been assured that its obligation was to make certain that safety shoes were worn by the employees working in specific areas of the plant. Thus, the company had no statutory nor regulatory obligation to purchase protective footwear for employees.

The company argued that the agreement between the parties did not require the company to pay for safety shoes that were required by OSHA regulations. Since the contract was silent concerning the purchasing of personal safety items, the company was not obligated to assume the cost of such items. The financial burden of protective wear was an item that was open for collective bargaining.

During previous contract negotiations between the parties, the union had proposed a provision to be added to the contract whereby the company would assume the cost of safety wear. However, the company rejected such a provision. The agreed-upon article (Article XV) did not require the company to purchase personal safety wear for its employees. Thus, it was clear that the company did not intend to be responsible for buying safety wear, and the union was clearly on notice of this position of the company.

Finally, the company contended that the practice of supplying certain safety items to the employees did not bind the company to supply safety shoes as well. The footwear required by OSHA was a personal item to the employee; these shoes could be worn at times that were of no benefit to the company. Supplying such an item differed greatly from the company's practice of supplying safety gloves, aprons, and glasses to employees. The company pointed out that it had consistently refused to be responsible for the purchase of personal safety items such as prescriptive safety glasses.

In summary, the company claimed that the union was attempting through this grievance to gain a benefit for the members that it had not been able to gain through negotiations. The company urged the arbitrator to deny the grievance.

APPENDIX

Relevant Clause of the Contract

Article XV—Safety and Health

Section 1. The company shall continue to make reasonable efforts to maintain its equipment and facilities in a safe operating condition. The company will also make reasonable efforts to maintain clean premises, and employees shall cooperate in keeping all facilities in a clean condition. Management alone may determine the specific means by which a safety hazard shall be corrected or eliminated, including closing such department or area. Employees must abide by management's health and safety rules, and misuse or disregard of safety devices or equipment are grounds for discipline including discharge. The company will comply with applicable state and federal laws and regulations concerning the health and safety of its employees.

QUESTIONS

1. Did Article XV of the agreement mandate that the company must pay the costs of the safety shoes under the circumstances of this case? Why, or why not?

2. Were the past practices in the company regarding safety equipment more supportive of the union's or the company's position? Discuss.

3. Was the union attempting to achieve through arbitration what it had failed to achieve at the bargaining table?

4. What are the precedent implications of the arbitrator's decision in this case?

51. Who's Telling the Truth?

Company:

National Car Rental System, Inc., East Boston, Massachusetts

Union:

International Brotherhood of Teamsters, Chauffeurs, Warehousemen and Helpers of America, Local 841

BACKGROUND

National Car Rental System, Inc., was in the business of renting out cars. The company operated a major facility near Logan Airport in East Boston, Massachusetts. Preparation of cars for rental took place in the firm's main car wash bay, which was a large building with a central heating system. During the winter months, employees often set the thermostat as high as 90°F. to keep the bay warm while they were working. This practice consumed a large amount of energy and kept the bay area warmer than necessary.

Because of the energy crisis that brought on a shortage and rapidly escalating cost of oil early in 1978, the company turned down the thermostat in the car wash bay to 72°F and requested employees not to change this setting. Some employees ignored this request and continued to turn the thermostat up to 90°F. Finally, on March 17, 1978, Peter Walton,[1] the assistant manager, set the thermostat at 72°F and installed a lock box on the thermostat to prevent continued misuse. He also posted the following notice on several company bulletin boards:

> The lock box and thermostat in the bay are not to be touched. The heat is set at the proper temperature and must not be altered.
>
> If I find this unit tampered with again, I will shut off the heat altogether.
>
> Also, if I catch you touching the unit, you will be terminated.

This notice was posted and a locked plastic box placed over the thermostat to prevent vandalism to the thermostat.

At about 4:30 P.M. on December 27, 1978, Walton noticed that the doors to the main car wash bay were open and letting in the cold air. As he entered the bay through the open doors he observed two employees, John Bosworth and Melvin Ziegler, standing in front of the thermostat

---

[1] Names of all individuals have been disguised.

about 20 feet away from him. Bosworth was holding a straightened metal coat hanger, a newspaper, and other trash. Peter Walton then thought he saw Bosworth insert the hanger into the locked plastic box and tamper with the thermostat. Walton shouted at both men to stop tampering with the thermostat, whereupon they turned around and stared at him, apparently startled by his voice. Walton then proceeded to walk toward them. When Walton got nearer, he noticed that the lock box had been cracked and the temperature setting changed to a setting of 85°F. Walton then escorted Bosworth to the shift manager's office and questioned him about the incident.

Bosworth stated that he had reported for work at 4:15 P.M. and immediately had started cleaning cars. He said that he and Ziegler had got to talking about the temperature in the bay, so they walked over to the thermostat to "check it out." Bosworth said he was still holding a coat hanger, a newspaper, and other trash that he had removed from one of the cars, when Walton walked into the bay. Bosworth claimed that he was merely checking the temperature, and that he did not insert the coat hanger into the locked box, did not break it, and did not change the thermostat setting in any way.

Bosworth admitted that he had read the notice dated March 17, 1978, prohibiting any tampering with the thermostat or its locked protective covering. He also stated that he knew that violators would be discharged.

John Bosworth was a 25-year-old high school graduate when he was hired in 1977. He had held various unskilled and semiskilled jobs in Boston and Hawaii before being hired as a service agent. His duties as a service agent included cleaning the interiors of rental cars, operating the mechanical car wash equipment, checking for certain deficiencies and defects, and checking gasoline, oil, water, and air levels.

His personnel records indicated the following prior disciplinary actions by the company: (1) June 27, 1977—oral warning for being late for work on four days out of five during one week; and (2) October 27, 1978—three-day suspension for "screeching tires while exiting the bay."

Walton did not believe Bosworth's story, and after reviewing his employment record at National Car Rental, Walton discharged him. The discharge notice included the following reasons:

> 12/17/78. Bosworth was observed using a coat hanger to change the thermostat inside the service bay. Locks had been put on these thermostats so that no one would tamper with them.
>
> Previous misuse of company property by Bosworth happened on 10/27/78.

The union filed a grievance on behalf of John Bosworth, protesting his discharge and requesting reinstatement with restoration of full back pay, seniority, and any other benefits.

POSITION OF THE COMPANY

The company argued that Bosworth was "caught red-handed" tampering with the lock box that covered the thermostat. Manager Peter Walton should be believed because there was no reason for him to fabricate such a story. Both Bosworth and Ziegler had a self-interest in denying that Bosworth had tampered with the temperature setting on the thermostat.

The company pointed out that Bosworth had a poor employment history, including a warning for excessive tardiness and a suspension for misuse of company property. Bosworth was clearly aware of the regulation prohibiting tampering with the thermostat, which warned of termination for violation.

In response to Bosworth's and Ziegler's statements about their work activities, the company contended that there was no reason for Bosworth to be carrying the trash items that he held when Walton observed him near the thermostat. Trash items removed from cars were to be thrown on the floor or in a trash bin to be removed at the end of the shift. It was more logical to conclude that Bosworth deliberately carried the metal coat hanger (and other trash items) to the thermostat with the intention of using the hanger to crack the plastic box over the thermostat.

The company claimed that it had ample "just cause" to discharge John Bosworth, under a contractual provision that required that disciplinary actions taken by the company must be for "just cause." Bosworth was observed by a manager engaging in an act that he and other employees had been notified would lead to their termination. The discharge action should be sustained, and the union grievance should be denied.

POSITION OF THE UNION

The union did not contest the company's right to post the notice that Peter Walton had posted on March 17, 1978. The union acknowledged that the reason for this company action was to conserve fuel consumption and energy costs.

However, the union stated that the company had failed to meet the required burden of proof that Bosworth had violated a company regulation by tampering with the thermostat. Both Bosworth and Ziegler were doing nothing more than standing in front of the thermostat to check the temperature when Walton entered the car wash bay. Ziegler, who was standing next to Bosworth when the incident occurred, had a clear view of what was going on, and he testified that Bosworth did not tamper with the thermostat. Ziegler also confirmed Bosworth's statement that the clothes hanger was part of the trash removed from the rental cars, and that it had not been used to vandalize the lock box. The union claimed that Bosworth and Ziegler had told the truth, and the company should accept their statement of events as true. Obviously, someone else had tampered with the thermostat, not Bosworth as claimed by the company.

In addition, the entrance to the bay was 20 feet from the thermostat. Walton could not possibly have seen a thin metal hanger at that distance. It was even more unlikely that he could have seen the hanger inserted into the thermostat, since both Bosworth and Ziegler were standing in front of it with their backs to him.

In summary, the company did not adequately prove that Bosworth had tampered with the thermostat. Therefore, Bosworth should be returned to his job, and be made whole for all monies and benefits lost as a result of the company's action.

QUESTIONS

1. Discuss the burden-of-proof issue, which is a central aspect of this case. Why do arbitrators generally place a heavier burden-of-proof requirement upon the management side in discharge cases?

2. How can the arbitrator resolve the conflict in testimony between the union and company witnesses?

3. If the arbitrator should resolve the credibility question in favor of the testimony of Walton, was the infraction involved serious enough to sustain the discharge of Bosworth? Why, or why not?

52. A Disciplinary Warning to the Union President

Company:

Reichhold Chemicals, Incorporated, Grand Junction, Tennessee

Union:

United Rubber, Cork, Linoleum and Plastic Workers of America, Local 672

BACKGROUND

The management at the Grand Junction plant had watched employees gradually stretch their breaks to the point where the practice was affecting morale, costs, and productivity. In order to regain control over the length of employee breaks, the company instituted a rule requiring employees to punch out and in on lunch periods and authorized breaks. A petition had been circulated among the employees challenging the propriety of the rule. The union president, Rodney Jacobs,[1] appeared at the office of the foreman, Lenny Walker, with the petition fastened to a grievance on Monday, May 1, 1979, shortly before 3:30 P.M., when he was scheduled to start his shift. He requested an immediate grievance meeting. Walker contacted the plant superintendent, Robert A. Yehle, who reminded the union president that he had bypassed step 1 of the grievance procedure; but Yehle agreed to meet on Tuesday, May 2, at 3 P.M. Jacobs was not satisfied with this but went to his job at 3:30 P.M.

At about 3:35 P.M. Jacobs returned to Walker's office with Bill Sperry, vice president of the union. He demanded, "We want to have the meeting now." The plant manager, Edward Arnold, was tied up in a conference with two of his superiors from the headquarters office and was unavailable. After checking with all management personnel involved, Walker and Yehle told the union officers that no meeting could be arranged, and that they would have to abide by the contract by having the employees first take this matter up with their foremen. Jacobs replied that Yehle could go to the foremen for them. Yehle explained to Jacobs that he was mistaken. When Jacobs and Sperry then tried to push their way into the plant manager's office, Yehle instead directed them into foreman Walker's office. Yehle tried to

---

[1] The names of all individuals have been disguised.

convince Jacobs that he should follow standard procedures, to which Jacobs replied that he could confer with the plant manager any time he wished. After further discussion, Jacobs agreed to meet with Yehle on May 2, as had been originally planned. However, they then postponed the meeting to the next day, May 3, at 3 P.M. in order that they could also discuss a different grievance that had been filed by another employee, Willis Jones.

The May 3 grievance meeting began at 3 P.M. as scheduled. Although several members of the union grievance committee were present, Yehle was the only company representative in attendance. It was anticipated that the meeting would last only about 30 minutes and that Jacobs would be back at work as a "relief man" at the start of his shift at 3:30 P.M. A short time prior to the meeting, Jacobs's foreman, Lenny Walker, told him that his attendance at the grievance meeting had been approved. Walker did not obtain a substitute relief man, however, since he expected Jacobs to report for work at the start of the shift.

Jones's grievance was quickly disposed of. Jacobs then asked Yehle to present the May 1 petition and grievance to the plant manager. Yehle informed the union committee members that he would not do so because the petition and grievance had not been properly presented through the established channels. At the close of the meeting, Yehle signed Jacobs's timecard, indicating that the meeting had ended at 3:30 P.M.

After leaving Yehle's office, Jacobs talked briefly with the other members of the union grievance committee and then went to the plant manager's office. He presented the May 1 grievance to Arnold, explaining that Yehle had refused to do so. At that point, Yehle entered Arnold's office, looking for Jacobs. Upon seeing Jacobs talking with Arnold, Yehle told Jacobs that his foreman had expected him to be at work and was looking for him. Jacobs did not leave, but rather asked Arnold to give him a written acknowledgement of having either accepted or rejected the grievance. Arnold supported Yehle's position in stating that it had not been properly processed, and that he would not initial it. Jacobs left Arnold's office at about 4:10 P.M. and returned to his job.

Shortly after Jacobs reported for work on the following day, his foreman handed him a written reprimand for having absented himself from his job on the previous day without permission from 3:30 to 4:10 P.M.

The union immediately filed a grievance in which it requested that the company remove the written reprimand from Jacobs's records. The parties were unable to resolve their dispute, and the union carried the grievance to arbitration. The union and company were unable to agree upon a statement of the issue that they wished the arbitrator to resolve. The company proposed the following:

> Did the company violate the contract by giving Jacobs a warning on or about May 3, 1979? If so, what should the remedy be?

The union declined to accept the company's statement of the issue and offered instead:

> Was the disciplinary warning given Jacobs on May 3, 1979, just and proper? If not, what should the remedy be?

POSITION OF THE COMPANY

The company charged that Jacobs possessed a distorted notion as to his role in employee relations. The company claimed that the petition presented by Jacobs had been drafted and circulated by him as a means of challenging the company's authority. Company witnesses cited several examples of Jacobs's behavior to support the company's position. For example, on May 1, when his foreman warned him not to be off the job and said, "If you do, we will be forced to take disciplinary action," Jacobs retorted without hesitation, "We'll see." Similarly, on May 3, Jacobs told his foreman, "I can come up and see the plant manager anytime I want to." At the same meeting, when asked if he had permission to be off the job, he responded with, "No, I didn't think that it was necessary."

The company claimed that during the grievance meeting on May 3, Jacobs stated that he was personally going to "try" the company, and that he planned to pick out something he was assigned to do, and then refuse to do it. Then after Yehle refused to waive step 1 of the grievance procedure and to accept the list of names on the petition as a grievance, Jacobs announced that he was left with no alternative other than to go to Arnold. In fact, he had many alternatives, including going back to step 1 and following the orderly steps of the grievance procedure without interfering with normal plant activities. But this would have been too tame for Jacobs. He preferred to go to Arnold immediately and complain because Yehle would not waive the contractual rights of the company.

The company contended that the arbitrator possessed no basis for upholding the grievance. Article II, Section 1, of the contract stated that the company retained all the functions, powers, and authority not specifically abridged, delegated, or relinquished by the contract. Except for the prohibition of discrimination contained in Article III, Section 6, the only limitation in the contract on the company's disciplinary authority was in Article V, which required that suspensions (including layoff) and discharges be given justly. The contract contained no such standard for the issuance of a warning or reprimand.

Further, Article III, Section 4, prohibited the arbitrator from adding to or altering any clause in the contract. Thus the arbitrator did not possess the authority to find that the company violated any clause in the contract in issuing a warning to Jacobs.

For all of these reasons, the company requested that the arbitrator deny Jacobs's grievance.

POSITION OF THE UNION

The union argued that all types of disciplinary action taken by the company against an employee could only be for just cause. The company was in error in contending that Article V required that only suspension or discharge must meet the standard of fairness. Oral warnings or any other form of discipline that may subsequently become the foundation or justification for suspension or discharge must also as a matter of logic be delivered only for just cause.

The union contended that the plant manager, Edward Arnold, had encouraged union officers, including Jacobs, to bring any problems that they could not resolve at lower levels to him for additional discussion and resolution. In several such statements to union leaders, Arnold had placed no limits on the type or scope of issues or problems that he would be willing to discuss with them in this manner.

The union claimed that Article XI, Section 17, included union representatives other than stewards, including the union president, when conducting union business with the company. The language of Article XI, Section 17, required only that a foreman be notified when a union representative must obtain permission from a foreman before leaving the job to investigate a grievance. The union opposed any change in the language of the section. Thus, it was clear that it was not necessary for Jacobs to obtain permission from his foreman to be absent from his work. It was only necessary that he notify his foreman of his need to be away on union business with the company. The company was using Jacobs and this grievance to obtain through arbitration that which it had been unable to obtain through negotiation.

The union pointed out that company rules listed "leaving assigned area, department, or job without foreman's permission" as constituting minor misconduct. However, this rule could not apply to instances where the union representative must leave the job to transact union business with the company. The conduct of union business was specifically covered by the contract language of Article XI, Section 17.

Finally, irrespective of all of the above, Jacobs did not leave his position without permission. His foreman, Lenny Walker, knew on the previous day that Jacobs would be in a meeting on union business at 3 P.M. on May 3, 1979.

For all the reasons cited above, the union claimed that the disciplinary warning given to Jacobs was unjust. The union requested that Jacobs's grievance be sustained, and that the written warning be removed from his records.

APPENDIX

Relevant Provisions of the Contract

Article I—Recognition and Representation

Section 1. The Company agrees to recognize and bargain with the accredited representatives of the Union, and the Union shall be the sole and exclusive bargaining agency for all production and maintenance employees of the Company's Grand Junction, Tennessee, plant. . . .

Section 2. There shall be no discrimination in respect to any term or condition of employment because of race, creed, color, religion, national origin, sex, or age. . . .

Article II—Management Rights

Section 1. All the functions, powers, and authority which the Company has not specifically abridged, delegated, or relinquished by the Agreement are and shall be retained by the Company.

Section 2. The Union agrees that (a) the management of the plant, (b) the direction of the working forces, (c) the operation of the plant and machinery, (d) the number and location of plants, (e) the nature of equipment or machinery, (f) the methods and processes of manufacturing, (g) the right, subject to the terms of this Agreement, to hire, promote, demote, suspend and discharge employees and to relieve employees from duty for lack of work and other causes, including the right to transfer employees from one department or job to another department or job, (h) the assignment of work, (i) the scheduling of work . . . is vested exclusively in the Company. The exercise of such authority shall not conflict with this Agreement.

Article III—A. Grievance Procedure

Section 2. Step 1: In the event that any dispute or grievance shall arise between the employee and the Company as to the application of any of the provisions of this Agreement, this matter shall first be taken up with the foreman involved by the employee, or the employee and Union representative. . . .

Step 2: If the grievance is not settled within twenty-four (24) hours from the time it is presented to the foreman in step 1, above, it shall be put into written form and presented to the supervisor within two (2) working days after the Company's answer in step 1 or the Company's answer shall be final. The supervisor and/or a member of management and the foreman involved shall meet with a Union Grievance Committee of no more than three (3) employees. . . .

Step 3: In the event no settlement is reached in step 2, the grievance may be submitted to the plant manager of the Company or a representative of management designated by him, who will meet and discuss the complaint with the Union committee. . . .

Section 3. (c) As in any arbitration, the Arbitrator will first decide any questions as to timeliness or arbitrability before rendering a decision on the merits, but there will be a single hearing on the entire case.

Section 4. The Arbitrator shall have no power or right to add to, subtract from, or alter any clauses in this Agreement. . . .

Section 6. The Company will not discriminate against any representative or employee properly participating in grievance matters or arbitration proceedings.

Article V—Discharge or Suspension

Any employee found to have been unjustly discharged or suspended (including disciplinary layoff) shall be reinstated into his former job with all rights and privileges including full seniority. . . .

Article X—Seniority

Section 2. For all employees, seniority shall be the governing factor in determining the filling of job vacancies, shift preference, job selection within a job classification, transfers, layoff, and recall in accordance with the provision of this Agreement, provided the employee possesses the skill and ability to do the job.

Article XI—Miscellaneous

Section 17. The proper Union Steward will be permitted to investigate grievances provided it does not interfere with the normal plant activities. The Union Steward will notify his foreman when necessary to leave his job to investigate a grievance.

QUESTIONS

1. Why is the exact wording of the issue being arbitrated of significance to the positions of both parties?
2. Evaluate the company's position that the arbitrator possessed no basis for upholding the union grievance.
3. Evaluate the union's position that by consistent reasoning all types of disciplinary action (e.g., a warning) must be for just cause.
4. Irrespective of the contractual issues involved, discuss the handling of the union president, Jacobs, by management personnel under the circumstances of the case. How could some of the problems have been avoided (or at least mitigated) by more astute management approaches?

53. The Sleepy Inspector

Company:
    City of Iowa City, Iowa
Union:
    American Federation of State, County and Municipal Employees,
    Local 183

BACKGROUND

Steve Edberg[1] was discharged from his job as a building inspector for the city of Iowa City on January 3, 1979, after Ed Koch, his supervisor, again found him asleep at his desk. This action followed a series of events that began during the latter part of 1977, when Edberg started to experience periods of "uncontrollable" drowsiness and sleeping while at work.

Koch had observed that Edberg was dropping off to sleep from time to time while sitting at his desk. After discussing the matter several times with him, Koch referred him to the city physician. A thorough medical examination revealed that Edberg was suffering from several medical problems including congestive heart failure, chronic obstructive lung disease, and obesity. These medical problems were so severe that he was hospitalized in the early part of January 1978. The city granted him a paid sick leave; when that was exhausted, the city granted him an additional unpaid sick leave.

Edberg returned to work on February 14, 1978. Both the city's personnel director, Sylvia Collins, and Koch counseled with him concerning personnel policies and practices. Edberg was informed that he would be unable to receive additional sick leave beyond his normally accumulated sick leave, which at that time had been completely expended. He was warned that he would be terminated from his job if further hospitalization were required. Collins informed Edberg that the city would be especially unsympathetic to his problem if further hospitalization were to result from his negligence in following the dietary suggestions of his personal physician and the city physician.

Edberg continued to have difficulty in remaining awake and alert at work. He was verbally warned on April 27, 1978, and was given a written warning on May 2, 1978. He was further advised on the latter

---

[1] The names of all individuals have been disguised.

occasion that he would be suspended for three days the next time he was found asleep on the job. On June 8, 1978, Edberg was again found asleep at his desk. For this he received a three-day suspension. Although he did not file a grievance concerning this suspension, Edberg stated that the reason for his drowsiness was that he had remained awake almost all night for the previous three nights helping his wife with her housework and visiting with his children, who were home on vacation from jobs in Chicago and St. Louis.

However, when he was terminated on January 3, 1979, Edberg through his union filed a grievance protesting his "unjust discharge." The grievance eventually was carried to arbitration.

POSITION OF THE CITY

The city pointed out that it had followed all the procedural steps outlined in the collective agreement when it warned, suspended, and discharged Edberg.[2] He had been warned on April 27, 1978, and again on May 2, 1978. He had been advised of the consequences of his continued sleeping at work on each occasion. He was suspended on June 8, 1978, and finally discharged on January 3, 1979. The city had taken steps to counsel Edberg in order to help him minimize the effects of his illness, and to enable him to perform his work. But Edberg had ignored this counsel and had failed to improve.

For example, during this time both supervisor Koch and the personnel director, Sylvia Collins, periodically had counseled with him in an attempt to get him to control his obesity and to conserve his energy. But Koch observed that Edberg continued to snack on candy bars and soft drinks several times a day. Koch testified that he spoke with him about this, but apparently with no effect. Koch testified, too, that he had urged Edberg to take walks when he felt an urge to sleep, or to get some fresh air, or get out in the field and perform inspections. Edberg similarly ignored these suggestions.

The city stated that it had "leaned over backward" to protect Edberg's job interests. Two other supervisors testified that they had observed him sleeping on several occasions, but they had taken no action since these observations had been made only by themselves and no corroborating witness could be produced before he woke up.

The city claimed that Edberg did not maintain his fitness for work. Both the city's physician and his personal physician had attempted to keep him from overindulging at mealtime as well as between meals. His supervisor also counseled with him about his poor eating and

---

[2] See Appendix to this case for relevant clauses of the contract.

sleeping habits. Thus, the city contended that it had afforded Edberg every opportunity to present himself in a fit condition for work. The city emphasized that Edberg had not been discharged for being obese, but rather because he could not stay awake at work. Such behavior made him unfit for work, and it constituted ample just cause for discharge as required by the labor agreement.

Finally, the city claimed that Edberg's behavior created a serious morale problem among other employees and citizen patrons. Other employees felt that they were being required to perform Edberg's work for him because he lost considerable time dozing and sleeping. Citizens visiting city hall would become angry to discover an employee sleeping on the job. They were already unhappy over their taxes. Discovering an employee asleep on the job would confirm their (unfounded) fears that the city was poorly managed.

For the reasons stated above, the city urged that the arbitrator uphold its discharge of Steve Edberg.

POSITION OF THE UNION

The union agreed with the city that willful sleeping on the job was a serious offense that could merit some form of discipline. However, the union argued that the termination employed in this instance was not merited and constituted unjust discharge. Edberg suffered from a medical condition that caused him to experience momentary periods of unconsciousness from a lack of oxygen in his blood. His periods of drowsiness and sleeping were uncontrollable, not a willful act on his part in defiance of work rules. Edberg's work performance was good, and his health problem caused no safety hazard to himself or to others. Edberg was not an irresponsible employee caught sleeping on the job. Rather, his was a case where an otherwise excellent long-service employee suffering from a medical problem was fired by the city, even though that problem neither interfered with his work performance nor presented a safety hazard to anyone. Edberg's periodic dozing should not be considered of sufficient harm to himself, his fellow employees, or the city to justify discharge. Rather, the city should be willing to accommodate Edberg as it would any other handicapped employee.

The union contended that the city was entirely unreasonable to discharge an employee with a medically related problem when it did not affect the employee's performance and did not affect the performance, health, or safety of others.

The union requested that Steve Edberg be reinstated with full back pay and benefits. It also requested that his personnel record be purged of all documents relating to the discharge.

APPENDIX

Relevant Provisions of the Agreement

Article II—Management Rights

Section 1.   Except as limited by the express provisions of this Agreement, nothing herein shall be construed to restrict, limit, or impair the right, powers, and authority of the city under the laws of the state of Iowa and the city's ordinances. These rights, powers, and authority include, but are not limited to, the following:

(a)   To direct the work of its employees.

(b)   To develop, implement and enforce work rules, safety standards, performance, and productivity standards.

(c)   To hire, promote, transfer, assign, classify, schedule, and retain employees within the operation of the city government and to develop and maintain qualifications, standards, and procedures for employment, promotions, and transfers.

(d)   To discipline, suspend, or discharge employees for just cause.

(e)   To maintain the efficiency of the governmental operation and to determine and maintain the nature, scope, and definition of city organization.

(f)   To relieve employees from duties because of lack of work, lack of adequate public financing, or for other legitimate reasons.

(g)   To determine the amounts, methods, and procedures for compensating employees and the definition of necessity for, allocation of, and nature of overtime and the method of compensating overtime.

(h)   To determine and implement the methods, means, tools, locations, equipment, and assignment of personnel by which its operations are to be conducted including but not limited to the right to contract and subcontract work.

(i)   To take such actions as may be necessary to carry out its mission.

(j)   To initiate, prepare, certify, and administer its budget.

(k)   To exercise all powers and duties granted to it by law.

QUESTIONS

1. Did the city have just cause to terminate Steve Edberg, or was this a medical/health problem that should have been approached differently? Discuss.

2. Evaluate the arguments presented by both sides in this matter. Which arguments are most persuasive?

3. Refer to the Rehabilitation Act of 1973 (as amended in 1974), which requires certain employers to adopt affirmative action programs and make reasonable accommodations for handicapped people. Might Steve Edberg be considered a handicapped person in the context of this law? Why, or why not?

54. A Weighty Problem

Company:
Bethlehem Steel Corporation, Sparrows Point Plant
Union:
United Steelworkers of America, Local 2609

Mary Weber,[1] a factory laborer, was terminated by the company within her first 520 hours of employment. The union filed a grievance on December 12, 1979, charging that Weber had been terminated because of her "physical structure," a euphemism for obesity in this instance. The union and company could not resolve their differences, and the case was submitted to an arbitrator for a final and binding decision.[2]

POSITION OF THE UNION

Union representative Fred Lewis stated that he had inquired of plant superintendent Jesse Dowell the reason for Mary Weber's discharge. According to Lewis, Dowell stated that, "Weber's physical structure was detrimental to her employment. Her job required a frequent need to climb up and down steep and narrow ladders and to crowd into and through narrow and low areas, but her physical structure caused her much difficulty in performing her assignments." However, Lewis testified as follows:

> We have many employees, male and female but mostly male, who outweigh Weber and are also as tall as she is; there are many others taller, too, if that's the way to say it. And we thought our investigation showed that her size was in no way detrimental to any of the jobs she was required to perform. So we felt it was discrimination just on that factor alone.

In response to a question by the arbitrator, "Discrimination based on what?", Lewis stated:

> On her sex, because we have male employees the same weight who would not be considered to be put out on the street just because they weigh 250 or 260, but yet they look at a female in the same way and determine in their own opinion that she can't make it.

---

[1] The names of all individuals have been disguised.
[2] See Appendix to this case for relevant clauses of the labor agreement.

The arbitrator then asked:

Do you know of any cases during your investigation where Weber was assigned to do a particular job and she could not fulfill it?

Lewis answered:

Not one, not one. I tried to look for those, just one. I tried to look for just one and I couldn't do it. Every job duty she was given, she performed.

The union requested that Mary Weber be reinstated and made whole for all losses in pay, seniority, and other rights and benefits.

POSITION OF THE COMPANY

The company did not cross-examine Lewis, or attempt to refute or challenge his testimony at the hearing before the arbitrator. Superintendent Dowell stated, "According to the contract, if we want, we can discharge an employee who is a probationary employee because he or she has green hair." He added:

I was prepared to put on testimony as to why Weber was not a satisfactory employee, but I don't think that is necessary. The union has not established sex discrimination; all they've established was that one person said it was because of her physical structure. Well, I submit physical structure isn't one of the reasons for discrimination. And we say the record is completely devoid of any evidence of any sex discrimination, and we ask that the grievance be denied.

The company reiterated that since the union could not prove sex discrimination had occurred in this case, the company could discharge Weber as a probationary employee for whatever reason it felt appropriate. The company urged that the grievance be dismissed in its entirety.

APPENDIX

Relevant Clauses of the Contract

Article II—Application of Agreement

Section I. Purpose and Intent of the Parties. (d) Nondiscrimination: It is the continuing policy of the Company and the Union that the provisions of this Agreement shall be applied to all Employees without regard to race, color, religious creed, national origin, or sex. The representatives of the Union and the Company in all steps of the complaint and grievance procedure and in all dealing between the parties shall comply with this provision.

Article X—Seniority

Section 6. New or Reemployed Employee. A new Employee and one who shall be reemployed after a break in his continuous service shall not acquire any seniority until the expiration of 520 hours of actual work following his employment and shall not receive any credit for continuous service during such period. If he shall be continued in the employ of the Company after the expiration of such 520 hours of actual work, the length of his continuous service shall be computed from the date of his employment or reemployment in accordance with the provisions of Section 2, Section 3, and Section 4 of this Article. During the first 520 hours of actual work, he may be laid off or discharged as the Management shall determine and his layoff or discharge shall not be made the basis of any claim, complaint, or grievance against the Company; provided that this will not be used for purposes of discrimination because of race, color, religious creed, national origin, or sex or because of membership in the Union.

Article XIII—Management Functions

The management of the Plants and the direction of the working forces and the operations at the Plants, including the hiring, promoting, and retiring of Employees, the suspending, discharging, or otherwise disciplining of Employees for just cause, the laying off and calling to work of Employees in connection with any reduction or increase in the working forces, the scheduling of work and the control and regulation of the use of all equipment and other property of the Company, are the exclusive functions of the Management; provided, however, that in the exercise of such functions the Management shall observe the provisions of this Agreement and shall not discriminate against any Employee or applicant for employment because of his membership in or lawful activity on behalf of the Union.

QUESTIONS

1. Did the union establish that the company had engaged in sex discrimination? Why, or why not?

2. Evaluate the company's contention that it had the right to terminate a probationary employee who "has green hair."

3. Why did the company choose not to present any testimony or evidence in support of its position? Is this approach apt to be persuasive to an arbitrator in this type of case situation? Discuss.

55. *The Jurisdictional Dispute*

Company:
> Rust Engineering Company, Chattanooga, Tennessee

Union:
> Tri-State Carpenters and Joiners District Council of Chattanooga, Tennessee, and Vicinity

On May 22, 1979, the Rust Engineering Company filed the following grievance against the Tri-State Carpenters and Joiners District Council in connection with a work stoppage on a construction project at the Bowater Southern Paper Corporation, Calhoun, Tennessee:

> Subject: Contract 21-1840 B. Project "Smoky"
>
> Bowater Southern Paper Corporation
> Calhoun, Tennessee 37309
> Grievance for Strike Damages
>
> Dear Mr. White:[1]
>
> This letter will serve as Rust's written grievance demand, pursuant to the Project Agreement at the Bowater Southern project in Calhoun, Tennessee, for the reimbursement to Rust for damages in the amount of $4,642 resulting from the illegal strike in breach of the agreement's "No-Strike" commitments by millwrights on May 17 and 18, and by carpenters on May 18, 1979. Our damages are computed as *(a)* direct extra expenses caused by the strike, *(b)* unproductive people directly assigned to millwright and carpenter work, *(c)* a pro rata share of overhead that is normally borne by production of the craftsmen who struck, and *(d)* legal fees to procure an end of the strike and resumption of work (but not legal fees for processing this grievance).
>
> The damages are:

Rental equipment	$ 445
Wages and fringes	2,053
Temporary facilities	144
Legal fees	2,000
	$4,642

---

[1] The names of all individuals have been disguised.

We consider this matter as step 2 of Article 9 of the Project Agreement. A copy is being sent to the international union. We will be glad to meet within ten (10) days or we will be willing to proceed directly to arbitration if you desire.

Please let me know how you wish to proceed.

The grievance was eventually submitted to arbitration.

BACKGROUND

The Bowater Southern Paper Corporation awarded the Rust Engineering Company on a cost-plus basis the entire construction contract to expand and modernize its newsprint manufacturing plant at Calhoun, Tennessee. One of the conditions precedent to awarding the contract to Rust by Bowater Southern was that, for this project only, all building trades unions having jurisdiction over local unions in the Calhoun area would agree upon comprehensive no-strike provisions in their agreements with the company and the Rust Engineering Company. The Carpenters Tri-State District Council of Chattanooga, which also included millwrights,[2] was one of the signatory unions to an overall Project Agreement that was negotiated between Rust and a number of local unions whose members would be employed on the Bowater job.

As part of the arrangements for implementing the special commitments made by the unions in the Project Agreement,[3] the above union agreed to inform its members of the necessity to abide by the agreement. Each worker in this union as well as members of other crafts, prior to employment, executed a written document acknowledging that he or she had been informed of the terms of the Project Agreement. Such acknowledgements were also signed by Harold F. White, the business agent of the carpenters-millwrights and all other stewards and foremen designated by the various unions.

The Tri-State District Council was given the right to designate all craft stewards, including the millwright and craft stewards; it also designated the business agents and assistant business agents; and it determined the general foreman as well as all craft foremen. The Council was designated as the agency to receive from Rust all pension and health and welfare payments on behalf of workers employed under the contract. The effective date of the special Project Agreement was August 30, 1977.

---

[2] Millwrights are skilled craftsmen who install, dismantle, move, and assemble machinery and equipment according to blueprints, layout plans, and schematic drawings. They use hoists, lift trucks, rollers, and hand tools to move equipment. They work with all types of building materials, such as wood, plywood, cement, and steel.

[3] See Appendix A to this case for relevant clauses of the Project Agreement.

On Thursday afternoon, May 17, 1979, at about 1:30 P.M., during their scheduled work hours, 52 millwrights, who were represented by the Council and were working at the Bowater Construction site for Rust, walked off their jobs because of a jurisdictional dispute between the millwrights and members of the ironworkers union. That morning a sheetmetal subcontractor for Rust had assigned to members of the ironworkers union certain drilling and tapping[4] work that the mill-wrights claimed as appropriately belonging to them. Representatives of both Rust and the subcontractor discussed the problem all that morning with Ralph Flint, a District Council business agent, who claimed the drilling and tapping work for the millwrights. Nothing was resolved, and they left the site at 12 noon.[5]

Rust's project superintendent, John Burgess, learned that the millwrights were walking out at about 1 P.M. He immediately notified his main office and sent a telegram to the Council notifying the union of the walkout. At about the same time, the millwright union steward came into his office and notified him that the millwrights were leaving.

The dispute had apparently begun before the Thursday morning work assignment by the subcontractor. On Wednesday afternoon, May 16, business agent Ralph Flint, while in Chattanooga, had received a telephone call from a union steward at Bowater concerning what he described as "a jurisdictional dispute and other working conditions and problems, including only eight toilets for 70 men, unsatisfactory drinking water facilities, and so forth."

While business agents Flint and White were eating lunch at about 1:30 P.M. on Thursday, May 17, at a diner down the road, they saw several millwrights pass the diner. They said nothing to them, although Flint had received earlier a telephone call from a millwright still on the job telling him that the millwrights were "fed up and that they had walked off the job." Flint and White then drove to Chattanooga, about 50 miles distance, arriving at about 4 P.M., "hoping to hear from someone from Rust." When they heard nothing, Flint went home and White drove to Cleveland, Tennessee, a small city situated about halfway between Calhoun and Chattanooga, as part of his investigation of the walkout, because "a lot of fellows live in Cleveland and go to the Cleveland local union meetings there." The Cleveland local union was comprised of both carpenters and millwrights.

White said that at a union meeting that evening, he told the members to return to work. He said that he specifically told them that

---

[4] Tapping is the mechanical process of forming threads for bolts or screws inside a hole drilled into metal.

[5] Most of the following "reconstruction of events" is based on testimony of various individuals during the arbitration hearing.

"if the union wanted them to walk off the job, he would let them know." There were only a few millwrights at the meeting, however. He left the meeting at about 10:30 P.M., and returned home without contacting any of the union officials or millwrights to insist that they return to work Friday morning. White returned to his Calhoun office at about 8 A.M. on Friday, May 18, and found three or four millwrights standing around. He said that after talking with them, he "found that the millwrights had left their jobs, again a confirmation that the walkout was about 100 percent." (Company personnel records indicated that 65 millwrights and 35 carpenters remained off the job on Friday.)

White told the three or four men who were present in the office to go back to work and use the grievance procedure. He said that he had not yet heard from Rust, and felt that the company had some responsibility to get in touch with him. A few millwrights, including a shop steward, eventually reported for work, but none went through the gate except for the millwright general foreman, Henry Mays. White apparently did not find out until later Friday morning that some of the carpenters had not reported for work either.

White claimed that Flint had started calling some millwrights on Friday morning, telling them to report for work; however, he was vague as to exactly when the telephone calls actually were initiated and as to how many calls were made.[6]

White added that he was contacted Friday morning by Rust's attorney, who advised him that there would be a court hearing, whereupon he referred the attorney to the union's attorney. He then went to the Federal Court at about 12 noon and remained there until 5:30 P.M.

He and other union officers began telephoning the millwrights Friday shortly after 5 P.M., immediately following issuance of a Temporary Restraining Order by the judge of the Federal District Court in Chattanooga, instructing them to return to work on Monday morning.[7]

Millwright general foreman Henry Mays attempted also to reconstruct the sequence of events on that Thursday and Friday. He recalled that at about 1:30–2:00 P.M. Thursday afternoon, he "had no millwrights." At about that time he had a conversation with a millwright steward about "where the men were," but this conversation was interrupted by an urgent message to report to the project superintendent. He claimed that he could not recall what was said at that meeting.

---

[6] White later admitted that he did not start telephoning millwrights to return to work until after being ordered to do so on Friday afternoon by the Federal District Court.

[7] On the company's motion, the Federal District Court issued a temporary restraining order on May 22, 1979, requiring that the union abide by its agreement with the company and order its members to return to work.

As was customary for him, Mays reported for work early, before the other men arrived. He talked about the situation with the carpenters' general foreman, Tom Burton. The arbitrator and Mays discussed that conversation:

Mays:

Well, Burton said that he looked for something like that to happen before then, see? In other words, before Thursday. He said there had been lots of mouthing around on the job for several days prior to Thursday.

Arbitrator:

Did he say what the mouthing had been about?

Mays:

Oh, just different things. They were squawking about one thing or another all the time. They would cry about the water and about materials and such as that.

Arbitrator:

I believe that you were the only millwright and Mr. Burton was the only carpenter to show up on Friday?

Mays:

I believe that's right, to the best of my knowledge.

Arbitrator:

Why did you decide to leave, after you had been there an hour?

Mays:

Well, I didn't know but that the boys would all be in, you see? And it was payday, also. I got my check and left.

Arbitrator:

All right. Later on that day, did you have any conversations with any of the other workmen, or other millwrights or carpenters about the walkout?

Mays:

No, sir.

Arbitrator:

Did you receive any calls from anybody in the union about the walkout?

Mays:

I did on Sunday. Actually, my wife received the call. I had already left home. We live in Alabama, and I was already on my way back up to Calhoun. When I telephoned her from a service station, she told me she got a call for me to report back to work on Monday, which I was going to do anyway.

A second millwright general foreman, Frank Bowers, also discussed his role in the walkout. Bowers, as were all the craft foremen and general foremen, was a member of a union. In this case, he was a member of Carpenters Local 654, which was associated with the Tri-State Carpenters District Council. He said that he was working at the finishing end of the paper machine when he learned from some of the millwrights that "several of the fellows were leaving." He also indicated that quite a few millwrights voiced considerable dissension as to working conditions before they left. The arbitrator queried Bowers:

Arbitrator:

Well, the millwrights who told you that they were walking off, did they ask you to walk off?

Bowers:

No, absolutely not. Nobody ever asked me to walk off. I met Mr. Peters, the mechanical superintendent, up in the building. And I said, "Looks like most of our men have left us," and he kind of laughed, and he said, "Yes, it looks like we might as well go with them."

Arbitrator:

Did Mr. Peters leave?

Bowers:

I don't really know.

Arbitrator:

Did you interpret Peters's comment to mean that you should leave, or did you join the walkout?

Bowers:

I didn't join the walkout. Me and one other fellow, one of my foremen, walked out together. But I never did see a mass walkout. I saw them trickling out one or two at a time through an opening in the building.

All millwrights and carpenters reported for work on Monday morning, May 22. None of the union members engaged in the work stoppage were fined for violating their no-strike agreement nor given disciplinary action by the union.

THE QUESTION OF TIMELINESS

The defense of "untimeliness" to the company's grievance was raised by the union.

On May 22, 1979, the company wrote the business agent of the Council and sent a copy of the letter to the international union. This letter was the grievance or complaint filed by the company. On May 24, 1979, business agent White wrote the project superintendent, acknowledging receipt of the company's letter of May 22, 1979, as set out which was the company's grievance. In the letter he questioned whether the walkout was grievable under the Project Agreement. He added that he would not be able to meet with the company representatives until 10 A.M., May 30. The company, by telegram, advised White of its acceptance of the date and time for a meeting.

There was no agreement at the May 30 meeting, and another meeting was held on June 11, which the company considered the "step 2 level." Again, there was no resolution of the company's grievance. By letter of June 13, the company exercised its right to proceed to step 3, and demanded that the grievance be submitted to arbitration.

The issues as stipulated by the company were:

1. Whether the arbitrator has jurisdiction over a strike damage claim where the work stoppage occurred as a result of a jurisdictional dispute.
2. Whether the union breached its no-strike commitment when all employees represented by it, including job stewards, struck in support of jurisdictional demands made by its business agent.
3. Whether Rust's alleged failure to follow the steps of the grievance procedure outlined in the Project Agreement has any effect on its right to bring claims before the arbitrator.

The issue stipulated by the union was:

Is Tri-State liable for the walkoff of millwrights for approximately two hours on May 17 and the refusal of the carpenters and millwrights to work on May 18. If so, what is the appropriate remedy?

POSITION OF THE UNION

The union contended that it gave its best and under the circumstances reasonable effort to get its members back to work. The company must bear a portion of the blame for the union's not acting sooner. The company failed to call or notify the union on May 17, as it had previously done in the past concerning even the most minor incidents.

According to the union, the rule followed by some arbitrators is that the union must make a prompt, reasonable, and sincere effort to get the employees back to work. At least half of the arbitrators, if not the majority, have held that in a wildcat strike situation, the union is not liable unless it instigated, encouraged, or prolonged the strike. The union did not instigate, encourage, or prolong the strike. Further, it took prompt action to attempt to return the strikers to their jobs once the strike occurred.

The union argued that the only applicable language in the Project Agreement was contained in Article 16, which declared that all crafts shall cooperate with Rust and with each other in the performance of any reassignment of duties that may become necessary because of the refusal by any craft to staff the project, until such time as the uncooperative craft ceases to be in violation of the agreement. There was no evidence whatsoever to show that the District Council did not cooperate with the company, or that it had attempted to block any reassignment of duties. However, the union charged that Rust failed to cooperate with the union by failing to notify it immediately about the walkout; and then when the company finally notified the union, it did everything possible to get its members back on the job. It accomplished this within 10 hours after they left their jobs.

The union pointed out that the grievance procedure established clear time limits. The Project Agreement provided that the impartial arbitrator be selected within five days from June 11. This language, drafted by Rust, does not state five working days, but just five days. In any event, even if the agreement were interpreted to mean "five working days," the time would have expired on June 18. It was not until June 19 that Rust's attorney even wrote for a panel of arbitrators. This is simply a case wherein Rust drafted an arbitration procedure aimed at preventing final arbitration for employees, and it overlooked the fact that it might want to use the arbitration procedure someday. The arbitration procedure backfired on the company.

The union next contended that the Project Agreement specifically provided under Article 11 that jurisdictional disputes will be settled through the Impartial Jurisdictional Disputes Board.[8] In this regard, the union held that a specific provision of an agreement has the effect of overriding a general provision. Article 11 provided the procedure for settling all union jurisdictional disputes arising on the construction project, which procedure included final and binding arbitration by an Impartial Jurisdictional Disputes Board located in Washington, D.C.

---

[8] This refers to the Impartial Jurisdictional Disputes Board of the AFL–CIO. For many years, labor organizations affiliated with the Building and Construction Trades Department of the AFL–CIO and various employer associations who employ their members have signed a stipulation to be bound by decisions of the Impartial Jurisdictional Disputes Board. In essence, when there is a dispute or potential jurisdictional dispute following an assignment of work, either the contractor(s) or labor union(s) involved may refer the issue to the Impartial Jurisdictional Disputes Board for a decision. There was a rather detailed procedure for both filing complaints and appealing rulings of the Board.

In June 1981, however, the IJDB was ended, and it was not until June 1984 that it was replaced by a new internal jurisdictional disputes procedure, which provides for arbitration as the final and binding step for settlement of certain jurisdictional disputes. See *Procedural Rules and Regulations for the Plan for the Settlement of Jurisdictional Disputes in the Construction Industry,* (Building and Construction Trades Department, AFL–CIO).

The contract language was direct and clear on this. The union conceded the strike was over a jurisdictional dispute, but claimed that the matter should have been resolved by the Impartial Jurisdictional Disputes Board.

The union also contended that there was no contract language providing for damages. The only means of resolving a jurisdictional dispute was to go to the Impartial Jurisdictional Disputes Board in Washington, D.C. The union further argued that Rust had the contract on a cost-plus arrangement and had lost nothing on which to base its claim for damages.

Finally, the union argued that the company was mistaken in regard to the law. The Supreme Court in the *Carbon Fuel Company* v. *United Mine Workers of America* case[9] took the position that the international union and its district and local unions could not be held liable for damages as a result of a wildcat strike.

In view of all the facts of the case, the union requested that the grievance be denied.

POSITION OF THE COMPANY

The company contended that the union had breached its no-strike commitment when all employees represented by it, including the union stewards, struck in support of the jurisdictional demands made by the business agent.

In the instant case, the Tri-State District Council did nothing to force its members to return to work until after the Federal District Court issued a temporary restraining order. Subsequent to the issuance of the order, no disciplinary measures were ever taken against any strike participants, although discipline was the function of the District Council. The conduct of the union in this case clearly showed the ratification of the actions of its members, and damages may be imposed against the union consistent with the rulings of the Court.

The company further contended that where a contract provides for the determination of jurisdictional disputes by the Impartial Board, the only issue to be decided by that Board is which union is entitled to the disputed work. As to damages that had been incurred by the company as a result of this illegal strike, that question had been appropriately submitted for arbitration despite the fact that the illegal walkout occurred as a result of a jurisdictional dispute. Therefore, Rust's submission of the jurisdictional dispute to the Impartial Board in no way would act as a bar to seek strike damages through the arbitration procedure.

---

[9] 444 U.S. 212, 62 Led. 2d 394, 102 LRRM 3017 (1979)—see Appendix B.

Rust maintained that it was entitled to an award of compensatory damages that should include the additional costs incurred for overtime hours worked in order to have the project completed on schedule, and a reasonable attorney's fee incurred in effecting a resumption of work on the project. In this regard, the company argued that the Carbon Fuel Company case was not applicable to this situation, for unlike that instance, the District Council, the local unions, and each individual member of those unions employed with Rust were signatories to the Project Agreement.

The company maintained that it could process its claim for damages even though it was operating on a cost-plus contract with Bowater Southern. In fact, it had a duty not to incur unnecessary costs in order to inflate its fee.

The company pointed out that any delays in the procedure for seeking arbitration should be charged to the union, and that the grievance was timely under provisions of Article 9, Section 3, of the agreement. The company within two days of the step 2 meeting notified the union of its intention to proceed to arbitration. It also requested in its letter to the union that its attorney contact the union attorney "to obtain a panel of arbitrators and proceed to hearing." According to the company, its request was not honored by the union.[10] Therefore, on June 19 the company attorney requested that the Federal Mediation and Conciliation Service provide a panel of arbitrators. The company argued that it had attempted to make arrangements for the selection of an arbitrator within the five-day period set out by the contract. If the company failed specifically to obtain a panel within the five-day period, so did the union fail to get in touch with the company with reference to securing a panel of arbitrators, as requested in the company's letter of June 13.

Finally, the company took the position that the arbitrator had jurisdiction of its strike damage claims. The company requested that it be compensated for the costs incurred as a result of the walkout by the millwrights in violation of the collective agreement. The company submitted an amended claim for damages that was more than the amount stipulated in its original grievance letter of May 22, 1979. In making this claim, Rust emphasized that it did not seek punitive damages against the union for its actions; it only wished to be made whole for the damages it suffered because of the strike. Rust requested that it be awarded the sum of $3,625.25, the cost of overtime premium pay necessary to make up for production lost during the strike. Rust

---

[10] The company attorney claimed that he had talked with the union attorney within the five-day period of step 2, but this was denied by the union attorney.

also requested that it be awarded the sum of $4,088.31 as attorney's fees expended to get the union members back on the job.

APPENDIX A

Relevant Clauses of the Project Agreement

Article I—Intention of the Parties

The purpose of this Agreement is to set out the conditions for the efficient prosecution of all work performed by Employer at the Bowater Southern Paper Corporation project being constructed at Calhoun, Tennessee, hereinafter referred to as the "Project," to establish and maintain harmonious relations between all parties to the Agreement, to secure optimum productivity and to eliminate strikes, work stoppages, lockouts, slowdowns, or delays in the prosecution of the work undertaken by the Employer.

The parties hereto agree and do establish and put into practice effective and binding methods for the settlement of all misunderstandings, disputes, or grievances that may arise between the union and its members and the Employer to the end that the Employer is assured of complete continuity of operation, without slowdown or interruption of any kind, and that labor/management peace is maintained.

Article 3—Scope of the Agreement

(5) This Agreement represents the complete understanding of the parties. Any provision of local and national collective bargaining agreement contrary to or in conflict with this Agreement or contrary to the intent and meaning of this Agreement shall not be enforced as to the Employer working under this Agreement.

Article 9—Grievance Procedure

Any controversy arising out of the interpretation and application of terms and conditions of this Agreement other than those pertaining to craft jurisdictional disputes shall be processed in the following manner:

(1) All controversies shall be referred to the appropriate craft business representative or his authorized agent and to the Employer's representative at the project site or his designated representative for adjustment.

(2) If the grievance cannot be settled it shall, within three (3) working days of occurrence, be reduced to writing and submitted to the appropriate International Union and the designated representative of the employer for consideration and settlement.

(3) If the grievance is not settled within ten (10) working days under step 2, it may be referred by either party to an Impartial Arbitrator for settlement. The Impartial Arbitrator will be selected within five (5) days and shall be selected from a panel of arbitrators submitted by and in accordance with the rules and regulations of the American Arbitration Association.

The decision of the Impartial Arbitrator shall be final and binding upon all parties.

The expense of the Impartial Arbitrator shall be borne equally by the disputing parties.

Article 11—Jurisdictional Disputes

(1) There will be no strikes, no work stoppages or slowdowns, or other interferences with the work because of jurisdictional disputes.

(2) Work shall be assigned by the Employer in accordance with the procedural rules of the Impartial Jurisdictional Disputes Board, and jurisdictional disputes will be settled in accordance with the procedural rules and decisions of such Board or successor agency.

(3) Where a jurisdictional dispute involves any union or employer not a party of the procedures established by the Impartial Jurisdictional Disputes Board and is not resolved between the unions, it shall be referred for resolution to the International Unions, with which the disputing unions are affiliated. The resolution of the dispute shall be reduced to writing signed by representatives of the International Unions and the Employer. The disputed work shall continue as assigned by the Employer until the dispute has been resolved. The provisions of Paragraph 1 will apply to disputes covered by this paragraph.

Article 16—No Strike-No Lockout

The unions agree that there will be no strike (which term shall include any collective action which will interfere with, or stop, the efficient operation of construction work of the Employer) for any reason whatsoever during the term of this Agreement. Participation by an employee, or group of employees, in an act violating the above provision will be cause of discharge by the Employer. If there is a strike, work stoppage, or picket line in violation of the Agreement by any craft, it is agreed that the other crafts will be bound to ignore such action and continue to man the Project without interruption. Further, it is agreed that all crafts shall cooperate with the contractor and with each other in the performance of any additional assignments of duties resulting from the refusal to man the Project by any craft until such time as the involved craft ceases to be in violation of this Agreement.

There will be no work stoppage on the Project due to local negotiations. In the event of the expiration of a local agreement, the Employer will continue to recognize those terms and conditions of the expired agreement, not in conflict with this Agreement, until a new agreement is consummated between the union and the recognized bargaining agents. The Employer will recognize those terms and conditions of the new agreement not in conflict with this Agreement on the effective date of the new agreement.

The "No Strike-No Lockout" commitment is based upon the agreement by the parties to be bound by the grievance and arbitration procedure of this Agreement.

APPENDIX B

Decision of the U.S. Supreme Court in *Carbon Fuel Company v. United Mine Workers of America* (444 U.S. 212; 102 LRRM 3017)

The Carbon Fuel Company and United Mine Workers of America (UMWA) were parties to the National Bituminous Coal Wage Agreements of 1968 and 1971, covering several of the employer's coal mines in West Virginia. Three local unions had engaged in 48 wildcat strikes in the employer's mines from 1969 to 1973. Efforts of both the international union and District 17, a regional subdivision of the international, were uniformly unsuccessful in persuading the miners not to strike and to return to work in each instance. The Carbon Fuel Company charged that the UMWA and District 17 were liable under Section 301 of the Labor Management Relations Act (LMRA) for the actions of the three locals.

The company charged that the international union and District 17 were obligated to use all reasonable means to try to control the locals' actions because the UMWA had agreed in the contract to resolve all disputes through the grievance procedure, and to arbitrate disputes as a last resort. The company further charged that the locals were agents of the UMWA, and that as a principal the parent organization was liable for the actions of the locals.

In December 1979 the Supreme Court ruled as follows:

1. The international union and District 17 were not liable for the actions of the locals under Section 301 of the LMRA. Section 301(b) provides that a union "shall be bound by the acts of its agents"; and Section 301(e) provides that the common law of agency shall govern "in determining whether any person is acting as an 'agent' of another person." This means that the principal (the international union and District 17) is liable for the wrongful acts of the agent (the three locals) only so long as the agent is acting within the authorized limits of the relationship, as established by the principal. Under the constitution of the UMWA, the local unions lacked authority to strike without approval from the international union and District 17. The locals did not obtain such authorization. Moreover, both the international union and District 17 had repeatedly expressed opposition to wildcat strikes.

Failure of the international union and its district subunit to use "all reasonable means" to prevent "wildcat" strikes by the local unions in violation of the collective bargaining contract does not make the international union and District 17 liable for damages to the employer, even though the contracts contained an arbitration provision. The international and district unions did not instigate, support, ratify, or encourage the work stoppages by the locals. They, in fact, consistently expressed their opposition to the stoppages and took measures to get the workers to resume work. The employer failed to prove agency as required in Sections 301(b) and 301(e) of the LMRA.

2. An agreement by an international or district union to arbitrate employee grievances does not impose an obligation upon them to use "all reasonable means" available to them to control the actions to their affiliated locals' actions that are in violation of the collective bargaining contract.

QUESTIONS

1. Why is it unusual for a company to file a grievance against a union as happened in this case?

2. Evaluate the issue of untimely handling of the grievance. Are the arguments of the union persuasive that the grievance was not admissible because the procedural time limits were not followed exactly? Discuss.

If the grievance was ruled to be timely by the arbitrator:

3. Evaluate the various arguments presented by the union. Which are the most compelling?

4. Evaluate the various arguments presented by the company. Which are the most compelling?

5. Would the arbitrator possess authority to order monetary damages in the event the arbitrator found that the union had violated the Project Agreement? Why, or why not?

6. To what degree is the *Carbon Fuel Company v. United Mine Workers* Supreme Court decision cited in Appendix B relevant or inapplicable to the issues in this case?

56. The Wastebaler and the Custodian

Company:

St. Regis Paper Company, Consumer Products Division, Vernon, California

Union:

Printing Specialties and Paper Products Union, District Council No. 2

At about 6 A.M. on September 25, 1979, Melanie Castle[1] and her co-worker, Doris Duncker, walked into production manager Earl Holt's office to report an alleged threat made against Castle by Henry Mangrum. Castle said that shortly after the 4 A.M. lunch break, Mangrum strode up to her and announced, "I'm going to get you; I'm going to rape you."

The "threat" was later denied by Mangrum, and of course there were several events leading up to the incident.

BACKGROUND

As of the date of this event, Henry Mangrum had been working as a wastebaler on the graveyard shift at the company plant in Vernon, California. He was 22 at the time and had been employed by the company for 13 months.

Sometime during the first half of the shift on September 25, Mangrum had an argument with Melanie Castle, who was 19 and had been working for the company about two months as a custodian. Her job entailed delivering waste paper to the baling machine where Mangrum was stationed. The nature of their argument was never clearly established, but it was either about whose job it was to throw the paper into the baler or about whether the paper she brought was the right kind to be put into the machine. Castle claimed that in the course of the altercation, Mangrum grabbed her by the collar and poked her in the chest with his finger, causing a soft drink in her hand to spill and wet her clothes. Mangrum later claimed that he merely "nudged" her, while John Woodson, who observed the incident and later testified for Mangrum, stated that Mangrum "pushed her away." Castle admitted

---

[1] The names of all individuals have been disguised.

that she threw the rest of her drink at Mangrum and kicked him in the leg. She also said to Woodson, "I'm going to get him fired." Mangrum was unable later to recall either having been kicked in the leg or hearing Castle speak to Woodson.

Castle promptly told her long-time good friend, Doris Duncker, what had transpired. Duncker had previously urged Castle to report to management some earlier encounters with Mangrum, but as Castle put it, she "didn't want to get him fired," and was afraid "different things would happen." Duncker insisted that this was the "straw that broke the camel's back" and went with her to meet with production manager Earl Holt.

Castle told Holt what Mangrum had said and done that day, as well as what he had done on three previous occasions. She told him that Mangrum had come up behind her about a month before and "felt my butt"; another time he lifted her up, but put her down when she started kicking; and he once put his arms around her waist from behind and tried to kiss her cheek.

Holt told Castle and Duncker to go to the stockroom and lock the door. Then he called Mangrum and the shop steward, Lloyd Roberts, into his office. Holt told Mangrum that he was "not going to tolerate any more of his threats."

Holt's comment about Mangrum's threats resulted in part from a three-day suspension levied on Mangrum for threatening to "knock a supervisor down." (An arbitrator had sustained the company's disciplinary action a few weeks earlier.) Several other employees had also complained about having been threatened with bodily harm by Mangrum, but all had refused to follow through on their complaints. Mangrum's work performance had been only marginal during his employment with the company, and he had received a number of written warnings for unsatisfactory work and absenteeism. Although he had been promoted to wastebaler only two weeks earlier, he also had been the only bidder; the union had urged his promotion on the ground that he would perform better as a wastebaler than as a custodian.

The meeting between Holt, Mangrum, and Roberts did not go particularly well. Holt refused to identify the complainants, including Castle and Duncker, fearing repercussions, especially since both women were still on the premises. The shop steward seemed to have known of the dispute that had occurred less than two hours earlier; without mentioning Castle's name, he charged that Holt seemed to be accusing Mangrum of threatening a single "employee" whom he would not name.

Holt discharged Mangrum at the close of the meeting. Holt alleged that later, when he and Mangrum were leaving the plant, Mangrum said, "I'm not finished with you yet," a statement that Mangrum later denied.

Subsequently, the union filed a grievance protesting Mangrum's "unjust discharge," which eventually was carried to arbitration.

POSITION OF THE UNION

The union argued that Holt, the production manager, had "summarily" discharged Mangrum "without any thorough investigation of the facts and without allowing him to give his version of what had occurred on and before September 25." Holt had conducted a "kangaroo court" by calling in Mangrum and reading him the "riot act" about various threats he had allegedly made against various unnamed employees. Mangrum was given no opportunity to defend himself or confront his accusers.

The union also contended that Mangrum's language constituted nothing more than "shop talk" and that his behavior was no more than what is customary in a shop employing both males and females. Mangrum's earlier encounters with Castle—"if they did, in fact, occur"— amounted to "harmless horseplay."

Several male witnesses testified for the union that Castle "likes the attention of men," has a "sexy walk," and so forth. The union noted that Castle's "handling" of those incidents "would lead Mangrum to wonder whether she really minded his alleged advances." The union pointed out that Castle apparently was unafraid of Mangrum, as evidenced by her having thrown her drink at him and kicking him.

The union also charged that her complaint arose out of "sheer vindictiveness" that had been supported by Duncker. Castle was obviously very angry after Mangrum had pushed her and caused her to spill her drink and get wet. In fact, she had on at least one previous occasion threatened to a few of her co-workers to "get him fired"; yet she did nothing on this occasion until almost two hours after he had allegedly threatened to rape her. It was only after she had spoken with her friend, Doris Duncker, that she complained to Holt.

Finally, the union pointed out that while the company had made many accusations about Mangrum's threats against his fellow employees, only Castle had identified herself as a complainant. The company had a duty to substantiate its charges of intimidation.

The union requested that the arbitrator reinstate Henry Mangrum with full back pay and all other benefits and rights he might have accrued had he not been unjustly discharged on September 25, 1979.

POSITION OF THE COMPANY

The company stated that Holt had not acted hastily in discharging Mangrum on the morning of September 25. First, he had called in the shop steward, Lloyd Roberts, before talking to Mangrum, even though the labor agreement did not require that safeguard. Second, Holt had acted upon firsthand reports of Castle, Duncker, and others who had refused to be identified. Third, both Castle and Duncker subsequently testified at a formal grievance meeting conducted a few days later to hear Mangrum's appeal. Finally, both Castle and Duncker were still on the premises on September 25 at which time Holt spoke with Mangrum. Holt was so apprehensive about their safety that he had even requested that they lock themselves in the storeroom.

The company pointed out that Holt's actions on September 25 were not those of an impetuous and inconsiderate manager. The company cited the previous occasion on which Holt had levied a three-day suspension on Mangrum as an example. On that occasion, Mangrum's supervisor reported that he had been threatened with bodily injury by Mangrum. When Holt questioned Mangrum about the threat, he denied having made it. At that point, Holt removed Mangrum from the job and arranged for a formal meeting to take place as soon as all the parties and evidence could be assembled, which was several hours later. Holt's action on that occasion, as on this, was deliberate and thoughtful, and gave full consideration to the safety and rights of everyone concerned.

The company noted that in making these procedural objections against the company, the union did not claim surprise. The union seemed to have already received all the facts, as the company detailed them, and was quite prepared to meet and counter the company's arguments and evidence.

The company argued that Mangrum's threat to rape Melanie Castle was only one of many evidences that Mangrum was an unsatisfactory employee. He had already received several written warnings for unsatisfactory work performance and excessive absenteeism. Several employees had already complained of having been threatened by him. He had been suspended for three days for threatening a supervisor. And following the threat of rape against Melanie Castle, he threatened Holt with some sort of retaliatory action for having discharged him.

The company requested that the arbitrator sustain its decision to discharge Henry Mangrum on September 25, 1979.

QUESTIONS

1. Was the statement about rape made by Mangrum to Castle a serious threat, or was it "harmless horseplay" or "shop talk," as claimed by the union? Discuss.

2. Did company manager Holt follow proper procedures in reaching his decision to discharge Mangrum? Should this aspect of the case make any difference in the arbitrator's determination?

3. To what degree was Mangrum's behavior influenced by the behavior of Castle? Why is this area of male/female relationships often a gray area in acting upon charges of sexual harassment?

4. Did the company have just (proper) cause to terminate Mangrum? Why, or why not?

57. *The Refused Assignment*

Company:
Interstate Brands Corporation, Springfield, Illinois
Union:
International Brotherhood of Teamsters, Chauffeurs, Warehousemen and Helpers of America, Local 916

BACKGROUND

On February 15, 1980, Teamsters Local 916 filed the following grievance on behalf of Donald K. Rebstock,[1] a driver-salesman employed by Interstate Brands.

> On Monday, February 11, 1980, the Interstate Brands Company apportioned the business of my route to other routes without taking into consideration my seniority with the Company.
>
> The working agreement between Teamsters Local 916 and the Interstate Brands Corporation, Section 1, of Article 4, provides that seniority shall prevail.
>
> The unilateral action by the Company in apportioning the business of my route to other routes and not giving me the opportunity to have one of the routes is a violation of my seniority with the Interstate Brands Corporation.
>
> I am requesting assignment to one of the routes affected consistent with my seniority.

On February 20, 1980, Ronald Schuessler, general manager of the Springfield plant, sent Jack Belding, president of Local 916, a reply denying the grievance. The essential portion of his letter stated:

> Received the letter on Mr. Donald K. Rebstock.
>
> This route was eliminated because it was geographically located so all accounts could be put on other routes with the least amount of miles and man-hours.
>
> As the contract states Article 4, Section 3 (in case of reduction in force the youngest man in seniority shall be laid off first), which is what we did, and placed Don Rebstock in his position. If and when a route becomes open for bid, Mr. Rebstock will have the opportunity to bid on it.
>
> Our position is that we followed the guidelines of the contract as stated in Article 4, and it is the company's position that this grievance is unwarranted and should be retracted.

---

[1] The names of all individuals have been disguised.

Rebstock was very displeased with the company's reply to his February 15 grievance. He was even more displeased when his supervisor, Tom Costello, informed him on Friday, February 22, 1980, to report for work on Monday, February 25, at 5:30 A.M. at the company's Litchfield terminal to work temporarily on a route there. He refused the assignment. On March 17, 1980, he filed the following second grievance.

> I was suspended for ten (10) days because I refused to accept work out of the Springfield Area and Teamsters Local 916's jurisdiction, where I hold my seniority.
>   I am requesting that I be paid for all time lost as a result of that suspension.

The parties were unable to resolve their differences, and the union invoked its right under the collective bargaining agreement to refer both grievances to an impartial arbitrator, whose decision would be final and binding upon both parties.

TESTIMONY AND EVIDENCE PRESENTED AT THE ARBITRATION HEARING

Interstate Brands in the Springfield, Illinois, area had been experiencing severe competition from other large baking companies, especially price competition from manufacturers of private brand merchandise. Early in January 1980, the general manager, Schuessler, decided that eliminating the least effective route by combining it with other routes would be one of several steps taken to reduce costs. It was Rebstock's route that was selected for elimination.

Donald K. Rebstock was a driver-salesman who had worked in that capacity for some 23 years for Interstate Brands. His major duties included loading his truck with bread and other bakery goods, driving to retail stores on his route, taking orders, placing merchandise on the store shelves, removing stale bakery goods to be returned to the Interstate distribution depot, and making collections for merchandise sold. He could also solicit new grocery outlets, as time permitted, and set up special displays for company promotion of special and seasonal items. He had a very good work record. He was an excellent driver, never having been involved in a driving accident. No disciplinary action had ever been levied against him for any aspect of his work or behavior.

Rebstock normally worked out of the Amos Street Depot in Springfield, although there is a second depot (also known as a terminal) in Springfield, identified as the Clearlake Terminal. Approximately 14 employees were in the bargaining unit. At the time of these grievances, Rebstock was operating a route in the western part of Springfield. It encompassed a three-mile area, and included some 26 stops. Rebstock was told early in January 1980 by his supervisor, Tom Costello, that the general manager had decided to eliminate his route. The actual elimination of Rebstock's route occurred during the first week of February.

Rebstock's previous route was allocated among those of a number of other drivers. Some of his previous stops were given to drivers who were senior to him, but six of his stops were assigned to James Flanagan, who was junior in seniority to Rebstock.

Rebstock was compensated at a rate of $122.50 per week, plus a 10 percent commission on all net sales over $450. Junior seniority sales-drivers hired after July 23, 1968, received $161.50 per week, plus a 7 percent commission on net sales over $475.

Schuessler and Costello met with Rebstock during the last week in January to explain the company's decision to eliminate his route. They also told him that he would be assigned to the swingman's route, currently held by Dave Hawley. Hawley was the most recently hired driver-salesperson, with only a few months seniority and service with the company. Rebstock protested against taking the swingman's route, and claimed that he should be able to "bump" Flanagan, who held 12 years seniority, the next highest seniority rank among the drivers, or any other driver with less seniority than himself. Schuessler would not agree with him on his proposed reassignment, and Rebstock went to work as a swingman on Monday, February 11. Swingmen are driver-salespersons who perform all the regular duties of that position; however, they have no regular route. They fill in when regular drivers are on vacation, ill, on jury duty, and so forth. They may also ride with a regular driver whose route required temporary additional time and attention. Rebstock immediately filed a grievance.

On Friday, February 22, Costello told Rebstock to report on Monday, February 25, at 5:30 A.M. at the Litchfield terminal, located 50 miles from Springfield, to work for a few days on a route with the regular driver who was returning to work following surgery. Sales on the Litchfield route were very large, averaging about $3,000 per week, as compared with $2,200–$2,400 per week on Rebstock's previous route. He would receive his full commission on all sales while assisting temporarily on the Litchfield route. He spoke immediately with his shop steward, Sam Montaldo, and his union president, Jack Belding. Both informed him that "he didn't have to go to Litchfield," and they assured him that the union would back him fully if he chose to file a grievance.

While Springfield drivers in the past had always accepted assignments at the Litchfield terminal, the union had always taken the position that they need not accept such assignments, since Litchfield was within the collective bargaining jurisdiction of a different Teamsters local union.

Rebstock refused to accept the Litchfield assignment. He was away from his job for 10 days, returning to work on Monday, March 10. He filed a second grievance on March 17.

The company and the union did not agree as to whether Rebstock had been suspended for 10 days, or had simply failed to report to work for that period. Rebstock claimed that at first he was told that if he did not report to the Litchfield terminal, he should not come in. According to him, he was first "terminated," but that action was later changed to a 10-day suspension. On the other hand, both Schuessler and Costello maintained that Rebstock was never told that he should not report for work, or that he was suspended or terminated. He simply failed to appear.

POSITION OF THE UNION

The union argued that the company ignored the seniority requirements of the collective bargaining agreement when it demoted Donald K. Rebstock from a driver-sales employee to a swingman. According to the union, Article 1, Section 4, of the agreement[2] recognized that the two positions are different; and, Article 2, Section 2, indicated that the position of swingman is below that of driver-sales employee in the job hierarchy by expressly stating that the former "shall have the opportunity to fill route job vacancies by the bidding procedure." Swingmen work under less favorable conditions than the regular drivers. The company acted correctly in following Article 4, Section 3, when it laid off Hawley, the employee with least seniority. However, it erred in assigning Rebstock, an employee with 23 years experience and who held number three rank among all driver-salespersons, to Hawley's swingman position. Rather, the union contended, "the number three man in seniority should be able to 'bump' any driver-sales employee less senior than himself, and take that less senior employee's route." In fact, the union argued, Article 4, Section 1, provided that "Seniority shall prevail, dated from the date of employment in the sales department."

Rebstock had 11 more years seniority than Flanagan, and should have been permitted to bump into the latter's job, or that of any driver-sales employee with less seniority. Flanagan, in turn, should have been able to bump into the route of any other driver-sales employee with less seniority than he.

---

[2] See Appendix to this case for relevant contractual clauses.

The union reinforced its claim for Rebstock by adding that the application of the seniority principle was not qualified in any way in the collective bargaining agreement. For example, the contract did not say that the company "may take into account seniority," thereby making seniority discretionary with the company; nor did it say that seniority was a factor to be considered in conjunction with other factors, such as versatility, educational level attained, physical capacity, and so forth. The language of Article 4, Section 1, made the seniority clause a "strict" seniority clause.

The union noted that Flanagan's commission rate was less than that of Rebstock. The company's motive in eliminating Rebstock's route was simply that of replacing a 10 percent commission with a 7 percent commission. As swingman, Rebstock's sales would fluctuate from week to week according to the amount of sales of the particular route he was working.

The union further argued that the company acted in an arbitrary and unreasonable manner in directing Rebstock to report to Litchfield on Monday, February 27, 1980, to run a route as a swingman. It held that the company compounded its previous action when it suspended him for 10 days when he refused the assignment. The hardships of the two-hour drive, the cost of gasoline, and the stresses of an unfamiliar route were great. The company treated a 23-year employee inconsiderately, and his response to the order should have come as no surprise. The union noted, too, that Interstate Brands had no contract with Local 916 in Litchfield. Since Rebstock held no seniority in Litchfield, the purposes of collective bargaining were subverted if the company was able to assign an employee to Litchfield, or some more distant city, and then discipline him or her for not accepting the assignment.

The union contended, finally, that the company had chosen to assign Rebstock to the Litchfield terminal in retaliation for his having filed a grievance on February 11, protesting against a demotion from position of driver-sales employee to that of swingman. In fact, on February 26 the union and Rebstock chose to file the following charge with the NLRB.

I have been a driver for the above-named employer for 23½ years. The employer is under a contract with Teamsters Local 916, which expires August 3, 1980. I am one of the senior drivers. Recently the employer did away with my route and assigned coverage to other routes. Under Article 4 of the contract, I am entitled to another route. See Article 4 of the contract attached. The company refused to give me another route. I filed a grievance on this matter about one week ago. The grievance has not been disposed of yet. Today the employer attempted to assign me to a different area, different unit, and outside the jurisdiction of the current contract. The other assignment would be in Litchfield, Illinois. His action, in making this assignment in derogation of the contract, is motivated by my having filed a grievance. The current attempted assignment is in fact a discharge. This action by the employer is discriminatory toward me because of my union activity and my filing a grievance, all in violation of the Act.

The union requested that Rebstock be restored to his position of driver-sales employee according to the principles of seniority, and that he be made whole for full pay and all other rights and privileges lost during his two weeks of suspension.

POSITION OF THE COMPANY

The company stated that its decision to eliminate Rebstock's route by incorporating it into those of other driver-salespersons was purely an economic one. Eliminating his route substantially reduced the mileage driven because a number of stops were located close to other routes. And the elimination of his route would produce considerably greater savings than the elimination of any other route. Schuessler pointed out that routes had been realigned on various occasions in the past, sometimes adding stops and sometimes deleting stops. The union had never previously protested this action by the company. In fact, the net effect of increasing the efficiency of the routes had always been to increase driver earnings by increasing sales on each route.

The company argued that to have granted Rebstock's grievance of February 15 would have resulted in wholesale bumping of employees. This would have reduced the efficiency of the sales program. required extensive retraining, and reduced the personal relationship of drivers with the grocers. Every driver potentially could have ended up with a different route.

The company contended that its treatment of Rebstock was consistent with both the terms of the contract and past practice. In fact, it held that during the most recent contract negotiations of January 1977 the union attempted to amend Article 4, Section 3, as follows:

> In the event a route is abolished, the driver-salesman effected shall be allowed to bump to whatever route his seniority will allow. Such displaced routeman shall be allowed same privilege until down to youngest man who shall take the layoff.

The company refused to accept this union proposal for the reasons cited above. The company held that the February 15 grievance, which was designed to permit chain bumping, was nothing more than an attempt to obtain through arbitration that which the union had proposed and failed to obtain in negotiations.

The company noted that nothing in the contract permitted Rebstock to bump any driver with less seniority when his route was eliminated. The only contractual limitation upon the company in managing any reduction in force is the provision of Article 4, Section 3, which required it to lay off personnel according to seniority. After abiding by Article 4, Section 3, the company's options regarding the operation of its business in a reduction of force were not limited by the contract. It chose among all the available options the one that was least disruptive; it reassigned Rebstock. The company cited the last sentence of Article 4, Section 4, as evidence of the high value it has placed upon minimizing changes of routes by driver-sales personnel.

The company further noted that the union knew that chain bumping was not required by the contract; otherwise it would not have tried to negotiate a change in the wording of Article 4, Section 3, in 1977.

The union's reliance upon Article 4, Section 1, to support its argument for strict seniority was misplaced, according to Schuessler. If the union's position were correct, there would be no need for Sections 2 and 3 of that article. Furthermore Section 4 of that article provides that "merit" and "capability" override seniority in the determination as to who will be awarded a job bid. The contract did not require a strict application of seniority. In fact, it made specific provision for other considerations.

As to Rebstock's grievance of March 17, the company took the position that he should have followed the important labor relations rule, "work now and grieve later." That is, what he did when reassigned on February 11 was what he should also have done on February 25. He had a duty to follow his supervisor's instruction to report for work at the Litchfield terminal. He also had the right to file a grievance concerning that assignment. Costello's job assignment was reasonable and proper. Even if Rebstock and the union believed that it was improper, both were bound by the contract to pursue their remedy through the grievance procedure, and Rebstock was bound to work until an arbitrator ruled otherwise. The union erred in telling Rebstock that he need not report for work at Litchfield.

The company pointed out that the contract contained no definition of a geographical area for any purpose. If a union for internal purposes restricts itself to a certain geographical area, that restriction had no effect upon the company. Furthermore, it was unreasonable for a local of the Teamsters union to argue that its drivers were not permitted to work beyond that local's claimed geographical boundaries. It seemed even more unreasonable for a union to want to reduce job opportunities for its members.

The company denied that it assigned Rebstock to the Litchfield route in retaliation for the February 11 grievance. The assignment was reasonable and proper, and other employees from Springfield had accepted these assignments in the past. All Rebstock was required to do was assist an ill driver-salesperson perform his job. Rebstock was not harmed in any way; his compensation would have been larger in Litchfield; his job duties would have been the same; he would have been working in an area in which the company recognized the Teamsters as bargaining agent. The claim of retaliation was entirely unfounded.

The company requested that the arbitrator deny both of the grievances in their entirety.

APPENDIX

Relevant Clauses of the Contract

Article 1—Employing Union Drivers

Section 1. All workers employed by the Employer and coming under the Union purely by reason of this Agreement shall be employees in good standing with the Union as long as the terms of this Agreement are in effect.

*   *   *   *   *

Section 4. It is understood and agreed that driver-sales employees and swingmen come under the jurisdiction of Local 916, and shall become members of this Union as provided for in Article 1, Section 1.

Article 2—New Employees

*   *   *   *   *

Section 2. Employees hired as swingmen shall be paid $151.50 per week while being trained. When trained and able to operate routes unassisted, he/she shall be paid the applicable base pay as stated in Article 2, Section 1, plus 7 percent commission on the net weekly average route sales of the depot where he/she is domiciled. It is further agreed that swingmen shall have the opportunity to fill route job vacancies by the bidding procedure.

Article 4—Seniority:
Driver-Sales Employees

Section 1. Seniority shall prevail, dated from the date of employment in the Sales Department.
Section 2. Driver-sales employees shall pick their vacations by order of seniority.
Section 3. In case of reduction in force, the youngest man in seniority shall be laid off first.

Section 4. In the event a route is open, or a new route created, that such opening shall be posted and any driver-sales employee can ask for the opportunity to advance providing:

(a) The driver-sales employee has been a routeman with the Employer for one (1) year.

(b) Such advancement is based on merit.

The Employer agrees to give such request fair consideration on the basis of seniority, and comply with the same if the driver-sales employee is capable. Should such move be made, it shall be the only change and the driver-sales employee making such a change shall make no further bids for advancement for a period of two (2) years.

QUESTIONS

1. Evaluate the union's arguments that Donald Rebstock should have been allowed to bump junior seniority employees to choose a preferred route.

2. Evaluate the company's arguments that the union was attempting to achieve through arbitration what it could not achieve through negotiations.

3. Did the company have the right to assign Rebstock to work out of the Litchfield terminal, which was not under Teamsters Local 916's jurisdiction? Why, or why not?

4. Does the arbitrator's decision depend in any way upon the determination of the NLRB in regard to the union's filing of unfair labor practice charges?

5. Evaluate the company's position that Rebstock and the union should have "worked now and grieved later." Surmise why Rebstock and the union did not follow this principle in this case.

58. Emergency-Leave Pay

Company:
    Basin Electric Power Cooperative, Bismark, Minnesota
Union:
    International Brotherhood of Electrical Workers, Local 1593

In July 1983, employees Melvin Kane and Roger Field[1] each filed separate requests for emergency leave without payroll deduction because of medical emergencies within their immediate families. Their claims were denied, and each filed a grievance. The parties failed to settle their differences, and the union requested final and binding arbitration as provided in the agreement. They agreed that the issue to be resolved was:

> Did the company violate Article XI, Section 4(c) of the Agreement when it denied emergency-leave pay to Melvin Kane for June 8, 9, and 10, 1983, and to Roy Field for July 5, 6, and 7, 1983, and if so, what is the appropriate remedy?

BACKGROUND

The Field Case

On June 21, 1983, Roy Field was on company business in Duluth, Minnesota, when his wife phoned and informed him that their daughter had a brain tumor. He immediately returned home and conferred with their physician for one and a half hours that afternoon. He was advised that there should be two operations, the first to relieve the pressure within the cranial cavity and, about a week later, the second would attempt to remove the tumor. The first operation was performed on June 23. Field was paid one and a half hours emergency leave for June 21 and eight hours for June 23.

The daughter remained in the hospital and the pressure subsided to the point that the second operation was scheduled for July 5. She was, however, permitted to return home for the preceding weekend as her physician thought she would be more relaxed there. After the operation she remained in intensive care on July 5 and 6. She continued to be in serious condition and under strict observation through July 7. At Field's request, his daughter's physician gave him a letter

---

[1] The names of all individuals have been disguised.

stating that the daughter had undergone emergency surgery and that her father was with her on July 5, 6, and 7.

The Kane Case

On April 4, 1983, Melvin Kane's daughter suffered an attack of asthma. She was admitted to the local hospital, where she received emergency treatment; she was released the same day. Following that episode she remained under the care of her physician, and she was "in and out" of the emergency room of the hospital in Bismark on several occasions. Kane was paid emergency leave for April 4.

During the course of her treatment, her physician and parents decided that she should be admitted to the University of Minnesota Hospital in Minneapolis for examination and consultation; an appointment was arranged for June 9. She was taken there by automobile on June 8. During that 450-mile trip she was on a life support oxygen system, and four or five stops were made to activate the system. She remained in the hospital for several days. The daughter's physician in Bismark wrote a letter to the company, in which it was stated that "this referral to the University Hospital was of the utmost urgency and was accomplished at the only time available. Mr. Kane's time should be covered as if it were an emergency situation."

Testimony of the Company

Both Field and Kane worked under George Connors, chief of transmission. He said that he denied both claims because he did not believe that they involved an emergency. He expressed the view that a medical emergency must involve major surgery or a serious accident or illness, and that it must be unforeseen and require immediate action. He stated that he had followed that definition in ruling on other employee requests for emergency-leave pay. Connors discussed both cases with the director of personnel who agreed because these events were "scheduled, not unforeseen."

POSITION OF THE UNION

The union held that both the Field and Kane cases constituted an emergency within the meaning of Article XI of the Agreement.[2] The union cited a definition from the *World Book* dictionary to substantiate its claim. The dictionary defines an emergency as "a sudden or unexpected happening or situation that calls for action without delay." It

---

[2] See Appendix to this case for this provision.

also states that it means a crisis that is a "trying or dangerous time or state of affairs." The union argued that the situations in both cases were trying or dangerous and a crisis of life-or-death nature. They were of a continuing nature, fraught with uncertainty, and renewed by the dangerous aspects of the treatment. The union argued that "emergencies can be created by man in quest of corrective treatment."

The union urged that the arbitrator sustain the grievances of Field and Kane.

POSITION OF THE COMPANY

The company took the position that the claims of Melvin Kane and Roger Field were properly denied, because the events were scheduled in advance, and therefore there had been no need for immediate action and no emergency. The company had consistently followed a policy of allowing emergency-leave pay only when a true emergency existed that had been unforeseen and that required immediate attention. This was not the case in these situations, and the company requested that the arbitrator deny the grievances of both Field and Kane.

APPENDIX

Relevant Provisions of the Contract

Article XI—Sick Leave

Section 4(c). Emergency leave, without payroll deduction, will be allowed for medical emergencies within the immediate family for the time necessary for such occasions, but not to exceed three (3) work days. Emergency leave shall be limited to serious accidents, illnesses, or major surgery. Doctor, dental, or eye appointments, or physical checkups will not be permitted. Immediate family shall mean those members of the employee's household and the following relatives who may not reside within the employee's household: Husband, wife, son, daughter, father, mother, sister, brother, father- and mother-in-law. Upon request, emergency leave for family members not residing within the employee's household must be supported by a medical certificate which statement shall certify to the nature of the medical emergency.

QUESTIONS

1. According to the Company, what is an emergency?
2. Is the Field case different from the Kane case? If so, how?
3. According to Article XI of the collective bargaining agreement, did either of the two cases constitute an emergency? Discuss.
4. Do you agree with Connors' interpretation of the concept of emergency? Why, or why not?

59. The Disputed Test

Company:

Star Manufacturing Company, St. Louis, Missouri

Union:

International Brotherhood of Teamsters, Chauffeurs, Warehousemen, and Helpers of America, Local 688

On April 14, 1982, Roy Camp,[1] a setup operator at Star Manufacturing Company, submitted the following grievance to his supervisor:

> The company has disqualified me from the model template and sample maker job. I feel that I can effectively perform the duties outlined in the job description.
>
> Settlement Requested: Granted a 90-day trial period as described in the job bid.

On April 21, plant superintendent Robert Decker replied to Camp and the union as follows:

> After considering testimony given in the grievance hearing of April 20, 1982, with regards to Roy Camp's qualifications for a model maker position, please be advised of the following:
>
> Consideration was given to Camp's work experience, along with the results of job-related tests that were administered by the company. These were then compared with the qualifications required to be able to perform the duties of the position in question.
>
> It has been concluded that the grievant lacks the overall ability to fulfill all the requirements of this job. This lack of ability includes areas that are critical to the basic performance of the job.
>
> Therefore, the grievant's job bid and grievance are being denied.

The parties were unable to resolve the dispute, and as provided in the collective agreement, they submitted the case to an arbitrator for a final and binding decision. The parties agreed that the arbitrator should address the following issue:

> Did the Company violate the Agreement by not awarding Mr. Camp the position of model maker on which he was senior bidder and by not giving him a reasonable trial period on this job? If so, what should be the appropriate remedy?

---

[1] The names of all individuals have been disguised.

BACKGROUND

Roy Camp had been employed by the company since 1973 and had been a setup operator since 1979. In describing his job he stated that it included such functions as reading and interpreting engineering blueprints, making setups on machines, and operating a number of machines, such as the shearing machine, punch press, and brake press machines. Camp had a good work record with no disciplinary problems. He also received extra compensation as a "lead man." He was one of 12 setup men performing duties similar to his.

The job of model, template, and sample making[2] is performed in a laboratory area separate from production operations. Camp stated that he had worked in the lab area on a number of occasions and that he had assisted several model makers whom he had known down through the years. While the model maker's job paid the same wage rate as the setup operator's job, Camp had bid on the former job in order that he "might learn something new and different." He said that the model maker operated many of the same machines and tools as that of a setup operator, but that it would not be difficult to learn the additional machines on which model makers work. He added that he had already operated much of the equipment in the lab. According to Camp a model maker primarily makes the templates (patterns) used in making the production items and from which a setup operator works in setting up and adjusting machines in the manufacturing process. The model maker develops a "prototype of what is manufactured in the plant."

Camp bid on the model maker's job in April 1982. He was the senior bidder on the list of those who bid on the position. Several days later he was administered a written test by the chief engineer, Joseph Shell.

Shell described the test as one requiring applicants to answer questions about various prints, reading caliper and micrometer measurements, and the like. The test placed special emphasis upon visualizing and conceptualizing three-dimensional drawings. There were 10 questions, requiring about 45 minutes to complete. Camp failed the test and was so notified about a week later. Shell later reviewed the test results with Camp, who felt that he had answered 7 of the 10 questions correctly. Shell, however, informed him that he lacked an essential skill in that he didn't have "the visual concept."

At the request of the union, Shell administered a second test to Camp. This test included a number of exercises in which he was

---

[2] See Appendix to this case for job description and relevant contractual provisions.

required to make forms, shapes, and items from drawings. Shell informed Camp that he had also failed the second test and that he had "no visual concept for form or views." Camp disagreed with Shell's evaluation of his abilities because he had "to work from blueprints as a setup person." He stated that he did have to visualize three dimensions from drawings in his present job. Further, as a setup operator it was necessary for him on occasion to make new parts or modify existing parts and dies. He claimed that a setup operator must be able to visualize and that he could learn the visualization that was necessary for the model maker's job.

TESTIMONY AND POSITION OF THE UNION

The union contended that the positions of setup operator and model maker were quite similar, although there were some important differences. For example, the model maker works from "beginning to end on each new model, puts the parts together, and tests the model to ensure that it functions as originally conceived." The union steward, Gino Bertelli, argued that the best experience for becoming a model maker would be to work as a setup operator. He also stated that to his knowledge, no black employee, such as Camp, had ever risen to the position of model maker. Bertelli stated that he had reviewed Camp's test results and felt that he had performed adequately to warrant a 90-day trial in that position. He also reviewed the test results of Robert Peters, the second most senior setup operator who successfully passed the test, and felt that he had done "only about equal" to the test performance of Camp. The steward noted that a model maker could readily obtain assistance and help from the engineers and inspectors if a model maker had a problem with a job assignment. While he minimized the significance of the test results, he acknowledged that tests had been used for many years for the model maker's job. Bertelli pointed out that the company had also used a similar test for the position of inspector since 1968. Camp had taken that test in 1975 when he had bid on the job of inspector. He failed that test; the company, nevertheless, gave him a trial period to qualify for the job. He successfully completed the probationary period for the position of inspector. And, subsequently, he was promoted to the job as a fully qualified inspector. Bertelli argued that Camp would qualify as a model maker, if given the 90-day trial period, in the same fashion as he had earlier qualified for the inspector's position. He claimed that Camp had earned the opportunity to try out for the position of model maker and should not be denied that opportunity because of race.

The position of the union was summarized in a post-hearing brief. Relevant excerpts from this brief follow:

Roy Camp was the senior qualified person bidding on the model maker job. The company's entire case is based on the subjective opinion of Joseph Shell that Camp was unqualified because he failed to prove on the tests to Mr. Shell that he had the ability to "visualize" properly. They did not in any manner contend that "relative" ability played a part in the management's decision to place the recently hired Leo Kelly in the model maker job since the collective bargaining agreement clearly is of the modified type which provides that the senior employee shall be given preference if he possesses sufficient ability. Under this clause the question simply is, "Can the employee in fact do the job?" In this case the company has admitted that no employee can step immediately into the model maker job and perform it. Training is necessary.

The union strongly believes that the company violated the intent of Article VIII by *solely* relying on the test results to determine that Camp was not qualified. The union has never contested the right of the company to administer a test to employees to aid management in determining an employee's ability to do a job. The key is that the test results must be *only one* of various methods and means of determining the issue of ability. In the instant case the company *solely* relied on the test results as judged by Mr. Shell.

Elkouri and Elkouri in *How Arbitration Works* (1973 edition) state: "It must be kept in mind that arbitrators generally take the view that while the test may be used as an aid in judging ability or as a "verification" of ability, the employer may not base his determination of ability solely upon the results of a test but must consider other factors and other evidence."

The union believes that the company failed to consider the grievant's excellent past performance in the job of "setup" which admittedly is one of the best training grounds for a model maker job. Mr. Camp's past experience was not given due consideration. Because the grievant on a couple of questions failed to convince Mr. Shell that he had the "visualization" ability, the company has unfairly prevented him from expanding his job future. The evidence is clear that the model maker position is a stepping-stone to a management position. Mr. Camp believed he had all the qualities and abilities to become a good model maker just as he had become a good setup person. Undoubtedly had Mr. Camp been required in 1975 to pass a test for "setup" he would have failed, just as he failed an identical type test for the inspector's job.

Elkouri and Elkouri in their book *How Arbitration Works* state on page 583: "Agreements sometimes provide for a trial or break-in period on the job to determine ability, and questions in connection with the interpretation and application of such provisions are frequently arbitrated. In the absence of contractual provision, the question arises as to whether management must give the senior employee a trial. Obviously, ability to perform the job, or the lack of it, may be demonstrated by a trial or break-in period on the job. As stated by arbitrator Carl A. Warns, "The best evidence as to whether an employee can do a job is to give him a fair trial on it." Arbitrator Vernon L. Stouffer stated that, "The purpose of a trial period is to afford an employee the opportunity to demonstrate that he has the ability for the job in question or can with some familiarization therewith achieve the necessary skills within a reasonable period of time to perform the job in an acceptable manner."

The grievant and the union have from the very beginning of this dispute only asked that the company give Mr. Camp a trial period. Article VIII, Section (e) of the contract clearly protects both parties and contemplates the use of such a trial period. The union urges that the company has been unfair in not utilizing the trial period provision.

Thus, arbitrators generally are inclined to the view that if there is a reasonable doubt as to the ability of the senior employee and if the trial would cause no serious inconvenience, it should be granted, but that a trial should not be required in all cases.

In order for management to fairly use test results, the test itself must be prepared, administered, and graded fairly and objectively. It is the union's belief that in the instant case the company has failed to prove that the above criteria were observed. Mr. Shell continually used the phrases "lack of ability to visualize" or "no visual concept" as demonstrating why he considered that Mr. Camp failed the test. But this observation by Mr. Shell is his subjective *opinion*.

For all of the above reasons, the union strenuously urges the sustaining of this grievance.

TESTIMONY AND POSITION OF THE COMPANY

The company first made considerable effort to establish the credibility and testimony of chief engineer Joseph Shell by pointing out that he had been employed by Star for 26 years, that he was an electrical engineer, that he had served as plant manager for several years, and that he had been "accepted as an expert in numerous federal and state trials as a professional engineer."

In discussing Camp's performance on the test, Shell described the test as being made up of 10 questions. Six of the questions were concerned with flat planes; Camp answered five of the six correctly. Three of the questions involved three-dimensional drawings and prints; Camp answered all three incorrectly. He stated that from the test results, he concluded that Camp was unable to "visualize parts in total and accumulate the kind of information necessary to perform the model maker's job adequately."

Shell stated that the model maker's job was different from the setup operator's job in three major respects: (1) the model maker must take sketches, prints, and verbal instructions from an engineer and convert these into parts (including their assembly) that had never before been produced; (2) a model maker must be able to make templates from a part and convert these to flat view sketches from which setup men adjust and set up various machines to produce items for production; (3) the model maker on occasion must also test various items produced from the sketches and drawings for electrical, chemical, and other properties. The test administered to Camp primarily addressed the first area, not the other two, which Shell claimed contained the primary differences between a model maker's and setup operator's job. The test primarily attempted to determine whether or not the applicant possessed the basic visualization skills necessary to perform the job. Management felt that it lacked the expertise to train a person to acquire conceptual skills and felt that this type of skill would be most difficult to teach under the best of circumstances.

Shell stated that after Camp and the union complained about the results of the first test, he agreed to give him a second test, although he had never done so before in this kind of situation. The second test contained five problems, of which Camp correctly answered two and correctly answered a third in part. Shell stated that the results of the second test confirmed those of the first—that Camp could not "visualize spatial dimensions," an ability that was absolutely essential for a model maker.

The company stated that Shell had administered basically the same test or tests to all other model makers in the plant since 1968. Those who were awarded the job of model maker had all passed the same test or tests as those given to Camp. These tests are "very practical and directly job related"; they included several blueprints and sketches typical of the work performed by a model maker.

Shell stated that applicants who failed the test were not promoted to the position of model maker. No one who had failed the test had ever filed a grievance in the 14 years that the testing procedure had been in effect.

The company pointed out that as a result of Camp's grievance, it employed an outside consultant to review the procedures and tests involved in this case. The consultant's report stated:

> In my opinion the testing procedure covers the various phases of the work which is to be accomplished, particularly since test questions are based upon common production parts and is therefore fair.

Shell testified that Robert Peters, the second most senior setup operator, was awarded the vacant position of model maker, but he stayed on that job only a week before deciding to return to his former job as setup operator. Subsequently, Leo Kelly, who was also on the bid list, was given the same two tests as Camp and Peters. Kelly passed both tests successfully and is currently a model maker.

The position of the company was summarized in a post-hearing brief. Relevant excerpts from this brief follow:

The contract is clear that this position is to be awarded, not on strict seniority, but to the senior "qualified" bidder. Consistent past practice has given this provision the meaning that, for the model maker position, the bidder "qualifies" by passing a test. This same practice has also consistently applied to the inspector position and was in 1980 extended to the setup position. On these facts it is difficult to see how the union can challenge the company's right to test model maker bidders.

Therefore the union must be challenging, not the company's right to test, but the result in the particular case of grievant Camp. Fundamentally the integrity of the tests depends upon the competence and integrity of the tester. The qualifications of Shell as an expert engineer were unrebutted and his testimony was unchallenged by any union witness with similar expertise. Normally judges and arbitrators accept the testimony of lay witnesses only as to what they saw or heard but not as to what they opine. The point of qualifying someone as an expert is that a tribunal is entitled to rely on that expert's opinion. The company submits that in an industrial setting both it and the arbitrator are entitled to rely on an engineer's opinion as to whether Camp passed tests within the engineer's competence to devise and judge. The union offered no expert testimony to the contrary.

The union noted that Camp failed the test for the position of inspector, at which he ably performed. But this does not show that the tests are unreliable. Camp's inspector test was taken in May 1975, over a year and a half before he was awarded the inspector position on January 20, 1977. Apparently he learned enough in that year and a half to become a successful inspector.

The union also argues that Camp's performance was similar to that of Peters, who passed. First, the company feels that it and the arbitrator are entitled to rely on the judgment of chief engineer Shell that Peters passed and that Camp failed. Moreover, we wish to point out that Peters did not exhibit the same consistent deficiency as Camp had. We concede that Peters' results were closer to those of Camp than to those of Kelly. Perhaps this is why Kelly is still on the job and Peters begged off after a mere week. If Peters, who tested better than Camp, lasted but a week, surely Camp was unqualified.

The union argued that Camp does not test well but he worked well. But chief engineer Shell took the test procedures from day-to-day work performed at the company. Therefore if you can't do the test, you can't do the work. If Camp could not do the relatively simple visualization required on common production parts used in the test, how could he produce parts from more complex prints? An independent industrial engineer validated the job relatedness and fairness of its tests. The union offered no such evidence to the contrary.

Chief engineer Shell's tests and judgment of them were considered fair by all employees who passed and failed them since 1968. At least no one grieved until now. Moreover when the union in 1980 agreed to testing for the setup position, they knew that chief engineer Shell would conduct these tests as he had all others. If he or his tests had been considered unfair, the union would never have agreed to expanding his testing jurisdiction to yet another position.

The union made an unworthy effort to claim racial discrimination. The truth is that these same tests have been given to employees, black and white, for years. When a black passed the test, no white grieved his being awarded the position. When a white failed the test, he accepted this result. Only Camp has grieved. In fact the only racial discrimination here is that, for the first time in its history, the company gave a bidder (Camp) two tests, something it had never done for a white employee. Instead of discriminating against Camp, the company bent over backward for him.

Moreover if one compared the union's description of the model maker's duties with Shell's description, one would never guess they were the same position. For purposes of this grievance the union protrayed the model maker as a glorified setup man. If that is all the model maker was, there would be no separate classification. Shell's description of the model maker's duties shows both the importance of the position and the reason for testing.

Finally, the union bore and failed to carry its burden of proof that the company violated the contract.

The company urged the arbitrator to deny the grievance.

APPENDIX

Relevant Provisions of the Contract

Article VIII—Job Vacancies

(a) All job vacancies or new positions and the number thereof shall be posted for a period of two (2) working days. Eligible employees not at work at the time of posting shall be notified by registered mail or telegram of the opening and will have two working days after receipt of such notice in which to notify the company of their intention to bid for such opening, provided that they return to work within 30 calendar days of the original posting of such an opening.

* * * * *

(c) Employees shall be entitled to bid on such jobs, and the job shall be awarded to the senior qualified employee bidding therefor within a period of five (5) working days and shall be paid at the appropriate rate of pay. If the senior employee bidding for the opening is not qualified to perform the work satisfactorily, the job shall be awarded to the next senior qualified employee who has bid for the job, subject to the grievance procedure. No employee's bid for an opening will be considered unless it would represent a movement to a job of the same or higher rate of pay, except by mutual agreement of the parties.

* * * * *

(e)   An employee awarded a job through the foregoing bidding procedure shall be given a fair trial for a period not to exceed 90 days, but it shall at the end of a fair trial be decided by the Employer (subject to the grievance procedure) that such employee cannot adapt to the new position, or if the employee desires, he or she shall be returned to his or her former position at the rate of pay for that position.

Relevant Job Description

Model, Template and Sample Making. Under the direction of his supervisor, the model, template and sample maker performs duties including, but not limited to, the following:

1. Uses hand tools, power tools, power machinery, spot-welders, grinders, etc. and employs soldering and brazing and other techniques to produce models, templates and samples as required.
2. Reads drawings and is able to make parts and templates from prints, sketches and verbal instructions or sample parts.
3. Performs other experimental and testing work as directed by the Chief Engineer and his assistants.
4. Must furnish and be proficient in the use of his own tools.
5. Keeps daily time card.
6. Maintains orderly working area.

The Job Bid Posted on the Company Bulletin Board

JOB BID

DATE POSTED_____4-06-82_____
TIME POSTED _____11 A.M._____
If qualifications are in doubt test will be given.
PROGRESSION RATE SCHEDULE
$6.67–$8.31
HOURS OF WORK * Unless otherwise stated, the hours of work will be the same as those worked by the general factory work force.
TRIAL PERIOD * Unless otherwise stated, the trial period will be from five (5) to ninety (90) days.
BIDS ARE TO BE TURNED IN TO A FOREMAN OR TO THE PRODUCTION OFFICE.

QUESTIONS

1. Is the job of model maker different from that of setup operator? If so, how? Are these differences significant to this case?

2. What was the skill that the company contended that Camp lacked?

3. Arbitrators often have applied the "head and shoulders" principle in some of their cases. This principle advocates that in certain selection or promotion decisions, the seniority of an employee should be the decisive criterion, unless a junior-seniority employee is significantly superior to a higher-seniority employee in ability and merit. Should this principle be applied to the circumstances of this case? Why, or why not?

4. Did the company have a duty to grant Camp a 90-day trial period? Why, or why not?

60. The Forbidden Nuptials

Company:
　　Distribution Center of Columbus, Inc., Columbus, Ohio
Union:
　　Columbus Warehouseman's Union, Local 102

Mark Fuller[1] was hired by the Distribution Center of Columbus in February 1978. He was terminated on November 22, 1983, because on October 22, 1983, he had married a fellow employee, Irene Fraser. Fraser was hired by the company in June 1976; on November 22, 1983, she had seven years and five months seniority, while her spouse had five years and nine months seniority. The company terminated Fuller, the less senior of the two, for having violated an administrative policy[2] prohibiting the employment of related persons.

BACKGROUND

Fuller and Fraser met while both were employed by Distribution Center. They began dating, and in April 1983 they began living together with the full knowledge of the company. This knowledge was both informal in that their supervisor knew of it, and formal by reason of Fraser's changing her address on company personnel records to the address of Fuller.

The administrative policy in question was an internal management document. It was not collectively bargained; nor was it part of the published work rules that were made available to employees when hired and that were posted. The administrative policy was not posted but its existence had been rumored among employees including Fuller and Fraser. However, it had never been seen in written form by any of the employees, nor by any union official, until Fuller made a formal inquiry to his supervisor. He was furnished a copy on October 19, only a few days before the couple was married.

Both Fuller and Fraser were classified as warehousemen. Neither supervised the other. Both had received awards for attendance for the first six months of 1983, and neither presented any disciplinary problems. Both were considered very good employees during this time.

---

[1] The names of all individuals have been disguised.
[2] See Appendix to this case for relevant provisions of both the contract and the administrative policy.

If Fuller had not married Fraser, he would not have been terminated by the company.

POSITION OF THE UNION

The union argued that the company had no right to enforce its policy when that policy had not been clearly communicated to employees. The union also argued that the policy was unreasonable, unjust, and contrary to public policy. Fuller and Fraser did not learn of the policy until they made formal inquiry and even then they received a copy only three days before their marriage.

The right of management to make reasonable rules does not override the "just cause" protection provided in the collective bargaining agreement.

The union urged the arbitrator to order the company to rehire Fuller with full back pay and seniority, to restore any rights and privileges lost as a result of the company's action, and to remove all reference to this disciplinary action from his personnel records.

POSITION OF THE COMPANY

The company contended that the discharge of Fuller was for "just cause," because he had knowingly violated the company's longstanding "no-spouse," antinepotism policy. The policy was a reasonable one and was supported by substantial business considerations. Further, the policy had been enforced in the past and should also be enforced in this instance. The labor agreement itself provided that the company could make and enforce reasonable rules and regulations.

Finally, the company argued that if the union's position were sustained in this case, this decision would abrogate the policy with respect to all present employees. This would seriously jeopardize the company's ability to protect itself against the detrimental effects that result from spouses working together.

The company urged the arbitrator to deny this grievance in its entirety.

APPENDIX

Relevant Provisions of the Contract

Article III—Management Rights

The company retains the right to make and enforce reasonable rules of conduct and regulations not inconsistent with the provisions of this Agreement. However, such rights can only be exercised to the extent that the express provisions of this Agreement do not specifically limit or qualify this right.

The company agrees that disciplinary action, including discharge, shall be only for just cause.

Relevant Provisions of the Administrative Policy Manual

Distribution Centers, Inc. has a policy which prohibits the employment of anyone who is related to another Distribution Centers Associate. This policy is a common practice which many companies adopt for a number of sound reasons, some of which are as follows:

1. Avoiding difficulties in scheduling work where two relatives desire the same hours of work.
2. Preventing family matters from distracting Distribution Centers Associates from their job duties.
3. Minimizing absenteeism, where one relative must take time off to care for another.
4. Avoiding conflicts involving the Associate's loyalties to the spouse or other relatives and his obligation to the Company.

This policy was initiated in January of 1970 and exceptions were made for any relative on the payroll at that time.

For these reasons, the company will not hire or continue the employment of relatives of any existing Distribution Centers Associates or of their spouses regardless of location or facility involved excepting those hired prior to January 1970, as indicated above. The term relatives includes those related by blood or marriage, and if used in this policy, means spouse, parent, children (including foster and adopted), brother, or sister. Should two Distribution Center Associates become related to each other, whether by marriage, adoption, or otherwise, one must resign within 30 days thereafter. If neither employee resigns the one with the least seniority with the company will be discharged.

QUESTIONS

1. Why did the company enact a rule prohibiting the employment of related persons?
2. Do you agree with the Company's position on this issue? Why, or why not?
3. Were Fraser and Fuller adequately advised of the rule?
4. Regardless of its outcome, why is a case of this type difficult to management from a policy point of view?

61. The Frustrated Bus Drivers

School District:

Des Moines Independent Community School District, Des Moines, Iowa

Union:

American Federation of State, County, and Municipal Employees, Local 2048

On June 22, 1983, Patricia Abbey, Jean Bass, Carol Real, Linda Sims, and Dana Tebo[1] each filed a grievance alleging that the "grievant has relatively equal qualifications, if not superior qualifications, and has greater total seniority within the unit" than the five persons selected for the position of transportation driver, class 2. Linda Sims filed a concurrent complaint with the Des Moines Human Rights Commission. The five employees were currently employed in the position of transportation driver, class 1, and each had bid on the class 2 position that had been announced in School District Bulletin 26, dated February 28, 1983.[2]

The grievances were processed through the grievance procedure to arbitration. The parties agreed that the issues to be resolved by the arbitrator were:

1. Is the grievance of Linda Sims arbitrable?
2. Did the employer violate the comprehensive agreement when it eliminated the grievants from consideration for the class 2 driver positions announced on February 28, 1983? If so, what is the appropriate remedy?

BACKGROUND

The collective bargaining agreement provided for three classifications of transportation drivers. Class 1 drivers work less than six hours per day and may be assigned daily routes or they may be unassigned. Class 2 drivers work more than six hours per day for 10 or 12 months per year and are assigned to specific routes. Class 3 drivers are at the highest classification and work full time but are unassigned.

---

[1] The names of all individuals have been disguised.

[2] See Appendix to this case for relevant provisions of the contract, state statutes, and job descriptions.

Forty-five applicants filed for the five positions that were announced to be open on February 28, 1983. The employer (Des Moines Independent School District) reviewed the applications of all those applying and selected Sheryl Smith, Daniel Wesley, Joseph Rohn, David Knox, and Lance Cary to fill the vacancies. The five grievants had greater seniority than those selected by the employer and grieved to be placed in the class 2 driver positions with full back pay.

On July 6, 1983, Linda Sims filed a racial discrimination complaint before the Des Moines Human Rights Commission. She recited essentially the same facts that she offered in her grievance to the employer.

Testimony of Linda Sims

Sims testified that she was a class 1 driver and had been with the School District since March 1, 1978. She stated that this was her seventh or eighth driving season and that she had applied five or six times for a class 2 driver position. In each instance, she was refused on the grounds that her qualifications "were not deemed equal." She alleged that many other positions were automatically filled by seniority but that the employer consistently discriminated against her. She affirmed that she had been convicted of speeding in February 1982, that she had several nonchargeable accidents, but that in 1981 she did not have a chargeable accident. She further acknowledged that she had received a written reprimand and that she had also been cited for insubordination by the School District. She reported that her absences were principally for surgery and maternity reasons and for injuries suffered in an automobile accident in which she had been involved. All of these, she claimed, were "excusable."

Sims stated that her claim pending with the Des Moines Human Rights Commission was separate from her grievance. She said that she filed it because there was a 180-day time limit in which to file a claim; she could not wait until after this grievance had been resolved to file a claim.

Testimony of Jean Bass

Jean Bass testified that she was a class 1 driver and had worked for the employer since September 1978. She stated that her performance evaluations had been good and that she had received commendations. She reported that her attendance was average and that she had no chargeable accidents. She further alleged that her absences were due to bronchitis and pneumonia. She affirmed that she was presently on maternity leave. She admitted that she had been off from her work for almost a year on approved leave and that even if she had been earlier selected as a class 2 driver, she could not have performed those duties until the present time. She stated that she had had her baby and that she was now available. She further acknowledged that she had not informed the School District of her present availability until this time.

Testimony of Patricia Abbey

Patricia Abbey testified that she had been a class 1 driver for the school since August 1979. She stated that her application for a class 2 position had been denied. She acknowledged that she had a high rate of absenteeism.

Testimony of Carol Real

Carol Real testified that she had been a class 1 driver since August 1979. She stated that she had applied for a class 2 position on four previous occasions and had been rejected in each instance. She pointed out that she had two letters of commendation in her file and that she had no chargeable accidents on her record. She affirmed that she had received a low rating on her personal evaluations by her supervisor, Sharon McCloud, but she claimed that these evaluations were unfair.

Testimony of Dana Tebo

Dana Tebo testified that she had been a class 1 driver for the employer since September 4, 1979. She alleged that the School District had used her 1980 evaluation in finding her not qualified for the position of class 2 driver instead of her 1981 evaluation. She acknowledged that she had had a change in name during this period. She also acknowledged that the low ratings she received for poor attendance in both 1980 and 1981 were correct.

Testimony of Peter Ellis, Chief Union Steward

Peter Ellis testified that he was the class 3 lead driver for the school district. Along with driving, he also trained drivers and assisted in their evaluation. He reported that he also held the position of chief union steward.

Ellis argued that the employer was unfair in its selection process. First, he criticized the selection of an applicant, David Knox, who had no previous experience driving a bus. This applicant's prior driving experience had been as a food truck driver. All other applicants with bus driving experience should have been recognized as better qualified. Second, Ellis alleged that the employer gave inadequate consideration to seniority. Seniority is important to workers; it should be given primary consideration; junior applicants should be given preference only when the employer can clearly establish that their performance, abilities, and qualification are "head and shoulders" above that of the senior candidates. He claimed that, in his opinion, all of the grievants had more than equal ability to those selected. They also had greater seniority. The criteria used by the employer were neither consistent nor fair.

Ellis spoke to the issue of the arbitrability of the Sims grievance. He argued that her grievance was filed to establish her "relatively equal" qualifications and greater seniority, whereas her complaint before the Des Moines Human Rights Commission alleged a different problem—that of continuous "racial discrimination."

The chief union steward also criticized the use by the employer of attendance records. This factor inherently was included in the factors of discipline and personal evaluation. Thus, attendance had been weighted much too heavily in evaluating the relative performance of the candidates.

Testimony of John Enders, Supervisor of Transportation

John Enders stated that he had been employed with the school district for 18 years and that he had served as the director of transportation for 4 years. He also indicated that he had driven buses, repaired them, and had extensive experience and training in the management of a school transportation department.

Enders testified that he gathered complete and accurate data on each of the 45 applicants on the following categories: seniority, driving records, attendance, discipline, and personal evaluations. He said that he prepared a chart on which he listed each applicant according to seniority. In separate columns he summarized the applicant's driving record, attendance, discipline, and personal evaluations.

Enders reported that he collected and analyzed the information on each applicant in an attempt to comply with an arbitration ruling rendered by John M. Gradwohl, arbitrator, on July 23, 1982. This earlier grievance concerned a similar dispute between the parties. It had been filed by other grievants who had been eliminated from consideration for class 2 driver positions that were posted by the employer on October 26, 1981.[3]

---

[3] See Appendix to this case for relevant text of the Gradwohl arbitration decision.

Enders explained that shortly after the Gradwohl decision, he and Dr. David Prince, assistant superintendent for personnel management, developed those five categories used in evaluating applicants for the position of class 2 driver.

He further explained that he assigned each applicant a point value on each of the four factors (driving record, attendance, discipline, personal evaluation), following guidelines established by Prince and himself. From this, he obtained a total point value for each applicant. He and Prince had established a minimum acceptable score on each of the four factors, as well as a minimum total score. From those who met the minimum established standards on each factor and who also met or exceeded the minimum total score, Enders prepared a list of acceptable candidates listed according to seniority. Those achieving satisfactory scores were further reviewed. Where the composite scores of applicants were equal or nearly equal, the senior applicant was selected. The five candidates selected by Enders and Prince were the most senior of the group considered to be clearly most competent.

Enders said that the applicant's driving record was relevant because of the safety factor associated with the transportation of students. He indicated that regular and prompt attendance was essential in order to let both parents and students know that the bus system operated on a dependable schedule and in order to maintain good discipline among those riding the buses. The disciplinary record of applicants was considered to be important because it related to their behavior, to the type of example they set for students, and to their eligibility for promotion. Enders stated that he reviewed the personal evaluations by the supervisors of the applicants, along with his own personal observations and opinions of each applicant based upon his observations of their personal behavior and work performance.

Enders stated that after going through this evaluation process, he reviewed the entire process with Dr. Prince. The final selection of the five new class 2 drivers was made after careful deliberation by both of them. He stated that they were particularly careful to comply with the requirements of the Gradwohl decision.

Testimony of Dr. David Prince, Assistant Superintendent for Personnel Management

Dr. Prince affirmed Enders' testimony to the effect that they had worked together in setting up the evaluation process. He stated that the criteria and the charts used to review the applicants were as fair and objective as circumstances permitted. He further stated that he was satisfied as to the propriety and fairness of the procedure utilized; and he felt confident that he and Enders had selected the right candidates.

POSITION OF THE UNION

The union argued that the employer's selection policies and procedures had not been consistent. Prior to the most recent instance of selecting class 2 drivers, the school district required that the applicant must have had previous experience with driving a bus. In the current instance, truck driving experience was deemed adequate. The employer erred in awarding a class 2 position to a food truck driver; all experienced bus drivers should have been evaluated as better qualified.

The union further argued that the school district gave inadequate regard to the factor of seniority. Repeating the testimony of the chief union steward Ellis, the union contended that the senior employees must be given preference, except where the employer could prove that the junior employee was "head and shoulders" above the senior employee. The school district did not prove this; therefore, the five grievants should be promoted to the position of class 2 driver over the five others recently promoted.

The union asserted that the Linda Sims grievance was arbitrable and that it did not conflict with Article XVIII of the collective bargaining agreement. The issue before the Des Moines Human Rights Commission involved racial discrimination while the issue presented to the arbitrator concerned relative ability and seniority.

The union urged the arbitrator to direct the school district to transfer and promote the five grievants to the position of class 2 transportation driver and to make them whole for any back pay and rights to which they would have been entitled if they had been promoted to class 2 positions at the time of the original selection.

POSITION OF THE SCHOOL DISTRICT

The school district contended that the Linda Sims grievance was not arbitrable under Article XVIII of the collective bargaining agreement. The wording of the complaint filed with the Des Moines Human Rights Commission was almost identical to that of the grievance filed with the employer. By the terms of the collective bargaining agreement, the arbitrator was barred from hearing her grievance.

The school district claimed that the selection criteria and process developed and utilized by John Enders and Dr. David Prince in the selection of the class 2 drivers from the applicants generated from the February 28, 1983 notice complied with the decision of arbitrator Gradwohl. The employer's selection system was designed properly and administered fairly in the consideration of each applicant for a class 2 driver position.

The district took the position that seniority was given primary consideration, but that the other factors were also properly assessed in making the selection decisions. Article IV of the collective bargaining agreement gives the employer the right to transfer employees and Article VIII provides that the needs of the employer, as well as of the employee, shall be considered in making transfers.

The school district requested that the arbitrator rule that the Linda Sims grievance be declared unarbitrable under the terms of Article XVIII of the collective bargaining agreement and that the arbitrator sustain the school district's action on the four other grievances.

APPENDIX

Relevant Provisions of the Contract

Article IV—Management Rights
Public Employer Rights

Consistent with this Agreement, the public employer shall have, in addition to all powers, duties, and rights established by constitutional provision, statute, ordinance, charter, or special act, the exclusive power, duty, and the right to:

* * * * *

2. Hire, promote, demote, transfer, assign, and retain public employees in positions within the public agency.

* * * * *

4. Maintain the efficiency of governmental operations.

* * * * *

6. Determine and implement methods, means, assignments and personnel by which the public employer's operations are to be conducted.

7. Take such actions as may be necessary to carry out the mission of the public employer.

* * * * *

9. Exercise all powers and duties granted to the public employer by law.

Article VIII—Transfer Procedure

Transfer shall mean movement of any employee to another job classification, or location within the District. A vacancy exists as a consequence of an employee's action or the creation of a new position.

Notice of such vacancy will be posted in the "Superintendent's Bulletin" and within seven working days of the date of the "Superintendent's Bulletin" employees may apply for the vacancy by filing a written statement with the office of the Executive Director of Personnel. The notice of the vacancy shall include job qualifications deemed necessary, hours of work, and location of the opening. The Executive Director of Personnel shall acknowledge to the applicant the receipt of such application, and shall notify the applicant when the position is filled.

The Employer shall consider the needs of the District and each applicant's qualifications. When two or more applicants have relatively equal qualifications, the employee applicant with the greatest total seniority within the unit will be given priority.

Article XVIII—Grievance Procedure

* * * * *

B. Rights of employees to representation

* * * * *

It is understood and agreed by the parties that the grievance procedure and the steps outlined in the grievance procedure are the appropriate method of resolving grievances which may arise during the term of this Agreement. If an employee formally files an alleged violation of this Agreement other than under the grievance procedure, then the Employer shall not be required to process the said claimed set of facts through the grievance procedure.

C. Steps in grievance procedure

* * * * *

Step IV Binding Arbitration

* * * * *

The arbitrator, in his/her opinion, shall not amend, modify, nullify, or add to the provisions of the Agreement. His/her decision must be based solely and only upon his interpretation of the meaning or application of the express relevant language of the Agreement. He/she shall be asked to issue his decision within 30 calendar days after conclusion of testimony and argument.

Relevant State Statutes

Section 20.7, Code of Iowa (1983). Public employer rights. Public employers shall have, in addition to all powers, duties, and rights established by constitutional provision, statute, ordinance, charter, or special act, the exclusive power, duty, and the right to:

1. Direct the work of its public employees.
2. Hire, promote, demote, transfer, assign and retain public employees in positions within the public agency.
3. Suspend or discharge public employees for proper cause.
4. Maintain the efficiency of governmental operations.

5. Relieve public employees from duties because of lack of work or for other legitimate reasons.

6. Determine and implement methods, means, assignments and personnel by which the public employer's operations are to be constructed.

7. Take such actions as may be necessary to carry out the mission of the public employer.

8. Initiate, prepare, certify and administer its budget.

9. Exercise all powers and duties granted to the public employer by law.

Section 20.17(6), Code of Iowa (1983).   No arbitrator's decision shall be valid or enforceable if its implementation would be inconsistent with any statutory limitation on the public employer's funds, spending or budget or would substantially impair or limit the performance of any statutory duty by the public employer.

Section 20.18, Code of Iowa (1983).   An arbitrator's decision on a grievance may not change or amend the terms, conditions of applications of the collective bargaining agreement.

Job Description Published February 28, 1983.

Transportation Driver
Class 2 (10 months)

Hours of work: to fit District's need.

Required experience/training: Valid chauffeur's license; driving record void of moving violations, convictions or suspensions; demonstrable leadership, communications and organizational ability; good personal attributes and physical qualifications.

Desired experience/training: High school diploma; previous bus or truck driving experience.

Special requirement of the position: Must qualify for State School Bus Driver Permit; physical attributes sufficient to meet the demands of the position—vision, lifting, climbing, etc. (physical examination on file); personal attributes—alertness, normal intelligence, capable of managing students and retaining their respect; safety oriented and responsible driver; disciplined with an adherence to the rules and regulations of the Iowa Department of Transportation, Iowa Department of Public Instruction, and the District concerning driving, driving habits and conditions of continuing employment; competitive rating on employee evaluation criteria as established by the District.

Qualified applicants should write to Dr. David Prince, Assistant Director of Personnel. Applications close March 9.

Relevant Sections of Text of Decision of Arbitrator John M. Gradwohl (July 23, 1982).

The Comprehensive Agreement states plainly in the Transfer Procedure Article:

The Employer shall consider the needs of the District and each applicant's qualifications. When two or more applicants have relatively equal qualifications, the employee applicant with the greatest total seniority within the unit will be given priority.

It is equally plain from the prescreening criteria and from the testimony at the arbitration hearing that the School District did not give effect to the contractual language "When two or more applicants have relatively equal qualifications, the applicant with the greatest total seniority within the unit will be given priority." The preceding sentence allows the School District to "consider the needs of the District and each applicant's qualifications." The safety and regular reliable attendance considerations are certainly important qualifications. The parties have agreed in the Comprehensive Agreement that, additionally, the School District will apply a seniority factor which gives a priority to the employee with the greatest total seniority within the unit when two or more applicants have relatively equal qualifications. The School District simply did not carry out its contractual obligation to take seniority into account in the present instance.

QUESTIONS

1. Assess the qualifications of each of the grievants for the position of transportation driver, class 2.

2. Does it make any difference that Linda Sims concurrently filed a grievance with the district and a charge with the Des Moines Human Rights Commission? Why, or why not?

3. Did the district simultaneously comply with the terms of the collective bargaining agreement and the terms of the decision of Arbitrator John M. Gradwohl? Discuss.

62. No Bread in the Store

Company:

Wolf Baking Co., Inc., Baton Rouge, Louisiana

Union:

International Brotherhood of Teamsters, Chauffeurs, Warehousemen and Helpers of America, Local 568

BACKGROUND

Route salesman Kevin Holt[1] was discharged by the Wolf Baking Company on October 6, 1983. The company charged that Holt's unsatisfactory work performance in antagonizing an important customer justified his summary dismissal without either previous warnings or without a written statement to either him or the union at the time of discharge.

Holt had been with the company for five and one half years and was responsible for the delivery of the company's baking products to customers on his route. He was compensated in part by a commission from sales. Routes were subject to bid and were awarded on the basis of seniority. His route included four convenience stores of the Little General chain.

On the morning of October 6, 1983, Holt was making his usual stop at the Little General store on MacArthur Drive in Alexandria, Louisiana. The store was in the process of being remodeled, and the display gondolas (including the bread racks) had been disassembled and taken outside. Despite the disarray and confusion, the store manager, Helen Jackson, had decided to remain open for business in the expectation that the remodeling would be completed later in the day.

Holt picked up the stale items and asked the store manager if he should make his delivery of fresh products. Jackson was not certain and asked her division manager, Barbara Bauer, who had come into town to supervise the remodeling. Bauer instructed her to tell Holt to come back in two hours, by which time it was expected that the gondolas would be back up. However, Holt replied to her request that he would be tied up in a delivery to Oakdale, some 40 miles round trip, and could not be back at the requested time.

Bauer then came over to talk to Holt about the problem and again

---

[1] The names of all individuals have been disguised.

requested that he make some arrangement to have the bread delivered in about two hours. Holt offered to leave the products on top of a video game machine or to come back after completing the rest of his route, but neither of these alternatives were satisfactory to Bauer. She became irritated at what she perceived to be Holt's lack of cooperation. She then telephoned the company's offices in Baton Rouge and talked to Peter Larson in sales and marketing, telling him that Holt had "refused" to make the delivery and that the company had better get the merchandise out to the store or lose the entire business of the entire Little General chain. Then, Bauer told Holt to leave and not come back.

Larson reported his telephone conversation with Bauer to his superior, Jack Helwig, who began to try to contact Carl Day, sales manager of Wolf Baking in Alexandria. Day was located a short time later in Natchitoches and drove immediately to Alexandria to see what was going on at the Little General store. He talked to Bauer, who was adamant that she did not want to allow Holt to continue serving her stores. Day promised to arrange for an immediate delivery.

In the meantime, Holt had attempted to contact his superior for instructions as to what he should do. He knew that his immediate supervisor, Clement Peyton, was at Fort Polk and unavailable, so he phoned the Alexandria office to try to reach Day. Day was out; the only person in the office was an employee who operated the company's thrift store on the premises. She told him that she did not know where he could locate Day. It did not occur to Holt to phone the Baton Rouge office. He decided, at that point, to go on to Oakdale and complete his route.

At about 3 P.M. Holt returned to Alexandria, where he was making a delivery to the A&P Store when Day, who had been looking for him, drove up. Holt and Day drove directly to the Little General store to attempt to make the delivery. Bauer was still there; she refused to allow Holt to enter the store.

After returning to the office, Day phoned Jack Helwig in Baton Rouge to discuss the problem. They concluded that it would be necessary to terminate Holt because he could not service his route. The union steward offered a compromise solution that would allow Holt to exchange part of his route with another salesperson, who was overextended. The company refused to accept this proposal. It made no other attempt to persuade the management of the Little General stores to rescind the ban on Holt.

On October 7, 1983, the union filed a grievance on behalf of Holt. It was processed through the grievance steps to arbitration.

POSITION OF THE UNION

The union argued that the discharge of Holt was procedurally deficient because it violated the express requirements of Article X of the contract.[2] This article required the company to give at least two written warnings, except for a specific list of offenses that require no warning notices. None of the items listed included the offense for which Holt had been charged. Thus, Holt should have received a written warning at most.

The union also contended that Holt was the victim of an unreasonable demand placed upon him by a customer, which, in order to satisfy, would have required him to delay service to his customers in Oakdale and which would possibly have antagonized them as well.

The union pointed out that this is not the only occasion on which customers and salespersons have had a confrontation. This same thing had happened at Natchitoches several months earlier with a salesman named Smith. In that instance the company interceded with the customer to let the salesman back into the store. The company made no effort to persuade the management of the Little General store to reconsider its hasty action.

Finally, the union stated that it had proposed a viable alternative—to switch part of Holt's route with that of another salesman. This would have cost the company nothing in extra commissions or downgraded service.

The union urged that the arbitrator restore Kevin Holt to his position of salesman and make him whole for all financial losses and benefits lost as a result of the company's action.

POSITION OF THE COMPANY

The company argued that Holt had disqualified himself from continuing as a route salesman by refusing to service his accounts. The company's business was extremely competitive, and its very survival in business depended on the goodwill created by its route salesmen in servicing their accounts; thus, any action that antagonized a customer had to be treated with the utmost seriousness.

The company asserted that there were situations where issuing a warning notice would be unwarranted. This was one of them. There was no way to resolve this conflict without either terminating Holt or losing a large and valued customer. It was not necessary for an offense

---

[2] See Appendix to this case for relevant contractual provisions.

this serious to be specifically listed in Article X any more than it would be necessary to list a large number of other offenses, such as fighting, thievery, and so forth.

Finally, the company contended that it was under no obligation to switch routes among salesmen, even if the union and other salesmen agree to the switch. Furthermore, such a switching of customers might have given rise to a grievance by the other salesmen.

The company urged the arbitrator to deny the grievance and sustain the discharge of Kevin Holt.

APPENDIX

Relevant Provisions of the Contract

Article X

The employer shall not discharge or suspend any employee without cause, and shall give at least two (2) warning notices in writing of the complaint against such employee to the union. . . . No warning notice need be given to an employee before he is discharged if the cause of such discharge is for dishonesty, drunkenness, drinking on the job, reporting to work while under the influence of drugs, narcotics, or drink, carrying unauthorized passengers, failure to report an accident, or for recklessness in damage to equipment, carrying firearms or dangerous weapons on company property, possession of habit forming drugs on company property, fighting on company property, commission of criminal acts on company property. Discharge must be by proper notice.

QUESTIONS

1. Was the discharge of Holt by the company procedurally deficient? Why, or why not? If so, would this justify his continued employment under the circumstances?

2. Had the company taken reasonable measures to intercede with the customer in behalf of Holt? Discuss.

3. Is the discharge of Holt justified? If not, how should the company have handled the problem?

63. One Last Chance?

Company:

 Ohio River Company, Cincinnati, Ohio

Union:

 United Steelworkers of America, Local 14262

At approximately 6 P.M. on December 13, 1983, the towboat *Jennifer Leigh* was passing through a lock on the Ohio River. Henry Thompson[1] and two other deckhands were called to the deck to "lock the barges through." This procedure required that the deckhands leave the vessel and work at the side of the lock. As the three men were returning to the vessel, Thompson fell overboard. He was rescued and admitted to the hospital. The admitting diagnosis read as follows:

Admitting Diagnosis

1. Blunt abdominal trauma.
2. Multiple rib fractures, bilateral. Rule out fracture of the right wrist.
3. Acute alcohol intoxication.

Upon investigation the next day, Thompson admitted to two company representatives that he had been drinking. Thompson was immediately discharged for violation of a posted company rule prohibiting drinking and intoxication on the job.[2]

BACKGROUND

Henry Thompson was hired as a deckhand on December 30, 1969, by the Ohio River Company, which conducts barge operations on the Ohio River.

The work schedule of the crews is 25 continuous days of work on board a towboat followed by 25 days off the vessel.

The *Jennifer Leigh* carried a crew of 10, which was divided into two teams of four each with the remaining two members being a cook and a floating deckhand. Each crew worked six hours on and six hours off during the time they were on the vessel. Vessel crews did not

---

[1] The names of all individuals have been disguised.

[2] See Appendix to this case for relevant provisions of the contract and the company rule.

remain together when crewmen were transferred from one vessel to another. The individual crewmen received new monthly assignments following their 25-day rest period.

Thompson joined the *Jennifer Leigh* at 2 A.M. on December 13, 1983. It was a company rule that when an employee boarded a vessel, he was required to sign a "boarding report." Thompson did not sign this boarding report, as he was assigned immediately to the loading of stores. Thompson asked the captain if he could use his seniority to displace another employee in the position of the swing man deckhand. This was agreed, and Thompson then went to bed.

During the night, Thompson went up to the pilot house and told the pilot that he had forgotten his glasses and did not complete his boarding report. He subsequently located his glasses and completed the report at 12 noon on December 13, 1983. The relevant portion of the report read as follows:

1. Have you been treated by a physician for an injury or illness during your accumulated time off? (Answered NO)

2. Have you (in the last 24 hours) or are you now taking any drugs or medications prescribed by a physician or bought over the counter? (Answered NO)

3. Are you aware of any condition that may impair your ability to perform all duties of your job classification? (Answered NO)

During the investigation following Thompson's accident and hospitalization, it was learned that at least some of the crew suspected that he was under the influence of alcohol when he came on board the vessel early that morning and also that he had been drinking later during the day. They did not convey their suspicions to the vessel's officers. There was also evidence that some of the vessel's officers suspected that Thompson had been drinking while on board; however, no one followed up on these suspicions.

POSITION OF THE UNION

The union stated that Thompson admitted that he had an alcohol problem, that he was drinking on the vessel, and that it was wrong to do so. He had not had a drink since the accident and had joined and had become a continuing member of Alcoholics Anonymous, going to meetings three to five times per week.

Thompson began serious drinking when a three-month strike occurred in 1983. Prior to that time he had quit drinking and had his problem under control. He lived alone and, therefore, his solitude had aggravated the problem when he was off the vessel for the 25-day period. This accident impressed upon him the seriousness of his illness.

On his own initiative he sought out and joined AA. He should now be considered a cured alcoholic.

The union alleged that the company had not enforced consistently its no-drinking rule. The union spokesperson testified that it was well known that on several occasions employees had come on board the vessel in an intoxicated state without the company taking any disciplinary action against them. It was also well known that the crew had put intoxicated crew members to bed to sleep off their drunken condition; the company took no disciplinary action in those situations either. Furthermore, in Thompson's case at least one of the vessel's officers knew, or should have known, that he had been drinking on board.

The union also contended that, since Thompson had admitted that he had an alcohol problem, had joined AA, and had not had a drink since the accident, he should be given one "last chance." The company should also consider his long and good service with no disciplinary record. Other employees in the past had been given "one last chance," and, following past practice and practicing fair and equal treatment to all, Thompson should also be given another chance.

The union strongly urged that the arbitrator reduce the penalty of discharge to that of suspension.

POSITION OF THE COMPANY

The company pointed out that Thompson was found to have an alcohol content of .3034 percent, which, according to the attending physician, was high enough to render a normal man unconscious. The company pointed out that most states consider a person with .10 percent alcohol in the bloodstream to be legally intoxicated.

Thompson had been drinking on the vessel—a clear violation of the rule against drinking posted on the bulletin board, given to him in a copy of the work rules, and included in a copy of the deckhands' manual.

In order to protect the safety of the employees and the safety of the equipment, the company had the right to enforce reasonable rules. The rule against drinking was reasonable and had been enforced on numerous occasions. The accident severely jeopardized Thompson's life and the safety of others and constituted an unnecessary expense to the company. The company had the right to terminate Thompson under the terms of Article V of the contract. In addition, the union had agreed in Article XII(b), that the "safety of operations and precautions against all hazardous conditions shall be a joint effort and mutual aim of the company and the union." Therefore, the union was required, by contract, to accept this reasonable safety rule.

The union also agreed in Article XIII, Section 3, that "it will not oppose the efforts of the company to obtain a normal day's work" and will combat employee practices that restrict or limit efficient operations. Being under the influence of alcohol and drinking on board the vessel restricts or limits efficient operation. The union should support the company in this discharge.

As to the union allegation that the company had not applied the rule consistently, the company claimed that the situations referred to by the union occurred more than three years previous. The company had been conscientiously endeavoring to tighten disciplinary standards. It did not condone either coming on board a vessel in an intoxicated condition or drinking alcohol once aboard. All of the situations referred to by the union involved coming on board in an intoxicated condition, and not to drinking on board, as Thompson had done.

The company argued that Thompson's plea to the effect that he no longer was an alcoholic revealed that he did not understand the philosophy of Alcoholics Anonymous, which states that "once an alcoholic, always an alcoholic." For example, when questioned during the investigation, he was asked:

Q. Do you regard yourself as an alcoholic?

A. Well, I would say I was. But I ain't now.

Q. You aren't one now?

A. No, I ain't.

Thompson did not understand his problem; he was still an alcoholic; he would certainly drink again.

The company urged that the arbitrator sustain the company's position and uphold the discharge of Henry Thompson.

APPENDIX

Relevant Provisions of the Contract

Article V—Management

Nothing herein contained shall be construed to limit the authority of the Master, Pilot, Chief Engineer, Company Officers or Designated Representatives in the discharge of their lawful duties. The management of properties, including boats, the direction of the working force, the right to hire and discharge and/or transfer are vested exclusively in the Company, and the Union shall not abridge these rights. The Company shall not discriminate against employees because of membership in the union.

Article XII—Safety & Health
(Boats and Terminals)

(b)   Safety of operations and precautions against all hazardous conditions shall be the joint and mutual aim of the Company and the Union, and every effort on the part of each party shall be directed to this end.

Article XIII—Miscellaneous
(Towboats and Terminals)

The Union agrees that it will not oppose the efforts of the Company to obtain a normal day's work on the part of its members and will combat absenteeism and any other employee practices which restrict or limit efficient operation. The Union further agrees that it will not oppose the Company in the Company's efforts to eliminate waste; conserve materials and supplies; improve the quality of workmanship; prevent accidents; and strengthen the good will between the Company, the employee, the customer and the public.

Company Rule Posted on All Bulletin Boards

—Post on Bulletin Board—

TO: ALL VESSEL EMPLOYEES, OHIO RIVER COMPANY—OHIO DIVISION
RE: DRINKING AND INTOXICATION WORK RULE

Boarding any company vessel or being on any company property under the influence of alcoholic beverages is prohibited. Bringing alcoholic beverages on company property, including vessels is prohibited. The consumption of alcoholic beverages on company vessels or property is also prohibited.

Any violation of this rule will result in an immediate suspension, possibly resulting in discharge.

Intoxication and the possession of alcohol aboard our vessels and property endangers not only the safety of the offending party, but also the safety of the crew. Therefore, the company cannot and will not tolerate any exceptions to this work rule and hereby gives advance warning to all employees that any violation of this work rule will be considered a matter of the utmost seriousness. It is the Master's and/or Pilot's responsibility to enforce this work rule.

s/John J. Egan, Jr.
Port Captain
June 17, 1958 (Original Date)
January 22, 1968 (Revised Date)

August 6, 1969 (Revised Date)
March 23, 1973 (Revised Date)
August 16, 1982 (Revised Date)
September 20, 1982 (Revised Date)
November 17, 1983 (Revised Date)

Grievant's Statement. In addition, on the grievant's employment application, he had signed the following statement:

I also understand that the use of intoxicants or being intoxicated or illegal use of narcotics during company time is sufficient cause to terminate my employment with the company. (November 17, 1983)

QUESTIONS

1. What is the fundamental issue in this case?

2. If the company had permitted crewmen to come to work drunk in the past without having taken any action, would this have any bearing on this case? Does the fact that the company had been attempting to tighten disciplinary standards have any bearing on this case? Discuss.

3. How important is the issue of safety?

4. How important is the fact that Thompson had become a member of Alcoholics Anonymous and had abstained from the use of alcohol for a considerable period of time after this incident?

5. Does Article XII(b) require that the union support the company's action? Discuss.

6. Was the discharge of Thompson warranted under all of the circumstances? Why, or why not?

64. *The Payroll Error*

Company:

    Hermann Oak Leather Company, St. Louis, Missouri

Union:

    International Molders and Allied Workers Union, Local 59

BACKGROUND

On December 7, 1982, foreman Charles Johnson[1] received written notice of a grievance from John Coffman, which stated:

> Company said they overpaid me for 22 weeks. They said I should have caught it and reported it to them. I feel that they fired me unjustly. I want to be paid average for all time lost.

And on the same date, Johnson received an almost identical grievance from Roger Bickford:

> Company said they overpaid me for 24 weeks. They said I should have caught it and reported it to them. I feel that they fired me unjustly. I want to be paid average for all time lost.

Both employees worked within the shipping area of the finishing department of Hermann Oak. Their jobs included the measuring, rolling, binding, and shipping of leather that had been processed from raw hides to finished leather.

The company primarily was involved in tanning and finishing leather for sales to manufacturers. It employed about 50 persons in the tanning and finishing departments.

On Thursday morning, December 2, 1982, Anne Beck, payroll manager, informed plant manager Jack Rand that there had been a major error in piecework rates paid to two employees in the shipping department. This was discovered because new piecework rates, to be effective in January 1983, were being programmed into the computer. Five different piece rates involving Bickford and Coffman had been programmed in error, resulting in overpayment to them. On the following day Beck reported to Rand that the overpayment had extended from June 1982 through the remainder of the year. These overpayments averaged $35 per week but were as large as $67. Bickford had been overpaid a total of $840.88 during the 24-week period, and Coff-

---

[1] The names of all individuals have been disguised.

man $780.64 during the 22-week period. (Coffman had been on two weeks vacation during that time.)

Rand met with both Bickford and Coffman later that day; he informed them that they had been overpaid and that they would be told later what would be done. According to Rand, Bickford then turned to Coffman and said, "I told you so." Neither man denied receiving the overpayment. On the following Monday, both men were presented copies of a compilation that had been prepared by Beck.

Subsequently that day, Rand and Beck met with Robert Henkle, president of Hermann Oak, and the company attorney to determine what action should be taken. A decision was made to terminate both Bickford and Coffman because both were considered to be guilty of major dishonesty.

The union appealed the company's action through the established grievance procedure without agreement. The case was submitted to arbitration. The parties agreed that the issue to be decided was as follows:

> Were the grievants, Coffman and Bickford, discharged for just cause? If not, what should be the appropriate remedy?

TESTIMONY OF THE GRIEVANTS

Coffman testified that he had been employed by the company for 14 years, during 12 of which he had served as a union committee person and steward. He indicated that during those years he had been involved in contract negotiations and grievance meetings, and that he had engaged in many "heated discussions" and "yelling contests" with management. However, he claimed that he had never received any disciplinary actions for his work. He felt that the company had terminated him for his union activity. To support this contention, he claimed that on one occasion Rand had said "he'd get me" following a heated grievance meeting.

Coffman admitted that he had pleaded guilty of embezzlement of union funds in the U.S. District Court and had been placed on probation in return for 200 hours of community service and restoration of the monies to the union.

According to Coffman, he "didn't know anything" about being overpaid for 22 weeks in 1982 until he was informed by the plant manager to this effect on December 3, 1982. He acknowledged that he had lodged several complaints during the earlier months about not being paid enough. But he said that he and Bickford had checked their pay only for about the first five months of 1982; since most of the time company calculations were correct, both he and Bickford stopped challenging their paychecks rather than engage in "aggravating" the company.

He claimed that during the meeting with Rand on December 3, the plant manager said that "the company would figure out some plan of restitution," but that this opportunity had never been offered to him and Bickford. He further claimed that during a grievance meeting protesting his discharge, he offered to pay the money back on a weekly installment basis if he could get his job back, but that his offer was not acceptable to the company.

Bickford stated that he had been with Hermann Oak for 16 years, during 10 of which he had served as a union committee person and steward. He, too, felt that he had been treated unusually harshly by management because of his union activities. He said that he had participated in many heated arguments during grievance meetings, and that he was not liked by several members of management because of his assertive behavior on behalf of his fellow union members. He stated that he had a good work record with the company.

Bickford testified that he had never been indicted nor charged with a crime by the grand jury, although he had been investigated by the U.S. Department of Labor for allegedly claiming and receiving more money from the union for negotiating time than he was entitled to collect.

He testified that he kept "a little black book" in which he kept detailed records of his piece rate earnings, but that he kept such records only at the beginning of each year until such time that he felt assured that the company was correctly calculating piece rates. In 1982 he stopped keeping records after satisfying himself that the company's calculations were generally accurate. He said that he was "not a good mathematician" and that his paychecks varied by as much as $50 from one week to another. It was only reasonable that he attempted to determine his earnings on a daily basis, especially when errors in company records were likely to occur.

He claimed that he had stopped maintaining accurate records of daily earnings late in May 1982, and that he had no personal knowledge of the overpayments from June through December. Like Coffman, Bickford stated that during his first meeting with Rand on December 3, the plant manager suggested that he would be allowed to make some form of restitution. However, subsequently the company refused to offer him this opportunity in exchange for reinstatement to his former job.

POSITION OF THE UNION

Lester Norvell, international union vice president, argued on behalf of Coffman and Bickford, as well as for the interests of all other members of the union. He pointed out that two other employees were also overpaid during the two weeks that Coffman was on vacation, but that they had not been either asked to refund the overpayments or disciplined in any manner.

He further argued that neither Coffman nor Bickford had falsified their time cards. The principal problem with the miscalculation of their pay was the incompetence of management in programming the computer and the failure of the company to monitor the operation of its bookkeeping system. This was not only a classic case of "garbage in, garbage out" but also of slovenly attention to what was happening in the bookkeeping department. Neither Coffman nor Bickford was either a computer expert or an accountant. They kept track of their earnings during the first few months of 1982, but did so with difficulty and the devotion of much time to the activity. They uncovered several errors in payroll calculations, one as small as $1.33, but usually in the $5–$10 range; after all, even $1.33 was important to a working man. However, after determining that their pay was being accurately calculated, they were only too happy to stop keeping detailed records, which they did toward the end of May 1982.

Norvell also pointed out that the collective bargaining agreement contained no provision, or even an implication, that required an employee to either compute his own pay or report an overpayment if such occurred.

Norvell argued that the company discharged Bickford and Coffman because of their tenacious defense of the rights of their fellow union members under the terms of the collective agreement.

The union urged that both Bickford and Coffman be reinstated to their former jobs, that they be paid for all time lost, that all references to the company's unwarranted disciplinary action be removed from their personnel files, and that their seniority remain uninterrupted.

POSITION OF THE COMPANY

The company charged that both Bickford and Coffman were guilty of major dishonesty because both men clearly knew for an extended period of time about the overpayments. In support of the company's contention, Thomas Howell, assistant plant manager and superintendent of the finishing department, stated that he had observed both Coffman and Bickford figuring and maintaining a record of their pay. According to him, they maintained a "little black book" in which they recorded their pay; he had seen this book in discussions with them. He said that they calculated their pay each day at the end of their shift and that they knew what pay was due them "to the penny." He stated that both men had discussed discrepancies in their pay at least a dozen times, and that when they did so, they always claimed underpayment. These discussions took place during the period of January–June, 1982.

During the period June–December, 1982, they raised questions about wages paid to other employees, although they did not question him about their own checks during those months. Howell indicated that he heard Bickford tell a fellow employee following the meeting of December 3, "Didn't I tell you that I was being overpaid?"

Payroll department manager Anne Beck also indicated that she had discussed payroll matters with both Bickford and Coffman at least a half dozen times during the past year. She claimed that both men calculated their pay on a regular weekly basis, and she cited several examples from payroll records where they contested alleged payroll errors prior to June 1982. All of the amounts were less than $10. Three examples were:

a. April 1979: $1.33 due Bickford

b. October 1979: $8.26 due Coffman and $8.54 due Bickford

c. April 1981: $6.40 due Bickford and $6.25 due Coffman

Beck also claimed that on many instances they brought to her attention payroll matters in which they were proven wrong. These, too, were minor discrepancies, usually involving less than $10. Beck stated that she was not sure who made the computer error, but she held that it was an "innocent mistake." Coffman and Bickford were the only two persons who were overpaid excessively during this period.

The company supported its contention that both men were dishonest in citing that Coffman had been found guilty of embezzlement of union funds in U.S. Circuit Court. And Bickford was under investigation by the U.S. Department of Labor for allegedly padding his expense account, thereby potentially defrauding the union of a considerable amount of money; the charge was that he claimed payment for more time spent in negotiations than he actually devoted to that union activity.

The company stated that only Bickford and Coffman had been disciplined because they were the only persons who knew that they were being overpaid over a long period of time. Two other employees who served as vacation fill-ins, for one week each, had no reason to know of the overpayments. Thus, the company considered them innocent of dishonesty.

The company acknowledged that both Coffman and Bickford were union officers, and that management found both men to be somewhat contentious in arguing the terms of the collective bargaining agreement and aggressive in supporting their perceived rights of other union members. However, plant manager Rand stated that on no occasion had he or any other member of management ever said to either man, "I'll get your job." On the other hand, Rand admitted that he had written an official warning to Bickford, dated March 15, 1976, which placed him on final warning for his part in supporting a work stoppage. The company maintained that dishonesty, not union activity, caused the company to terminate both employees.

Finally, the company argued that it was absolutely essential that employees in the shipping area be honest in their actions, since these men measured and weighed valuable materials shipped to customers. Both men were responsible for reporting rate figures to the company on which the company relied; and both men also calculated their own pay on a regular basis and had challenged the company on numerous occasions for errors. They knew how to calculate their pay; they regularly did so; and they knowingly accepted for many months overpayments to which they were not entitled. Such gross dishonesty could not be permitted in such responsible positions as held by both Bickford and Coffman.

The company urged the arbitrator to find the company's action reasonable, the discharge to be for just cause, and to uphold the termination of both Bickford and Coffman.

APPENDIX

Relevant Provisions of the Contract

Article VI—Management Rights

The direction of the work and the selection, promotion and transfer of employees, except as limited in this Agreement or by law, shall lie with the Company. All employees shall observe rules and regulations made by the Company for the conduct of its operations. Any employee shall perform any service at any time in the Company's operations which he is required to and is in the opinion of the Company qualified to perform. Except as herein limited, the hours of labor, the assignment of duties and tasks and the general conduct and management of the Company and of its production processes and facilities, rest with the Company. Nothing herein shall be so construed as to impair or abate the right of the Company to change, modify or cease its operations, processes, or production in its discretion; and in the event of such change, modifications or cessations, the Company shall be the sole judge of all factors involved, including, but not limited to, the efficiency, usefulness and practicability of machinery, processes, location of business, and personnel required by it. The Company will, however, discuss with the Union, on its request, any such change, modification or cessation which would affect the wages, hours or working conditions of the employees. The Union will not interfere with the sales policies of the Company or with its source of supplies of raw materials, equipment, supplies, power, services, or other articles and services required by it in its unlimited discretion.

Article VII—Seniority

4. Seniority shall be lost and employment may be terminated for any of the following:
A. Discharge for cause.

QUESTIONS

1. Did Coffman and Bickford knowingly accept monies to which they were not entitled? Discuss.
2. Should the responsibility for these payroll errors be attributed to the payroll manager? To Coffman and Bickford?
3. Are the past backgrounds of Coffman and Bickford of any direct relevance to the issues in this case?
4. Were the discharge actions justified? Why, or why not?

65. *The Unrecorded Purchase*

Company:

    Furr's, Inc., Albuquerque, New Mexico

Union:

    United Food and Commercial Workers Union, Local 1564

Jane Eyer[1] was employed as a food clerk by Furr's, Inc., from October 25, 1973, until her suspension on March 24, 1984, and her discharge on April 2, 1984. She was discharged for a violation of the company's "Failure to Ring Up Purchases" policy.

The union filed a grievance in behalf of Eyer. It was processed through the grievance procedure to arbitration. The parties agreed that the question before the arbitrator was as follows:

1. Did the company have just cause to discharge Jane Eyer for violation of the "Failure to Ring Up Purchases" policy?

2. If not, what is the appropriate remedy?

BACKGROUND

Jane Eyer reported for work on March 23, 1984, having missed the previous two days because of illness. At approximately 11:20 A.M., a customer named Celia Tamm approached Eyer's checkout station with her baby, pushing a grocery cart filled with grocery items that she desired to purchase. Tamm had divided the groceries into two groups. The first group included items to be paid for with a "Women, Infant, and Children Nutrition Program" check ("WIC" check); the items in the second group were to be purchased with Tamm's personal check. The WIC program was conducted by the State of New Mexico; it provided certain grocery items to qualified persons at no cost. The mechanics of a purchase under the program provided that a qualified person, such as Tamm, was entitled to purchase certain specified food items with a WIC check drawn on the State of New Mexico.

According to Eyer, she noted the items that were being purchased by Tamm with the WIC check and compared them with the items that Tamm was authorized to purchase. Tamm completed the name and

---

[1] The names of all individuals have been disguised.

address portion of the WIC check and gave it to Eyer. Eyer did not, at that point, complete the transaction on her cash register or place the WIC check in the register drawer. Eyer then rang up the other items, which Tamm paid for with a personal check that Eyer deposited in the register drawer. During that time, Tamm's baby was crying very loudly, disturbing both the baby's mother and Eyer. (Tamm corroborated Eyer's recollection of the details of the transaction.)

After Tamm left the store with her purchases, Eyer waited on two or three additional customers before realizing that she had not either rung up the purchases for the WIC check or deposited the WIC check in the register drawer. In attempting to rectify this mistake, she first made an error in the proper amount of the WIC check. She stated that she confused the proper amount of Tamm's WIC check with the dollar amount of the purchases of one of the subsequent customers she had waited on in the meantime. Further, she claimed to have had difficulties in getting the register to function properly.

Each cash register had a transaction number that identified each transaction. Tamm's personal check was identified as transaction number 4239. The last transaction involving the WIC check was number 4255. If Eyer had followed company procedure precisely, the WIC check would have been deposited before the purchase involving Tamm's personal check and would have been recorded as number 4238.

At some time between transaction 4239 and 4255, the head clerk noticed that Eyer was experiencing a problem with her register, asked her about it, and upon receiving an affirmative response, pushed the "clear" key on the register to clear the machine.

At the end of the day management personnel examined the "detail tape," which recorded each transaction on the register. The next day company security personnel conducted an investigation of Eyer's failure to ring up the WIC check. At the end of her work shift on March 24, Eyer was suspended, and she was discharged on April 2, 1984.

An audit of Eyer's transactions on March 23 revealed that there was no shortage; instead, there was an overage of $1.34.

Furr, Inc., had had a "Failure to Ring Up Purchases" policy for more than 10 years prior to this incident. Each new employee was advised of the policy at the time of hire and was required to read and sign the written policy statement when first employed. Each time the policy was changed or revised in any way, a copy of the new version was issued to all employees to be read and signed. The last revision occurred in August 1978, and it had been read and signed by Eyer.[2]

---

[2] See Appendix to this case for copy of the "Failure to Ring" policy.

POSITION OF THE UNION

The union contended that Eyer attempted to ring up the WIC check within 10 rings but was unable to do so because of a malfunction of the cash register. She became quite nervous upon discovering that she had failed to ring up the WIC check properly. The malfunction may have been caused, at least in part, by some misstep on her part, but it did occur.

The union also pointed out that the acts of Eyer were not willful, deliberate, or intentional violations of the "Failure to Ring Up Purchases" policy. As soon as she discovered her error, she immediately attempted to rectify it. She was not attempting to defraud the company; she ultimately recorded the transaction properly; the company lost nothing.

Eyer had a long record of excellent service. She was a loyal and competent employee with no prior disciplinary record for any reason. The company had no just cause for discharge.

The union urged the arbitrator to restore Jane Eyer to her position of food clerk with full back pay and restoration of all benefits.

POSITION OF THE COMPANY

The company argued that the penalty for a violation of the "Failure to Ring Up Purchases" policy had always been discharge on the first offense without any prior warning. The policy had been invoked consistently and without exception. The penalty was appropriate because of the serious nature of the offense.

The company cited the text of an earlier decision by arbitrator Donald Daughton, who had heard a similar case involving a violation of the company's "Failure to Ring Up Purchases" policy:

First, in the judgment of management the company's policy on "failure to ring" is essential to maintaining inventory and cash control at the retail store level. Second, the establishment of such a policy by other retail grocery chains is the norm rather than the exception. Third, the employees of the company were specifically advised of the policy, and that a violation of the policy would result in discharge on first offense. Fourth, the policy had been uniformly applied by the company.

Food clerks play a vital role in the operations of the company inasmuch as all the payments for purchases must go through their hands. Consequently, it is necessary that the company policy governing the receipt of monies be meticulously adhered to. Given the crucial role which food clerks play in the operation of a retail grocery business, arbitrators have uniformly acknowledged the right of the company to impose the penalty of discharge for a first violation of a company policy of the kind involved in this arbitration.

The company urged that the arbitrator sustain the discharge of Jane Eyer.

APPENDIX

Relevant Clauses of the Contract

4.2—DISCIPLINE—The employer shall have the right to discharge, demote or suspend any employee for just cause. However, prior to such action being taken, at least one (1) written corrective action notice on a related or similar offense must be given to an employee, except in those cases where there is just cause based upon a particular offense.

Relevant Company Policy Read and Signed by Employee Jane Eyer

Failure to Ring up Purchases
Revised Rule 8–78

The primary responsibility of every checker is to make an accurate record, by use of the cash register, of all purchases made by a customer, to receive correct payment for same, and to place all money, checks, food stamps, and coupons received into the cash register.

Money or legal tender is to be placed in the register immediately after each complete customer transaction. Failure to do this shall constitute failure to ring and the penalty for violation of this rule is DISCHARGE WITHOUT WARNING.

An employee will be discharged on first offense if he/she fails to ring up money received by a customer for a purchase whether or not the money so received is placed in the cash register.

If an additional sale is made to the same customer, it will be treated as a separate sale and handled by ringing up the purchase, placing the money in the cash register, and issuing the customer receipt and tape to the customer.

In the event that a customer gives you, or leaves you the correct amount for a purchase while you are recording another sale, the money will be placed on the change plate of the cash register. This sale must then be recorded as the next immediate transaction even if other customers are in line. The money received in this type of sale must be recorded on your register and not issued to another checkstand.

Customer's money or the company's money, saving stamps, coupons, or food stamps shall not be mixed with personal funds or kept on your person. Violation of this rule shall result in immediate discharge.

Professional shoppers are retained by Furr's who act as customers to shop employees periodically to determine if the above rules are being followed. A typical examination of this kind is conducted by two or more shoppers working in conjunction so that at least one shopper can observe or identify the transaction of the other shopper who will tender exact change for a purchase and not wait for a detail tape. Employees who fail to record monies received in this manner will be discharged for failure to ring.

The detail tape will be used to identify the transaction and if the money so tendered is not indicated on the detail tape within 10 transactions it shall be defined as failure to ring.

If you have any questions on the above procedures, please ask your immediate supervisor.

I have received, read, and understand these procedures.
/s/ Jane Eyer 11/18/78 #22
(Signature   Date   Store No.)
Each checker should keep the first copy for his/her personal file and return the second copy to his/her store manager signed and dated.

Employee's Name: ___Jane Eyer___
                    (Please Print)

QUESTIONS

1. Should the fact that Eyer had been employed as a food clerk for over 10 years influence the arbitration decision?
2. Do the circumstances surrounding her failure to ring up the purchase have any influence on the arbitration decision?
3. Was the company's rule on ringing up purchases reasonable? Why, or why not?
4. How has the company enforced the rule in the past?
5. Had Eyer been adequately informed of the rule? Discuss.
6. If you had been the manager of this store, how would you have handled this case?

66. Do New Hires Include Rehires?

Company:
> Owens-Illinois, Inc. (Libbey Glass Division), City of Industry (Los Angeles), California.

Union:
> American Flint Glass Workers, Local No. 705

NEGOTIATING BACKGROUND

During negotiations in 1983 for a new collective bargaining agreement that was to take effect November 16, 1983, the company presented a "two-tier" wage-scale proposal for all new hires. The union initially rejected the company proposal, and there was little or no discussion regarding the specific language in the company proposal. Throughout the negotiations, however, the company continued to press the union to accept the two-tier wage proposal. The chief negotiator for the company, Gus Triplett,[1] argued that the proposal did not affect any current employees, but only would impact upon "nameless, faceless people."

In the final agreement, the union reluctantly agreed to the two-tier wage provision, since it would be difficult for the union membership to take a strike over this issue, which did not affect currect employees. Union negotiators, however, said that they were opposed in principle to inclusion of the two-tier wage provision, because of the potential problems it could cause among employees in the future.

As drafted by the company and as included in the new collective bargaining agreement, the two-tier wage contractual provision was as follows:

Article 50—New Hire Wage Progression

All new hires in Schedule A (Excluding the Forming Department) shall be paid at a rate of $1.50 per hour less than the qualified rate for the job that they are performing. Such employees shall be increased by 25¢ per hour in each succeeding six months period. They shall also receive contractual increases as they occur.

Such an employee, who is laid off prior to having attained the maximum base rates of the job classification and who is reemployed at the plant within two years from the last day worked, shall receive a rate

---

[1] The names of all individuals are disguised.

upon reemployment which has the same relative position to the maximum base rate of the job classification as had been attained by the employee prior to layoff.

Upon such reemployment, the credited rate progression period of the employee's prior period of employment at the plant shall be applied toward his rate progression the maximum base rates of the job classification.

An employee who has received the New Hire Rate Progression, is assigned or continues to be assigned to a job classification that has an extended training period but has not completed the required time in such classification to receive the maximum base rate, will continue at the current rate or the rate specified for time worked in such classification, whichever is higher. Thereafter, the specified time limits and rate schedule will be the same as those in the labor agreement for other than new hires.

THE GRIEVANCE DISPUTE

In April of 1984, Local Union President Miller Brooks first became aware of the problem that led to this grievance dispute. Brooks was contacted by employee Ellen Ferguson, who asked him, "What is going on?" She told Brooks that she had just recently been rehired and that she was making $1.50 less per hour than the other employees who were working in the same jobs. She indicated that there was a man in the warehouse at the same wage grade level who also had just been rehired by the company, and who was being paid $1.50 more per hour than she was getting. Brooks then visited the warehouse facility and talked with Willy Smith, the rehire that Ellen Ferguson had mentioned. Smith stated that he had been rehired by the company, and he was being paid the old rate of pay for the job.

Brooks next approached the company personnel director, Collin Miles, and informed her of the difference in pay between Ferguson and Smith. Miles then went to Willy Smith, and she told him that his pay would be reduced by $1.50 per hour in accordance with Article 50 of the labor-management agreement between the company and union.

About a week or so later, Emily Parker, another employee of the company, quit to take a test for the California State Highway Patrol. Ms. Parker failed the test, and two weeks later she returned and reapplied for a job. Upon rehire, Ms. Parker was informed that she would receive $1.50 less per hour. Several days later, Miller Brooks was approached by employee Penny Ward, who stated that her job was at the same wage level as the other three employees (i.e., Ferguson, Smith, and Parker). Ward reported that she had worked for the company, quit, and subsequently was rehired at a $1.50 per hour less rate of pay.

On July 19, 1984, Miles Brooks filed a grievance on behalf of the four employees; Brooks also inquired of company management to determine whether he had identified all of the grievants in this dispute. Brooks was advised that the four grievants constituted all of the rehires of the company at this point in time. After exhausting the grievance procedure, the matter was placed before an arbitrator for a final and binding resolution.

POSITION OF THE UNION

Union witnesses pointed out that Article 50, the "new hire wage progression" provision in the contract, was opposed by the union to the very end of the previous negotiations. The union finally gave in, because it would have been a difficult strike issue. Present employees were unwilling to strike about an issue that would not affect their wages.

Counsel for the union claimed that the words *new hire* did not mean or include *rehires*. Since 1965 the company had utilized the word *rehire* in the contract to identify those employees who were hired more than once. Article 22 in the present contract stated as follows:

Article 22—Retirement Program

* * * * *

Section 14.   Restoration of Service—An employee who is rehired by the Company and who then works at least three (3) years from the date of such rehiring shall be given credit toward pension rights for prior service with the Company provided such prior service with the Company was at least two (2) years.

* * * * *

Thus, an employee who was rehired and who worked at least three years from the date of such rehiring was given credit toward pension rights for prior service, provided such service was at least two years.

Counsel for the union further pointed out that company management had proposed and written Article 50. During negotiations, reference was made by the company's chief negotiator to "nameless, faceless people," that is, people who had never worked at the company. The Union submitted that the term *new hires* within Article 50 meant exactly that—i.e., hires that were new to the plant, and this did not include rehires. The grievance should be sustained, and the Company should be ordered to reimburse the four grievants the full amount of lost wages as appropriate, which should be revealed by company records.

POSTION OF THE COMPANY

Counsel for the company argued that the union was trying to read something into Article 50 that was never intended to be there. The company had drafted Article 50, but the parties really did not bargain about its wording. The union was not as diligent in regard to this matter as it should have been. The company claimed that a *new hire* and a *rehire* were the same thing. That is to say, the purpose of the two-tier wage system under Article 50 was to have a lower wage rate for all employees who were to be hired after the effective date of the new contract, irrespective of whether or not they previously had worked at the company.

Since the union had failed to negotiate any specific wage considerations for so-called rehires under the new two-tier wage system, then rehires must be treated the same as new hires. This was the company's intent in developing Article 50. If the union desired to achieve certain rights and privileges for rehires, these should come through the collective bargaining process and not through the grievance-arbitration mechanism.

The company urged that the union grievance should be denied.

QUESTIONS

1. Evaluate the union's position that the term *new hires* did not include rehires.
2. Evaluate the company's position that the term *new hires* was meant to include rehires under the new labor agreement.
3. Why is the negotiating background of this dispute somewhat contradictory to the resolution of the grievance? Discuss.
4. Does it make any difference in interpreting Article 50 that the current and previous contracts between the parties contained special provisions for rehires. Why, or why not?

67. The Right to Work Overtime

Company:
   Fashion Shoe Products, Sullivan, Missouri

Union:
   Local No. 284, Amalgamated Clothing and Textile Workers Union—Shoe Division

BACKGROUND

The union grievance heard in arbitration had been filed on February 28, 1984, by Shirley Hildebrand,[1] an employee in the company plant. The nature of her grievance was stated on a union complaint form as follows:

> A lower seniority employee was required to work and I was refused on Saturday, February 25. I feel all losses should be made whole.

As framed by the parties, the issue for the Arbitrator's determination was as follows: Was the company obligated to assign overtime work to a higher seniority employee, Shirley Hildebrand, on February 25, 1984? If so, what should be the appropriate remedy?

POSITION OF THE UNION

Testifying on her own behalf, Shirley Hildebrand stated that at the time of her grievance she was a team leader who was part of a divisional group called Quality Assurance (QA). Her actual job classification was as a team leader in the Polyurethane Molding Department. According to Ms. Hildebrand, she was ready, willing, and able to work overtime on Saturday, February 25, 1984. Two other employees had been told that they would have to work, because certain products that had been returned needed sorting and inspection. One of these employees, Mabel Keller, did not want to work and she had less seniority than Ms. Hildebrand. After Ms. Hildebrand had inquired at about noon on Friday, February 24, she was informed by her supervisor, Eleanor Stroup, that the plant manager, Willis Jerald, had decided that the other two employees would be required to work on this Saturday.

Hildebrand said that there was nothing specifically in the labor agreement about assigning overtime by seniority, but she asserted

---

[1] The names of all individuals are disguised.

that there was a well-understood practice in recent years that the company would offer overtime first to those employees with highest seniority who were qualified and available to work. Further, the company would, if necessary, even "force" higher seniority people to work overtime. The job in question was to sort good parts from defective parts, and Ms. Hildebrand said that she had performed this work and had received training for it. She acknowledged that her normal inspection job in the Polyurethane Department was somewhat different from the inspection job in the Finishing Department where the overtime work was done.

Testifying also for the union was Alberta Sloan, vice president of the local union. Ms. Sloan testified that overtime in recent years had always been offered first to higher seniority employees, and in most cases senior employees were required to work. Ms. Sloan stated that the union believed it was now an established practice that senior employees, if qualified, would be given first opportunity to perform overtime work. She stated that she could not remember that the company had ever "hopscotched by seniority" in overtime scheduling in recent years. Ms. Sloan also said that in past years, the company would require junior seniority people to work overtime, but for the last several years the company would force higher seniority people to work overtime.

The position of the union was summarized in a post-hearing brief submitted by George Sullivan, Union Field Representative and chief spokesman for the union. Excerpts from his brief included the following arguments:

It is the union's position that:

1. The grievant had received training in this type of work and was assigned to the Quality Assurance Division.
2. The company had established a policy of both offering and requiring the oldest operator by seniority to work overtime.
3. The grievant called attention to the error in time for it to be corrected before the overtime work was performed.
4. The company is still continuing to force the oldest employee experienced on the work to work overtime.
5. Working overtime for extra pay is not corrective discipline.

The company manager stated that he required the junior operator to work overtime as "punishment." The work that was returned and required rework was performed in the same division where the grievant was a team leader. Although the employees who were forced to work should have caught the poor quality work when it reached their department, they were no more responsible than the original operators.

The company has methods of punishment available to it to control poor workmanship. The requirement of an employee to work overtime for extra pay would not be corrective discipline. It is not in the best interests of employee and management relations for a company to establish a policy and then change it back and forth at will.

The grievant should be compensated at time and one-half her hourly wage of $5.99 for a total of eight hours, or $78.84.

The grievance should be sustained in favor of the grievant.

POSITION OF THE COMPANY

Appearing as the sole witness for the company was Willis Jerald, plant manager. Jerald gave extensive testimony concerning the nature of the products manufactured by the company and the departments involved in manufacturing operations. Within the Quality Assurance Division, the Polyurethane Molding Department primarily performed the function of molding products, such as plastic heel molds for shoes. The Finishing Department primarily was involved in lacquering and inspecting products before shipping to customers. According to Mr. Jerald, the grievant, Shirley Hildebrand, was a team leader who did inspection work in the Molding area; the junior seniority employee, Mabel Keller, who was required to work on the date in question, was a team leader or inspector in the Finishing Department. Mr. Jerald stated that a customer had sent back some products identified as "Marion" because of quality problems in the Finishing Department. Because there was nothing in the labor agreement that specified how overtime was to be assigned, he said his practice had been to answer a three-part question about overtime assignments, namely, how would the assignment affect safety, quality, and production? Jerald said that from time to time lower seniority emplyees would be assigned overtime work. Normally he did not permit higher seniority employees to bump junior seniority people across departments. On Saturday, February 25, 1984, he wanted the two operators who had made the mistakes to work the overtime. This was consistent with his practice of training such employees, which even could lead to disciplining of employees who did not improve.

Under cross-examination, Mr. Jerald acknowledged that Shirley Hildebrand could have done the work, and she was qualified to do so. However, his first preference was to have those employees who made the mistakes to work the overtime to correct them. He emphasized that his decision was made so as not to compromise quality, safety, or production. He also acknowledged that the company did require higher seniority employees to work overtime if needed.

The position of the company was summarized in a post-hearing brief submitted by Albert Lukins, attorney for the company. Excerpts follow:

There are three reasons why the union cannot prevail in this case. First, there are no contractual restrictions on the company's right to make assignments of overtime. Implicit in this is the fact that the company has altered its methods of selecting employees for overtime purposes, as the union affirmatively testified. In years past, the company had selected the junior employees and then unilaterally switched to a procedure where it selected more senior employees. That is the most concrete evidence that it is the company who makes the selection of the individuals to work a particular overtime assignment.

Secondly, the union cannot prevail because the company followed its consistent pattern of making overtime assignments by department. While the grievant belonged to a Quality Assurance Division for purposes of work assignment, her department was the Polyurethane Molding Department and not the Finished Goods Department in which the individual who received the overtime worked. The company as Mr. Jerald testified, did not permit bumping around from department to department. It has consistently followed more of a "man-on-the-job" principle of overtime assignment.

Thirdly, and lastly, the company has traditionally used such assignments for purposes of training when individuals who have made mistakes can be identified. In this instance, the Saturday overtime was for purposes of rechecking goods which had been allowed to go to a customer. When the finished goods inspector who made the error could be identified, that individual was assigned the rechecking of the goods. Thus the union's suggested relief is not specified under the collective bargaining agreement, it is contrary to past practice, and it is inconsistent with the company's uniform procedure for using overtime periods for retraining when returned goods can be attributable to a given quality assurance employee.

The grievance should be denied.

QUESTIONS

1. Evaluate the union's arguments that a past practice of offering and requiring overtime among senior employees should decide this grievance in the union's favor.

2. Evaluate the company's arguments that the alternating past practices should decide this grievance in the company's favor.

3. Should overtime work at premium pay be considered as an employee right or benefit, or as an employee obligation including for corrective training purposes? Discuss.

4. Since the contract in this case is silent concerning overtime assignments, does management have the right to assign overtime according to its own preferences? Discuss.

68. *The Revised Payroll Period*

Company:
   Creative Data Services, Inc., St. Louis, Missouri
Union:
   International Brotherhood of Teamsters, Chauffeurs, Warehousemen and Helpers of America, Local 688

BACKGROUND

On December 3, 1985 Jeb Wilcox,[1] a printer in the production department, filed the following grievance on behalf of the union bargaining unit employees:

> The company is in violation of the contract by changing the pay period from one week to two. This violates ARTICLE 25.02, Hours of Work, and also ARTICLE 33, Maintenance of Standards, and any other article that may apply.[2]
> Settlement Requested. Change back to one week pay period.

The grievance was also signed by the union shop steward, Will Davis.

The company's answer, dated December 6, 1985, and signed by plant manager Max Ulrich, was as follows:

> The company has reviewed Article 25.02, Hours of Work, and Article 33, Maintenance of Standards, and changing the pay period is not in violation of these articles.

The union grievance was eventually carried to arbitration.

POSITION OF THE COMPANY

The company explained that during the third or fourth week of November 1985, management decided that it would change to a biweekly basis for paying employees in its St. Louis facility. The company had another facility in Los Angeles, whose employees had always been paid on a biweekly basis; St. Louis employees had always been paid on a weekly basis. According to the company's chief financial officer, Joseph Mills, his review of accounting and administrative functions revealed that in 1985 three employees in St. Louis were

---

[1] The names of all individuals have been disguised.
[2] See Appendix to this case for relevant provisions of the agreement.

involved in payroll work. He testified that there had been numerous payroll errors and expenses that were excessive for the size of the facility in St. Louis. St. Louis employees were paid on a direct-deposit basis with the Commerce Bank of St. Louis; employees received notice of direct deposits of their wages and salaries to their individual accounts at the bank. Mr. Mills stated that there had been many errors and corrections in forms and journal entries, and therefore the company decided to go to a biweekly payroll for all employees in the St. Louis operation. The bargaining unit represented by the union contained from 29 to 34 employees, depending upon production levels; additionally there were approximately 75 to 80 nonunion employees at the St. Louis facility.

The change to the biweekly pay schedule was made in the second week of January 1986. The company stated that it now had a "streamlined" payroll system that was free from the many errors in the past and that functioned with one fewer employee than formerly.

The company pointed out that on November 26, 1985, Mr. Mills sent a memorandum to all employees apprising them of the impending change to a biweekly payroll schedule beginning December 30, 1985. In addition, Mr. Mills sent a memorandum to all employees on December 2, 1985, offering to prepare an analysis as to what an individual employee's take-home pay would be on a biweekly basis. However, no one sought information or help from him.

Mr. Mills acknowledged that it was his understanding that St. Louis employees had been paid on a weekly basis ever since the union had been organized in about 1976. He further testified that there had been a number of management meetings concerning the payroll question and that Rob Pinter, director of human resources, and Janis Gueriny, vice president for planning and administration, both assured him that a change to a biweekly payroll schedule would not violate the labor agreement. Mr. Mills also acknowledged that Article 25.02 of the agreement used the term "payroll period," and that the company was now using a "work week" definition that was also in the agreement as a basis for paying people biweekly. Mr. Mills emphasized that the change from a weekly to a biweekly pay period did not affect anything other than the frequency of payment of employees.

The position of the company was summarized in its post-hearing brief, the relevant portions of which follow:

The grievance and the union's presentation of the grievance reflect a fundamental confusion about payroll periods, work weeks, and paydays. Paragraph 25.02 follows:

25.02 The payroll period shall be the seven day period from 12:01 A.M. Sunday through 12:00 midnight of the following Saturday. A "work day" shall mean the twenty-four (24) hour period beginning with an employee's starting time. "Work week" means a period of seven (7) consecutive days, beginning with an employee's starting time on the employee's first work day of any payroll period. A "shift" shall be deemed to be worked on the day the shift starts.

Paragraph 25.02 does not contain the term "pay-day," nor does it, in any way, state when an employee will be paid. This paragraph defines the "payroll period" and defines a "work week" in order to fix the appropriate periods for determining an employee's right to overtime in two (2) ways. There are contractual rules, and there is the Fair Labor Standards Act. The definitions make it easier to determine when the employee is eligible for overtime or premium pay. This section does not fix the time or frequency of payment of wages.

The union also relies on Article 33, Maintenance of Standards, for the proposition that the company could not change when emplyees are paid. That Article states:

"All conditions of employment relating to wages, . . . shall be maintained at not less than the highest standard in effect at the time of the signing of this Agreement . . ."

This article is a catch-all clause to cover various benefits not contained in the agreement which are too numerous for the union to set forth in detail. Such individuals are frequently referred to as "red circle rate" employees. The union will argue that payday is a benefit or condition of employment relating to "wages." The company, of course, does not agree. While the frequency has changed, there has not been a reduction in wages—only the frequency of pay days has been changed.

The decision to go to biweekly paydays was based upon sound accounting and good business reasons and was beneficial to the employees. One of the unacceptable circumstances existing at the time of the decision was an excessive error rate in the preparation of the payroll. The company believes that the number of errors was affected by the weekly pay day and the fact that three different employees were involved in preparing the payroll. These employees were experienced and competent employees; nevertheless, there were excessive errors. The errors increased the cost of preparing the payroll. The errors also caused problems for the employees—getting the right amount of money and, on occasions, any money at all. Since the company consolidated the payroll function and went to the biweekly payday the errors have been reduced, costs have been reduced, and the company is one system.

Prior to doing its own payroll, the company had two operations; one in St. Louis, and one in Los Angeles. The West Coast operation had been on a biweekly payday from its inception. The bargaining unit is slightly less than a third of the total payroll. The change to paydays biweekly consolidated the whole company on one system, resulting in a smoother operation subject to fewer errors, and made it less costly.

Joseph Mills was asked on cross-examination if his estimates of savings included the use of money for the period of the first week in the two (2) week cycle of paydays. He replied that it did not.

In making an interpretation of the contract, we cite the familiar concept that the contract must be viewed as a whole. A careful examination of the contract reveals that the company and union have gone to great effort to detail the rights and obligations of the company, union, and employees. Thus, the absence of a specific reference to a specific payday is significant. Where there are limits to the company's authority, they are enumerated. Surely, if the parties intended to restrict the company's right to change the paydays, they would have been specific in making such limitations.

The grievance should be denied.

POSITION OF THE UNION

The union did not present any witnesses in the arbitration hearing. The union only argued its position that the company had violated the agreement when the company decided in late 1985 to change the basis of payment of bargaining unit employees from a weekly period to a biweekly period. The union pointed out that the company had paid bargaining unit employees on a weekly basis throughout the history of the collective bargaining relationship between the parties. The union further indicated that the union grievance predated the actual change in the basis of payment, that is to say, the union filed its grievance when the company announced such a change but before it was actually implemented.

The union position was summarized in its post-hearing brief, the relevant portions of which follow:

> The union submits the issue as: Did the company violate the collective bargaining agreement by converting from a weekly to a biweekly payroll period?
>
> The undisputed facts are that the company, through its chief financial officer, unilaterally decided to reformulate the payment policy at Creative Data Services. The employees were notified of the policy change through correspondence dated November 26, 1985. Neither the union's representatives nor the members were notified of any intent to alter the payment policy until the decision was finalized.
>
> The aforementioned decision directly violates Article 25.02 of the collective bargaining agreement, which defines "payroll period" as "the seven day period from 12:01 A.M. Sunday through 12:00 midnight of the following Saturday. Until January 1986, the company's employees had been paid weekly, receiving a payroll check on each Wednesday in compensation for the previous payroll period. Thus, "payroll period" was the period for which each employee was paid and prior to January, 1986, the company and the union had always interpreted "payroll period" in this way. In fact the language in Article 25.02 has been in existence since the original collective bargaining agreement negotiated in 1977, and the employees have always been paid based on the contractual defintion of the payroll period. The language is clear and a definite standard has been established.

The company now claims that "payroll period" is not used to determine when employees are paid, and that changing to a biweekly payment basis does not violate Article 25.02. However, if in fact, the company does not use the definition of "payroll period" in Article 25.02 as the determination of when employees are paid, then the term "payroll period" becomes meaningless. The collective bargaining agreement provides for other defined periods for every other calculation necessary in Article 25. In his testimony, Joseph Mills admitted that since January, 1986, the "payroll period" as defined in the collective bargaining agreement has not been used for any calculation at all and this is meaningless according to the company's current practice.

Accepted principles of contract interpretation dictate that all agreements be construed as a whole, and that all words used in an agreement be given an effect.

* * * * *

The company also argues that the "payroll period" has not changed. They contend that the company is merely paying employees for two payroll periods in each paycheck rather than one. However, this argument still does avoid the aforementioned alteration or disregard of the Article 25.02 definition of "payroll period." Indeed, in answering the grievance the company acknowledged that it changed the payroll period.

The collective bargaining agreement also contains a section on "Maintenance of Standards." This Article states that:

"All conditions of employment relating to wages, hours of work, overtime differentials and general working conditions shall be maintained at not less than the highest standard in effect at the time of the signing of this agreement."

Through their past practice of paying each employee weekly, according to the payroll period, the company had established a standard. Clearly, the company violated this standard by changing the payroll period and failing to maintain Article 25.02 on "Hours of Work."

Joseph Mills testified, and stated in his November 26 correspondence, that the decision to convert to a biweekly payroll period was made to "reduce the number of people and hours it takes to process payroll." In turn, the company would save money. Thus, the company contends that cost efficiency is justification to alter the terms of the collective bargaining agreement. The union does not deny that the company could save money by adjusting the payroll period. But, the fact remains that the company entered into an agreement with the union and it is bound to uphold those terms. Certainly the company could avoid numerous other costs by ignoring the collective bargaining agreement. However, both parties bargained in good faith, have agreed to abide by the terms of the contract, and are therefore obligated to do so regardless of the cost or inconvenience. The employees have a right to be involved in decisions affecting or changing the collective bargaining agreement. In this case, the company ignored that right.

For the reasons stated above, the union urges the arbitrator to sustain the grievance and to enforce the payroll period as defined in the collective bargaining agreement.

APPENDIX

Relevant Provisions of the Agreement:

ARTICLE II
MANAGEMENT

11.01 The management of the company and the direction of the working force, including the right to hire, promote, discipline, suspend, transfer or discharge for cause, the right to schedule hours, schedule overtime work, and the right to relieve employees from duty because of lack of work or for other reasonable causes, is vested exclusively in the company; provided, however, that no action may be taken by the company which is contrary to the provisions of this agreement.

11.02 The company shall have the sole right to establish reasonable rules, decide the processes and types, kind and amount of machinery and equipment to be used, types and quantity of products to be made, quality of material and workmanship required, number of employees required for various operations, selling prices of product, method of making and selling products, personnel to be employed in supervisory, clerical and management positions and policies. The foregoing is intended by way of illustration and not in limitation of any customary or usual function of management, all of which are expressly retained by the company; provided, however, that no action may be taken by the company which is contrary to the provisions of this agreement.

ARTICLE 25
HOURS OF WORK

25.01 All references in this agreement to "days" refers to calendar days unless the context in which the word is used clearly indicates a different meaning; and the term "working day" refers to days on which the company's plant is actually engaged in production work, regardless of the calendar on which such working day may occur, or refers to the days on which an employee actually works, as the context may require.

25.02 The payroll period shall be the seven day period from 12:01 A.M. Sunday through 12:00 midnight of the following Saturday. A "work day" shall mean the twenty-four (24) hour period beginning with an employee's starting time. "Work week" means a period of seven (7) consecutive days, beginning with an employee's starting time on the employee's first work day of any payroll period. A "shift" shall be deemed to be worked on the day the shift starts.

25.03 The work week shall consist of forty (40) hours a week, which may be five (5) days of eight (8) hours per day or four (4) days of ten (10) hours per day or both a five (5) day and a four (4) day work week. This provision is subject to certain limitations in paragraph 25.12. The company may have multiple work week schedules. An employee may select a work schedule by seniority. An employee's starting time may be changed by notice given at least seventy-two (72) hours in advance. The company may schedule shifts and work weeks in order to meet customer requirements. A schedule of individual starting time may be established by mutual agreement between the company and the employee. An employee's scheduled off days will include Sunday. An employee working four (4) ten (10) hour days will have three consecutive days off, one of which will be Sunday.

ARTICLE 33
MAINTENANCE OF STANDARDS

33.01 All conditions of employment relating to wages, hours of work, overtime differentials and general working conditions shall be maintained at not less than the highest standard in effect at the time of the signing of this agreement, and the conditions of employment shall be improved wherever specific provisions of this section shall not apply to inadvertent or bona fide errors made by the company or the union in applying the terms and conditions of this agreement if such error is corrected within ninety (90) days from the date of knowledge or error.

33.02 This provision does not give the company the right to impose or continue wages, hours and working conditions less than those contained in this agreement, nor does this provision apply to terms or conditions substituted or changed during the course of negotiations for this agreement.

QUESTIONS

1. What was the issue to be decided by the arbitrator? Do you agree with the union's statement of the issue? Discuss.

2. Did the company's action violate Article 25.02? Article 33?

3. The parties did not discuss Article 11. If you were the company representative in this case, would you have cited Article 11? Why, or why not?

4. How would you have ruled in this case, if you had been the arbitrator?

69. The Pregnant Laboratory Analyst

Company:
  Cities Service Company, Lube Plant, Lake Charles, Louisiana
Union:
  Oil, Chemical and Atomic Workers International Union, Local No. 4-500

BACKGROUND

Lisa Hall[1] was first employed by the Cities Service Company (hereafter to be referred to as CITGO) in July, 1979, as a laborer in the Lake Charles plant. About two years later, she bid on and was awarded a job in the laboratory department. There was only one job classification in the laboratory, that of *analyst.* This job, however, was divided into three job assignments—*tester, sampler,* and *utility pool*—and such assignments were based on seniority progression. The most desirable job was that of tester, who worked at a laboratory table using various chemicals. The tester's job required little physical exertion. It was also the most interesting and challenging of the three jobs. On the other hand, it also presented a potential health hazard to those few persons who were allergic to certain toxic chemicals utilized in the tests, even though the laboratory was well ventilated, was outfitted with modern safety equipment, and utilized state-of-the-art safety procedures. The sampler's duties, however, required considerable physical exertion as the samples had to be collected throughout the plant and brought to the laboratory. The utility pool employees worked as samplers, on the sampler truck, or at the testing table to fill in as needed. Exercising her seniority rights, Ms. Hall had bid for and been awarded the position of analyst on July 1, 1981. She was assigned to duties as a sampler. In August or September, 1981 Hall became pregnant. After becoming pregnant, she attempted to continue her work on the sampler truck, but soon discovered that the physical exertion, climbing and lifting, caused her to have cramps and to bleed. She approached her supervisor, Robert Jenkins, and requested that she be allowed to transfer into the utility pool, where there were some vacancies at the time. Hall said that she felt that she could perform the job assignments

---

[1] The names of all individuals have been disguised.

in utility without difficulty, since she had previously worked in that area and knew that a sustained level of physical exertion was not required. Furthermore, she knew of two other women who had worked in the utility pool almost the entire term of their pregnancies.

This request was denied by supervision, however, on the grounds that Article III, Section 6(i) of the labor agreement stated that, "After an employee is awarded and/or accepts a permanent job vacancy, he is not eligible to bid for one (1) year unless he is disqualified from his new assignment."[2] Ms. Hall then requested a transfer as a hardship case. This request was likewise denied.

Hall then requested that she be scheduled to work at the laboratory testing table, which required less physical exertion than the sampler position, and that a more senior person work the truck until an anticipated opening at the table occurred. Her supervisor likewise refused this request.

The only remaining alternative for Lisa Hall was to request sick leave. She and her union steward claimed that she was advised by her supervisor, Jenkins, that the only way that she could obtain sick leave was to secure a doctor's statement certifying that she could not work around toxic chemicals because of possible damage to the unborn child. Her supervisor later disputed her statement about this, saying that he did not give her such instructions. In any event, Hall secured a medical statement to this effect from her doctor, and she then applied for and was granted sick pay, which she subsequently exhausted along with all vacation pay benefits. After depletion of these benefits, Hall was without a source of income during the remaining months of her pregnancy.[3]

About two years later, in October 1983, Hall and her union steward discovered that another employee, Roy Ruger, had requested an accommodation similar to that which Hall had requested in 1981. The difference, however, was that his request had been granted. Ruger had a gallbladder operation in August, 1983. As he was nearing exhaustion of his full sick pay benefits, his supervisor, again Robert Jenkins, arranged for him to return to the laboratory and work on the testing table, and a more senior employee, Mary Okum, was assigned from the testing table to the sampler truck. There was a dispute as to how the switch was actually accomplished. The union contended that it was a simple case of "inverted seniority." The senior tester, Okum, without her consent, was scheduled to work the more junior sampler job, and Ruger was temporarily assigned to the table. The company, however,

---

[2] See Appendix to this case for relevant clauses of the contract.

[3] Lisa Hall was off work because of her pregnancy from October 1981 until August 1982.

maintained that the switch was made by mutual consent. Ms. Hall further discovered at this time that Ruger, as well as other employees, had been permitted to transfer into the utility pool, even though they had held their previous assignments for less than one year.

Lisa Hall and the union concluded that she had been discriminated against by the company, and a grievance was filed on October 28, 1983. On November 14, 1983, the company, through her supervisor, Robert Jenkins, responded that:

> This grievance is not timely and the validity of this complaint as a grievance is questionable.
>
> In answer to the complaint as filed, the company's position on limited duty is that it does not accommodate non-job-related medical conditions and has historically only allowed employees to return to work when they can return to full duty. In Mr. Ruger's case, however, supervision deviated from its position due to the short period that Mr. Ruger needed a special assignment to accommodate his condition (1 week). The company, however, now fully realizes that it erred in its judgment and wishes to assure the union that it will not again occur.
>
> This complaint refers to 'Inverted Seniority,' however, the current labor agreement contains no provisions for artificial separation of duties in the analyst classification. As negotiated in 1977, an employee within the analyst classification is subject to perform any job to which he/she may be assigned.
>
> In conclusion no discrimination or other violations of the labor agreement occurred in this case.

The parties failed to resolve the dispute through the various steps of the grievance procedure. The union issued a demand for final and binding arbitration as provided in the collective agreement.

The parties were unable to stipulate the wording of the issue and requested that the arbitrator determine the exact wording of the issue(s) to be resolved. The union version of the issue was:

> Whether Ms. Lisa Hall had been discriminated against by CITGO in contravention of Article XVI, the antidiscrimination article. This would be . . . on the basis of her sex. . . . If so, what would the remedy be?

The company's version of the issue was:

1. Was the grievance filed timely?
2. Does grievant have standing to complain about action the company took concerning Mr. Ruger?
3. Did the company discriminate against Ms. Hall on the basis of sex in 1981 by refusing to assign her the lighter duty of tester?"

POSITION OF THE UNION

The union argued that Lisa Hall, a pregnant female, was denied her requests to bid into the utility pool and/or be scheduled to the laboratory table, where the job duties were relatively less strenuous than on the sampler truck. Her requests were based upon her physical inability to work the truck due to her condition. Hall was treated unequally in that the same or similar requests were granted to others, particularly Roy Ruger. The company had failed to establish a legitimate reason for these disparities. Accordingly, the grievance should be sustained.

In support of this position the union offered the following evidence and conclusions:

First, Article XVI of the agreement prohibited any kind of discrimination based on sex. Lisa Hall was pregnant in late 1981. She was unable to perform her regularly assigned sampler duties because of the physical exertion that was involved in working on the truck. The employee requested that she be allowed to bid into the utility pool. There was no credible evidence that she could not have performed utility duties; indeed, two other employees had successfully performed utility duties during the full term of their pregnancies. Despite the fact that the agreement stated that a permanent employee in the laboratory or in another department could not bid into utility until she or he had held a prior position for one year, Mr. Ruger—as well as other employees—was allowed to do so. This contention was not refuted by the company. Thus, Ms. Hall was discriminated against because of her pregnancy.

Second, although the company contended that the cases of Ms. Hall and Mr. Ruger were quite dissimilar, such was not actually the case. Mr. Ruger was scheduled to work on the laboratory testing table, while a more senior employee was scheduled to leave the table and work on the sampler truck. This was not a voluntary swap in positions mutually agreed to by the employees involved. The union also noted that Mr. Ruger was medically incapable of lifting heavy objects for a four-week period. Ms. Hall was offered no help by Mr. Jenkins in her time of distress. Yet he readily accommodated a male employee.

The union offered the following exchange during the grievance hearings in support of its position:

Union Attorney:

> Mr. Jenkins, you didn't attempt to get a volunteer or even suggest that. However, you were ready, willing and able to suggest that with respect to Mr. Ruger. And not only that, you didn't ask, you just told Ms. Okum that you were going to do that, and she just shrugged. Correct?

Jenkins:

That's correct.

The union also referred to the following conversation involving Roy Ruger from the grievance hearings:

Union Attorney:

Relate to me what occurred when you came back to work. How did you arrange to work on the testing table?

Ruger:

Well, I can't remember who called who, but I remember the conversation between myself and Mr. Jenkins. The conversation was basically that my doctor was not going to release me to do heavy lifting for another two weeks, that's what Dr. Visser had told me. And Mr. Jenkins said, if it's the truck keeping me from coming back to work, that we could work around that, I believe that is just about exactly what he said. I said, yes, it was the truck keeping me from coming back to work. He said, get a release from your doctor and see the company doctor, which is exactly what I did. And the doctor wrote across the release, no heavy lifting, I believe it said for two weeks, if I am not mistaken.

Third, while the company contended that Lisa Hall could not work as a tester because of a potential toxic chemical danger, the union argued, "The truth is that when her requests were denied, she had no alternative but to request sick leave. And the only way she could obtain sick leave, as she was instructed by her supervisor, was to secure a doctor's certificate that she could not work around the chemicals. Thus, the doctor's certificate only reflected instructions from Mr. Jenkins. Nor was management able, through the testimony of the company doctor, to prove that the chemicals listed were fetal-toxic. Actually, the employer had no policy which would have prevented Ms. Hall from working at the laboratory testing table."

Fourth, the union maintained that the company's argument that the grievance was untimely had no merit. A person could not be expected to file a grievance until he or she was aware of the action upon which the grievance was based. Hall's requests were denied in 1981; however, the circumstances creating the basis of her charge of unequal treatment were not apparent until October 1983. Upon discovery of these circumstances, the grievance was filed within the ten-day grace period and thus was timely.

The union held that the grievance was fully meritorious; that Lisa Hall should have been given a position within the classification of analyst that she was able to perform during her pregnancy; and that she be made whole for all losses sustained as a result of the company's action.

POSITION OF THE COMPANY

Both in the arbitration hearing and in its post-hearing brief, the company contended that the evidence clearly indicated that Hall's supervisor, Robert Jenkins, dealt with Hall in an honest and open manner, doing everything he could to help her at the time. In Mr. Ruger's case, Mr. Jenkins did everything he could to help him. That was equal treatment, not sexual discrimination. There had been no evidence presented by the union to establish that the company intended to discriminate on the basis of sex.

Ms. Hall failed to file her grievance within the time limits established by the agreement. She had no basis for complaining about any company action taken in regard to Mr. Ruger. Additionally, she was not able to prove her *prima facie* case because, according to the medical report in evidence, she was physically and medically unable to do the work. Further, even if she had been able to work, there was no one willing to trade functions with her for seven months.

The company maintained that Hall did not prove that there was sexual discrimination in her case, and in fact, there was sufficient evidence to show that there was, in fact, no sexual discrimination.

In its post-hearing brief, the company requested that the arbitrator take particular note of the following:

> First, the grievance was certainly untimely in that it was filed in November 1983, yet Ms. Hall complained about an incident which occurred in September 1981. In September 1981 the employee suffered no loss of seniority or loss of pay. The agreement requires that a grievance be filed "within ten (10) working days after the occurrence." This the union failed to do.
>
> Second, Lisa Hall had no standing to complain about the company action in regard to Mr. Ruger when the assignments were switched between Okum and Ruger. Ms. Hall was not adversely affected in any way. The only person who was possibly damaged was Ms. Okum, and since she had agreed to the change no grievance was filed.
>
> Third, the company did not discriminate against the employee on the basis of her sex by refusing to assign her to the light duty as a tester. Ms. Hall cannot even show a *prima facie* case of sexual discrimination. She simply was not qualified to work as a tester for a number of reasons. Her own physician stated that she could not work around toxic chemicals because of the effect of chemicals on the fetus. Furthermore, supervision could not force a senior tester off the table and allow Ms. Hall to claim that job. No one volunteered to trade with her, and management could not force a change in work assignment. In the Ruger case, Ms. Okum volunteered to make the change, thus this case has no bearing on the charge of sexual discrimination. The truth is Mr. Jenkins did everything that he could do to help Ms. Hall. The grievance therefore, is completely without merit. It should be denied and dismissed in its entirety.

APPENDIX

Relevant provisions of the agreement follow:

Article III—Seniority

Section 6(i). After an employee is awarded and/or accepts a permanent job vacancy, he is not eligible to bid for one (1) year unless he is disqualified from his new assignment.

Article XVI—Discrimination

Section 1. Discrimination—There shall be no discrimination against any applicant for employment or against any employee in regard to promotion, discharge, layoff, sickness, accident, insurance, thrift plan or retirement plan benefits, on account of sex, race, national origin, creed or color or on account of any activity undertaken in good faith in his capacity as a union representative of other employees.

Article XVIII—Grievance and Arbitration

Section 1. If any differences, disputes or complaints arise over the interpretation or application of the contents of this agreement, there shall be an earnest effort on the part of the parties to settle such promptly through the following steps: . . . .

Section 6. No grievance may be presented later than ten (10) calendar days after the occurrence from which such grievance arose.

QUESTIONS

1. The parties were unable to stipulate the wording of the issue to be decided by the arbitrator. If you were the arbitrator, how would you word the issue?

2. Had Lisa Hall been treated differently from other employees under similar circumstances? Why, or why not?

3. Why is a case of this nature of particular concern to both the company and the union? Discuss.

4. If you were the arbitrator, how would you rule in this case? Explain your reasoning.

70. The Police Detective's Request for a Switch of Shifts

Employer:
Town of Wilton, Massachussetts

Union:
American Federation of State, City, and Municipal Employees, Local 1492

BACKGROUND

On September 10, 1986, police detective Kevin Tarrell[1] submitted a request to switch shifts with detective Eric Bell on September 23, 1986. Tarrell was scheduled to work the 3:00 to 11:00 P.M. shift; Bell was scheduled to work the 7:30 A.M. to 3:30 P.M. shift. Bell had agreed to the switch. Tarrell's desire to switch was prompted by his desire to referee a tag football game at 4:00 P.M. and also engage in a 6:00 P.M. game of tag football as a player. Unless he switched shifts with detective Bell, he would miss the games. These games were the first league games of the season and his attendance was very important to detective Tarrell, especially since he had helped organize the league and was one of its three sponsors.

Following standard procedures, detective Tarrell filled out the proper form well in advance and submitted it to police Captain Raymond Towle, who denied the request. The captain's denial of the request was affirmed by Chief of Police Carlos Tallio.

Detective Tarrell worked his scheduled shift, missed out on refereeing the tag football game, and would have missed playing in his football game, except that it had been canceled. Detective Tarrell stated that had he been granted the switch in shifts, he would have been able also to perform a traffic control job at a local plant from 9:00 to 10:00 P.M. that night, for which he would have received $40. He also would have received $10 for refereeing the tag football game.

The parties were unable to resolve their dispute, so the issue was referred to an impartial arbitrator according to provisions of the agreement.[2]

---

[1] The names of all individuals have been disguised.

[2] See Appendix to this case for relevant provisions of the contract.

POSITION OF THE UNION

Detective Tarrell testified that he had switched shifts on several previous occasions for various reasons. At times he switched to play football or baseball, and the requests were always granted. The union introduced about 60 requests for switching shifts by several police personnel, showing that they were granted. Detective Tarrell claimed that he lost $50.00 because the switch had been denied by Chief Tallio. Tarrell also said that the game he had been planning to play had been canceled after he requested the shift change, and that he had not been notified of the cancellation until an hour prior to the game's scheduled start.

Detective Eric Bell testified about the history of Article VII, Section 5, governing switch changes. Section 5 first appeared in the August 1983 agreement. Its purpose was to permit officers to switch shifts at any time. He stated that after it had been signed, no one had ever been denied a request, except in this instance.

Sergeant John Ferris also testified that as the former union president, he was familiar with the negotiations over Section 5. The town, according to him, did not even request any limitation as to the conditions under which requests to switch would be honored. He acknowledged that before August 1983, some requests had been denied.

The union requested that the arbitrator require that the town grant all requests for switching shifts in the future and reimburse detective Kevin Tarrell in the amount of $50 for income lost as a result of the town's refusal to grant his request to switch shifts with detective Eric Bell.

POSITION OF THE CITY

In denying detective Tarrell's request to switch shifts with detective Eric Bell, Chief Carlos Tallio set forth his reasons for his action in a long letter dated September 27, 1986.

Chief Tallio stated in the letter that switching to play football was "an abuse of the reason" for having the switch provision in the contract. He indicated he had no opposition to shift changes "to attend a function or conduct business of an important nature that could not be carried out at any other time, and is of a special nature in that it is important to the officer, his family, or marks a special event or occasion." He wrote that "playing football was of little consequence and not of special significance" and "did not fit into the criteria" under the contract section governing switches.

The letter then referred to Tarrell's recently broken hand. Chief Tallio expressed concern that it was not fully mended. He also stated that Tarrell's doctor had not given him permission to play football, and that Tarrell's plan to play with his hand in a cast was a foolish course of action. The letter pointed out to Tarrell that during the past three years, "You have sustained three major injuries all related to playing sports. The last injury of July 1986, resulted in the loss of 23 sick leave days at a cost of $2,625.99 . . . for no service rendered. . . . In addition, you missed 21 sick days plus eight leave days because you injured your face in 1982; and, you missed six sick days in 1985 because of a knee injury. . . . You risk your future health, your position as a police officer, and career in the law enforcement profession, and the safety of your fellow officers, when you cannot work or work to full capacity." The letter further stated that, "while I cannot prohibit your participation in these activities, I do not feel that it is the responsibility of the police administration to provide special time allotments or shift changes to accommodate scheduling of your recreational activities."

The town of Wilton argued that it had the right to reject Tarrell's shift switch because: (1) his reason for switching swifts was frivolous and was not consistent with the town's intent of accommodating the serious needs of officers to switch shifts; (2) it was not consistent with efficiency, as set forth in the preamble to the agreement; (3) Tarrell had been seriously injured three times in four years while engaged in sports activities; and, (4) he was still recuperating from a sports injury.

Chief Tallio testified that "this decision to deny the switch was appropriate, sound, and consistent with the agreement and in the best interests of both the town, as well as Detective Tarrell." The town also pointed to Article I, Section 3, as giving it inherent authority to refuse a request for a switch. Chief Tallio testified that on occasion requests were denied, although he was unable to produce any written denials, other than that of Tarrell.

The town also contended that the request for a switch of shifts was not merely a notice that police officers intended to switch. It was a "request" that had to be approved and signed by the chief of police. This implied the power to disapprove and reject. The town maintained that Captain Towle, who reviewed these requests, would consider: (1) the level of coverage, such as duration, nature of assignments, etc.; (2) whether the two officers were capable of performing each other's work; (3) whether the officers were of the same rank; and (4) the reason for the request. With respect to denial of requests for switch of shifts, Chief Tallio testified that he once denied a request for a change of shifts by Sergeant Lambio. He said that he made that decision because the officer with whom he was asking to switch could not perform dispatching duties, which were part of Lambio's responsibilities, and also because the reason that Lambio wished to switch was to attend a Saturday night party.

For the reasons cited above, the town requested that the arbitrator deny the grievance in its entirety.

APPENDIX

Relevant Provisions of the Collective Agreement

PREAMBLE

This agreement has been made in order to . . . ensure the efficiency, and continuity of the department and the performance of the duties of its personnel. . . .

ARTICLE I

Section 3. There are no provisions in this agreement that shall deem to limit or curtail the Town in any way in the exercise of the rights, powers and authority which the Town had prior to the effective date of this agreement, unless and only to the extent that, provisions of this agreement specifically curtail or limit such rights, powers and authority.

ARTICLE VII

Section 5. The practice of officers switching shifts and days off shall be allowed whenever they choose, providing the shifts are covered and both individuals are in agreement between them. If someone is assigned overtime the employee shall be permitted to give it away and worked by another employee, at no additional cost to the Town, but in the event the employee is unsuccessful in getting another to work in his place the employee shall be required to work the overtime.

QUESTIONS

1. Prepare a statement of the issue that the arbitrator must address in this case.
2. Why did chief of police, Carlos Tallio, refuse Detective Tarrell's request to switch shifts with Detective Bell? Were these valid reasons under the collective bargaining agreement?
3. How would you have ruled in this case? Discuss.

71. The Lunch-Time Tipplers

Employer:
Kalamazoo County Road Commission, Kalamazoo, Michigan
Union:
Teamsters State, County and Municipal Workers, Local 214

BACKGROUND

On July 8, 1986, two employees of the Kalamazoo County Road Commission were patching roads adjacent to a public golf course. During their lunch period, which was from 11:30 A.M. to 12:00 noon, they drove their truck to the restaurant at the golf course for lunch. During the course of the luncheon, Paul Grainger[1] consumed two to four bottles of beer and Roy Steen consumed one or two wine coolers. The precise amount consumed later became a matter of dispute between the two employees and Herbert Larger, manager of the Road Commission. When the two employees returned to the Commission yard shortly after 3:00 P.M. (their work day started at 7:30 A.M. and ended at 4:00 P.M.) they were each handed the following written disciplinary suspension, signed by Larger:

> You are hereby suspended under the provisions of Article III, Section 1 of our current Union contract. This disciplinary action is assessed for violation of Art. XV, Sec. 2(a), Rule (h), "Drinking, possession or use of any alcoholic beverage or controlled substance without a doctor's prescription on Commission's time, premises or equipment, or reporting to work while under the influence of alcoholic beverages or controlled substances without a doctor's prescription."
>
> On 7/8/86 you consumed alcoholic beverages during working hours at the golf course on East C Avenue. This was reported to us by the owner of this facility. A determination as to further disciplinary action, including possible discharge, will be made within the next five (5) regularly scheduled working days.[2]

This matter came to Larger's attention on the afternoon of July 11, when the owner of the golf course telephoned to complain that two Road Commission employees working nearby had tracked tar onto the clubhouse carpet. During the conversation, the golf course manager asked if the Road Commission had a policy of allowing its employees to

---

[1] The names of all individuals have been disguised.
[2] See Appendix to this case for relevant contract provisions.

drink alcoholic beverages with their lunch. Larger was out of the office at the time, but when he returned from lunch at 1:20 P.M., he called the club owner, who was out of his office. They were able to arrange a telephone conversation at approximately 2:30 P.M. In the conversation, the club owner confirmed that the two individuals had been in the club for lunch, and he said that they had consumed three or four beers and a couple of wine coolers. Larger immediately wrote up the notice of suspension that he handed Grainger and Steen when they returned to the yard.

On July 11, following a brief meeting on July 9 that included Larger, Grainger, Steen, and the union business agent, Larger issued the following notice of termination to both employees:

> I have reviewed the situation and occurrences which resulted in your suspension under the provisions of Article III, Section 1 of our contract on July 8, 1986. I have also reviewed your work record.
>
> The decision reached as a result of these reviews is that your employment with this Commission will be and is terminated as of 4:00 P.M., July 11, 1986.

Both Grainger and Steen protested the action taken by the Commission. Grainger filed the following grievance on July 14:

> On 7/8/86 Roy Steen and I were assigned to patch East C Avenue from 40th Street to the County Line. At 11:30 we were close to the Maple Golf Course. I suggested to Steen we have a hot sandwich; with the sandwich I consumed two beers and Steen had one wine cooler. This was reported to KCRC by the owner of the facility—though the KCRC never verified this statement by calling or visiting the golf course.
>
> At a meeting with Herbert Larger and my Union representative on 7/9/86, Herbert stated that the half hour for lunch was "our" half hour, not the KCRC's, but returning to work under the "influence of alcoholic beverages" was his concern. If KCRC thought Steen who was drinking or myself were "under the influence of alcoholic beverages," why didn't they come out to talk to us or relieve us of the equipment. Three and a half hours later we were handed reprimand notices back at the KCRC offices. This was done without any questions asked about what we did or didn't do for lunch. The KCRC had taken it upon themselves to convict us of "under the influence of alcoholic beverages" without a question being asked about the incident. No one seemed to care about the persons using the equipment until three and a half hours later, after we had driven from Gull Lake to Kilgore Road. I am requesting immediate reinstatement of my job at KCRC and all seniority rights and back pay without any reprisals. Due to the actions taken by the KCRC in my above statement. Signed: Paul Grainger

Steen filed a similar grievance on July 12:

> On July 8, 1986, I was suspended from work for supposedly drinking on
> the job. I was not drinking on the job. With my lunch I had one bottle of
> wine cooler at the golf course on C Avenue east of 46th St. on my 30
> minute lunch—one half hour for which I'm not paid.
>
> Article X, Section 3 paragraph (a) does not define our lunch period as
> paid hours of work. Therefore, I was not working at the time. I did not
> drink on Commission property or in a Commission vehicle or on the job
> or Commission time. If the Commission was so concerned about the
> condition I was in after lunch, why didn't my foreman come out and
> check us out on the job? The one drink I had with my lunch did not in any
> way, shape, form, or fashion keep me from doing my job as it had to be
> performed after lunch was over.
>
> I feel it is only right to reinstate my employment with full back pay.
> Signed: Roy Steen

The grievances were processed through the grievance procedure
and were eventually submitted to arbitration. The parties presented
the following issues to the arbitrator:

> 1) Was the dismissal of Paul Grainger from his employment with the
> Kalamazoo County Road Commission for "cause"? If not, what shall the
> remedy be?
>
> 2) Was the dismissal of Roy Steen from his employment with the
> Kalamazoo County Road Commission for "cause"? If not, what shall the
> remedy be?

POSITION OF THE UNION

The union argued that the Commission failed to show that
Grainger and Steen were "drinking on Commission time, premises or
equipment." The unpaid lunch period was not work time or the Commission's time. The two employees worked the full 8 hours on July 8
and the full 40 hours during that week. The eight hours worked on
July 8 did not include the one-half-hour lunch period. Article X, Section 3(a) specifically provided for an "unpaid lunch period at or near
the mid-point of their eight (8) hours shift."

The union further claimed that the Commission did not support
the charge that Grainger and Steen were guilty of reporting to work
under the influence of an alcoholic beverage, since Larger did not
discuss the matter with them when they returned at 3:00 P.M. and did
not test them. No one from management visited the work site between
12:00 noon and 3:00 P.M., and no one prevented them from operating
the equipment during that period of time.

The union contended that there was a difference between "consuming alcoholic beverages" and "being under the influence of alcoholic beverages." In fact, the Commission had recognized this difference in the past, when it called crews in to work overtime on emergency snow removal. It permitted employees to operate equipment, even though it was known to management that some employees had consumed alcoholic beverages between the end of their regular work shift and the time at which they were recalled to operate snow removal equiment.

The union pointed out that a .10 percent blood alcohol level must be shown in the State of Michigan to prove that an individual was "operating a vehicle under the influence" of alcohol. A blood alcohol level of .07 percent indicated that the individual was "impaired." Any reading below the level of .07 percent indicated that alcohol had been consumed, but such consumption did not violate the statutes of the State of Michigan. The union also cited the ruling of the court in the *City of Lansing, Michigan* case that "under the influence" was synonymous with the terms "drunk" or "intoxicated." The Commission had not supported the charge that Grainger and Steen were either drunk or intoxicated.

The union further pointed out that the courts in the state of Michigan had determined that one element in determining whether an individual is "under the influence" is the effect of the substance on the individual, and that for an individual to be shown to be "under the influence," it must be shown that the ability of the individual to operate a vehicle was "substantially and materially affected." The Commission failed to prove that the ability of the two employees to operate a vehicle was less than that of an ordinary, careful, and prudent driver.

The union asserted that no one in management noticed anything wrong with the behavior of Grainger and Steen or indicated that they observed any signs that they were "impaired," such as slurred speech or unsteady gait. Larger was not aware that the two men had been drinking until he received a call from the bar owner. Larger did not then take action to observe the two men, nor did he drive to the scene to take charge. In any event, even if the men had been "impaired" in any way, the effects of the alcohol would have worn off during the three hours that they had worked unobserved by management.

The union contended that the Alcohol Awareness Calculator, on which the Commission relied for much of its case (a technique for estimating the alcohol level in the blood), was an unreliable method for determining the state of sobriety of an individual who had consumed alcohol. At best, it provided only a very rough estimate based upon estimated weight of the individual, rate at which the alcohol is consumed, and several other variables. However, the union pointed out that a given quantity of alcohol affected each individual differently, depending upon rate of consumption, type and quantity of food consumed during the period in question, and individual body tolerance for alcohol. Furthermore, there was no scientific proof that the blood alcohol level of an individual consuming two drinks in one half hour would be double that of the same individual consuming two drinks in one hour, as the Commission contended.

Finally, the union argued that the statements made by the golf course owner must be dismissed as hearsay, since he admitted that he did not personally observe Grainger and Steen consume the alcoholic beverages; rather, he was told by the person serving the drinks how many drinks had been consumed by the two men. Further, neither the golf course owner nor the persons serving the drinks was available to testify as to the amount of alcohol consumed by the two employees.

The union contended that the Kalamazoo County Road Commission did not sustain the burden of proof that Paul Grainger and Roy Steen were guilty of violating Article XV, Section 2(a), Rule (h) of the contract as charged, and they should be restored to their former positions and be made whole for all losses sustained as a consequence of the Commission's action.

POSITION OF THE ROAD COMMISSION

The Commission took strong issue with Grainger's and Steen's claim that they did not violate Article XV, Section 2(a), Rule (h) because they did not drink on the "Commission's time," but were rather free to do as they wished, since they were on their unpaid lunch period. The Commission argued that even though the lunch period was unpaid, it "was a part of the work day and shift" during which the Commission was responsible for the actions of its employees. If the Commission allowed its employees to drink alcoholic beverages during their unpaid lunch period and someone were injured as a consequence, the Commission would be liable. Rule (h) had been negotiated into the contract for this very purpose precisely because of the Commission's liability for the conduct of its employees during the work day.

With reference to the rule, the Commission pointed out that it stated that employees shall not possess or use alcoholic beverages on the Commission's time. Technically, the alcoholic beverage is in the employee's possession after being ingested because it is in his or her stomach and is being "used" for the next 40 to 70 minutes per drink as it is being assimilated into the blood stream. Therefore, since Grainger and Steen consumed somewhere between two and four drinks during a half-hour lunch period, they were in possession of an using alcoholic beverages on the Commission's time.

The Commission contended that these two employees were under the influence of alcohol when they returned to work, since the club owner stated that they had consumed three or four beers and a couple of wine coolers and the employees admitted to having at least two beers and one wine cooler.

The Commission argued that according to the Alcohol Awareness Calculator, both employees had blood alcohol levels between .06 and .08 percent, which put their condition, according to the Calculator, in the category of "Reflexes, vision, judgment and powers of concentration affected. Driving should not be attempted."

The Commission's claim that these two employees were "under the influence of alcohol" was based on their admission that they had consumed two beers and one wine cooler, although the golf course owner claimed that they had consumed about twice that amount. According to the Commission, the Alcohol Awareness Calculator indicated, that since each of the two men weighed about 200 pounds, their blood alcohol level would have been between .04 and .03 percent, if each had consumed two drinks in one hour. However, since each had consumed the alcohol in a period of 30 minutes, the blood alcohol level should be doubled, to .08 and .06 percent. This higher level of blood alcohol, according to the Calculator, put them in the range of being "under the influence of alcohol."

The Commission contended that the negotiated term in Rule (h), "under the influence," was intended to mean that the use or consumption of any alcohol or controlled substance by any Road Commission employee was prohibited in the interests of safety to the employee, his or her fellow workers, and the general public. Many employees, such as Grainger and Steen in this instance, must often work without close supervision for lengthy periods of time at considerable distances from the Commission yard. Management must be able to depend upon responsible behavior from these employees. They worked under conditions where the potential for injury to themselves and others was very high. They must be in full possession of all their faculties at all times. They must be alert, careful, and sensitive to situations that carry with them a high potential for an accident that may result in damage to property and equipment, injury, and even death. Larger stated most emphatically that there was no justifiable reason for any employee driving Road Commission vehicles to use alcohol or a controlled substance during the work day, and the unpaid lunch period was a part of the work day.

The Commission admitted, however, that on occasion emergencies had arisen when it had not been possible to monitor its policy on the consumption of alcohol as closely as it felt necessary. These emergencies had arisen during the winter, when sudden snow storms required management to call in crews to operate snow removal equipment. On occasion, one or more of these employees had consumed alcoholic beverages before returning to the job. The Commission stated that in those rare instances, it relied upon its observation of the behavior of the employees and their good judgment. It was a situation that it recognized to be undesirable, but one in which it had to weigh the danger of a possible accident from the failure to remove snow against the danger from an occasional employee's escaping detection and becoming involved in an accident because he or she was less than fully alert.

Larger admitted that no one in management noted any "impairment" of Grainger or Steen when they returned to the yard at about 3:00 P.M. on July 8. He pointed out, however, that any ill effects of the alcohol would probably have disappeared during the three-hour lapse between the consumption of the alcohol and the time that they returned to the yard. He further admitted that he did not observe them on the job that afternoon. His duties required that he visit job sites at various locations where job difficulties necessitated his presence. He was out of his office at the time that the golf course owner telephoned; by the time that he learned of the incident, Grainger and Steen were already returning to the yard.

The Commission reported that the consumption of alcohol or other controlled substances was not a problem and that no other cases of drinking during the work day had come to its attention. The Commission had made no arrangements for testing employees suspected of having consumed alcohol or other controlled substances during the work day, and it had not discussed the issue of possible testing with the union up to this time.

The Commission contended that both Grainger and Steen were well aware of Rule (h) and knew that the consumption of alcohol during the work day was a violation of the rule.

The Commission urged that the grievances submitted by Paul Grainger and Roy Steen be denied in their entirety.

APPENDIX

Relevant Provisions of the Agreement

ARTICLE II—GRIEVANCE PROCEDURE, ARBITRATION

Section 6(a).   All matters submitted to arbitration shall be submitted to the Michigan Employment Relations Commission in accordance with its procedures, within the time specified above and such procedures shall govern the arbitration hearing. The arbitrator shall have no power or authority to alter, amend, add to or subtract from the terms of this Agreement, and shall be required to render his decision within thirty (30) days after the close of said hearing.

Both parties agree to be bound by a proper award of the arbitrator and that the costs of any arbitration proceeding under this provision shall be borne equally between the parties. The expenses and salaries of witnesses and representatives of the Employer shall be borne by the Commission and the expenses and salaries of witnesses and representatives of the Union shall be borne by the Union.

ARTICLE III—DISCHARGE/DISCIPLINE

Section 1. The Commission agrees that employees shall not be discharged without cause from and after the date of this Agreement, and the Union will be furnished with a copy of such notice, but that in all instances in which the Commission may conclude that an employee's conduct may justify discharge or discipline, such employee shall first be suspended.

In all cases of suspension, the Commission shall allow the suspended employee an opportunity to discuss his suspension with his steward before being required to leave the property of the Commission. Such initial suspension shall be for not more than five (5) regularly scheduled working days. If the suspension is converted into a discharge, the decision of whether to discharge will be made within five (5) days after the initial suspension. During the period of initial suspension, the employee may, if he believes he has been unjustly dealt with, request a hearing in a meeting between the Union Grievance Committee, the Superintendent and the Engineer-Manager. After such hearing or if no such hearing is requested, the Engineer-Manager shall decide dependent upon the facts of the case, whether the suspension without pay already given is considered sufficient, should be extended, should be converted into a discharge or that no discipline should have been given. In the event the employee believes he has been unjustly disciplined, it shall be a proper subject for the Grievance Procedure, provided a written grievance with respect thereto is presented to the Engineer-Manager pursuant to the Second Step of the Grievance Procedure within two (2) working days after the Engineer-Manager makes his decision as set forth above.

Section 2. In the event it should be decided under the Grievance Procedure that the employee was unjustly discharged or suspended, the Commission shall reinstate such employee and pay full compensation, partial or no compensation as may be decided under the Grievance Procedure which compensation, if any, shall be at the rate of the employee's straight time earnings during the pay period immediately preceding the date of the discharge, less such compensation as he may have earned at other employment during such period and less any worker's or unemployment compensation received.

ARTICLE X—HOURS OF WORK

Section 1. *Day/Week Defined:* The normal work day shall consist of eight (8) hours and the normal work week shall consist of forty (40) hours.

Section 3(a). Employees shall be required to be ready to start work at the start of their shift and shall be required to remain at work until the end of their shift except for one fifteen (15) minute rest period at about the mid-point of the morning and another at about the mid-point of the afternoon, and except for the unpaid lunch period at or near the mid-point of their eight (8) hours shift.

ARTICLE XV—MISCELLANEOUS

Section 2(a), Rule (h). Drinking, possession or use of any alcoholic beverage or controlled substance without a doctor's prescription on Commission's time, premises or equipment, or reporting to work while under the influence of alcoholic beverages or controlled substance without a doctor's prescription is strictly forbidden. Employees violating this rule will be subject to discharge.

QUESTIONS

1. Was the Road Commission responsible for the acts of Grainger and Steen during their unpaid lunch period? Did it make any difference whether or not they used the Commission's truck to go to the restaurant? Discuss.

2. How do you assess Larger's decision-making process? Does his handling of this case meet the requirements for taking disciplinary action? Discuss.

3. How do you evaluate the Commission's reliance upon the Alcohol Awareness Calculator to support its claim that the two employees "were under the influence"?

4. Does it make any difference that Road Commission employees often must work for long periods of time without close supervision?

5. Section 2(a), Rule (h) is very specific and very stringent in its prohibition against the drinking, possession, or use of alcoholic beverages and drugs during working hours. How do you evaluate the Commission's action in the light of this Section?

72. Vacation Time After Recall?

Company:
> Hess Oil Virgin Islands Corporation

Union:
> United Steelworkers of America, Local 8526

BACKGROUND

On May 23, 1986, the union filed the following grievance on behalf of 39 employees who had been laid off on March 5, 1986, and who subsequently were rehired:

1. These employees are eligible for vacation time and pay as of January 1, 1986. The layoff has no bearing on their time for vacation.

2. Nature of Grievance: The company has refused to give the recalled employees time off for vacation as due them.

3. Settlement requested in Grievance: That the employees be given their time off for vacation as requested.

On March 5, 1986, a total of 83 bargaining unit employees were placed on layoff as a result of a serious reduction in plant operations. All 83 employees received their accrued vacation pay at the time of layoff. Subsequently 39 of these employees were called back to work prior to the filing of this grievance on May 23.

The union had no dispute with the company concerning the amount of vacation pay that the employees received at the time of layoff, and the matter of the amount of vacation pay was not at issue in this grievance. Rather, the issue centered on the interpretation of ARTICLE 10, VACATIONS,[1] of the collective agreement. As framed by the parties, the question was: After recall, was the company required to provide vacation time off without pay to employees, who, when placed on layoff, received all accrued vacation pay due them?

POSITION OF THE UNION

The union argued that a vacation meant more than pay. Vacation time was a right under the terms of the agreement, which provided that employees receive both vacation pay and time off. The 39 employ-

---

[1] See Appendix to this case for relevant clauses of this contract.

ees in question had received their accumulated vacation pay, but they were still due their time off.

The union pointed out that the last sentence of Section 10.7 of the agreement provided that the company had discretion only as to the scheduling of time off for vacation. Section 10.1 bestowed upon employees the right to vacation with pay, and nowhere in the agreement had this right been altered or taken away.

The union contended that past practice supported its position. Between 1973 and 1983 there had been several layoffs and recalls. While the company claimed that no employee ever raised the question of vacation time off without pay after recall after being paid for vacation at time of layoff, employees had always, without exception, been allowed time off without pay on a case-by-case basis. The union challenged the company to identify any employee who had been denied vacation time off following recall. The union stated that in the last 13 years, for which it had records, the company did not refuse the request of a single employee for unpaid vacation following recall.

Finally, the union claimed that employees were not on vacation while they were on layoff. Employees could not leave the island while on layoff, since they were required to report each week to the territorial unemployment office, as well as accept job interviews each week when referred by the territorial unemployment office. The practical effect of being on layoff was that employees could not visit friends and relatives off the island. According to the union, this did not constitute a vacation as that term implied under the collective agreement.

For the reasons cited above, the union requested that the arbitrator require that the company permit employees who had been laid off to take unpaid vacation time that had accrued up to the time of layoff, according to the schedule provided in the collective agreement.

POSITION OF THE COMPANY

The company asserted that this was the first claim by the union for accumulated time off for employees who had been laid off and subsequently rehired in the 18 years that the union had represented employees in the bargaining unit.

The company argued that there was no basis in either the wording of the collective agreement or in past practice that would entitle an employee to vacation time off without pay when recalled to work following a layoff where he or she had received all vacation money due at the time of layoff.

The employee relations manager admitted that, following the layoff of 1983, the company granted five requests for time off without pay after recall. He stated that vacations without pay following a layoff were not approached from the standpoint of "you're entitled to time off without pay." All requests by employees were received and dealt with on a case-by-case basis. The plant manager who had been employed at the Virgin Islands facility for many years was unable to provide the names of anyone who had been denied unpaid vacation when the employee requested such; but he said that he was certain that "not all requests had been granted." The employee relations manager also testified that he had studied the records of all employees who had been laid off, paid accumulated vacation allowance, and later rehired. As far as he could determine, the company reviewed every vacation request, and made a decision based on the needs of both the company and the individual employee.

The company requested that the arbitrator deny the union's claim that employees who had been paid their vacation allowance at the time of layoff had a "right" to receive an unpaid vacation upon recall to work.

APPENDIX

Relevant Provisions of the Agreement

ARTICLE 4
MANAGEMENT RIGHTS

Section 4.1. The parties hereto agree that management has and retains for itself, all rights to manage its business and properties, including but not limited to, the direction of its work force, the right to establish jobs, workloads, work schedules, and reasonable work rules, and to hire, assign, promote, demote, lay off, . . . or relieve employees from duty because of lack of work or reduction of work force, provided that the exercise of any such rights by the company shall not violate any of the explicit provisions of this agreement. However, it is agreed that this Section shall not be used to discriminate against any member of the union and any such discharge or disciplinary action shall be subject to the grievance procedure clause of this agreement.

ARTICLE 10
VACATIONS

Section 10.1. All covered employees shall be eligible for a vacation with pay beginning January 1st of each year as follows:

After one (1) continuous year of service with the company and up to the fifth year of service—fourteen (14) consecutive days (80 hours pay).

After five (5) continuous years of service with the company and up to the tenth (10) year of service—twenty-one (21) consecutive days (160 hours pay).

After ten (10) continuous years of service with the company—twenty-eight (28) consecutive days (160 hours pay).

Employees with less than one (1) continuous year of service on January 1st of each year shall be entitled to a vacation of 5/6 of a day times the number of complete months of service prior to January 1st.

In the case of an employee whose vacation is scheduled to start on a Monday and where such employee's regular work week is Monday through Friday, the company will endeavor to refrain from scheduling work for such employees on an overtime basis for the preceding Saturday and Sunday.

Section 10.2.   Vacation for each year shall be deemed earned as of January 1 of each calendar year of his employment. The amount of vacation to which an employee is eligible will be prorated on the basis of the number of full months which an employee is paid for prior to January 1st, i.e., one-twelfth ($1/12$) for each full month worked. An employee shall receive credit for having worked a full month if he works or is paid for at least fifteen (15) of his regular scheduled days during that month. "Paid" under Article 10 is defined as compensation for unworked holidays, vacations, military encampment and/or sick leave (excluding accident and sickness benefits). Compensatory illness or injury lasting not more than six months shall be deemed as time worked for vacation eligibility purposes. Any employee who works or has been paid for a minimum of 1,560 straight time hours in the vacation earning year, consisting of 2,080 hours, shall be entitled to receive full vacation benefit as provided under Section 10.1.

Section 10.3.   Pay for any vacation earned in accordance with Section 2 above shall be computed on the basis of the employee's permanent base rate of pay immediately prior to when such vacation is to be taken and shall be prorated according to the number of full months worked during the twelve month period prior to January 1st. An employee shall receive credit for having worked a full month if he works or is paid for at least fifteen (15) of his regularly scheduled days during that month. See Section 10.2 for definition of Paid.

Section 10.4.   Payment of vacation money to each active employee shall be made at the start of such employee's vacation time off, but not before January 1st. However, employees who are discharged or laid off or resign from employment during the twelve-month (12-month) period immediately preceding January 1st, shall be paid accrued vacation pay on the basis of one-twelfth ($1/12$) for each full month worked at the time of their discharge or layoff or resignation. Employees laid off, or terminated, during their probationary period, as herein defined, shall not be entitled to any vacation leave or any vacation pay accrued therefor.

Section 10.5.   If an employee is deceased, his beneficiary will receive pay for his accrued vacation. If an employee is inducted into U.S. Military Service, he will receive pay for his full accrued vacation through the end of the calendar year.

Section 10.6.   Vacations are noncumulative and must be taken before December 31st of the year in which they are due.

Section 10.7.   Employees will be requested to signify their desired vacation period by November 15 of the previous year. Employees will be requested to designate a first and second choice for the vacation period. Employees with 3 weeks or 4 weeks vacation will be allowed to split the vacation period one time.

The company will endeavor to grant vacations when requested and endeavor to give preference to the employees with the most company service. However, employees requesting split vacation periods will only be given preference for one vacation period. The final right in determination of the vacation period of the employee is reserved to determination by the company in accordance with its operational requirements.

QUESTIONS

1. When does a "practice" become a precedent? Had the company established a "past practice" that set a precedent that it could not unilaterally eliminate?

2. Did the language of the contract restrict the right of the company to deny these employees an unpaid vacation allowance? Discuss.

3. How would you decide this case? Explain your reasoning.

73. "Restructured" Out of the Company

Company:
> Flowers Baking Company of West Virginia, Inc., Bluefield, West Virginia

Union:
> International Brotherhood of Teamsters, Chauffeurs, Warehousemen and Helpers of America, Local Union No. 549

BACKGROUND

The Flowers Baking Company operated a bakery in Bluefield, West Virginia, with several distribution points in that and neighboring states. It had a warehouse at Big Stone Gap, Virginia, as well as warehouses at Harlan and Hazard, Kentucky.

Up until November 24, 1986, the company employed checker-loaders and route salespersons as full-time employees in these warehouses. Employees in both classifications were members of the Teamsters Union. The checker-loaders took empty trays brought in by route salespersons on their trucks and stacked them for return to Bluefield. The route salespersons assisted in this. Checker-loaders then took each salesperson's order according to customer, separating various breads, rolls, pastries, cookies, etc. These orders were loaded onto the trucks. The checker-loaders also were responsible for keeping their respective warehouses clean.

On November 24, 1986, the company restructured its distribution system. It eliminated the route salespersons and instituted a network of independent contractors who owned and operated their own trucks. They were each given a specific area within which they were licensed to sell the company's products.

The grievant, Paul Lowe,[1] had worked for the company at its Hazard facility from March 1980 until April 1984 as a route salesperson; since then he worked as a checker-loader. Lowe worked 40 hours per week and continued in his job until December 26, 1986, when his job was abolished and he was placed on layoff. At that time Lowe was offered custodial work of one hour per day, five days a week, an offer that he declined. The independent contractors owned and operated

---

[1] The name has been disguised.

their trucks, but they also performed on their own behalf the duties formerly performed by the checker-loaders.

This owner-operator system was installed at the same time at the Big Stone Gap and Harlan facilities. However, these installations were somewhat larger and continued to employ checker-loaders on a part-time basis. Also, these warehouses were somewhat different in that the product trays were stacked 22 high, requiring two people to raise them to that level. The product trays were stacked only 17 high at the Hazard warehouse, and this could be done by only one person, the owner-operator under the new system. Also, the product mix was more varied at the Big Stone Gap and Harlan installations than at Hazard, thus requiring more time to complete making up the orders.

After the conversion to owner-operators had been completed, Big Stone Gap and Harlan each had five routes with five owner-operators, and Hazard had eight routes with seven owner-operators.

Bakery products were transported from the Bluefield bakery to the distribution centers in large transport rigs, known in the trucking business as "eighteen wheelers." Previously the truck driver and the loader-checker together unloaded the transport rigs at each facility. The elimination of the checker-loader position at Hazard put 2.19 additional hours per week upon the transport drivers. The transport drivers at the Big Stone Gap and Harlan warehouses continued to have the assistance of the part-time checker-loaders, who continued to perform other duties on a limited basis. The checker-loaders at these two warehouses each worked about 20 hours per week.

On behalf of the grievant, Paul Lowe, the union filed a grievance that challenged the elimination of Lowe's position as a checker-loader. The grievance was eventually carried to arbitration.

The company and the union agreed that the issues to be resolved by the arbitrator were:

1. Did the Company have the authority under the labor agreement to eliminate the checker-loader position?
2. If not, was the position required to be a full-time or a part-time position?

POSITION OF THE UNION

The union challenged the company's sense of fair play, pointing out that Lowe had been a dedicated and very competent employee. His attendance and performance record was outstanding during the 15 years that he had been with the organization. In all those years, he had never been late for work, and he had been absent because of illness for only five days. The union urged that the company recognize Lowe's long and loyal service by finding other duties for him until such time as he was able to find other employment. The cost to the company would be minimal, since he earned $6.50 per hour. Furthermore, Hazard, Kentucky, was a small depressed city with few employment opportunities; Lowe would find it difficult to locate alternative employment.

The union also argued that the company violated Article 3 of the agreement,[2] which stated that "all conditions of employment . . . relating to wages, hours of work, and overtime differentials shall be maintained at not less than the highest standards in effect at the time of the signing of this agreement . . . . This provision does not give the employer the right to impose or continue wages, hours and overtime differentials less than those contained in this agreement." According to the union, the company could not eliminate Lowe's position under the written terms of this Article.

In addition, the union challenged the company under Article 12, which stated that, "All full-time hourly employees shall be guaranteed forty (40) hours per week. . . ." Clearly, the union held, the five hours per week that the company offered Lowe did not meet this requirement.

Finally, the union contended that the company violated Article 13.14, which provided that, "The company is not required to have a checker-loader unless the branch has six (6) or more routes." Under the newly structured sales and organizational setup, the Hazard facility had eight routes.

The union, on behalf of Paul Lowe, requested that the company be required to reinstate him as checker-loader, and that he be made whole for all losses suffered as a consequence of terminating him from his job.

POSITION OF THE COMPANY

The company contended that the union failed to carry its burden of proof, since the union had not proved that: (a) the decision to eliminate Paul Lowe's job was not acted on in good faith, and (b) that there existed a specific contractual prohibition against eliminating such a position.

The company argued that it had the right to eliminate the classification of checker-loader at the Hazard warehouse. In elaborating upon its position, the company held that Article 3.1 related to conditions of employment regarding wages, hours of work, and overtime differentials. It did not guarantee that the company must continue every

---

[2] See Appendix to this case for relevant provisions of the agreement.

classification and job as they existed at the time the labor agreement was executed. To hold otherwise could bankrupt any company.

The company further held that when it eliminated the position of checker-loader and went to the owner-operator independent contractor system of distribution—which the agreement did not prohibit—there were no longer any routes at the Hazard or other warehouses (as routes were spoken of in the labor agreement). At the time that the labor agreement was executed, the company was still employing bargaining unit employees as salespersons. After changing to the owner-operator structure, the company no longer had any routes. It sold areas of operation to owner-operated distributorships, who then determined what routes the independent owner-operator would have. Thus, the company held that the union's argument that Article 13.14 prohibited the elimination of the checker-loader classification at Hazard was incorrect. The same was true of the union's argument regarding Article 12.1. This Article only guaranteed "full-time hourly employees" 40 hours per week of employment. Lowe could not claim reinstatement and pay for lost wages under this provision, since he was not an employee of the company.

For the reasons listed above, the company requested that the arbitrator reject the grievance in its entirety.

APPENDIX

Relevant Provisions of the Agreement

ARTICLE 2—MANAGEMENT RIGHTS

2.1. The company reserves the right in accordance with its judgment to reprimand, suspend, discharge or otherwise discipline employees for just cause; hire, promote, demote, transfer, layoff and recall employees to work; determine the starting and quitting time and the number of hours and shifts to be worked; maintain the efficiency of employees; close down any branch or any part thereof or expand, alter, combine, transfer, assign or cease any job, division, operation or service; control and regulate the use of equipment and other property of the company; determine the number, location and operation of divisions and departments thereof, the products to be sold, the schedules of work, the assignment of work, and the size and composition of the work force, make or change rules, policies and practices not in conflict with the provisions of the agreement; introduce new or improved research, development, production, maintenance, services and distribution methods, materials, equipment, and otherwise generally manage the operations, direct the work force, and establish terms and conditions of employment, except as modified or restricted by a provision of this agreement.

ARTICLE 3—MAINTENANCE OF STANDARDS

3.1. The employer agrees that all conditions of employment in his individual operation relating to wages, hours of work, overtime differentials shall be maintained at not less than the highest standards in effect at the time of the signing of this agreement, and the conditions of employment shall be improved whenever specific provisions for improvement are made elsewhere in this agreement.

Any disagreement between the local union and the employer shall be subject to the grievance procedure with respect to this matter.

This provision does not give the employer the right to impose or continue wages, hours and overtime differentials less than those contained in this agreement.

ARTICLE 12—HOURS OF WORK

12.1. For the purpose of this agreement, the term 'work day' shall refer to a work shift and shall not refer to a calendar day. A work day commencing on one calendar day and ending on another calendar day shall be considered as one (1) work day. There shall be no split shifts for regular employees at any time. All full-time hourly employees shall be guaranteed forty (40) hours per week and pay at time and one-half (1½) for all hours worked in excess of eight (8) hours in any one (1) work day;

* * * * *

12.8. Part-time employees shall not be used to deprive regular full-time employees of the opportunity to work a full work week. A part-time employee is an employee hired to work less than thirty (30) hours per week and is not eligible for the forty (40) hour guarantee.

ARTICLE 13—GENERAL PROVISIONS

13.14. The company is not required to have a checker-loader unless the branch has six (6) or more routes.

This amendment will be initiated as per Article 18, Section 18.2, of the Agreement between West Virginia Baking Company, Inc., and Teamsters Local Union No. 549 dated November 20, 1983.

This amendment is mutually and jointly agreed to by both parties as prescribed under Article 18 and as follows:

Pertaining to the classification of checker-loader as set forth under Schedule A, a part-time employee shall be employed to work twenty (20) hours per week and restricted to the Big Stone Gap warehouse. This employee will not be eligible for (1) the forty (40) hour guarantee as set forth in Article 12, Section 12.1, or (2) the health and welfare plan as set forth in Article 10, Section 10.1. All other provisions of the Agreement will apply.

Either party to this amendment shall have the right to void this Agreement if they give the other party thirty (30) days written notice to that effect.

QUESTIONS

1. Do Articles 3, 12, and 13 carry less or more weight than Article 2 in determining whether or not the company could eliminate the checker-loader position? Discuss.

2. Compare and discuss issues and circumstances in this case with those in Case 32, "Was the Union Contract Proposal a 'Hot Cargo' Clause?"

3. How would you decide this case if you were the arbitrator?

74. COLA Takes a Dip

Company:

E. M. Smith & Company, Peoria, Illinois

Union:

International Association of Machinists and Aerospace Workers, AFL-CIO, Local Union 360

On May 23, 1986, the company sent the following letter to all members of the union and the union officers:

> The cost-of-living adjustment provided for in the May 1, 1986, Agreement with Local 360 effective the first pay period beginning on or after June 1, 1986, is $1.52.[1]
>
> The Base Index (January, 1981) stood at 260.7. The Comparison Price Index (Price Index for February, March and April 1986, averaged) is 321.6 (321.6 − 260.7 = 60.9 ÷ .4 = $1.52). The $1.52 represents a $0.04 reduction in the cost-of-living adjustment of $1.56 placed in effect the first day of the first pay period beginning on or after March 1, 1986.

On June 2, 1986 the company reduced COLA wages from $1.56 to $1.52 per hour.

BACKGROUND

Dating from 1974, a succession of collective bargaining agreements between the company and union provided for a Cost of Living Allowance (COLA) based on quarterly averages of the Consumer Price Index (CPI: 1967 = 100). In the years following 1974, the Index rose consistently; each quarterly recalculation resulted in a COLA increase. During the 1980s, however, the inflationary spiral slowed, leveled, and in the first quarter of 1986, the Index dropped eight-tenths of one point. When that occurred, management applied the contractual adjustment formula and lowered COLA wages four cents per hour across-the-board. The reduction was made upon the advice of the company attorneys and accountants who performed the COLA audits.

The union protested the reduction, contending that the company misinterpreted both the language and the intent of the COLA provision of the agreement. According to the union, the agreement contemplated only raises in COLA wages, not reductions; the allowance was

---

[1] See Appendix to this case for the relevant clause of the contract, including the formula for calculating COLA.

vested when granted and could not be unilaterally canceled. In a policy grievance on behalf of every member of the represented work force, the union demanded that all employees be compensated for the lost four cents per hour beginning June 2, 1986.

The company denied the grievance, claiming that COLA was an add-on to base wages intended only to protect purchasing power. Management maintained that the agreement called for quarterly calculations, which were entirely neutral; the contractual formula was simply an arithmetic function. According to the company, increments did not vest, and the company successfully resisted during the period 1974–86 numerous union negotiation proposals to roll COLA increases into base wages.

The grievance eventually was submitted to arbitration for final determination.

POSITION OF THE UNION

The union contended that while the language of the agreement might appear on the surface to be clear in its meaning, this was far from the true situation. The meaning of Section 18 was more clearly revealed by the way the COLA provision had been administered over the past 12 years than by a "sterile, insensitive, concentration on literal contractual words." Section 18 was not so clear as to mandate adoption of the company's position to the exclusion of every other possibility. The union urged that the arbitrator consider past practice and bargaining history. In the 12 years that the COLA provision had remained substantially unchanged from agreement to agreement, the company never imposed a wage reduction. Through time a practice developed that bound the company to one-way COLA adjustments: wages could go up, but never down.

The union asserted that it was not claiming that lack of negative adjustments created a binding practice, but rather that COLA wages had been handled in such a way that they had been mutually recognized components of base-wage rates, not independent add-ons.

The union admitted that it was unsuccessful in bargaining for base-wage roll-ins. Nevertheless, it insisted that the parties routinely treated the quarterly increases as base wages. COLA wages influenced far more than hourly compensation for work performed. They were incorporated into vacation pay, holiday pay, overtime pay, bereavement pay, and shift differentials. Moreover, every new employee received base wages plus COLA wages from his or her date of hire. The union maintained that the company had neither asserted nor preserved any substantive distinction between "regular" and COLA wages. The two had been lumped together as a single wage rate.

The union claimed that the company's pay reduction was nothing more than a "cynical attempt to seize an illegitimate advantage from inexact contractual language." It cited bargaining history to substantiate its position. The union agreed to modest wage increases only because it felt that the COLA increments were guaranteed. Union officers consistently had accepted relatively low increases each contractual term and were able to obtain ratification from the members because of tacit assurances that negotiated base rates were not actual rates—i.e., that the pay each employee would receive would be the composite of his or her base rate plus the protected COLA wage. The union asserted that management's negotiating teams accepted this presumption. There was a clear meeting of the minds on this issue. If there had been disagreement, the company negotiators most certainly would have held out for more definitive language. In fact, when the union attempted on two occasions to modify the contract so as to roll the accumulated COLA into the base rate, the company negotiators resisted, claiming in part that the language of Section 18 was clear and that any change was neither necessary nor desirable.

The union emphasized that the company never attempted to obtain contractual language authorizing reductions in COLA wages. It argued that such provisions were standard in industry and were well known to management negotiators. The union submitted the following section of a current contract between the IAM and an Oconomowoc, Wisconsin, machine shop as an example of a typical COLA contract clause:

31.3. Should the difference between the base figure in the first month and the last month of a specified period represent an increase in the cost of living, each full four-tenths (0.4) of a one (1) point rise in the Index shall mean a one cent (1¢) increase.

31.4. Should the difference between the base figure in the first month and the last month of a specified period represent a decrease in the cost of living, each full four-tenths (0.4) of a one (1) point fall in the Index shall mean a one cent (1¢) decrease.

Finally, the union pointed out that the company had, in fact, on two previous occasions rolled the accumulated COLA into the base rate. The union had successfully negotiated for wage increases on top of a roll-in of the accumulated COLA of $.53 at the end of the 1974–77 three-year agreement. At the end of the 1977–80 agreement, the company sought a change. The accumulated COLA was $1.03. The company proposed rolling in $.93 per hour and floating the remaining $.10 per hour. The union rejected the proposal, and the company retreated from its demand. The entire $1.03 was merged into the 1980–83 rate base.

The union admitted that the parties were unable to agree on rolling in the accumulated COLA increment of $.79 at the end of the 1980–83 agreement, and the entire $.79 was allowed to float with the CPI. Further, the parties were also unable to agree upon a provision to roll-in the accumulated COLA at the end of the 1983–86 agreement, which by that time had grown to $1.56 per hour since the 1980 roll-in. The union held that its demands for COLA roll-ins since 1980 were merely "housekeeping" items of no real significance, and its acquiescence on the roll-in of the accumulated COLA in no way altered the fact that the company was not permitted to reduce wage rates, even though the CPI declined.

The union urged the arbitrator to uphold its position and award all employees represented by the union the sum of $.04 per hour from June 2, 1986, to the present and to require that the company include the entire $1.56, plus any other COLA increases due under the contract until it expired in 1989.

POSITION OF THE COMPANY

The company argued that the COLA language was unambiguous and its meaning clear. It pointed out that Section 18 called only for quarterly adjustments, and it did not vest any adjustment through a wage roll-in. Unlike base wages, COLA wages stood alone, open to adjustment from quarter to quarter. The word "adjust" means to bring something into balance with an external condition. The external condition under Section 18 was the Base Index, that is, the CPI for January 1981. According to the company, the provision set a clearly defined pattern for each quarterly adjustment—a pattern "wholly premised on an impersonal mathematical computation." The company claimed that the only cause for a legitimate grievance would be a mathematical error, and since the union conceded that the calculations were accurate, the grievance had no merit.

The company pointed out that there had not been a decline in the CPI during the 12 years preceding the first quarter of 1986; adjustments had to reflect the continually increasing CPI. No binding practice could be found from this condition, since a practice was a "tacitly consensual reponse to repeated circumstances." In order for the union to claim the benefit of practice, it must establish that there had been a uniform reaction to substantially changed conditions over time. Twelve years was a substantial period of time; if the CPI had fluctuated upwards and downwards since 1974 without COLA reductions, a binding practice might have been established. But until the first quarter of 1986, there had been no downward movement. Management further asserted, "It is absurd to hold that the lack of COLA reductions in 12 years became a binding practice even though there was not a single quarter when a negative adjustment was possible under the contractual formula."

The company pointed out that the $.53 per hour COLA roll-in in 1977 was an issue of serious negotiation between the parties; it was not a mere "housekeeping" item as claimed by the union. The same was true of the $1.03 COLA roll-in in 1980, when the company attempted to negotiate a $.93 COLA roll-in.

The accumulated COLA increment in 1983 was $.79 per hour. Again the union demanded that the entire amount be incorporated into the base wage rates. The company countered with a proposal to continue floating the $.79 until June, 1984. Neither party accepted the other's demand, and the conflict was a major factor responsible for a three-day strike from May 1 to May 4, 1983. When the agreement was finally ratified by both the union and the company, it contained no mention of a roll-in. Thus, the $.79 increase from the previous contractual term continued to float throughout the 1983–86 term.

The company pointed out that the issue was again addressed in 1986. The union apparently was intent upon putting the issue of COLA roll-in to rest. To that end, it introduced the following proposed amendment to Section 18:

> SECTION 18; Cost-of-living: Change the wording of the last paragraph of "C" to read:
> ". . . in the case of the adjustment amount computed for the adjustment date next preceding the termination date of this Agreement, such adjustment shall form the base rate for the next labor agreement."

The proposal was rejected by the company. Nothing was rolled into base wages, and the six-year accumulation of $1.56 continued to float. Less than a month after the 1986 agreement was ratified, the CPI dropped and the company applied the $.04 reduction.

The company also asserted that the union was well aware of the fact that the company intended that the COLA continue to float. During the 1986 negotiations, the company's chief negotiator commented that the anticipated CPI reductions would result in lower total wages. The union negotiator took strong exception, insisting that Section 18, as it had continued to read since 1974, did not permit COLA reductions.

Finally, the company argued that when other companies and unions intended that COLA increments should be rolled into the base rates, they typically stated as such. The company cited the relevant clause from the current agreement between Kaiser Aluminum & Chemical Corporation and the United Steelworkers of America to illustrate its point:

Annual cost-of-living roll-in: In order that the annual rise in the cost-of-living adjustment may be fully reflected in the standard hourly wage scales, the cost-of-living adjustments . . . shall be calculated . . . and **included in the employee's standard hourly wage rate** in the calculation of pay for all hours paid for commencing on the respective October 6 adjustment date and continuing thereafter. . . . [Emphasis added]

The chief spokesman for the company concluded by stating that:

The contract is unambiguous and should be interpreted according to its clear meaning. The cost-of-living provisions mandate a quarterly, de novo, calculation of the cost-of-living adjustment. The mathematical process set forth in the contract determines the extent of that adjustment. The employer has followed the applicable mathematical process since 1975, and the June 1986 cost-of-living calculation accurately conforms to the contractual requirement.

The company urged, therefore, that the arbitrator should hold that the issue of COLA increment roll-in had been fully discussed during the 1986 negotiations, that no past practice for automatic COLA roll-in existed, that the contract was completely silent on the issue of rolling COLA increments into base wage rates, and that the grievance should be denied.

APPENDIX

Relevant Provisions of the Agreement

SECTION 18: COST-OF-LIVING CLAUSE

Cost-of-Living adjustment will be made in accordance with the succeeding provisions of this Section on the basis of changes in the Consumer Price Index For Urban Wage Earners and Clerical Workers (Revised CPI-W) published by the Bureau of Labor Statistics, United States Department of Labor (1967 = 100) hereinafter referred to as the "Price Index". For purposes hereof:

A. Base Index means the Price Index for January 1981 (260.7).

B. Comparison Price Index means the Price Index for February, March and April (averaged) next preceding the June adjustment date:

* * * * *

C. Adjustment Date means the first day of the first pay period beginning on or after each June 1 . . .

* * * * *

For each Adjustment Date, there shall be computed an adjustment amount which shall be an amount equal to one (1) cent per hour (without fractions) for each full 0.4 point by which the Comparison Price Index relating to that Adjustment Date exceeds the Base Price Index, and such adjustment amount shall remain in effect from the adjustment date for which it was computed only until the next succeeding adjustment date.

QUESTIONS

1. What are the major issues that the arbitrator is being asked to resolve?
2. Discuss past practice as it applied to this case.
3. Had COLA, in effect, been rolled into the basic wage? Why, or why not?
4. How would you, as arbitrator, be influenced by the fact that the parties discussed rolling COLA into the basic wage rate during contract negotiations? Discuss.
5. How would you rule in this case?

75. The "Rehabilitated" Employee

Company:
   Navistar International Corporation, Indianapolis, Indiana
Union:
   International Union, United Plant Guard Workers of America

BACKGROUND

On November 19, 1985, Anna Pelton[1] was working the second shift (3:00 P.M. to 11:00 P.M.) as a plant guard. At approximately 4:50 P.M., she was working in the gatehouse, which housed the plant protection headquarters. At that time, her supervisor, Lieutenant Raymond Varley, observed her slurred speech and abnormal behavior and became convinced that she was under the influence of either drugs or alcohol. He consulted the company's medical director, Dr. R. K. Dobson, who also observed her. In response to Dr. Dobson's questions, she denied that she had been drinking.

After being informed that she would be considered to be intoxicated, on the basis of observations of plant personnel, Pelton agreed to submit to a laboratory test for intoxication at Community Hospital. She was driven to the hospital by another plant guard.

A blood alcohol test administered to Pelton at approximately 6:29 P.M. on November 19, 1985, showed an alcohol reading of 22 milligrams per deciliter, or .232 percent of alcohol in the blood. Under Indiana law, *prima facie* evidence of intoxication is evidence of .10 percent or greater of alcohol in the blood (Ind. Code §9-11-1-7). Pelton was thereafter driven from the hospital to the plant accompanied by an acquaintance at approximately 7:52 P.M. Dr. Dobson received the results of the blood alcohol test by telephone on November 20, 1985, and he received the written results of the test shortly thereafter. On November 20, 1985, Pelton was discharged by the company for being intoxicated while on duty, in violation of company Rule 3.

The union did not refute the company's contention that Anna Pelton was under the influence of alcohol while at work on November 19, 1985. Rather it contended that the company treated her unfairly in comparison with its treatment of other company employees under like circumstances, who were represented by the United Auto Workers (UAW).

---

[1] The names of all individuals have been disguised.

Company Rule 3 provided as follows:

> Any employee who is under the influence of alcohol and/or drugs on company property, including parking lots, will be discharged.

Despite the specific language of Rule 3, labor relations director Stanley Poindexter stated that Navistar's treatment of other union-represented employees who had been found guilty of being intoxicated had been much different. While they had been discharged for the first offense, as provided by the rule, the company would reinstate an employee after six months to a year if he or she filed a grievance, and after discharge, successfully completed a company-approved alcohol rehabilitation program. The employee received no pay during the time off the job. Further, the employee, the union, and the company all had to sign a "last-chance" letter of agreement setting forth the terms under which the employee would be permitted to return to work for the company.

Typically, the last-chance agreement verified the company's rule concerning intoxication while on company property, as well as its rules concerning absenteeism, lateness, safety, and work performance. The agreement also required the discharged employee to conform to a continuous rehabilitation program tailored to the particular employee. The agreement concluded with a provision stating that if the employee were again observed on company property in an intoxicated condition, he or she would be required to undergo an alcohol test; if the individual refused or if this test evidenced the presence of alcohol in his or her system, the employee would be summarily discharged. In the case of those employees represented by the UAW who had been discharged for intoxication on company premises, the company also paid the employee's rehabilitation expenses for the first full month following the employee's discharge.

The company had followed this practice for six employees who had been represented by the UAW. The company did not argue that this practice was not applicable to plant guards represented by the United Guard Workers as well. Rather, it contended that had it complied with this practice when it discharged Anna Pelton.

Anna Pelton had previously been discharged by the company on April 28, 1985, under a charge that she had been intoxicated on the company's premises. She filed a grievance, denying that she had been intoxicated, contending instead that she had been under medication. She did not attend an alcohol rehabilitation program at that time. The parties settled her grievance on August 22, 1985, when they entered an agreement that provided in its entirety as follows:

> This grievance is resolved effective today, August 22, 1985 as follows: Anna Pelton will be reinstated effective Monday, August 26, 1985.

Anna Pelton will receive eight (8) weeks back pay at the straight time rate with payment being made as soon as practicable.

According to Pelton, her discharge on November 20, 1985, made her aware for the first time that she had lost control over her alcohol consumption and she needed help. She then voluntarily entered the Koala Center rehabilitation program in Lebanon, Indiana, which started out with a thirty-day inpatient program that was followed up by extensive ongoing aftercare outpatient care.

This Koala program was one of the programs that was approved by the company, but the company did not participate in Pelton's rehabilitation program as it had in the rehabilitation programs for the UAW employees. In the case of the UAW emplyees, the company closely monitored their rehabilitation through continuous progress reports it received directly from the Koala Center. In Pelton's case, the company was not apprised of her participation in the Koala program until after she had filed a grievance requesting reinstatement.

Pelton admitted at the grievance proceedings that she was currently a recovering alcoholic. She stated that she had not taken an alcoholic drink since her discharge on November 29, 1985. She was currently taking Antabuse and could not state whether she would be directed by her doctor to continue taking it for the rest of her life. She testified that she regularly attended Alcoholics Anonymous from three to six times per week. She also said that she remained under the care of Dr. Daniel Black, who provided her with a letter dated October 22, 1986, which stated in part that:

> She has been cooperative in treatment with me. She is taking Antabuse and cannot drink even very small amounts alcohol without becoming deathly ill.

The parties were unable to resolve the issues raised by Anna Pelton's grievance, and they requested that the arbitrator determine the issue(s) and render a decision.

POSITION OF THE UNION

The union acknowledged that the company practice regarding the rehabilitation of employees was a fair and just one. The union particularly commended the company for reinstating employees after a first offense of intoxication on company property, subject to their undertaking a rehabilitation program and thereafter being reinstated under the terms of a last-chance letter. However, the union argued that the company did not follow this practice in Pelton's case, and that she was, in effect, denied this second opportunity. In that regard, it contended that her discharge on April 28, 1985, was not a first occasion of intoxication on company property. Intoxication was never admitted by the employee or substantiated by the company. The final settlement of the April 28 incident was arrived at on August 22, 1985, and this made no mention of discharge for intoxication, nor did it contain any of the provisions included in last-chance letters provided the six UAW members.

The union pointed out that the labor-management agreement required that the company must show "just cause" to discharge an employee. The union held that the company, by its previous consistent past practice, had defined "just cause" for discharge because of intoxication. The company strayed from that past practice in the case of Anna Pelton; hence, the company had failed to establish that it had "just cause" to terminate her employment.

The union requested that the company reinstate Anna Pelton with full back pay and restore to her all other rights lost as a consequence of the company's action.

POSITION OF THE COMPANY

The company stated that it was sympathetic with Anna Pelton's battle with alcoholism, but the company held that the relevant question in this case was whether or not the company was obligated to provide its employees with an alcohol rehabilitation program.

The company argued that it had not treated Pelton differently in this case from the UAW employees who had been charged with intoxication on company premises. The company described the union's argument as creating a "revolving door" that would require the company to fire and rehire an employee until the employee was rehabilitated.

The company further argued that its practice gave an employee a second chance after a first discharge for intoxication, and that the UAW employees took it upon themselves to seek rehabilitation. In view of its reinstatement of Pelton on August 26, 1985, the company felt that it had given her as many chances to seek rehabilitation as it had given the UAW employees.

Finally, the company contended that as a result of her work as a plant guard, Pelton was fully aware of Rule 3; she was responsible for her own behavior and had a special duty to abide by company rules, including Rule 3. The company took the only action it could, considering that it had reinstated her after her first discharge for intoxication on the job.

The company requested that the arbitrator deny Anna Pelton's grievance.

QUESTIONS

1. What is the issue to be decided? If you were the union representative, how would you word the issue? How would you want to word the issue if you were the management representative? How would you state the issue if you were the arbitrator in this case?

2. Did the agreement signed by the union and the company on August 22, 1985, constitute Anna Pelton's "last chance"? Why, or why not?

3. Had the company treated Anna Pelton differently from other employees?

4. As a plant guard, should she have known of the seriousness of being intoxicated on the job? Does it make any difference that she was a plant guard, rather than a production employee? Why, or why not?

5. How would you rule in this case?

76. No Smoking in the Restrooms

Company:

National Pen and Pencil Company, Shelbyville, Tennessee

Union:

United Food and Commercial Workers, Local 1557

BACKGROUND

On March 17, 1982, the union and company signed a "Memorandum of Agreement" that read as follows:

Agreement On Monitoring Going To the Restroom:

When the Company can factually demonstrate abuse in a department or departments, the following will apply.

1. A letter will be given to each employee in the department stating that there is abuse in the department and if it is not corrected within one week the department will be monitored.

2. During this short term monitoring period employees will notify in some manner that they are going to the restroom to the person designated by the company.

Employees will not, however, have to leve their work station to make such notification. (It is sufficient to say something like, "I'm leaving", waving to the supervisor, pointing, etc.)

3. Monitoring periods will not exceed two weeks.

4. In some monitoring situations it will not be necessary to notify a supervisor that the employee is going to the restroom although someone (fellow worker closest to the exit) will be notified.

The parties to the basic collective agreement, which had been negotiated and signed on January 1, 1982, had agreed that management was encountering problems with "restroom abuse" in early 1982. The memorandum was concerned with time spent in the restrooms, over and above what was felt to be reasonable and proper for the performance of necessary biological functions. The memorandum was not incorporated into the 1982 agreement, nor was it discussed during negotiations or incorporated into the agreements of January 1, 1984, and January 1, 1986.[1]

On August 12, 1985 the plant manager sent all employees the following memorandum:

---

[1] See Appendix to this case for relevant clauses of the collective agreement of 1986.

The restroom privilege is being grossly abused and this must be corrected. I do not intend to deny anyone the use of a restroom, when it is truly needed, but I feel people are using them as a place to meet and/or smoke and talk. Too many people are going at once and staying too long.

In an effort to correct this situation, the following rule will go into effect immediately: Anyone going to the restroom must be released by a supervisor or floor person while they are gone. If this does not correct the problem, I will seriously consider eliminating smoking in the restrooms.

The union took no action with respect to the plant manager's memorandum, even though the union had not been consulted and the company had placed a formal limitation on smoking for the first time.

On April 23, 1986, the plant manager posted a new memorandum, establishing a new rule concerning smoking and the use of restrooms:

The restroom privilege is continuing to be abused by a considerable number of employees. The company does not intend to eliminate the rights of employees to smoke. It is, however, very concerned over the continued use of restrooms for the purpose of taking frequent and extended smoking breaks. Starting May 1, 1986 smoking will be confined to your designated rest areas and to the lunchroom. You will be able to smoke, if you wish, during your ten-minute paid break period in the middle of each half shift and during your thirty-minute unpaid lunch period. There will be no smoking in the restrooms at any time.

The union filed a grievance on April 29, 1986 as a class action on behalf of all employees, alleging that the collective agreement had been violated by a unilateral change in the company's work rules. The union also requested that the preliminary grievance procedure be waived in order to proceed directly to arbitration.

The parties were unable to agree upon a statement of the issue to be decided upon by the arbitrator and requested that the arbitrator both state the issue and render a decision.

POSITION OF THE UNION

The union argued that the memorandum agreement of March 17, 1982, a plan to control restroom privilege abuse, had been agreed upon and never revoked by the parties; therefore, the memorandum agreement was still in effect and binding on the parties. The company's unilaterally fashioned action, dated April 23, 1986, marked a substantial departure from the mutually agreed upon memorandum for "monitoring going to the restroom" negotiated in 1982.

The union also contended that in changing the work rules, which were subject to the 1982 memorandum agreement, the company violated the purpose and spirit of collective bargaining as clearly stated in Article 1 of the current agreement.

Finally, the union strongly stressed the fact that smoking in restrooms was historically allowed by the company. Permission to smoke thus constituted a well-established practice and condition of employment that could not be changed unilaterally by either party.

For the reasons given above, the union requested that the arbitrator uphold its grievance and require that the company rescind its memorandum of April 23, 1986.

POSITION OF THE COMPANY

The company held that it possessed express authority under Article 10 of the collective bargaining agreement "to establish and maintain reasonable work rules covering the operation and reasonable rules governing employee conduct. . . ." The company held that it was within its rights to attempt to correct the smoking problem by establishing additional work rules. While not mentioning the abuse of the smoking privilege in the 1982 memorandum, it was a matter of mutual concern to the union and the company as early as that time. The rules instituted by the company since 1982 were intended only to ensure plant productivity, while still maintaining the right of employees to smoke at reasonable times.

The company further argued that smoking during company paid time—except during the designated paid ten-minute breaks twice each full work shift—was not an employment right, and this included time in the restroom. Employees could also smoke during their lunch period while in the lunchroom. However, they would not be permitted to take additional breaks in the restrooms for the purpose of smoking.

Finally, the company contended that the memorandum agreed upon on March 17, 1982, was not made a part of the collective agreements of 1982, 1984, or 1986, nor was it mentioned during negotiations. Therefore, it had no effect on the current contract.

The company, for the reasons cited above, requested that the arbitrator deny the union's grievance in its entirety.

APPENDIX

Relevant Provisions of the Agreement:

ARTICLE 1—INTENT AND PURPOSE

The employer and the union each represents that the purpose and intent of this agreement is to promote cooperation and harmony, to recognize mutual interest, to provide a channel through which information and problems may be transmitted from one to the other, and to set forth the agreement relative to rates of pay, hours of work and other conditions of employment for the employees covered hereby. The employer and the union recognize that the success of the employer is both vital to management and to its employees, and agree to work to the end that efficient economical and profitable operations are maintained at the employer's plant covered by the agreement. The parties to the agreement will cooperate fully to secure the advancement and achievements of these purposes.

ARTICLE 10—MANAGEMENT RIGHTS

The right to manage the business and direct the working force, including but not limited to the right to plan, administer, direct and control plant operations, hire, and discipline for just cause, transfer or relieve employees from duty because of lack of work or for other legitimate reasons, the right to study or introduce new or improved production methods or facilities, and the right to establish and maintain reasonable work rules covering the operation and reasonable rules governing employee conduct, remain with the employer, provided, however, that this right shall be exercised with due regard for the rights of the employees and provided further that it will not be used for the purpose of discrimination against any employee.

ARTICLE 18—MEAL PERIOD

There shall be an unpaid meal period of thirty (30) minutes in the approximate middle of each shift.

ARTICLE 19—BREAKS

There will be a ten (10) minute company-paid break in the approximate middle of each half shift worked.

QUESTIONS

1. The parties failed to reach a mutually agreeable stipulation of the issue to be submitted to the arbitrator. Prepare a statement of the issue. How might the union wish to state the issue? How might the company wish to state the issue?

2. Was the memorandum of March 17, 1982, still in effect, or did it end with the expiration of the two-year agreement negotiated January 1, 1982? Discuss.

3. Was it the intent of the parties to control smoking in the restrooms in the memorandum of March 17, 1982?

4. Does Article 10 of the agreement give the company the right to prohibit smoking in the restrooms? Explain.

77. Too "Punk" to Work?

Company:
  Fisher Foods, Incorporated, Youngstown, Ohio
Union:
  United Food & Commercial Workers Union, Local 880

Fisher Foods operated a chain of grocery supermarkets throughout northeastern Ohio. The grievants, Thomas Peters and Harold Half,[1] were both part-time baggers at "Carl's Food and Drug Warehouse Supermarket," which was one of the company's supermarkets located in a blue collar neighborhood on the near west side of Youngstown, Ohio. Both were students in the local area—Peters at nearby Youngstown Fitch High School and Half at Youngstown State University.

On May 29, 1986, Peters was confronted at work by store manager Roger Zeis, who asked him why both sides of his head were shaved to the scalp in front of his ears and for about two inches above his ears. Peters said that his brother's hand had slipped while giving him a haircut the previous night and that shaving had been necessary to cover up the mistakes. Zeis made it clear that he disapproved of Peter's appearance, although he took no disciplinary action and permitted Peters to remain at work.

The following day Peters reported for work with a further modification of his hair style. He had extended the two-inch high shaved "white sides" beyond his ears to a "V" shape at the back of his skull. The hair above the shaved area remained long, however, so that the resulting effect was "somewhat bizarre," as Zeis described it. Zeis confronted Peters upon his arrival and advised him that he would not be permitted to work with his hair in that style, but that he could return to work when he had modified his hair style to one that would be less offensive to customers. Peters conferred with his union steward, filed a grievance over not being permitted to work, and left.

During the following week the union steward contacted Zeis regarding Peter's hair style. During the ensuing discussion, Zeis offered to restore Peters to work if he would wear a suitable wig until his hair grew out enough to minimize the "strangeness of his appearance." The matter was dropped when the union demanded that the company bear the cost of the wig. Peters was permitted to return to work when he

---

[1] The names of all individuals have been disguised.

reappeared a week later with a butch haircut, which nearly conformed to the length of the stubble that had regrown on the sides of his head.

A few weeks later, on July 2, Harold Half reported to work with a "punk" hair style that involved long hair in an "afro" style on the top of his head, short hair on the sides, and two shaved lines above his ears, through which his scalp was visible, and which extended from the front hairline to meet in a "V" at the back of his skull. Manager Zeis took him aside and advised him that his hair style was inappropriate to work with, and in view of, the store's customers. Half responded that his hair was arranged in the latest style and that, in his opinion, customers would not be offended by it. As he put it, "Everyone's beginning to wear their hair like this now. Why, I bet that if you let us sport a New Wave look, it'll even attract extra business because the public will think of us as a progressive, front-of-the-pack organization." To this the store manager replied, "Sorry, but until your appearance conforms to our work rules, I want you and that bizarre haircut out of here."

Half acknowledged that he was aware that Peters had not been allowed to work because of his haircut. Store manager Zeis gave Half a leave of absence until such time as his hair styling conformed to company rules. Nine days later Half reported to manager Zeis with the shaved lines partially grown out and colored with eyebrow pencil. He was offered immediate work for which he was already scheduled; he declined this, and returned to work the following Monday, July 14.

Harold Half also filed a grievance, seeking payment for wages he had lost during the July 2–14 work period. Half's grievance was processed by the union with Thomas Peters' grievance; Peters, too, was seeking back pay for the work days he had lost in May and June. Both grievances were eventually carried to arbitration.

BACKGROUND

The company and the union negotiated an agreement in 1985 that, in part, governed the hours and working conditions of employees in the bargaining unit.[2] The company had for many years posted and published established standards governing the physical appearance of its employees. These standards included a dress code and regulations governing length of employees' hair, employee grooming, and other matters of personal appearance. The company handbook read as follows:

---

[2] See Appendix to this case for relevant contract provisions.

The Company takes great pride in the appearance and decor of its supermarkets, and in the presentation of its products to its customers.

The appearance and behavior of its employees is of special importance in establishing the image it wishes to create to the public. All employees are expected to be friendly, courteous and helpful at all times. Their dress should be conservative and appropriate to their position, duties and responsibilities. It is particularly important that employees who have close contact with the public reflect the desired behavior and appearance—meat cutters, produce handlers, stock personnel, checkout clerks, baggers, etc.

Appropriate appearance means conservative style dress for both male and female employees. While it is not possible to list all unapproved apparel, the following are among those items considered inappropriate; miniskirts; low cut blouses; tank shirts; shorts. It is expected that all clothing will cover the midriff and that socks will be worn by men and stockings by women. Clothing will be clean and pressed. The company will provide aprons, gloves, hard hats, insulated jackets and other special clothing necessary to the performance of certain jobs.

Hair must be neat and clean, not to cover the eyes. Mustaches, if worn, must be neatly trimmed. No beards are permitted by employees having close contact with the public, such as checkout personnel, packers, meat cutters, etc. Sideburns must not extend below the ear lobes.

Store managers are authorized to have an employee check out until he or she reports in proper uniform.

Baggers received particular attention with regard to matters of grooming and general appearance, since they worked in the public view and were often the first employees seen by a customer entering the store or the last seen by a departing customer. The company felt that baggers often conveyed the first impression or last impression of the store to customers, and their appearance was considered by the company to be vitally important to the success of the store. At the time of hire, each new bagger was given a copy of a document entitled "Principles of Bagging," which contained an employee dress code prefaced: "All employees must maintain an overall neat, clean and well-groomed appearance." This document further emphasized in several places the importance of baggers in the employer's customer relations activities, stressing the importance of displaying a "positive image" through demeanor, appearance, and performance.

Although the subject was not mentioned in this document, both Peters and Half were aware that they were not permitted hair styles in which the hair extended over the shirt collar.

The established appearance standards were made known to the employees through the distribution of various printed documents, postings on employee bulletin boards, and discussion at store meetings.

Additionally, supervisory personnel frequently ordered employees, within hearing of other employees, to straighten ties, button blouses, remove earrings, get haircuts, or otherwise attend to their appearance. Offending employees were, from time to time, disciplined or suspended for noncompliance, and these actions were common knowledge and the subject of scuttlebutt among the other employees.

POSITION OF THE UNION

The union did not dispute the generally accepted principle that management had an inherent right to adopt "reasonable" rules governing employee conduct and appearance. It held, however, that where the implementation of a rule, promulgated unilaterally by management, resulted in disciplinary action or a refusal to permit an employee to work, management had the burden of establishing: (1) that the standard or rule was reasonable; (2) that the standard or rule was clear, concise, specific, and capable of being understood by employees; and (3) that the employees involved had violated the standard or rule in question. According to the union in this case, management had "utterly failed to establish any of these three critical elements."

The union agreed that reasonable rules or standards relating to employee appearance have been upheld by arbitrators where the employers' image had been shown to be critical to its ability to compete and where the rule in question was reasonably related to the protection of that image, or where health and safety were involved. The union took the position that, since health and safety risks were not at issue in this instance, the company had the burden of proving that the rules in question were reasonably related to the protection of its image and that that image was critical to its ability to compete. The union held that the company established neither.

The union argued that the image of the employer in this case was a *de minimus* factor in its overall ability to compete in the local grocery market. It claimed that "one need go no further than today's media to conclude that, unlike the situation of the corner grocery store of yesteryear, today's competitive environment within the grocery industry is primarily based upon price, location, quality, and availability of a variety of products, not upon 'image.' No supermarket advertises the appearance of its employees, or any other 'image' factor as an enticement to potential customers. Rather, supermarket ads concern themselves with prices, discounts, and brand names available."

According to the union, image was only one small factor in determining a supermarket's ability to compete, and the hair styles (as contrasted with cleanliness, overall grooming, and dress) of its baggers were only one small factor in protecting its image. The union claimed that arbitrators have held that in other industries where competition is based primarily on price and other factors, rather than on image, employee hair styles are no longer a predominant factor in determining competition, if they ever were. The union argued that the competitive environment in the grocery industry, and indeed, the dress and hair styles of its customers, led to public acceptance of a wide variety of hair styles worn by grocery store employees. "Management has offered only the opinion of its store manager that he thought that the grievants' hair styles might affect the store's image and might be offensive to customers, and not one shred of probative evidence in support of the manager's opinion."

The union contended that the company had failed to establish any relationship between the rule as applied in this instance and its image, and between that image and its ability to compete. Arbitrator Elliott Beitner[3] had declared a similar rule unreasonable for the same reason. Furthermore, Fisher Foods' rule was patently unreasonable and totally inapplicable to the circumstances of the case involving Peters and Half. According to another arbitrator, reasonableness is "dependent upon an objective evaluation of all the relevant facts and circumstances existing at the time."[4]

According to the union, the facts were that the hair styles adopted by Peters and Half in this case were not the subject of any standard or rule ascertainable by them. On the subject of hair, the only written applicable references, either direct or indirect, found in the "Employee Dress Code" set forth in the employer's "Principles of Bagging" were: "All employees must maintain an overall neat, clean, and well groomed appearance," and, "Hair—neat and clean—not to cover eyes." Orally, the employees were advised that hair styles were not to cover the shirt collar. The union added that "in a poll of all checkers and baggers in the store, they indicated that Peters and Half appeared to be neat, clean, and well groomed, and that their hair did not cover either their eyes or their shirt collars." The company's rules had no application to the hair styles of Peters and Half, as viewed by their fellow employees who worked with them on a daily basis.

The union contended that the company bore the burden of establishing the reasonableness of its employee dress standards; it was not enough for it merely to assert that certain hair styles, such as those of Peters and Half, had a possible deleterious effect on its public image. The company had to present *proof* of the public's real attitude and reaction, as well as proof of a demonstrable relationship between those

---

[3] Roskam Baking Company, 79 LA 993.
[4] Rome Cable Communications, 70 LA 28.

attitudes and the rules intended to nurture its "positive public image." The union cited a large number of arbitrators who agreed with this position.[5] It also cited cases where the arbitrators required that the employer show that the employee's attire had an actual adverse effect on the company's business,[6] or an adverse effect on its public image,[7] that complaints had been received,[8] or that customers had been lost.[9]

Finally, the union stated that a review of these authorities disclosed that the following elements must be present to justify an employer's establishment of standards or rules governing the appearance of employees for the sake of uniformity of appearance or "image" alone:

1. There must be a reasonable relationship between the image of the employer and the potential success of the employer's business.

2. There must be a reasonable relationship between the physical appearance of the employees to be regulated and the employer's image as perceived by the public or by his customers and potential customers, or by his employees themselves.

3. The employer's establishment of standards of employee appearance must be a good faith effort on the part of the employer to protect his business image, and must be undertaken without prohibited or improper motivation.

The union argued that the company had not met these three criteria in establishing its rules on the hair styles of Peters and Half. The union requested that they be reimbursed for all wages lost as a consequence of their required absence from their jobs.

POSITION OF THE COMPANY

The company maintained, first, that it was a contract interpretation case, not a disciplinary action case. Peters and Half had frivolously rendered themselves temporarily unfit to perform their work duties by their voluntary adoption of bizarre hair styles espoused by a few "punk" or New Wave rock and roll fans. They were not suspended for a violation of the company's rules governing employee conduct, but they were merely required to conform to its well-known personal appearance policy before being permitted to work with, and in the view of, its conservative customers. This was evidenced by the

---

[5] Pacific Southwest Airlines, 73 LA 1209; United Parcel Service, Inc., 60 LA 147; Giles and Ransome Corp., 70-1 ARB 8319.

[6] Pacific Southwest Airlines (Supra); Texaco, Inc., 75 ARB 8198.

[7] Missouri Public Service Co., 77 LA 973.

[8] Monroe Concrete Co., 56 LA 15.

[9] Hillview Sand and Gravel, Inc., 39 LA 35.

company's willingness to permit them to work if they would wear wigs or otherwise modify their hair styles to something more acceptable. Each was permitted to return to work as soon as natural growth of hair, modification of the style of their remaining hair, or darkening of shaved areas with eyebrow pencil rendered their appearance acceptable under the prevailing community standards.

The company held that under the well-established rule that in a contract interpretation case the party alleging a breach of the contract bore the burden of establishing the contractual violation, "the bizarre hair styles of these employees constituted 'self-inflicted wounds' which necessitated their absence from work until they were again fit to perform their duties. Under these circumstances, these voluntary 'exiles' had undertaken nothing more than a conscious challenge to management's contractual right to establish and enforce a reasonable personal appearance policy."

The company maintained that the contract did not limit the company's inherent right to formulate reasonable rules governing the conduct and appearance of its employees. It contended that arbitrators have long recognized that right, especially as it related to employees who come into contact with the public and whose appearance affected the employer's "public image." The key factor in upholding this right was that employee appearance "can reasonably threaten the company's relations with its customers."[10] Consistent with this general arbitral doctrine, arbitrators have consistently upheld reasonable personal-appearance policies in the retail food industry.

The company argued that it acted reasonably and was within its rights in establishing an employee-appearance policy. The company expended tremendous sums of money on advertising and on the appearance of its stores in an effort to attract and retain customers in a highly competitive business. "Management's authority to regulate the appearance of its employees is critical to its public image and to its financial success in an industry already faced with the ominous specter of increasing nonunion competition. As supermarkets compete strenuously for each and every customer, it would be a harsh injustice for a unionized store, such as this, to endure the handicap of unregulated employee appearance while nonunion competitors could maintain a consistent public image in addition to other competitive advantages."

The company continued, "Employee-appearance policy established by the company was patently reasonable. The general policy, as set forth in the pamphlet, 'Principles of Bagging,' which was provided to both Peters and Half, was that all employees must maintain an overall

---

[10] Dravo-Doyle Co., 54 LA 604, 606.

neat, clean, and well-groomed appearance. Under this general rule appeared a specific requirement, 'Hair—neat and clean—not to cover eyes.' Clearly, 'neat and clean' was merely a guideline. The company could not be expected to anticipate all of the radically shifting styles adopted by various subcultures of society and to formulate specific written prohibitions against each. It would be plainly impossible to proscribe all unconventional, bizarre, and potentially offensive types of appearance and hair styles that might be adopted by high school and college students." The company argued that the underlying principle of the appearance policy was that employees, while at work, were to present to the general public, and to the store's customers, as attractive and conventional an appearance as is practical, avoiding any appearance that might be offensive to residents of its market area. The grievants knew, or should have known, this.

The company maintained that these employees were aware of the company's appearance policy and its underlying principle, and knew that in adopting such radical hair styles they risked not being allowed to work. Not only were they provided with copies of "Principles of Bagging," but they participated in various employee meetings at which they were advised that employees' hair was not permitted to extend over the collar. They were frequently subjected to individual instructions or orders regarding their personal dress or grooming. They saw and heard other employees being corrected regarding matters of personal appearance; in the case of Half at least, they knew of other employees who had been refused work on the basis of their hair styles, which the company found to be so unconventional as to be potentially offensive to customers. Under these circumstances, to the extent that any employee chose to make a radical change in his heretofore acceptable work appearance, it was incumbent upon employees that they assure themselves that their resulting appearance would be acceptable under their employer's appearance policies, and any question in that regard should have been raised with their employer before the change was adopted.

The company steadfastly maintained that it had acted reasonably in refusing to permit these employees to work with, and in view of, its customers in light of their "bizarre appearance." Management was justifiably afraid that some, or all, of its customers would be so offended by the appearance of Peters and Half that they would take their business elsewhere. It stated that in considering the reasonableness of an employer's belief that an employee's appearance could be harmful to its business, arbitrators have given great deference to the judgment of the employer on that question. It cited arbitrator Paul Kleinsorge, who ruled in another case:

The Arbitrator does not believe that the company needs to show that complaints were lodged against the grievant, or that certain customers were lost. If the danger is there, and if application of the rule will remove the danger, the company is acting reasonably in attempting to protect itself.[11]

The company took the position that its rule to regulate employee appearance met all the elements it felt to be necessary in order to be enforceable:

1. There must be an identifiable objective which the rule is intended to attain, e.g., uniformity of appearance among employees so that they are easily identified as employees, or employee conformance to a conventional appearance "norm," generally accepted by the community, so as to avoid the potential for offending perceived public or customer prejudices against the dirty, the unkempt, or the bizarre.

2. The rule in question must be consistent with the objective for which the right is being exercised.

3. The rule must not be vague—its requirements must be clear and understandable to the employees.

4. The rule must be communicated to the employees who are subject to its application, and its content made known to them.

5. The rule, and the enforcement of it, must be neither arbitrary nor capricious, and its application must be uniform and without prohibited discrimination among employees.

Citing various authorities, the company also argued that many arbitrators merely require a showing of a *reasonable belief* on the part of the employer that an employee's appearance could reasonably threaten its relations with its customers or other employees.[12] The company contended that the employer may regulate employee appearance when it might affect the company's business adversely, or that "a danger existed which could be removed by the application of rules governing employee appearance";[13] the employer could also regulate employee appearance where the controlling factor was not the reasonableness of the prejudice against a particular style of appearance, nor the absolute existence of it, but the reasonableness of management's belief that it existed and that its existence represented

---

[11] Allied Employers, Inc., 55 LA 1020.

[12] Frank Elkouri and Edna Asper Elkouri, *How Arbitration Works,* 4th ed., (Washington, D.C.: Bureau of National Affairs, Inc., 1985), pp. 764–65; Dravo-Doyle Co., 54 LA 604, 606.

[13] Allied Employers, Inc., 55 LA 1020, 1024.

a danger that some segment of its customer base will be offended.[14] As stated by arbitrator Philip Neville:[15]

> The arbitrator holds to the view that an employer should be free reasonably to regulate, and to prescribe standards of, personal appearance for its employees so as to require of them a certain degree of conventionality and approximate conformation to the norm.

The company also cited arbitrator George S. Bradley,[16] who said:

> The rights of individuals are necessarily limited by the rights of other individuals, the community, the government, and the employer. While a man has the right to wear his hair in any length, shape or form he desires, he also has the obligation, if he desires to work for the company, to have his hair conform to the grooming standards of the company, provided the same are reasonable . . . where the two are in conflict he makes a choice—meet the grooming standards or not work for the company. It is a very simple matter and all he has to do is decide whether he prefers to wear his hair the way he wants it, or work for the company.

In summary, the company argued that it had acted properly in not allowing Peters and Half to work as baggers until such time as their hair had grown out to the point where it met the company's dress and appearance standards. It requested that the arbitrator deny the grievances filed by Peters and Half, who were seeking payment for wages lost during the time they were not permitted to work their normal work schedule.

APPENDIX

ARTICLE 10
Management Rights

It is recognized and agreed by the union that the management and operation of all facilities and the direction of the work force are the sole and exclusive right and responsibility of the company and that in the fulfillment and accomplishment of these activities, the company has and retains all of the rights, powers, and authorities it would have in the absence of this agreement. The company recognizes and agrees that nothing in this paragraph shall supersede any other provision of this agreement. The subjects and topics contained in the various articles of this agreement shall be subject to the grievance and arbitration procedure provided herein.

---

[14] Western Airlines, Inc., 55 LA 1288.
[15] Northwest Publications, 48 LA 120, 122.
[16] Kroger Co., 58 LA 950.

QUESTIONS

1. Discuss the decision by Peters and Half to appear for work with their unconventional hair styles. Discuss the company's response to their behavior.
2. What were the company's major arguments? How persuasive were they?
3. What were the union's major arguments? How persuasive were they?
4. How would you rule in this case? Discuss.
5. Both parties cited decisions by other arbitrators. Why? How persuasive were the decisions of the other arbitrators in causing you to decide as you did in this case?